The Unlikely Voyage
of
Jack de Crow

A Mirror Odyssey from North Wales to the Black Sea

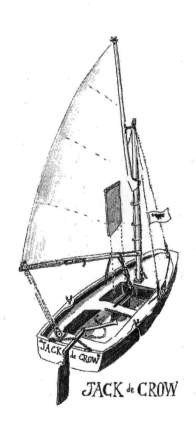

JACK de CROW

The Unlikely Voyage of
Jack de Crow

A Mirror Odyssey from North Wales to the Black Sea

By A.J. Mackinnon

SEAFARER BOOKS

SHERIDAN HOUSE

© A. J. Mackinnon 2002

First published in the UK by:
Seafarer Books
102 Redwald Road
Rendlesham
Woodbridge
Suffolk IP12 2TE

2nd impression 2002
3rd impression 2004
4th impression 2007

And in the USA by:
Sheridan House Inc.
145 Palisade Street
Dobbs Ferry
N.Y. 10522

A CIP catalog record for this book is available from the Library of Congress, Washington, DC

UK   ISBN 0 95381 805 5
USA ISBN 1 57409 152 2

Typesetting and design by Julie Beadle
Cover design by Louis Mackay

Illustrations and maps by A. J. Mackinnon

Printed in Finland by WS Bookwell OY

Acknowledgements

There are very many acknowledgements to be made, and these fall into two categories: first are those who lent support and practical aid in the writing of this book, and second are those, almost countless, who made the whole voyage possible in a variety of ways.

In the first category, I would like to express my heartfelt gratitude to Martin and Debbie Clewlow whose parting gift of a fountain pen wrote much of the book as I travelled; to Edward Lea, who persuaded me of the virtues of a word-processor once back on dry land; to Matt and Narelle Stone who took on the burden of searching for agents and publishers while I gallivanted abroad; to Carolyn Henshawe and Frank Clarke who tirelessly proof-read, edited and thereby greatly improved the original manuscript; and to Annie McQueen for advice, encouragement and much professional work on the artwork involved. To these, I must add Patricia Eve and all her associates at Seafarer Books whose faith in the final product and cheerful rallying along the way have been instrumental in bringing the book to fruition.

In the second category, the list is very much longer. It includes impromptu carpenters and boat builders encountered at timely intervals, such as Phil Simpson, Alan Snell, Paul Stollerof-Zambinski, Peter Pohl and a host of anonymous donors of expertise, varnish and screwdrivers along the way. In this list, I include warm thanks to my cousin Clive James for his gift of not one, but two, Union Jacks, the second sent to me post-haste when the first was stolen in Germany. To this must be added the kind hosts, either known to me beforehand or complete strangers, only a fraction of whom could be included in this account. Some of those who escaped mention for reasons of space are: Michael Charlesworth of Shrewsbury; the Reverend Michael and Jenny Goode of Abingdon; Cubby Fox (who saw me safely into and out of hospital in Kingston); David Halstead in Bulgaria; and most especially, Tim and Babette Gunstone, two newly-weds whose provision of bunk-space aboard their narrowboat for several weeks within yards of the marital bed went beyond the bounds of normal hospitality. Lastly, there were the countless river side dwellers across Europe who opened their doors and hearts to me; so numerous were they, and often so potent was their hospitality, that their names had vanished into an amnesiac haze by the next morning. To all these, I am immensely grateful.

For those whose names and deeds of kindness I have been able to record in the body of the book, there is the dubious privilege of seeing themselves portrayed in print. I should add here that when I first heard a former Headmaster, after telling some improbable anecdote in his annual Speech Day address, follow it with the terse explanatory note "I exaggerate for effect, of course," I nearly whooped with joy at finding at last a suitable personal motto, something in the same style as those arrogantly brief Scottish clan mottoes such as "I Shine, Not Burn."

"I Exaggerate For Effect" ... I was born for that motto. Let those who find themselves parodied or lampooned in return for their kindness towards a stranger understand that here, more than ever, the motto is true. Indeed, the greater the caricature, the deeper runs my gratitude and affection.

A third category exists: those whose support made both the book and the voyage possible. Of these, the foremost are my family, and, in particular, my sister Margaret, my father and my mother. While I have been enjoying the luxury of improvised voyaging in the realms of Fantasy, both my father and Margaret have allowed me to sustain the illusion of 18th Century roving by tirelessly dealing with bank statements and credit card payments, and those elements of the modern world that don't really disappear after all.

My father has been doing this for years now, and can hardly be thanked enough for this labour of love. Margaret, during this voyage in particular, spent much of her spare time away from finding a cure for malaria, concentrating on what at the time seemed to me a greater priority: namely, forwarding mail and engaging in long reverse-charge phone calls from Eastern Europe when it had all become too much to bear. She was my anchorline to the real world, and occasionally to sanity when the Keats and the endless willows had begun to take over.

Lastly, I wish to thank my mother. Caricatured and gently parodied in these pages, she nevertheless typed the entire first volume from my handwritten pages and resisted (generally) the sore temptation to edit as she went. Her encouragement and enthusiasm for every aspect of both the voyage and the writing process has been characteristically boundless throughout... as has her love for sailing, falling in the water, coming up laughing, and making a good story out of it for as far back as I can remember.

It is to her, therefore, that I dedicate this book.

Foreword

Sandy Mackinnon arrived on the doorstep of the Headmaster's House at Ellesmere College in much the same way as his bird-friend Jack was to arrive some weeks later, not in a basket but completely out of the blue. As his employer I probably should have a better recollection of how he came to be a teacher at the school of which I was at that time Headmaster, but in truth it just sort of happened --- one day he wasn't there, and the next day he was. Brought up in schools Sandy has on the one hand a certain conventional approach to schoolmastering which is the reassuring quality that any Headmaster would want to add to his staff; on the other hand there is an imaginative originality about him which leads to the unexpected and makes things happen differently. His journey to England from Australia, for example, which had brought him overland through Asia, had involved him being detained by Chinese border guards after straying across the frontier armed with some suspicious looking maps. It took Sandy a few days to persuade his captors that these maps were in fact the prototype for some crazy game he was in the process of inventing while strolling through the jungle, and not the wherewithal for espionage. We, too, at Ellesmere soon became used to the unusual where Sandy was concerned. His adoption of Jack the injured jackdaw, as told in the early pages of this story, his reinterpretations of Shakespeare as directed by him on stage, his creation of initiative tests for outward bound enthusiasts, and last but by no means least his parting gift to Ellesmere when he left --- a treasure hunt in the spirit of the quest for the Holy Grail with real buried treasure and clues in a series of seven paintings --- were all in their different ways evidence of the free thinker within him, and of the notion that anything is possible. As well as being a philosopher, he is also a poet, an artist and a dramatist (you may need to take the occasional pinch of salt with bits of what you are about to read!), and those creative urges combined with a free spirit to produce the journey that is the story of this book.

It was, typically of Sandy, an unusual journey, and it makes an unusual story. It may not have the daring duel with death of a Shackletonian adventure, but the voyage on board *Jack de Crow* is full of an excitement of its own created by strange twists and turns (both literal and metaphorical), and you will meet some wonderful characters on the way. For this is another of Sandy's many attributes, an uncanny ability to engage (engagingly) with anyone and everyone, to find something in common with the person with whom he is conversing, and to turn the whole experience into something enriching for both parties concerned. He even says that those Chinese border guards and he parted as the best of friends, and it would not surprise me!

Sandy Mackinnon is a "one-off", his journey was unique, and its story will fire your imagination with some moments of pure magic. Enjoy it!

David Du Croz

Contents

List of Illustrations

Part One

Bumping Into Places

The Teacher's Thief

'For there is an upstart crow, beautified with our feathers that with his tiger's heart wrapped in a player's hide is well able to bombast out a blank verse.'

Robert Greene - *A Groat's Worth of Wit.*

This is an account of a journey made from North Shropshire in England to Sulina on the Black Sea, sailing and rowing over three thousand miles in a small Mirror dinghy. It was in many ways purely an accident that it happened at all. I originally intended to spend a quiet two weeks travelling just the sixty miles or so down to Gloucester on the River Severn. Somehow things got out of hand - a year later I had reached Romania and was still going...

I have many heroes. They are mostly drawn from the world of children's literature, I confess: the White Queen who made it her daily habit *'to believe six impossible things before breakfast'*; a boy in a children's story whose title I have long since forgotten; he had a magical sailing ship called *Skillibladir* that flew through time and space but folded away into a pocket when it was not needed. But the earliest hero I can remember is Doctor Dolittle, that plump and kindly figure who lived in Puddleby-on-the-Marsh and talked to the animals. It was not this last attribute that first entranced me, however. It was the illuminated capital letters at each chapter heading which made a high-pooped, billow-sailed little galleon of each capital 'S', or turned an 'A' into a frame of leaning palm trees... and above all the marvellously casual line:

'Doctor Dolittle sailed away in a ship with his monkey and his parrot, his pig and his duck, and bumped into Africa.'

Bumped into Africa! Here was the way to travel! No timetables, no travel agents, no dreary termini clanging with loudspeaker announcements. No grubby platforms, no passports, no promises of postcards to be sent on safe arrival... just the little ship slipping down the river to the sea. Indeed the chief attributes of all the good Doctor's voyages seemed to be simple enough; a cheerful optimism and a beloved hat, both of which I happened to have. There was clearly nothing stopping me doing the same.

I had been working for six years as a teacher in a place called Ellesmere College. This is a minor public school set amidst the meres and meadows of Shropshire - a flat Shire land of grazing cattle and placid canals where narrowboats gay with painted flowerpots glide serenely across the countryside. In the distance rise the first blue hills of Wales, an altogether wilder and more enchanted land.

And some of that dark Welsh magic must have leaked from those nearby valleys, seeping across the prosperous plain to lap about the confines of Ellesmere College. For in my first year there something happened which has a bearing on all this present tale, and which you will forgive now as I recall it to mind before we set off in our little ship down the river to the sea.

In my first few weeks at Ellesmere College, amidst the busy routine of a new term in a new place, there grew in my mind a faint but persistent daydream, a niggling ambition of the most childish and unlikely sort: namely to own a tame crow.

One does not, of course, share such daydreams readily with others. They have a habit of wilting on contact with the breezy light of outside scrutiny, like poppy petals whose glossy scarlet silk crumples and fades within seconds of gathering for the drawing room vase. But when my oldest friend rang to see how I was settling in to my new life at Ellesmere, I did confide to him, half jokingly, self-mockingly, my avian fancy. Well, Rupert has long ago become accustomed to this sort of thing from me, so after expressing a polite but distant acknowledgement of my latest daydream, he neatly turned the conversation to more immediate issues such as the quality of school food, coming holiday dates and whether I'd purchased a car yet.

'Tell me, where is Fancy bred?
Or in the heart or in the head?' asks the poet.

Of this particular fancy, I have no idea of its source. Something to do, perhaps, with the feel of my new academic gown hanging on my shoulders, as heavy with power as Prospero's cloak, and the need to procure a familiar, an Ariel of my own. Perhaps such fancies are not so much wishes as faint psychic previsions of what will be.

For the next day, the very next day (and here we see some of that Welsh magic at work) I received a brief note in my pigeon-hole via the College receptionist. *"Crow arrives Friday next. Prepare."*

Rupert had, in the course of his veterinary work, stumbled across a tame, slightly injured jackdaw that needed an owner.

Thus it was that my daydream crystallised into reality with the sure speed of an arrow thudding home into the gold. The bird arrived in a cat basket in the middle of the House Singing Competition and, from the moment he arrived, divided the entire College into two camps - those who adored him, and those who loathed him to the least of his sooty black feathers. The first camp consisted of the Headmaster's family, the laundry ladies, and me; the second camp was simply everyone else, who regarded him more as a Caliban than an Ariel.

I called him Jack de Crow as a pun on the Headmaster's surname "du Croz" - though his full name was actually "Jack Micawber Phalacrocorax Magister Mordicorvus de Crow," a wild and marvellous name spun out of some dark, dog-Latin, cobwebby corner of my brain which defies rational explanation. The Headmaster was, I think, suitably flattered.

Jack de Crow found a wide field of play for his talents at Ellesmere, and he rose to the challenge magnificently. In the first week he had burgled the Bursar's bedroom and stolen Mrs. Bursar's ruby earring, demolished an important set of exam papers in the office of the Director of Studies and brought to a halt an important hockey match by sitting on the hockey ball and unpicking all the stitches before he could be shooed away. Week Two ended with the loss of a

The Master Summons His Familiar

gold pen and a bunch of keys from my Housemaster's desk, and the steady increase amongst the students of "Crow-ate-my-homework" style of excuses. As for Weeks Three to Fifty-three... well, some memories are better left unrevived.

Once he had recovered, Jack strutted and swooped and thieved his way around College, taking refuge at times of crisis in the hallowed precincts of the Headmaster's orchard garden under the protection of his kindly namesake. If I stepped outside and raised my arm and called "Jack, Jack, Jack, Jack!" he would come fluttering down from some lofty chimney-pot to perch on my wrist and so live out my dream, but as the months passed he flew free and squabbled amongst the other jackdaws in the rooftops or wheeled and tumbled in the sweet blue sky as God's Fool, somersaulting playfully for the delight of his Master.

Then one day, he was gone. Many of my colleagues breathed a sigh of relief and even I felt that life might be a little easier... I had been held largely to blame for Jack's list of crimes. But something ever so slightly magical had faded from the landscape, and my Enchanter's Cloak reverted once more to a simple academic gown. Time and routine and normality rose to obliterate that first dream-like year in a tangle of timetables and curricula, meetings and lesson plans, sporting fixtures, rehearsals, and the slow grinding of the academic year, and the name of Jack Micawber Phalacrocorax Magister Mordicorvus de Crow faded from the memories of men.

Until five years later when I decided it was time to move on and Jack de Crow was gloriously revived.

Five years had fled by. My feet were itchy and I felt it was time for a grand gesture and a dramatic farewell, and to have lots of people say touching things about me. Finally, I hit upon it. The very thing! I decided to leave Ellesmere - not by the Inter-City 10.15 to Birmingham with a suitcase in each hand, not by a lift to the airport checking the whereabouts of my passport every three minutes, not even by hitch-hiking off between the dusty July hedgerows with a cardboard sign outstretched - but, like my dear Doctor Dolittle, by sailing away in a jolly little galleon and seeing what I bumped into on the way.

The Dinghy and the Dreamer

'There was a merry passenger,
A messenger, a mariner,
Who built a gilded gondola
To wander in...'

J.R.R.Tolkien - *Errantry.*

Just over the fields from Ellesmere College lies a little mere, fringed with tall trees, dotted with ducks and coots and the odd haughty swan, and on Wednesdays and Saturdays, suddenly alive with the skim and swoop of white sails. This is Whitemere, and on the northern shore a grassy strip of meadow comes down to the lapping waters, sprinkled with daisies and blue speedwell and fringed with water mint. Here on this strip lie thirty or forty little sailing boats - the fleet of the Whitemere Sailing Club. Here are the gaudy pink and blue of plastic Toppers, constructed seemingly of Lego and Tupperware; the slim white forms of Lasers, half gull and half shark; the tiny wooden Optimists like little floating armchairs. But right at the back of this meadow strip in a corner of the fence, half smothered in thistles and golden ragwort, is the upturned hull of an ancient Mirror Dinghy, lowliest and least of the College sailing fleet. Its deep curved wooden hull is a fading, peeling yellow. Its square pram nose is lost in a tangle of blackberry brambles and out of the dark slit of the centreboard case a dozen spiders battle for supremacy with the scuttling woodlice.

It is a sad and forgotten derelict, no match for the streamlined Lasers and nifty Toppers out there darting across the mere like fibreglass damselflies. But it is a Mirror, a Mirror Dinghy, and my heart swells suddenly with a deep nostalgic pang.

A Mirror is to the sailing world what a Volkswagen Beetle is to the world of motoring. Everyone, anywhere, without exception, who has ever sailed a dinghy, seems to have learnt the basic skills in one of these gallant little tubs with their distinctive scarlet sails, almost invariably taught by some eccentric great aunt wearing a big straw hat and calling out "Swallows and Amazons for ever!" with every tack and turn.

People will tell you that they were first designed in the 1950s in response to a competition initiated by the Daily Mirror, but, frankly, I don't believe it. No, it was clearly designed some time in the 1900s as a joint project between Arthur Ransome and Heath Robinson, with Ernest Shephard chipping in occasionally on the blueprints. Looking down at the familiar lines of this upturned dinghy lying in the hot May sunshine, I am suddenly struck by an odd notion.

"Phil!" I call out to the Master-in-Charge-of-Sailing. "Does this Mirror float?"

He straightens up from some screw-tightening task on a nearby boat trailer and wades through thistles to join me. We both gaze down at the patchy hull in the hot sunshine.

"Hmm. Not sure. It did once, I assume."

"When?"

"1946, I think. No, no, I tell a lie. It was before the War, I reckon. Why?"

"Well, I've just had this sort of idea..."

We turn it over, revealing a patch of sun-starved tendrils and blanched stems, a nest of five fieldmice and eight million woodlice, but, remarkably, a reasonably unscathed interior. I pondered. A couple of coats of varnish. A good sand down. A tin of paint. She might just do.

"Er, Phil... could I borrow her, do you think? Just for a bit. I'm thinking I might take her on a trip when I leave College - sail away in her, even. What do you think?"

Phil gazed out across the blue-silver waters of Whitemere, surrounded on all sides by woods and hilly fields, and stroked his beard.

"Well, yes, of course, only..." He sounded doubtful.

"Yes?"

"Well, setting off from here, I don't think you'll get very far. No one's discovered a north-west passage out yet. Twice round the Mere and I think you'll be getting bored somehow. Still..."

But it was decided. In six weeks' time I would put the newly refurbished Mirror in the nearby Llangollen canal (a more promising through route than Whitemere) and see where I got it to - Gloucester near the mouth of the Severn, I thought. Phil, that saintly man, even promised to drive down to wherever I reached and pick it up in a trailer to return it to its weedy retirement at Whitemere, leaving me to continue by balloon, elephant, in the belly of a whale or whatever else would avoid the tedium and predictability of International Air Travel.

Meanwhile, much work was to be done. Paint and varnish and sandpaper were to be purchased, the Mirror's rigging and sails to be dug out from ancient mothballs in the sailing loft, maps consulted, oars and rowlocks obtained, and a dozen other things, all on top of the end-of-term scramble that each year leaves the College dizzy with the sheer pace and volume of things that need doing.

Three weeks had gone by before I even gave the derelict dinghy another thought, during which I had rounded off my examination classes' teaching programme and imparted last minute snippets of wisdom and advice, ("*Don't answer any questions on 'Animal Farm', chaps, it wasn't on the syllabus apparently...*")

By the time I got around to thinking about the dinghy, I found that Phil had quietly organised for the boat to be brought up to College, stripped, sanded and varnished and painted, and there she was, looking as bright and sturdy as a toy duck in buttercup-yellow with her timbers honey-gold inside. The only thing left for me to do was to decide on a name. After three seconds' thought, armed with a pot of gloss black, I painted in wobbly letters on her transom and both sides of the prow, the proud appellation: *Jack de Crow*.

Just as I had arrived at Ellesmere with a daydream solidifying around me in the form of that notorious bird, so too would I depart with Jack accompanying me in his new guise; a new guise surely but still, I suspected, with the same quality of waywardness that had been the original Jack's trademark.

It is appropriate here, I suppose, while I am standing over the dinghy in the warm sunshine waiting for the black paint to dry, to describe a Mirror dinghy for the benefit of those not privileged enough to have had a nautical Swallows-and-Amazons aunt. I comfort myself with the thought that all the classics are unashamedly dull when it comes to describing the minutiae of nautical travel and seafaring adventures. Half-an-hour's perusal of any Ransome book will enable even the most landlubberly of readers to rig up a mainsail jury hitch with belayed cross-over, and in *Robinson Crusoe*, there are detailed instructions for such things as converting a goat into a pair of moccasins without fatally damaging the original animal. So...

Jack de Crow is eleven feet long and four feet wide. Her nose is not pointed like most dinghies, but cut off square, giving her a sturdy, snub-nosed look. There is nothing even remotely aggressive or shark-like about a Mirror. She looks about as streamlined and racy as a toy hippo. The front three feet consist of a flat deck beneath which are two door-less lockers. This is where your aunt stows away bottles of ginger pop and pemmican sandwiches and more serious sailors store spare bits of rope or sail or shackles. It was where I was to stow all my worldly possessions to last me for a year of sailing: a space about the size of your average vegetable crisper.

Three broad decks or seats run right around the cockpit, making a Mirror the most sofa-like of all small dinghies to sail, and enabling several First Mates, an Able Seaman and a Ship's Boy to be deployed in relative comfort about the dinghy. Across the middle, however, is a sturdy thwart where a solitary oarsman will sit to row. Slotting into the gunwale on either side to hold the oars are the rowlocks, pronounced "rollocks", much to the amusement of the Third Form when attending sailing lessons. (*Yes, all right, settle down, Smithers, settle down...*).

So much for the dinghy as a mere rowing boat. However, she is primarily a sailing vessel and as such needs a mast, rigging, a centreboard and a rudder. These may be briefly explained thus.

A Mirror's mast is only about ten feet tall, not nearly tall enough to take a full sized sail, so it makes use of a *gaff*. This is a long light beam of wood with a hollow groove along its underside into which the thick leading edge of the sail is threaded. It is this gaff that is hauled aloft and when fully erect, (*All right, Smithers, I've warned you once*) projects out another six feet or so above the mast top, providing the necessary height for the sail.

By modern design standards this is a clumsy contraption, but was ideal for my purposes. You see, unlike most dinghy sailors out for a quick skim on a local reservoir, I would be encountering bridges and it is a very rare bridge that is generous enough to allow a fully masted dinghy to sail beneath it with impunity. With the ability, however, to simply lower the gaff and dip the peak and still keep sailing onwards, I was sure that I could escape being mauled by all but the lowest and meanest of the bridge tribe. Such confidence...

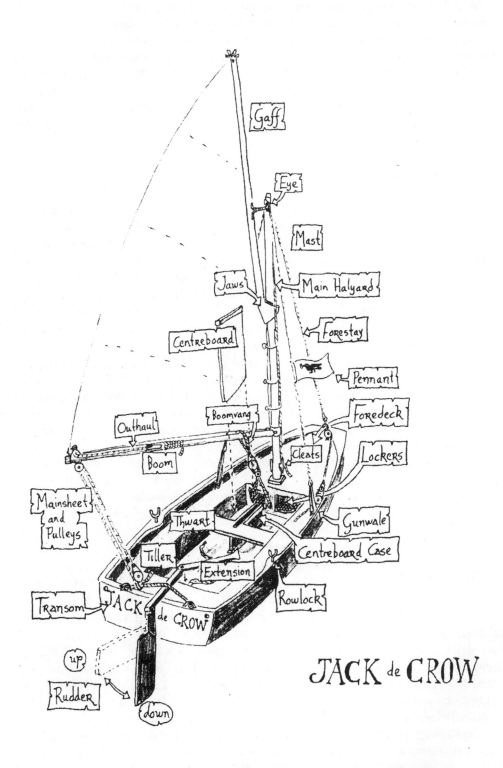

Gaff

Eye

Mast

Main Halyard

Jaws

Forestay

Centreboard

Pennant

Boomvang

Foredeck

Outhaul

Cleats

Lockers

Boom

Mainsheet
and
Pulleys

Thwart

Gunwale

Tiller

Centreboard Case

Extension

Transom

JACK de CROW

Rowlock

up

Rudder

down

JACK de CROW

We have just hauled up the *mainsail* and noticed that along its bottom edge is a long, heavy and potentially deadly wooden beam called a *boom*. This is what swings about in a gale in a Conrad film and sweeps hero and villain off into the raging seas to battle it out there once all the poop deck fighting has become tedious. At the outer end is a dangling pulley through which a rope, the *mainsheet*, threads. This then runs through a series of pulleys, but ends up in the skipper's hand, allowing him to haul in or let out the mainsail with ease. The only thing you need to know about this is that of all the myriad pieces of tackle and equipment on a sailing boat, this is the one that will jam, tangle or catch at every opportunity and cause imminent death by drowning, strangulation or sheer bloody bad temper.

Nearly finished. A smaller sail known as the *jib* runs up the forestay and this is apparently invaluable for sailing into the wind for some mysterious aerodynamic reason which I've never been able to fathom. Very soon after setting off, I abandoned the additional complexity of a jib, and the appropriate Law of Aerodynamics went off in a sulk somewhere and *Jack* and I got on perfectly well without its pedantic presence. So much for science.

The *rudder*, I assume, hardly needs explaining unless, dear Reader, you have grown up entirely as a member of some desert dwelling tribe without even the scantiest knowledge of boats, the sort of people Odysseus went looking for in his dotage. Nevertheless I will explain that it is the most vulnerable piece of the dinghy's equipment, being prone to ploughing into underwater obstacles, crushing against lock walls, jamming against banks and so on but, by some divine mystery, by the end of the whole trip, it was the single part of the entire boat that had not needed patching, mending, replacing or discarding.

As opposed to the *centreboard*, in fact, a hefty solid slab of hardwood that seemed to break at every opportunity, and the last item in this over-technical catalogue. The centreboard is simply a slim but heavy vane of timber that slots down through the hull and projects like an upside-down shark's fin several feet below the keel. When down it provides stability and prevents the dinghy drifting sideways in certain sailing conditions. When drawn up and out of the long centreboard case, it lies around, barks your shins and, if you are going fast enough, allows the foamy brine to well up through the case like a bubbling spring and fill half the dinghy with water before you notice what is happening.

So there you have a Mirror Dinghy described. Any questions? No, not you, Smithers, put your hand down, I don't want to know. Dismissed.

Or rather, that is only one aspect of the Mirror described. In one of C.S.Lewis's Narnia books the children meet a retired star, a silvery old man named Ramandu who has come to rest awhile from the great celestial dance on a remote island. One of the children on hearing his tale, splutters out in disbelief, '*But Sir, in our land a star is just a huge flaming ball of gas*'. Ramandu replies, '*My son, even in your world, that is not what a star is, but only what a star is made of.*'

By the same token, I have told you not what *Jack de Crow* is, merely what he was made of. To tell you what that gallant little boat is, I must borrow from the poets and the songs of voyagers everywhere. For *Jack* is all these: a stately Spanish galleon, sailing from the isthmus, dipping through the tropics by the palm green shores - Tom Bombadil's cockle-boat, otter-nudged and swan-drawn, up the Withywindle as the day draws down - a gilded barge bearing King Pellinore to Flanders in Malory's romance, or the magic flying Viking ship of that forgotten childhood story. He is Madog of the Dead Boat in his dark coracle beneath the shadow of the Welsh Bridge - Captain Cook's '*Endeavour*' sailing into Botany Bay in the bright, banksia-scented sunshine - or even that other little Mirror many years ago where a small boy sailed between lonely isles on the lake in the Snowy Mountains, dreaming of Doctor Dolittle, treasure maps, pith helmets and the rivers of old England where I knew I would one day voyage.

Departure and Dismay

'...Farewell, happy fields,
Where joy forever dwells; hail, horrors!'

Milton - *Paradise Lost.* Bk.1, L.249

Clop, creak, splosh.
Clop, creak, splosh.
Clop, creak, RAM, tangle, splosh.
I was off.

It was a mild, golden evening, the second day of September. Some hours earlier, I had trailered the good ship *Jack de Crow* over to the canal at Colemere Woods. Here a little redbrick bridge carries a farm track over the canal where it runs between Yell Wood and a wide field running up to a gentle horizon. In summer this field is a Monet's palette of scarlet poppies and sky-blue linseed, and one large solitary oak treetops the rise, a lonely giant against the sky. But this evening, fifty or so of my friends and colleagues and a handful of students had thronged the bridge, each with a glass in hand, and cheered as my dear friend Debbie officially christened the boat with a bottle of home-made hawthorn brandy. This clear amber liquid I had distilled some years previously from hawthorn blossom collected one sunny May afternoon on the banks of Whitemere, and it had been from the very start utterly undrinkable. It was good to find an appropriate use for it at last.

Debbie had dressed superbly for the occasion in an Edwardian outfit and her short speech was touching and apt, but she was clearly unfamiliar with the usual format of ship-launching procedures. Instead of the customary shattering of the bottle on the prow, for reasons she has yet to adequately explain, she uncorked the bottle and proceeded to pour the rancid fermenting liquor *into* the dinghy, liberally scattering it over thwart and deck and rucksack. Three thousand dancing midges dropped like confetti out of the air over a fifty foot radius, the merry throng on the bridge above us reeled back clutching their throats momentarily and the newly varnished deck started to bubble and peel like frying bacon as the hawthorn brandy got to work on the timbers. Deliberate sabotage to prevent my leaving? I like to think so...

Nevertheless, *Jack de Crow* slid down the bank and into the canal and bobbed, a buoyant little vessel, impatient to be off. There were no longer any excuses to linger. All my farewells had been said, all my worldly goods stowed, the mast and rigging lay in a long neat bundle down one side, the oars were in their rowlocks and the light was fading. It was time to go.

Clop, creak, splosh.
Clop, creak, splosh.
Clop, creak, splosh.
Clop, creak, splosh.

And the last the good folk of Ellesmere College saw of me was a small pith helmeted figure rowing away into the shadowy blue dusk beneath the beech trees, a silver V of dim ripples at the bow diminishing to nothing until a bend of the woody canal hid me from sight and I was gone.

The deliberate drama of the occasion, the classic rowing away into the sunset, the stage-setting of the gloomy woods and blue shadows - as enchanted as a backdrop for *A Midsummer Night's Dream* - these had been exactly as I planned. But as the silence closed about me, I suddenly felt flat and rather tired. A romantic gesture it had been, and I had been playing the star role - but it was a real farewell too, with all that that entails. From tonight onwards, I was, quite literally, homeless. I had no job to go to. I had left behind irrevocably six years of familiarity and friendship and ease, and I had only the vaguest notion of where I was going. As the dusk deepened to darkness, the water about me became a black mirror etched only with fine silver-point. Sharp silhouettes of leaf and stem and stalk stood high on the banks against the dimming apple-green of the sky - the serrated hair-tips of nettle, the stiff stems of meadowsweet, the classic drooping grace of plantain all in a black cut-out frieze. Somewhere an early owl hooted. Under my very bows something turned with a clop in the water and sent rings of light rippling across the canal waters, silver on Indian ink.

As I rowed past the darkening sheet of wooded Blakemere, I thought of local legends: Jenny Greenteeth who dwells in those sombre depths, her pale skull plastered with thin hair like green slime, her bone-white fingers creeping from beneath submerged tree roots to drag down unwary children at dusk; of a troop of local scouts who in the '60s vanished into the treacherous bog beneath these very alder trees, just metres from the canal path; of the Grey Lady who walks the lakeside path in the grounds of Otley Hall, just beyond the trees.

A sense of desolation seemed to rise like a mist from the very waters beneath me. I wondered whether my fanciful evocation of that '*wood outside Athens*' had called up perhaps the darker side of that enchanted World - for every Oberon there was, after all, a crueller Llud, and Puck's other persona was the black-browed Phooka. Midges whined in my ears; my hands upon the oars were already slippery with sweat and the dinghy seemed to skid from tangled bank to bank as I made my unsteady progress down the dark tunnel of trees. It was with some relief and feeling a little foolish that I emerged finally into a clearer stretch of the canal running between two fields and out of that sinister run by Blakemere. The sky was now fully dark, a lovely deep Prussian blue spangled with warm stars and, as I reached the junction where the short arm turns right towards Ellesmere Town, the main canal wound away to the left inlaid with the reflecting constellations. A meeting of ways. A fork in the road. '*Two roads diverged in a wood, and I? I took the one...*' All the magic of roadways and lanes, crossroads and paths and routes rose up to meet me in the neat foursquare signpost that glimmered white at the junction. It dispelled the last clinging webs of Blakemere's dark spell, the smell of weed and stagnant water, and there in the starlight I hummed to myself the words that Bilbo spoke, off on his own adventure to Wilderland.

'The Road goes ever on and on
Down from the door where it began,
Now far ahead the Road has gone
And I must follow if I can,
Pursuing it with eager feet
Until it joins some larger way.
Where many paths and errands meet...
And whither then? I cannot say.'

I cannot say. But happier now and with a sort of calm excitement, I turned my dinghy westward and rowed away into the night.

That evening, I row only another mile or so, and curl up on the towpath under a little humpbacked bridge carrying a disused farm lane between two fields. Snug in my sleeping bag and my head pillowed on a fleecy jacket, I lie awake awhile listening to the night noises around me: the breezy rustle of dry leaves in the sloe hedge, the distant bark of a dogfox, the cough of a nearby cow.

Just beyond that far hedge are the playing fields of the College, and just up the hill my friends are settling down for the night, all in their cosy apartments, high in some redbrick tower or grey-gabled wing. In ten short minutes, I could walk there and knock on any of a dozen doors for a late night whisky or mug of coffee. I could even beg a bed for the night instead of this damp and lonely towpath. Perhaps I will. One more night. One more evening of warmth and companionship. They'll understand. I've had three farewell parties already so a fourth won't matter, surely. That cow is coming closer. I don't want cow-cough all over me. Better start tomorrow, I think. Debbie could christen the boat properly this time. Properly. *Cough, cough...* Rustle...

Snore.

I woke with a start. The sky was an early morning grey, a brambling was singing in the hedge above me, and the grass was pearled over with dew. In the next field, a flock of blackheaded gulls was pecking over the newly ploughed soil, occasionally rising into the air in a swirling, white flaked cloud before settling again further on. Now, looking back on that scene, my eyes are screwed in concentration to see if I can remember, can visualise... some bulkier shape, perhaps? A different bill? No... ? No... It's no good. If there *was* an albatross amongst those gulls, I never noticed it. There was certainly nothing whatsoever to indicate that the next eighteen hours were to be the most disastrous of my life.

My plan, as far as I had one, was this. On consulting the Shrewsbury Ordnance Survey Map (OS 126) a few days earlier, I had been pleased to note that the Shropshire Union Canal that ran past Ellesmere wound its way westward for a few miles and then forked. The right hand branch turned northward towards Llangollen via a spectacular aqueduct and several long tunnels, but the southern branch lolloped along in a less dramatic fashion towards Welshpool and the Breidden Hills. There at Welshpool, the canal ran parallel to the upper reaches of the River Severn, separated only by a strip of road. Once I had made it to there (two hours? three hours?), it would surely be the work of a minute to commandeer some cheerful loitering youths, the yeomanry of Welshpool, and haul *Jack de Crow* over the twenty feet or so from canal to river. In fact as I saw it, that would be the only major obstacle between me and the Bristol Channel. Once on the broad bosom of the rolling Severn, I'd probably be in Bristol by tea time of the next day. I was very young in those days.

I had been sitting in Lynn's Antique Shop and Tea Rooms the previous day, my OS map spread before me cheerfully telling anyone who would listen of my proposed route when a rather grubby figure slurping tea in the corner spoke up.

"Ellesmere to Welshpool, ye say, young maister? Along that theer thicky canal? Ee, but ye'll 'ave a deal o' moither gittin' a boat beyond Maesbury on that bit o' water, that ye will. Heh, heh, heh."

A little miffed at this interruption to what had been turning into a splendid little outline of the coming voyage to a group of admiring customers (as long as I kept talking, they kept buying me tea-cakes), I turned and replied in the sort of confident tones that Phineas Fogg himself might have used to some doubting crony in the Athenaeum,

"My good man, we're not talking about a common barge or motor launch here. Though you may be right in pointing out the limitations of such common craft, (*Yes, thank you. Cinnamon toast would be splendid, Ma'am,*), my little *Jack de Crow* can go anywhere, Sir. She is a pioneering vessel, Sir, a feather-light, flat-bottomed skiff whose very delight is those winding waterways, those reedy backwaters closed to the World and its dog. I think you need not worry on that account, Sir!"

"Ahrr well," said the rustic cynic in the corner, shrugging his shoulders and downing the dregs of his Lapsang Souchong. "Suit yerself. All Oi knows is that Oi graze my goats on that theer stretch o' the canal. Still you'm knows best, Oi'm sure. Marnin'!"

Ah...

A second, closer scrutiny of the OS Map amongst the teacups, did reveal that yes, beyond Maesbury Marsh, the solid pale blue line indicating the canal did seem to thin out a little... in fact, became distinctly dotted... and I might have to revise my route.

Damn.

Some of my admiring audience were clearly losing faith in my skills as an explorer and were beginning to drift away, so I had to make up my mind quickly. Ah, yes, here. This thin blue thread on the map. The very thing. Perfect.

"I *will*, gentlemen," I rapped out, snapping all attention back to me, "be taking the ship down..."

Yes? Yes?

(A nifty flourish of a handy teaspoon...)

"... the Morda Brook."

Gasp!

"*Yes indeed. Another pikelet, I think, thank you Ma'am.*"

That'll show 'em, I thought. There's always a way. Yes indeedy. The Morda Brook. So that was the plan. A breezy sail down the canal to Maesbury Marsh where surely some ox-eyed yokel would be standing by to await orders, a quick lift and heave of the featherweight skiff into the limpid waters of the Morda Brook, and an easy ride on the current down to the Vyrnwy River and the cottage of a friend and colleague, Keith, who would expect me for a gin and tonic and early supper that evening.

A plan beautiful for its spontaneity, simplicity and utterly hopeless optimism...

After two hours of rowing in good spirits between banks heavy with ripe blackberries, I came to Frankton Locks, a series of three locks stepping down a long decline of about six hundred yards. I had been mildly apprehensive about how *Jack* and I would be greeted here. I had no idea whether small unpowered vessels were allowed through them. There was also an uneasy doubt in my mind concerning licences. Did I need one? Surely not for such a harmless little tub. So it was with a few well rehearsed winning smiles and persuasive banter that I approached the first of the three locks.

"Ah," said I, to the young red-haired lock-keeper who appeared. "There's no problem I assume in taking this little fellow down the locks, is there?"

"Yep."

"Ah. Meaning 'Yep, I can'?"

"No. Meaning 'Yep, there's a problem.' No unpowered boats in the locks, I'm afraid. Sorry."

"I've got oars," I said brightly, waggling them at him.

"Sorry," he said, and turned on his heel.

I had a brief but miserable picture of me rowing back to the College, poking my head round the Common Room door and saying, "Hi! Remember me! The Traveller returns. Brilliant trip. I'll tell you about it one day. Meanwhile, anyone got an Intercity timetable I could borrow?"

This I quickly dispelled and hurried after the lock-keeper.

"Um, hello, sorry. Me again..."

A blank look...

"Chap with the dinghy, yes? Look, there's a barge coming along now. What if I get towed through? Is that okay?"

Red looked me up and down, looked at *Jack de Crow* wallowing hopefully beside me, and made up his mind.

"Nope. Sorry. No towing."

Sigh.

Right, right. *Right.*

I took a deep breath, and hurried after him once more.

"Okay. Here's what I'll have to do. I'll empty her of all her luggage, remove the bundled rigging and somehow lift her out of the canal. Then I will drag her bodily down the towpath to beyond the lowest lock. I assume there's no serious objection to that, no?"

There followed a few seconds of teeth-sucking cogitation, and he finally grudgingly agreed.

"But if you start cutting up the towpath," he added, "I'll have to ask you to stop. We can't have British Waterways property damaged, you know."

It was at this stage that I began to suspect that Mr Ginger-mop was not fully behind me on this project. This suspicion was confirmed when, having removed the luggage, the rigging, the oars and all extraneous weight, it came to lifting bodily the entire dinghy up the sheer three feet of concrete canal bank onto the towpath; a two-man-and-a-small-crane job if ever there was one.

"Right, ready," I called breezily to Mr Stickler-for-the-Rules who'd been patiently sitting on a nearby bollard lighting up a pipe.

"Ready? For what?"

"Er... well... I wonder if you could possibly help me to lift... um, it's a bit tricky for one person you see, and... er..."

"Oh no. Can't do that, I'm afraid. Not my job, see. Can't get involved."

And he took another contented puff on his pipe.

Flinging *sotto voce* a few happy statistics about tongue cancer and pipe smokers over my shoulder, I set to hauling the dashed boat out of the dingety-danged water by myself. Actually, with several pints of indignation-induced adrenaline sloshing about my arteries, I found the task easier than I had suspected. Marginally, that is. The method I adopted was to haul up *Jack*'s bows as far as I could until the dinghy's keel was resting on the concrete lip of the canal, her rear two thirds sloping sharply down into the water. Then, putting all my weight on the front third and ignoring the ominous cracking sounds of splitting timber from her keel, I levered the stern up level until the boat was horizontally hanging out seven feet over the water. Finally, I pivoted the whole boat around parallel to the canal and safely onto the towpath.

This method brought on only the mildest of hernias and was one I had occasion to use later at various intervals throughout the trip, so I was actually very grateful to Mr Carrot for his passive encouragement to develop a solo technique. That gratitude does not extend, however, to remaining silent about his next piece of churlishness. Oh indeedy no.

I started to haul *Jack* down the towpath, a long and mercifully grassy slope of about six hundred metres, but by a third of the way down was reduced to a sobbing wreck. I recalled my conversation in the tea shop. Feather-light skiff? *Hah!* Light-winged dryad of the waterways? *Pshaw!* Bobbish little jollyboat? *Phooey!* She felt as if she were constructed of solid plutonium, and was about as draggable on dry land as a dead dugong. The fact that it had begun to drizzle a thin wetting rain did not improve my spirits one little bit.

Just then, when I was picturing in my mind's eye the warmth, comfort and grace of a British Rail Intercity second-class carriage (clearly delirious, you will note), there came a friendly call. "Need a hand, mate?"

Two burly workmen scraping some windowpanes on a refurbished lock side cottage were watching with kindly pity my painful progress down the towpath, and had decided I needed help. In a trice, I had directed one to take the prow and the other to join me in carrying the stern, and with a quick heave-ho we had covered the next fifty yards in a matter of seconds. In two minutes more I would be afloat and on my merry way again, a free spirit, a lissom Ariel, a bird of...

"OY!"

The call floated down the towpath from the top lock where the lock-keeper was standing beckoning to the two workmen to drop what they were doing and come immediately.

They did.

They returned.

"Sorry mate," they intoned together. "The boss says we're not to get involved, and we have to get back to work on 'is window frames. Sorry. Good luck though," and off they trudged to the cottage. Ah. I see. So when the lock-keeper said he couldn't get involved, he clearly didn't include in his policy of non-involvement the act of telling *other* people not to get involved. Right-o. Just so long as I know...

Well, to skip over the next dreary hour, I shall simply record here that I finally managed the task, and then had a further two trips up and down to collect my baggage and the rest of the boating paraphernalia from where I'd left them by the top lock. I didn't see Captain More-Than-Me-Jobs-Worth again - he was probably demonstrating his non-involvement by writing out a Complaint form in his cottage. But you know, inexplicably, in that last trip down to the lower lock, my boots seemed all over the place somehow, scuffing up the turf, loosening the edges of the bank, scattering stones and gravel on the grass, gouging divots in the tow path. Really, I don't know how I could have been so clumsy.

Back on the water at last and all the gear re-stowed, the canal lay before me in a featureless three mile stretch across the dreary waste of Rednal Flats, and I set off rowing once more, sculling into a thin drizzle borne on a stiffening headwind. There is, I discovered that day, an art to rowing, and it was an art that I did not in fact possess. My progress that day across the Rednal Flats was a sorry zigzag of crashes and curses from bank to bank, the oars flailing ineffectually in the rowlocks and my back and arms beginning to ache abominably. I spent more time trying to extricate myself from bankside vegetation than in forward motion and I began seriously to doubt the wisdom of the whole foolish venture.

Another miserable doubt was looming. A quick perusal of the map had shown three thick black chevrons across the blue line of the canal, a symbol I would come to loathe in the months to come; namely, another flight of locks a mile or so ahead. Aston Locks, three of them spread over more than a kilometre. Would I encounter another officious lock-keeper? And what really were the rules anyway about rowing boats in locks? Would I find this impasse all the way down the Severn? If so, I may as well give up now, sink the dinghy in this hellish canal and sneak off to a train station somewhere. I could always sit in a rented bed-sit in Bournemouth for six months and make up fictitious letters to all my friends about my wonderful nautical adventures. It has been done before. Yes, (*heave, slosh, crunch*) that's what (*heave, swing, jam*) I would do (*heave, thud, rustle*).

Sigh.

Then we were at Aston Locks, and there was a smiling, cheery looking chap in the standard British Waterways green uniform.

"Now look," I started up defiantly. "Dinghies. Rowing boats. Are they allowed in canal locks or not? Because..."

"Oh, aye. No problem there, boyo."

Pause. Welsh. Has possibly misunderstood.

"You mean, unaccompanied, just on their own?"

"Oooh yes. Don't see why not. They're boats, after all. Got to get down somehow, isn't it?"

Another pause...

"I'm sorry. Are you telling me that this boat, unpowered as it is..."

"Unpowered? No. You've got oars there, boyo. That's powered in my book."

"And this is legal, is it? Right down the Severn as well?"

"Oh yes, isn't it. All over England and Wales, far as I know."

(*Oh, thank you, thank you God, what a beautiful day it is all of a sudden. How bright the rosehip on the briar, how sweet the birdsong in the sedge...*)

"And so, let me get this quite clear. I, meaning *me*, could take *this* boat, *Jack de Crow*, down through *these* three locks, unaccompanied? Yes?"

He looked at me cheerfully, encouragingly, kindly.

"Oooh yes. No problem. After April, next year. Out of use since 1956, see. But come April, and they'll be like new pins. Cheerio!"

The newly developed Mackinnon 'Swing and Hernia' method of removing a dinghy single-handedly from a canal came into its own that dark and dismal afternoon. Three times I unloaded the boat, three times dragged her an inch per heave across gravel, boulders, marsh and broken concrete to send her scraping once more into the black and stagnant waters of the Aston Lock flight. I started to calculate that considering the distance she'd done overland since leaving Ellesmere, I'd have done better to equip her with a set of sturdy Dunlops rather than oars. Perhaps I could convert the wretched thing into a sort of caravan and save an awful lot of trouble all round.

And even when we finally reached the open canal again beyond the third lock, it was difficult to tell where land stopped and water began. The stretch of sedge-grown, log-jammed pond that masquerades under the title of the Maesbury Long makes a trip on the *African Queen* seem like a jollyboat jaunt on the Serpentine. The canal here narrows to a humid green lane, only a boat's width, between towering bulrushes and creeper-clad alders, making every stroke of the oars a frantic struggle akin to beating anacondas to death every five feet. The lurid green of duckweed grew so thickly that it looked as though I was ploughing across a velvety bowling lawn, leaving an inky black trail behind me.

The rain had stopped and down low amongst the waterweeds the air had become warm and damp and oppressive. My shirt stuck to my back and under my arms like a leprous shroud, and never did Amazon explorer welcome the sight of base camp and a stiff G & T as I welcomed the sight of the Navigation Inn and the Maesbury Marsh bridge.

The Inn - of course - was closed for renovations, but by the bridge, just before the canal runs out as my tea shop goat-herd had warned me, there is a tiny shop selling drinks and sweets run by a woolly-haired canal enthusiast. I asked to use his phone, and reckoning with all the confidence of a seasoned non-watch wearer that it was about one o'clock-ish, I phoned Keith. On his answering machine I left the cheery message that I was past the worst, would soon be on the Morda Brook and bobbing merrily downstream to arrive at his cottage by five-ish. Prepare the G & T, ice and lemon please. Cheers.

(Keith, I later discovered, was somewhat puzzled to receive this hearty assurance that I'd be arriving at five because my call was in fact made at ten past five, and not one o'clock as I'd guessed.)

Over a quick can of lemonade, I told my woolly-headed host of the morning's trials, especially of the redheaded keeper of Frankton Locks.

"Ah, 'im! 'E's a right bugger, that one, is young Norman," retorted he with some energy. "D'you know, 'e reported one of 'is mates, 'im who works up there at Frankton alongside 'im, for fishin' in the lock-cut of an evenin'. Reported 'im to the Authority, 'e did, 'is own neighbour. Ee, I don't know," said Woolly, shaking his head. "What 'e needs," he added, leaning confidentially towards me, "is a good woman. A big black mamma to spank some joy into 'im! Aye."

The Morda Brook, despite my breezy assertion in Lynn's Tea Rooms, is by no stretch of the imagination a navigable waterway, but it was my only route out. So it was that at the reedy dead end of the canal, I hauled *Jack de Crow* out of the water for the fifth time that day and dragged her a hundred yards down a narrow lane to slide her over the ford and into the dank, black waters of the least navigable stretch of water in Britain - the Morda Brook.

The Morda Brook, oh the Morda, the moist and morbid Morda, the Morda of my nightmares. Actually, no, at first, it was quite fun. Once away from the ford, the brook turned into a sparkling stream, cutting between high clay banks lined with alder and overhanging willow, little more than five feet wide in most places. I soon found that the easiest way to proceed was to stand in the boat and pole or paddle my way along with a single oar in the manner of a Venetian gondolier - albeit a rather muddy, leaf-plastered one - and be carried onward by the steady chattering current beneath the keel. Every five minutes or so I would have to leap out into the shin-deep waters to drag *Jack* bodily over a bar of shingle or round a particularly tight bend but the change from the monotonous slog of rowing was a welcome relief.

There was a lightening of the air as well. The afternoon had turned golden and blue; high white clouds were tinged by the westering sun and for the first time that day I felt touched by a sense of adventure and high spirits. This was exploring if you like!

Occasionally there was a greater obstacle to overcome - a black many-clawed alder tree that swept its low branches down over the stream's surface and had to be worked around, or a half-submerged log that needed heaving aside. But these were merely grist to my adventurous mill and simply added to my growing elation.

All the time as I progressed the banks of the Morda reared higher about me until I was alone in a narrow world of dark water and steep clay sides clothed in wild mint and Himalayan balsam. This last is a wonderfully triffid-like plant, with a complicated pink flower rather like a snapdragon smelling of peaches. The seed pod - a tightly sprung contraption explodes at the lightest touch into a tangle of curlicues sending hard black seeds like buckshot shooting in every direction. With every stroke of my paddle, half a dozen of these pods would instantly recoil with a soft splitting pop and the decks of my little galleon would rattle with tiny cannon-shot, and the air would grow yet heavier with the drowsy scent of peach balm.

But night was falling apace. The strip of sky above me deepened to dusk, the gold faded from the landscape and white stars began to glimmer out in the clear evening blue, and what with the meandering wriggles of the brook, I had no idea what distance I had covered. I knew that there was an old road bridge only half a mile up from the confluence of the Morda and the wider Vyrnwy. I knew also that Keith's cottage (where even now a sparkling, clinking, lemon-sliced gin and tonic would be awaiting) was only a mile or so across the fields from the Vyrnwy in the hamlet of Rhos Common. So when I poled around a sharp bend and saw the last gleam of twilight making a perfect disc beneath the arch of a bridge ahead, I breathed a heartfelt sigh and calculated that I would be sitting down to supper within the half-hour.

With renewed vigour I paddled onwards beneath the bridge's black arch and round the next bend where surely the waters would suddenly widen into...

Well, all right. Around the next bend then, surely, to find the infant Morda meet her bigger sister, the graceful Vyrnwy, just about...

Hmm. Perhaps a little further than I thought, until yes - clearly the current was slowing up as one would expect of a tributary mere yards before curving round one final bank to find...

Damn.

Better consult the map.

Too dark. Better find the torch. Too dark to do that either...

Make mental note: leave torch handy in future.

Ah, here's the torch. Where is map? Ah, here...

Make mental note: keep map in waterproof cover in future.

Unfold soggy map. Tears soggily into five pieces.

Make mental note: buy sticky tape.

Find relevant section. Yes, as I thought. There *is* a bridge just five hundred yards up from Vyrnwy. So where has blasted Vyrnwy disappeared to? Stupid map.

Make mental note: write stiff letter of complaint to Royal Ordinance Survey Office.

Sudden horrid idea. Check map again... Damn, damn, damn, damn, damn! There are *two* bridges - the one I have just passed which is only an inch on the map away from Maesbury, and then the second bridge more than four inches on the map - six miles - to go from here. Only *then* comes the Vyrnwy, the cottage at Rhos Common and the gin.

Make mental note: check out guest house bookings in Bournemouth at first available opportunity.

There is nothing for it but to keep battling on downstream. So on I went, into an increasing nightmare. Unseen willow branches raked across my face and clutched at the dinghy's gunwale. Grounding on to a shallow bed would have me stepping out, not onto an ankle-deep shoal of sand, but into a thigh-deep sludge of black mud. Log jams and barbed wire tangles occurred round every bend and the mosquitoes rose in whining clouds about my head undeterred even by the lingering vitriolic fumes of the hawthorn brandy. But at last after four black hours of this thrashing, hacking, blind progress, I bumped my way under the second bridge and knew that this time, truly, honestly, the Vyrnwy was only five hundred yards downstream... and beyond that, the lighted windows and warm welcome of Keith's cottage.

"*Sing ho! for the life of a bear,*" I sang, "*Sing ho! for the life of a bear...*" and all of a sudden the stars above seemed extra sparkly and silver in the black night sky. But the Morda Brook, that spiteful, black-hearted witch of a stream, knowing she was about to lose me forever had one or two last tricks to play. It was not over yet.

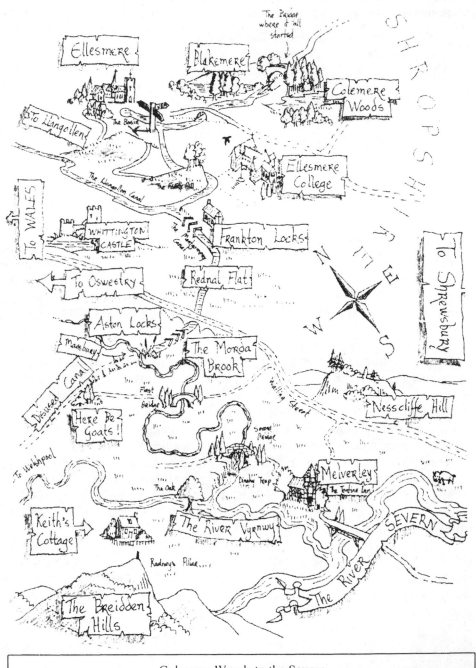

Colemere Woods to the Severn

Sweeping under a low alder tree the boat caught for the hundredth time that day in some overhanging bough, as black and scratchy and crooked as only an alder branch can be. More impatient than ever now that the end was so near, I levered the dinghy forward using an oar with all my might and heard a most satisfying splintering crack of wood as the boat groaned, strained... and then shot clear into a broad starry pool, trailing broken branches and twigs on all sides.

'Hah! hah! hah! Hee! hee! hee!
Alder witch, you can't catch me!' I sang in happy delirium.
'Alder witch, I'm Jack de Crow,
I break your bones, and off I go!' I burbled to myself as I leant over to clear the debris that draped around the gunwales and the rowlocks.

Rowlocks?
Rowlock. Singular.
Gunwale. Singular.

In the pitch dark, my groping hands told the awful truth. The splintering crunch I had heard as I tore free of the alder had not been the tree's branches breaking; it had been the entire starboard rowlock ripping away and taking a two foot section of the gunwale along with it. My blind fingers felt the smooth, sturdy woodwork end in a splintered mass and groped hopelessly for the cold metal horseshoe of the rowlock. Gone. Torn away. Lying, presumably, in the black depths of the pool beneath that malicious alder's waterlogged roots, while its niggly twigs and arid leaves hissed out in the sudden night breeze a mocking lullaby:

'Jack de Crow! Jack de Crow!
You won't get far if you cannot row.
Crippled Crow, don't mock me.
I'm the Witch of Morda, the Alder Tree!'

Too weary and numb even to think about the consequences of having lost in one fell swoop the power to row properly (except round and round in very small circles) I drifted on around the final bend... and into the final trap.

Here, only a hundred yards upstream from where the Morda lost itself in the greater Vyrnwy, the brook narrowed into a sheer-sided gully between cliffs of slippery clay and thick nettles rearing twenty feet either side in a near vertical slope. Across the stream at this point stretched a taut, black, double-twisted strand of barbed wire, as rigid and unyielding as an iron bar. This lay one foot above the water from bank to bank, attached either end to solid ancient willow stumps, so old and immovable that the wire had grown deep into the bark and become part of each stump itself. It was a dinghy trap, and utterly impassable.

In the blanketing darkness, I tried blindly dunking the dinghy low enough in the water to scrape beneath the wire, but to no avail. Even at her lowest the boat had a foot and a half of freeboard. I considered hauling her *over* the rigid wire but between the sheer banks there was not the slightest foothold for me to stand on to perform this operation, and a prodding oar confirmed my suspicion that the stream at this point was over six feet deep. Another approach was needed; technology.

In the midnight blackness, I rummaged around in the half ton of leaf mould, mud and debris that filled the bottom of the dinghy and located my Leatherman tool, a wonderfully useful parting gift from the Common Room, and equipped with, amongst other things, a sturdy pair of wire-cutters. However, twenty minutes later, twenty minutes of straining with sweat-slippery and blistered hands trying to snip through the blasted wire resulted only in a sudden twang, a plop and my suddenly empty hands. The torch revealed the wire still uncut but the Leatherman nowhere to be seen - clearly another trophy claimed by the Morda Brook.

It was at this point that I made my first sensible decision of the day. I was cold, hungry and exhausted, I was only one mile - two at the most - from Keith's cottage, and he had been expecting me since five o'clock. It was now nearly eleven, I guessed, and if I hurried I might catch him before he gave up waiting and retired to bed. The boat would go nowhere in the night - in fact, would probably still be there for the next few millennia - and I could leave the problems for the morning and broad daylight. A quick saunter by starlight across open fields while I was still relatively dry and cheerful, and all would be well.

Leaving most of my things in the boat, I somehow scrambled up the nettle-grown bank (what were a few stings when salvation was so near at hand?) and identified, with some relief, the lights of Rhos Common across the flat plain, no more than six fields away.

"*Ah! First the gin, I think, Keith, thank you,*" I murmured as I tripped my way across the first starlit pasture.

"*And if you could perhaps be running a hot bath while I drink this? Good chap,*" as I negotiated a stile into the next field.

"*Now, supper. We'll start with soup, ox-tail if possible, Keith,*" (avoid cow-pats) "*and move swiftly on to..., let's see now... Smoked salmon? Excellent!*" (Head for gap in hedge) "*But meanwhile, a warm, fluffy towel and a Noel Coward dressing gown embroidered with Chinese dragons, if you would be so good.*" (Those lights were distinctly closer) "*Ah. So kind.*"

I strode cheerfully across the open flat meadow towards the distant lights. One of them, I reckoned, I could even identify as Keith's kitchen window...

All of a sudden, I stopped dead.

I had to.

At my feet, the meadow stopped abruptly in a cliff that dropped twenty feet into the broad, starlit waters of a gleaming river. A wide river. A swift, deep river. A totally unfordable river. The long sought after Vyrnwy River, lying between me and the bright, hazy dream of Keith's cottage, now a thousand miles away.

I do not remember much after that. Possibly I fainted. Possibly I was overcome by a black, Berserker rage blotting out all conscious action for the next hour. Even now, as I struggle to recall my actions and emotions on discovering that I was cut off from Keith's cottage without my boat, only snatches come back to me like brief cloudy glimpses seen through the flying spume on a day of storm and gale.

I remember a furious stamping stride back across the fields - a hasty, but painful, plunge back down the nettled bank into the oil-black waters of the Morda. I remember sinking immediately over my head down, down, till I found the oozy bottom - then on hastily resurfacing, cracking my head so hard into the keel of the dinghy underwater that everything went rather swimmy for a bit. I remember that somehow, incredibly, and possibly helped by a blind, bitter, sheer bloody temper, I heaved that dinghy up onto the barbed wire strand from underneath, flailing about in deep water, and scraping her over the rusty strand in three great hoicks while the barbs gouged out deep grooves in her hull. I remember the sudden rush of elation as I realised she was over at last, and the floundering, clay-splattering manoeuvre that got me out of the water and into the dinghy like an epileptic seal, hardly heeding the long sound of ripping cloth as the barbed wire shredded my trouser-leg from knee to cuff as a last spiteful blow. Then the short paddle around the final bend out onto the broad bosom of the Vyrnwy, the delirious attempt to row to the opposite bank with only one oar and wondering vaguely why the stars were spinning so crazily in circles above me.

Finally, there came the blessed scrunch of keel on fine shingle, and the half-hearted tug of *Jack*'s nose up onto the little beach by a spreading oak, followed by the determination to just walk away, walk away, and never, *ever* come back. Ever.

It wasn't over yet. While waltzing deliriously through the middle of a wide meadow, I suddenly felt a sharp jolt as though someone had flung a pebble and caught me on the funny-bone. I also seemed unable to move forward, try as I might.

Ping! The jolt came again. An invisible elf-bolt out of the darkness. And still I was rooted to the turf.

Ping! A sling-shot to the nerves again. In English folklore there is a phenomenon called a 'stray sod', a patch of grass enchanted by the faeries to bewitch and bewilder any Mortal careless enough to stumble upon it. I had clearly found one, put there - possibly - by the same malicious wight who had designed the Morda Brook.

Ping!

It is some measure of my clay-smeared, nettle-stung, bone-weary condition that it took me some twenty seconds and five shocks later to realise that I was standing up against an electric fence in the darkness. I am sure it was only the additional amps that gave me the energy to get to Keith's at all.

And so this long and weary chapter comes to a close at last. At half past midnight, I clawed at the cottage window like some hideous swamp creature from a B-grade horror movie and startled Keith into a near heart attack. He opened the door to a gibbering, mud-oozing wreck, Jenny Greenteeth's husband, my face liberally peppered with nettle rash, my head garlanded with alder twigs, willow bark and leaf mould. One trouser leg flapped open to reveal a gashed and bloody calf and the hands held up in supplication were a mass of cuts and blisters beneath the grime. Several internal organs had ruptured, one eye was swollen and closed where a hail of Himalayan Balsam seeds had scored a direct hit, and a puddle of silt, river water and fresh liquid cow dung was spreading at my feet. I was still twitching every four seconds as the last of the amps chased one another playfully through the nervous system.

"Any chance of a gin?" I chirruped brightly, before pitching headlong into the hallway and measuring my length on the floral carpet.

"Ice and lemon, please. I'll have it here on the floor. Thanks."

Sails and Stained Glass

'Never in his life had he seen a river before - this sleek, sinuous, full-bodied animal, chasing and chuckling, gripping things with a gurgle and leaving them with a laugh, to fling itself on fresh playmates that shook themselves free, and were caught and held again. All was a-shake and a-shiver - glints and gleams and sparkles, rustle and swirl, chatter and bubble.'

Kenneth Grahame - *The Wind in the Willows*

Day Two.

Day Two?!

My level of exhaustion, my battered state, the haunted look behind my eyes; these rather gave the impression that I had single-handedly rounded the Horn and was approaching Tahiti at least.

Day Two was not going to be remotely like Day One if I could help it - nor were Days Three, Four, Five and through to Eternity. No, sir.

Rules would have to be made, and as I awoke to a bright and breezy morning and went through the cheerful ritual of waking up properly, I listed them.

Rule 1. Stop before nightfall. Never, ever sail after dark again. Ever.

Rule 2. Stow everything properly, in strong untearable waterproof bags.
(My carefully chosen bright orange plastic rucksack bags had been torn to shreds after two minutes of the Morda Brook).

Rule 3. Stick only to waterways marked clearly as thick pale blue lines on the map. Thin dark blue lines are mere culverts, brooks and drainage ditches and not to be entertained as even remotely navigable. However...

Rule 4. Don't try sailing on Motorways. These are also shown as thick blue lines, (see Rule 3.) so be careful.

Rule 5. Consult map carefully and often.

Rule 6. Stay dry.

It was with these carefully considered rules in mind that I ate a wonderful breakfast, said my heartfelt thanks to Keith and apologised for the six inches of rich river silt in the bottom of his bath. Then I sauntered happily back across the meadows to see what could be done about *Jack de Crow* and her various injuries.

The sun was strong and warm, high white clouds drifted like snowy galleons across a forget-me-not sky and my heart was unaccountably high. I don't know why. As far as I knew, I was returning to a half wrecked dinghy full of sodden luggage, with a large section of her gunwale missing, one rowlock irretrievably lost, my Leatherman multi-tool likewise full fathom five at the bottom of the Morda Brook, and therefore any chance of repairing any damage gone with it.

But, as I say, the day was warm, the fields were wide and peaceful, and I felt like Mole hurrying for the first time, the sunshine hot on his fur, across the Great Meadow for his life changing appointment with the River.

Hang whitewashing!

And besides, I had my six Golden Rules, my six sensible, well considered, easy-to-keep rules. Especially the last one. I liked that one. *Stay dry. Stay dry. Stay... dry.*

When I reached the Vyrnwy's bank and the little shingle beach by the spreading oak tree where I'd pulled *Jack* up the night before, I decided suddenly on a Seventh Golden Rule.

Rule 7. Tie the dinghy up each night. Firmly.

Jack had vanished.

Same shingle beach. Same massy oak. Same broad bend. No *Jack*.

Day Two was beginning already to look a lot like Day One after all.

So tired and careless had I been last night, that I had done barely more than hoist her bows onto the shingle. Now, on an extra six inches of floodwater, she was gone.

I found her half-an-hour later a mile downstream, caught in a tangle of osiers and willow in midstream. Golden Rule No 6. flicked tauntingly at my mind for a few seconds. (*What's the good of making rules if you're just going to break them, Sandy? I mean, really...*) and then after one last forlorn repeat of that pitiful mantra, 'Stay dry,' I stripped off and plunged in.

Swimming down to *Jack* was easy. Boarding her was accomplished by the epileptic seal method again. Rowing her back upstream against the considerable current with only one oar was a task that would have challenged Odysseus. My similarity to that nautical hero was emphasised by the fact that, just as he is depicted on all those Greek vases, I too was stark naked. It was indeed fortunate that this stretch of the Vyrnwy meanders through wide flat water-meadows empty of all but placidly grazing Friesians and the odd heron, none of whom took the slightest interest in the naked, pith helmeted gentleman rowing in tight circles in a little yellow dinghy.

It was *unfortunate*, however, that a small party of canoeists consisting of one young chap and three delightful looking lasses should choose that morning to be out practising their craft on the broad bosom of the waters on their way from the Llanymynech Bridge to lunch downstream at the Tontine Inn at Melverley. It is a pleasant but dullish run, this stretch, and does not generally afford the canoeist much in the way of interest to look at. But I think there are four people now who may disagree with me on that score. All I will say is that despite my cheery wave and smile - and despite my attempts to use my pith helmet in the manner for which fig leaves are generally reserved - this small party did not seem inclined to stop and chew the fat or pass the time of day. I cannot think why. The traditional comradeship of river users everywhere seems sadly in decline on those lower reaches of the Vyrnwy, alas.

Once they had paddled on, I somehow managed to zigzag *Jack* ashore, climb back into my clothes and then start the long but satisfying task of setting things to rights. This perhaps seems strange, but I cannot think of a time when I have been happier or more blissfully contented as slowly through the long noon tide, there on the warm grass under a wide sky, surrounded by miles of empty, lonely fields, *Jack* and I thoroughly sorted ourselves out.

Firstly, I found to my relief that the splintered off section of the gunwale still holding the rowlock had fallen, not into the brook as I had thought, but into the dinghy. Secondly, likewise, my Leatherman was lying buried in the half ton of debris in the bilges and had not fallen overboard last night. The Morda had only been teasing.

I hauled *Jack* up and spent a happy hour shovelling out the twigs, the weeds, the leaves, the balsam seeds and alder cones, the clay and silt and shingle that had collected in her yesterday. Then propping her on her beam ends with an oar, I sluiced her out from stem to stern with the bailer full of water. Finally I wiped her down inside and out with a big sponge until she was gleaming clean again.

Meanwhile I had unpacked all my luggage - soon every grassy tussock and thistle clump was draped with damp underwear, shirts, socks and pyjamas drying in the hot sun until the meadow looked like Mrs Tiggywinkle's washing day.

I had assessed the damage to the hull from yesterday's overland expeditions and found, surprisingly, that apart from a good many scrapes and gouges in the canary yellow paintwork, there did not seem to be the cracked and splitting timbers I had expected. The hull remained watertight.

The main damage, of course, was topside, especially that awful broken gunwale. This is a stout thickened length of wood running right around the rim of the boat, making a sort of solid lip to the hull. At the point where the rowlock sits on either side, it broadens out in a gentle curve to allow a hole to be drilled down through it. Into this hole drops the pin of the rowlock, without which, manoeuvring an oar effectively becomes impossible. It was this section of the gunwale that had snapped away completely, and now needed to be fixed before I could hope to proceed.

Now I am no carpenter, not in a million years. When in woodwork lessons at school other lads were knocking up drop-leaf coffee tables and walnut roll-top bureaux to take home to their adoring parents, I was struggling to produce a jam stirrer. A jam stirrer, I should add, is not as my mother thought when I told her I was making one, a complex sort of wooden egg beater with rotary paddles and a turning handle demanding the cabinet-making skills of Grinling Gibbons. No. A jam stirrer is a simple stick of wood with a tapering handle and bevelled edges. Mine didn't even manage the bevelled edges. It was therefore with some trepidation that I faced the task of rebuilding the gunwale. What it really needed was some proper wood glue, that white milky stuff that 'sets harder than the wood itself,' as it claims on the bottle. But apart from attempting to manufacture some glue by boiling up some cow dung and willow sap, I would have to do without. I did however need screws, and I suddenly noticed what an awful lot of extraneous fittings were dotted about the decking of *Jack de Crow*. In its heady days of racing back before the war, no doubt, it had flaunted all sorts of fancy rigging - staysails and spinnakers and what not - and all these had demanded various eyelets, cleats and runners that were now obsolete, each one sporting a pair of perfectly serviceable screws.

So I spent a happy couple of hours removing obsolete fittings and with my Leatherman screwing the smashed section of gunwale back into place as a temporary repair job. It would certainly do until I got to Shrewsbury where there was a chandlery and boat repair workshop open six days a week, and which could provide me with expert advice, proper wood glue, and even bevelled edges if need be.

Finally, I made a thorough check of all the rigging. Mast, gaff, boom, sails, halyards, sheets and stays, all needed untangling and unfurling, and shaking out the remarkable amount of river vegetation that had found its way even into the centre of the tightly rolled sails. Once I had finished, I felt that I now knew every inch of the little ship, top to toe. The whole exercise had forced *Jack* and myself into a more intimate acquaintance, and when I relaunched her, I felt she had become in some sense truly mine. We had survived our first major ordeal together, and though both a little battle-scarred, were to set our faces downstream with hopes high and heads unbowed, to take whatever adventure might befall as we journeyed into the wide blue southern yonder.

Late that afternoon we reached Melverley. A gentle row downstream proved the mended rowlock to be bearing up well and my luggage, nice and dry, sat snugly wrapped in my waterproof cagoule. The afternoon continued fine and the steep sided Breidden Hills, rearing vertically from the plain in three lofty peaks, swung to all points of the horizon as the Vyrnwy meandered in broad loops between its buttercup meadows. These three hills seen from afar look like an illustration on the dust jacket of an old book of fairy tales - *The King of the Golden Mountain* or *The Enchanted Giant*. In fact there was something giant-like about the way the blue, sun-crowned mass seemed to tiptoe silently about the landscape, now straight ahead, now peering over my shoulder, now retreating coyly behind a nearby copse of oaks.

After the slog of yesterday, the going was pleasant indeed. There was the odd shingle bar to negotiate, the odd moment when the current swept us too close to an entangling willow, but all in all it was the stuff of dreams. I was Ratty in *The Wind in the Willows* out for a gentle punt; Bombadil on a good day, back from picking waterlilies; Tom Dudgeon from *Coot Club* off to inspect a grebe's nest and the Hullabaloos far, far away.

Even when I arrived at Melverley Church late that afternoon, standing all in magpie black and white above the steep river bank, and an attempt to hop ashore plunged me up to my waist in the water, I was no more than mildly amused. The World and I were on excellent terms, and even such an unceremonious breaking of Rule Six for the second time that day could not seriously discomfit me.

I spent a happy half-hour exploring the exquisite little timbered church amongst its smoky yews. As I climbed to the tiny Minstrel's Gallery inside, the ancient timbers creaked comfortably underfoot. Every winter for almost a thousand years, these frail timbers have withstood the river floods that make Melverley an island each year. God willing, the equally frail timbers of *Jack de Crow*'s nautical reincarnation would do likewise.

That night, I dined in the Tontine Inn. I sat down, placed my beloved pith helmet on the table beside me and started ordering the grilled chicken. The waitress-barmaid, somewhat to my surprise, on seeing the pith helmet broke off in mid-order, clapped a hand to her mouth and ran off into the kitchens. She soon emerged behind the bar dragging the chef with her, and with much muffled giggling and whispering, pointed me out in the corner, only to collapse into giggles again. The chef gave me a long amused stare, shook his head, and vanished kitchenwards again. After a minute or so, back came the waitress clearly attempting to control her mirth, and I'd got as far as deciding on baked rather than new potatoes when she collapsed again with a barely stifled snort of laughter that threatened to choke her and ran for the door.

Now, I have become quite accustomed to mild amusement at the sight of the pith helmet. It is, I admit, a reasonably eccentric piece of headgear to wear about the highways and byways of Britain but that is partly its purpose. There is nothing wrong with a little harmless idiocy to put people off their guard before they suddenly find themselves talked into lifting a dinghy over twenty metres of towpath or doling out a free meal to a complete stranger. But I had not yet encountered a reaction quite as extreme as this at the sight of my headgear. Finally, an older woman appeared. She was clearly the landlady, presumably taking over from the mirth struck waitress who, one could only pray, was suffering a choking fit somewhere far from medical aid. She approached the table, glanced at the hat, smirked, but completed taking the order.

"...and afterwards, the Black Forest Gateau, thank you."

"Certainly sir. Um,... ?" She paused.

"Yes?"

"If you don't mind me asking, sir, but do you by chance have a rowing dinghy?"

"Well, yes, I do actually... but how did you..."

"A *yellow* rowing dinghy, by any chance?"

"Yes, yellow," I replied, wondering where this was leading.

"Ah," said she. "Good oh." She nodded. Then she leaned over and whispered reassuringly in my ear. "They're a bit old-fashioned hereabouts, see, pet. Me, I'm broad-minded as they come, but all the same, I think you was right to put on a suit of clothes before you came in here tonight. Anything to drink then?"

It was clear that my four canoeists had made it to the Tontine for lunch then. And equally clear what the main topic of conversation had been over the sherry trifle. But, hopefully, with a good current and a following wind I could be over the border and into Worcestershire before the news hit the Shropshire Star the next day. An early night that night, and an early start on the morrow, and they'd never catch me.

Day Three. (You see, we *are* getting on quicker now.)

Day Three saw the very first hoisting of sail, and a whole host of new delights, new challenges, new near-death experiences to savour.

Only half a mile down from Melverley's magpie church, the River Vyrnwy flows into the River Severn, the longest river in Britain and my highway from here to the sea some two hundred miles away. Once on to this relatively broad thoroughfare, I decided it was time to start doing things in earnest. I would hoist the sail.

I rowed in to a little beach of shingle and spent a contented half-hour unwrapping the mast and rigging from their neatly furled bundle, stepping the mast and attaching the long wire stays to their three respective fittings - port beam, starboard beam and prow. Once these were adjusted and tautened, the mast stood proudly erect and *Jack* already looked more like a sailing ship than a common little rowing boat. Getting the stays exactly the right length and tied off firmly with one hand while holding the mast upright in the other, is no easy task and I was pleased to have got the job done so smoothly.

Getting it down again one minute later was even easier, as it tends just to fall on top of one like a felled redwood. The reason I had to take the mast down again so quickly was because I had forgotten to thread the two halyards through the top eyehole before erecting it. Once these were pulled through, I went through the tricky mast-balancing, one handed rope-tying stunt again, and stood back to admire my handiwork - the gallant little vessel, ten foot mast standing high, framed against the blue sky and the old road bridge just downstream.

Road bridge?

Road bridge!... Sigh. Down came the mast again and ten minutes later I had rowed *below* the road bridge with its niggardly nine foot head clearance and was setting the wretched thing up for the third time.

Once my problems with the mast were over, the rest was relatively easy. The rudder was in place, the sheets were clear and soon I was ready to hoist the scarlet mainsail. There is something exhilarating about this action no matter how many times you have done it before. Even many months later, when I was hauling up the sail for the thousandth time, I could not help thrilling to the sudden bellying out of the red canvas, the sail's peak soaring into place against a bright sky in three swift, easy glides, the clunk of the main pulley lifting free of the gunwales and the smooth run of the mainsheet as the boom swings fully out.

There is always the faint, stirring lilt of the Onedin Line music as the sail goes up, the ghostly drift of sea spray on the high bows, and it always takes me a second or two for me to realise that I am not in fact a Bristol clipper heading out into the Atlantic in the last century, but a small dinghy on inland waters about to ram a coot's nest again.

The fact is that once a boat is sailing she is alive, and that every time those halyards hoist the peak to the heavens with a gentle breeze following there is a little resurrection of sorts. I once saw a sick and dying horse lying in a stable-yard, an ungainly, sweat-darkened tangle of inert legs and neck and hooves on the dusty cobbles. Then the vet stepped back having administered some injection. In ten seconds, with barely a twitch between near-death and full consciousness, the horse rolled, unfolded its legs and shook itself upright in one swift movement and was off, skimming across the field in a gliding canter. The sudden sail-shaking resurrection of *Jack de Crow* that morning on the upper Severn was as heart-thumpingly beautiful as that.

For the first time so far, I was actually sailing. The weary *creak-thud* of the oars was now replaced by that loveliest of all sounds, the light rippling music of water on the wooden drum of the hull. I could sit in the dinghy facing the way I was travelling rather than in the neck-craning posture of the oarsman who must travel through life backwards. The sheets were easing and flexing as the light breeze nudged the mainsail out; the tiller thrummed beneath my fingers, gently tugging to one side as it should but kept in check by my steering hand. *Jack* was wonderfully alive again, for the first time in years.

Wonderful it was, but the hazards remained. I have been sailing on and off since I was five, but I still have not learnt the importance of *not* letting go of the tiller. In a car you find that if you take your hands off the steering wheel you have a good half minute's grace to prise the lid off a polystyrene cup of coffee before the car starts veering dangerously into the oncoming traffic and needs your full attention again. In a small dinghy, however, if you remove your hand from the tiller for so much as half a second, the rudder swings out of control, the boom takes a murderous lurch at you and you find yourself ramming the dinghy into a willow tree.

The willow tree on this first of many such occasions, a mile or so above Shrawardine, was a particularly clingy specimen and managed to get its green-grey twiggy fingers thoroughly enmeshed in the stays and halyards before I knew where I was. I had spent a few minutes carefully trying to wiggle the boat free, snapping off a twig here, bending back a bough there, before I gradually became aware of a large and furious presence six feet above me on the bank, the sort of nautical hazard that the ocean-going skippers of the Onedin Line rarely had to cope with ...

A bull.

Now, I've always been a great fan of Warner Bros. cartoons and I realised then, as I was forced to observe this bull at close quarters for a further heated fifteen minutes, that this specimen was in fact an exact model for the Warner Bros. cartoon team. It stamped. It snorted. It pawed the ground, sending great sods of turf and soil down the steep bank and into the dinghy. It had a shiny, spittle covered brass nose ring. It had two mad, little piggy eyes that turned to two spinning red spiral discs as its temper grew. It tossed its massive head and stubby

horns in frustrated rage at being unable to find a way down the sheer bank to
gore me to death. In fact, I would be almost prepared to swear that steam whistled
out its ears and nostrils and formed humorous little skull-and-crossbone puffs of
white smoke in the air while Bizet's *El Toreador* played in the background. It
struck me with some force at the time that a major design flaw in the Mirror
Dinghy is its bright red sails. To my mind, it is simply asking for trouble.

And all this while, with trembling hands and making ineffective bull soothing
noises, I was trying to get that damned willow to let go of my damned stays so
that I could drift quietly away and not bother nice Mr. Bull in his nice meadow
any more.

Eventually the last willow twig snapped away. Wiping sweat and bull-spittle
from my ashen face, I pushed away from the bank and out into the current once
more. The gentle westerly breeze blowing down from the Welsh hills behind me
filled the sail once more. *Jack* gave a shake and a ruffle as if to say "Concentrate,
Sandy! Concentrate," and we were on our way once more. Two miles later the
bull's bellowing had faded over the fields and I had stopped shaking enough to
think about lunch.

The God of Spontaneous Lunch Offers was not slow in manifesting his
bounty. Since escaping the bull I had bowled merrily along, and was just
approaching Shrawardine and its overgrown castle mound clothed in fading
dog's-mercury, when a voice hailed me from the bank.

"Twenty years I've been on this river," it barked, "and I've never seen a sail.
Come and have lunch!" Well, my friends say I'm slow at many things (catching
a Rugby ball, picking up a joke when I'm the object of amusement, for example)
but when it comes to free lunch invitations, my reactions are those of a striking
cobra. I put the tiller over, gybed neatly, and came to a graceful halt on a grassy
bank below a wall bright with purple aubretia and snow-in-summer. At the top
of this wall on a sunny terrace sat my host, a gruff, iron browed gentleman with
a gammy leg, reclining in a garden chair. He introduced himself in clipped,
military tones as Kiril Gray and waved me towards the French windows behind
him.

"In there, on the right. Kitchen. Cold roast beef. Bread. Help yourself. And
bring another bottle of red out, would you?"

A few minutes later, I was out again in the warm September sunshine, a roast
beef and horseradish sandwich the size of a Bible in one hand and a goblet of
superb red wine in the other. We chatted of this and that, Mr. Gray snapping out
shrewd brief questions about my plans hereon and expressing a gruff admiration
for my courage.

"Courage?" I queried. "Why do you say that?"

Suddenly I was worried.

"Ever been to Ironbridge Gorge, hmm? And before that there's Shrewsbury
Weir of course. Didn't they tell you? Ah well, you'll find out soon enough," he
murmured, a grim smile creasing his eyes. A silence, while I swirled the wine in

the glass, watching the sun make a bright ruby in its dark heart. It was very peaceful, very quiet...

"Isn't that gorgeous," I said. "That colour... It's like a garnet... or the colour you get in old stained glass."

"Funny you should say that. My wife's not here at present. She's putting a new window in Shrewsbury Abbey today. Won't be back till late. More wine?"

"Yes please." I held out my glass. "A window? In the Abbey?"

"That's right. Jane Gray by name. May've heard of her. Quite well known actually. Makes stained-glass."

Ah. I had a vision of Mrs. Gray, a little faded perhaps, a Parish Worthy, busy over her small retirement hobby with some Make-It-Yourself Craft Kit, piecing together garish glass kingfishers or improbably coloured autumnal sprays in circular frames for polite neighbours to hang in their front parlour windows. At this very moment, I thought, the Rector of Shrewsbury Abbey was diplomatically accepting some well meant offering in coloured perspex ("*I call it my Rainbow Prayer, vicar*") and wondering where he could best lose it in some dark side aisle or dusty apse.

"Care to see her workshop?"

"Lovely," I enthused politely, and considered launching into how, too, my mother kept herself busy making Victorian Christmas Decorations, silk flowers and ceramic kittens for the parish jumble sale. The moment I saw the workshops, however, and a portfolio of Mrs. Jane Gray's work, I realised that she and my mother were in somewhat different leagues. The glasswork was utterly magnificent. Photographs and designs for vast windows all around the country spilled into my lap: castles, cathedrals, cenotaphs, museums, and such a blaze of saints and angels, swords, lilies, fountains and flames, glowing like rich jewels... and these were only the photographs. How they must look in real life with God's good sunlight transmuting into sapphire and garnet, honey-gold and cool amethyst I could only imagine with awe. I determined there and then to stop at the Shrewsbury Abbey as I sailed past in the next day or two and see the new window in its place. But talking of Shrewsbury, if I wanted to make it there by nightfall I had best be off, so making my heart-felt thanks and farewells to my grim, ironic host, ("*Best of luck! Regards to the Weir...*") I hurried down to the dinghy, hoisted sail once more and rippled on my way.

I was immensely happy and grateful, not just for the slabs of roast beef, horseradish and wholewheat bread settling comfortably into my belly, nor for the ambrosial wine sloshing rosily into my bloodstream, but for the chance kindness of a stranger, the spontaneous call across the river at the sight of my red sail that was to set the pattern for the next three thousand miles.

Mr. Gray was the first to be warmed and delighted by the sight of *Jack de Crow* and to reflect that warmth straight back like a clear mirror; the first of many to send a small part of himself winging down the river with me into the wide lands beyond. And if this sounds uncommonly like an epitaph, then I'm afraid to say that that is in fact the case. Sadly, Mr Kiril Gray died three days later, but not before receiving a postcard from a pith-helmeted stranger somewhere downriver, assuring him of a successful outcome with Shrewsbury Weir and the Ironbridge Gorge, about which he had remained so disturbingly tight-lipped, with only his shrewd eyes gleaming with amusement.

Above Shrewsbury the River Severn runs in a huge placid loop around an isthmus known as 'The Isle.' The river by this time had become a deep, beautiful dark green running between rich pastures and glossy rhododendron woods and every now and then overlooked by some gracious manor house across shaven lawns. Horses grazed in the lush meadows and white Charolais cattle browsed beneath spreading chestnut trees, knee deep in the late summer grass.

As there was still a fair following breeze, I had the sail out full and was beginning to relax into the way of things. I had found it was possible to sit down low in the stern, my back propped for comfort against my folded life jacket (such a useful thing; I had been right to bring one) and steering the tiller with an idle elbow. The nice thing about running downwind as opposed to tacking into it is how calm and gentle and sunny things appear. With both the current and the breeze going your way, there is no alarming gurgle of water racing under the keel, no pushy wind tugging fitfully at the sails, nothing in fact to indicate that you are moving at all except for the smooth retreating glide of the distant banks...

Until you stop dead, that is.

I had just closed my eyes for a second or so, my face upturned to the warming sun, identifying the sweet trilling of what I thought was possibly a skylark somewhere above me in the pure serene, when BANG! Something clutched at the centreboard, held it fast. The placid green waters of the Severn, seemingly so dreamy a second before, became an inexorable muscle of torrent sluicing past the bows as *Jack* turned side on to the current. The barely perceptible breeze that had lulled me along so sweetly ripped off its benign mask and revealed itself as a bullying braggart of a wind, pushing, pushing, *pushing* the sail over until the dinghy was heeling at forty-five degrees and water was pouring over the submerged gunwale.

Whatever had snagged the centreboard beneath the boat was still holding it fast, and any minute the wind and current would capsize me completely. The orderly sheets and lines had been instantly transformed into a snarled tangle of sodden ropes in the bottom of the boat. The jammed mainsheet was holding the sail hauled in, rather than safely spilling the wind. The life jacket was half overboard, clearly making a bid for shore and leaving me to sink or swim.

I tried pulling up the centreboard but the wretched thing was clearly stuck on whatever had caught it. Finally, with an almighty heave and a horrid gouging sound, up it came like a cork from a bottle. I reeled backwards, sprawling into the flooded bottom of the dinghy, while the flying centreboard did a graceful somersault into the air before landing with a crack across my ribs.

I lay for a few seconds, wild-eyed and breathing hard. Floating ropes and a foot of river water sloshed gently about my buttocks as I glared up at the sky and listened to the river rippling on the hull. But all was calm again, instantly, miraculously, the moment *Jack* had been freed from that underwater claw. Now that once again we were going with the elements the Severn was murmuring its silken whispers under the keel, calm and placid, and the faintest of breezes was saying with some surprise:

"*Us? Violent? The dear old river and I? No, you must have been dreaming, old son. We're your friends. Now, what were you saying about skylarks...?*"

(I examined the centreboard later that evening, and found two deep scores gouged its entire length, so have come to the conclusion that it was either an underwater strand of barbed wire or there is something pretty huge in the freshwater crayfish line up around there, and that if entire cows are going missing as they go down to drink in the river at dusk, then I think I know what's doing it).

Finally, after baling out the dinghy, restoring some sort of order to the sheets and halyards and considering scrapping Rule No. 6 about staying dry as too impractical to enforce, I took the errant life jacket and put it on. I had just come up with a Rule No. 8. *Life jackets to be worn at all times.*

Life jackets have a certain magical quality that make them invaluable on any boating trip. This is that, invariably, within two minutes of donning the life jacket, rough weather conditions subside to halcyon tranquillity. Howling gales fizzle out to idle zephyrs. Tempestuous seas flatten to oily calm. When it has just taken you half-an-hour to zip up the life jacket with icy fingers in a numbing gale, the elements conspire to render the damned thing completely needless.

Marvellous things, life jackets.

Three minutes after firmly strapping myself into the life jacket, the breeze dropped to nothing, the current abated as the river widened, and small knots of ignorant people appeared along the bank who, glancing meaningfully at the mirror-like water and pacific sky, seemed to find the sight of a chap up to his ears in padding, a sort of orange Michelin Man, a trifle entertaining. Not normally one to bow to public opinion, nevertheless after ten more minutes of rowing in time to the jocular remarks thrown my way, I sent Rule No. 8 the way of Rule No. 6 and put the life jacket to better use - thwart padding. Besides, with it on, I had been hardly able to bend my arms. They had stuck out either side of the excessive padding like sticks on a tangerine-coloured snowman, and made rowing needlessly more complicated.

It was important at this point that rowing was as simple as possible, partly because evening was drawing on and I still had five miles to go, but also because my temporary repair job on the left rowlock was coming to the end of its warranty. With every oar stroke, the section of gunwale I had screwed into place the day before was slowly working loose again. Already the screws were at the cardy-snagging stage that is a trademark of Mackinnon carpentry, and I knew that by tonight I had to be within a very short drift of the Frankwell Boat Yard, upon which I was relying for wood glue and expert help on the morrow. Saturday? Yes. Good old Frankwell Boat Yard, I'd been told, open six days a week, come rain or shine, flood or fire. I'd be all right.

   Those last few hours of Friday afternoon were rather splendid. Despite the
loosening rowlock, I managed to row reasonably steadily past the last richly
pastured estates, and so to the first signs of Shrewsbury town. These are tall
Victorian houses perched high up on the steep right bank, looking somewhat
snootily across the river to the desolate Showground beyond, and with a strip of
common ground at the cliff's foot, a wilderness of long damp grass, hawthorn
and elder bushes, rabbit runs and sedges. Here I pulled gingerly in just as the sun
dipped below the high roof-line above and the air turned suddenly cold with blue
shadow. I tethered *Jack* to a hawthorn ruddy with berries, hoicked my rucksack
onto my back, sang out "Goodnight, *Jack*. Sleep well," and set off to find my
own bed for the night.

Rapids and Repairs

'But oh! that deep romantic chasm which slanted
Down the green hill athwart a cedarn cover!
A savage place; as holy and enchanted
As e'er beneath a waning moon was haunted
By woman wailing...'

Coleridge - *Kubla Khan*

After supper I went out for a walk in the cool night air. I have always loved Shrewsbury, and, though I would be sailing around her tomorrow on the river loop that almost completely encircles the town, I wanted to say a few quiet goodbyes in the lonely night.

For a Friday evening, the town was eerily quiet. Like so many other English towns nowadays, I'm afraid, Shrewsbury is generally given over to the lager lout and nightclub crowd on Friday and Saturday nights. Usually, I'm sorry to say, by eleven p.m. the streets are noisy and crowded and one must thread one's way between broken glass and reeling parties of young drunks. Decent folk tend to shun the town centre and stay at home. But on this night even the youths seemed to have abandoned it.

As I walked across the suspension bridge and up through the lovely riverside park called the Quarry I saw why. At the top of the park just by the big blue and gilded gates opposite St Chad's Round Church there is a little marble rotunda which houses a wonderful bronze statue of St. Michael slaying the Dragon. Tonight it housed something else. There in the dark silence of the park glimmered a hundred or so white candles, their golden flames glinting on a huge pile of cellophane-wrapped flowers. These buried the winged St. Michael up to his waist and spilt out onto the grass beyond the warm halo of candlelight, and every bouquet carried a tender card of condolence bearing the same theme: *We Love You, Diana, Princess of Wales*. This was the 5th of September, 1997, and the eve of the most publicised and widely mourned funeral in modern times.

As I wandered on between the Georgian houses of Swan Lane and up the narrow Tudor beamed Bear Steps to St Alkmund's, I saw with astonishment that every shop window was piled high likewise with flowers or bore a photo-portrait of the Princess and some caption of grief. Some, too, had candles burning all the night through. The War Memorial column at the top of Pride Hill was laid with wreaths and bouquets up to the halfway mark, and throughout the whole town, not a soul stirred.

I suppose that it was partly due to having arrived by river instead of the familiar road routes, but what with the candles, the photos, the flowers and the silence of the steep little lanes, I felt as though I had arrived after a long sea journey in some foreign port, some little island in the Mediterranean perhaps, on the eve of some great and holy festival. I half expected to see a midnight procession of donkeys, black head-scarfed peasant women and solemn Orthodox priests to come chanting down Pride Hill bearing candles, or to find that St Alkmund's graveyard had sprouted olive trees or orange groves, scenting the warm air with the perfumed blossom of an Aegean night.

It seems churlish to say it (and one dared not say it at the time) but I found the mass grieving that gripped England over those few weeks uncanny and disturbing. A beautiful Princess, mourned by a nation and buried in an island shrine on a lake; this is perfect when it occurs in Malory or Tennyson. But in reality, in the 20th Century, underpinned by the vast media machine? The mood of those weeks had the uncrushable, brittle glitter of cellophane, the acres of cellophane that smothered Britain in a crackling rainbow film that weekend... and equally as non-degradable.

I could almost have wished for the lager louts back... but not quite.

I have confessed already to being somewhat slow on the uptake in certain things. It will come as no surprise, therefore, to learn that I returned to my dinghy in a jaunty and optimistic mood the next morning, confidently expecting to row around the bend and have Frankwell Boat Yard provide the urgently needed service of rowlock repair. They were, after all, open every Saturday in the year, nine to five, come rain or shine, come flood or fire... but not, it seems, come Royal Funerals.

As I rowed around the bend and saw the closed and shuttered shed doors and realised that wood glue and expert advice would not be found the length and breadth of Britain that day, my heart sank. Already in that short stretch of rowing, the damaged gunwale had worked almost completely loose. A minute later it gave way with a crunch and fell into the dinghy. Crippled, unable to row, I drifted broadside on towards the ancient stonework of the Welsh Bridge as the bells of St Mary's and St Alkmund's chimed eleven. The fear of smashing sideways into the bridge was suddenly replaced by another thing to worry about. On the bridge stood a policeman. As the last of the chimes rang out the hour, he held up a solemn white-gloved hand and instantly, the road traffic on the bridge came to a halt. The background throbbing of engines died as the drivers switched off their ignitions. As I listened, I could hear a wide pool of silence spreading throughout the town as a thousand motorists all over Shrewsbury did likewise. Pedestrians halted on the riverside pavements; children in the park playground were hushed by mums who rose from the park benches and stood with heads bowed - not a soul, not a vehicle, not a living being moved for two minutes as all England fell silent to remember Princess Diana at the eleventh hour.

Except, of course, me. Unable to help it, I drifted helplessly down the current, scraped beneath the Welsh Bridge with a hollow thud and clang of hastily lowered mast on echoing stone vault and emerged in a tangle of ropes and stays into daylight on the other side, furiously whispering *Sorry! Sorry!* to the silently outraged mourners on the banks.

So frosty were the glares I received from the populace of Shrewsbury and the traffic policeman in particular that I was mildly surprised that the Severn did not freeze solid from bank to bank. I wasn't sure which fate would overtake me first: an arrest on the capital charge of high treason, or a town mob lynching. Either one, I was not in a position to escape.

But ten minutes later a minor miracle occurred, as befitted the sanctity of that day. A silvery-haired gentleman on the bank called out as I struggled by,

"Good Lord, is that a Mirror?"

"Yes," I called back. "A Mirror. Want to buy one?"

He watched me benignly for half a minute, then spoke again.

"Probably a silly question, old son, but why are you rowing round and round in small circles?"

I explained.

"Ah, now what you need is some wood glue, old boy. And a little expert advice. Pull in here. I may be able to help you."

And that is how I met Alan Snell, who just happened to have a waterside boat shed at his back, and who just happened to be building a wooden sailing-dinghy in his spare time, and so happened to have wood glue, screws, planes, files, chisels and bags of expertise. He also had rather a nice bottle or two of Chardonnay - it seemed that fine wine was becoming a regular feature of these unscheduled riverside stops.

For two hours Alan helped me mend the damaged gunwale and kept refilling my glass, and, by the time we had finished, the whole thing was as solid as the Rock of Gibraltar, which is more than could be said of the pair of us. As well as gluing it, he had, in fact, taken a strip of steel, drilled screw holes through it, curved it to the shape of the gunwale's swell and bolted the whole thing on with this reinforcing strip. It is a matter of record that for the rest of that long, long voyage, that gunwale and rowlock never gave the slightest trouble again.

It was with tears of gratitude that I finally set off again with both oars pulling strongly once more. The fact that I was still going in circles is, I suspect, entirely due to the third glass of Chardonnay.

Shrewsbury lies in another great loop of the Severn and is almost an island. The Romans came and placed a castle at the narrow neck of the isthmus and threw up walls with the river serving as a natural moat. In later centuries, the Normans added to the defences, built an abbey, improved the castle, and the town thrived behind its impregnable bastions, keeping the enemy hordes at bay for nearly a thousand years before a major breach in security let in the Town Planners who wrecked the place.

Still from the river it remains an attractive town on the whole, a mixture of Tudor and Georgian architecture and wide riverside parks. On I rowed, past the Shrewsbury School boathouses in mock Tudor, beneath the gilded blue of the iron tollbridge, and so on to the huge red stone Abbey and my promised stop to see the newly installed Jane Gray window. This depicts St Benedict and is every bit as glorious as I had hoped. The style is neo-medieval: that is, bold leadlines, clearly drawn figures and deep, rich stains in the wealth of symbolic emblems that crowd the back-ground - corn sheaves, flaming swords, the Chi Ro, the Lamb of God bearing its banner aloft. For *Jack* and me, there was the sinuous river loop that encircles Shrewsbury, a map in royal blue glass winding across the bottom frame. And for those enthusiasts of Cadfael, Ellis Peters' fictitious monastic sleuth is represented here also by an open book and quill and a diagrammatic herb garden down the left side. An even lovelier window, also by Jane Gray stands opposite, showing St Winifred crowned with stars and her holy fountain springing in silver-blue arcs at her feet.

By the time I left the Abbey, the warm glow of the morning's Chardonnay had faded from my veins. This allowed me to row in a relatively straight line, but was otherwise a pity, because approaching Shrewsbury Weir I felt in particular need of a little Dutch courage. This is the most fearsome obstacle to navigation the entire length of the Severn, chiefly because it is not in fact meant to be navigated at all. There is no boat pass, no side channel, no lock - nay, not so much as a fish ladder. It is simply an eight foot concrete wall built across the river from bank to bank over which the pent-up waters pour in one unbroken, white, roaring fall. At the foot of this thunderous cascade is a great trough of seething foam where the waters roll endlessly back on themselves. This is known to kayakists as a 'stopper', for the very good reason that it stops things - kayaks, canoes, canoeists and so on, holding them there in an eternal tumble of crushing waters until other things stop as well: breathing, pulse and neural activity, for example. Nothing that goes into this trough ever comes out again. For all anyone knows, there are the whitened bones of Norman soldiers, Tudor suicides and pre-Roman coracle fishermen revolving in an endless whirl at the foot of the weir, held there spinning in a restless watery grave, and soon possibly to be joined by a Late 20th Century dinghy sailor.

To this day, I do not know the proper technique for getting a small dinghy down an eight foot weir... there must *be* one surely... but here is the method I invented. I do not recommend it.

1. Moor up well above the weir.
2. Walk along and look at the layout.
3. Blanch slightly.
4. Decide that if and when the boat goes over, one will be somewhere safely on the bank at the time.
5. Rally five or six old-age pensioners who are dozing on park benches nearby.
6. Organise said pensioners into a chain gang to shift entire contents of boat by land to some point below weir.
7. Tie painter, halyard and mainsheet together to make one long, long towrope and attach one end to dinghy.
8. Pause to chivvy back into line one or two pensioners attempting to sneak back to their benches before job fully done.
9. Hold other end of towrope tightly.
10. Smile bravely.
11. Push dinghy out into midstream with one foot.

12. Walk alongside drifting dinghy on bank clutching rope.
13. Walk more briskly.
14. Trot...
15. Break into panicky gallop...
16. Scream as rope races out through hands, removing most of skin in process.
17. Watch with utter astonishment as good little dinghy plunges over the fall, breasts the maelstrom unharmed, and bobs like a cork over the rolling bones beneath her, laughing all the way.
18. Make short but heart-warming speech of thanks to pensioners, spectators, dogs, ducks, etc, before rowing away downstream, using only the undamaged tips of my fingers to hold the oars.

Many months after this escapade I read Sam Llewellyn's superbly witty account of a very similar exploit, *The Worst Journey in the Midlands*. In his book he describes his disastrous attempt to row an ancient dinghy in 1982 from Welshpool to London via the Severn and various Midland canals, and it came as no surprise to discover that we shared many common experiences. The boat-handling pensioners at Shrewsbury Weir were one of them... do they go there for the weekly exercise, I wonder, or had they just crept cautiously back after a fifteen year absence reckoning it was now perhaps safe to return to some peaceful riverside dozing?

And talking of other dinghy trips, it would seem to be a more common exercise than I had thought. One of the pensioners there told me with a misty gleam in his eye as he limped by clutching my sleeping bag that he had set off down the Severn in just such a boat many long years ago. "Really?" I enquired eagerly. (Perhaps I wasn't so foolhardy after all.) "Where did you get to? What happened?"

"I got as far as Stourport and was hit by a tanker," he replied, shaking his head sadly. "Sank of course." He sighed. "The leg's never been the same since..."

Right. Um.

Below Shrewsbury the river runs swiftly and strongly again in several more loops, and by mid-afternoon a good breeze had sprung up that stiffened to a fair wind over the next few hours, a wind that whipped steely ripples from the river's surface and sent silver-white squalls amongst the osier leaves.

I will not dwell on the horrible half-hour I spent jammed firmly in a riverside willow's branches while the greeny current attempted to suck the keel out from under me. I will pass lightly over the horrid scraping bump as I grounded on the shingle bank below old Atcham Bridge. This is, apparently, where all the drowned bodies end up - those released by the weir, that is. Legend tells of a mermaid that dwells in the deep pools by Atcham, and the story is perpetuated by the fine inn of that name that stands by the double bridge there. More modern tales tell of a giant eel also that lives in the umbrous shadows of the arches. Year by year it grows in stature, feeding on corpses and cockle-boats, defying all attempts to capture it. In the minds of local anglers it has now assumed the proportions of Jormungander the World Serpent - it would not surprise me to learn that the two tales, of mermaid and monster eel, are of equal antiquity... and veracity. I, alas, saw neither.

I skimmed on downriver and just as dusk was falling, saw that the stream divided into two on either side of a thickly wooded island. Which way to go? Where was the main channel? Wind and current were bearing me swiftly down and I had no way of telling the safer route. Just then a flash of blue skimmed out low across the water in front of me and zipped down the left hand channel. A kingfisher! An omen! I have always loved these jewel-like birds - who does not? - not only for their sapphire and flame-orange plumage but for all the myths and magic that fly with them. First to fly from the Ark, legend has it, the kingfisher flew up and drenched its then drab feathers in the dazzling hues of the first rainbow. Such a symbol of summer days and cloudless skies, old bestiaries claim that it lays its eggs on the silken surface of the sea when it is glassy calm. Such days of tranquillity are known therefore as 'Halcyon days' after the kingfisher's Greek name. I, too, have always made a personal connection between this secretive bird and the equally elusive Fisher King of Arthurian myth, mysterious keeper of the Grail in his hidden River Kingdom. Thus it was that with the whirring spark of turquoise leading me down the eastern channel, I silently thanked the gods and steered after my bright guide into the dark tunnel of trees.

Whenever a river is interrupted or split by any obstacle, the pier of a bridge, a sandbank or an island, the current either side suddenly intensifies to become a mill race, and this was certainly the case now. It was almost pitch black under the crowding trees, and the channel narrowed to a dark, wrangling torrent that swept over submerged logs and around out-thrust tree-roots. Down came the sail in a flurry. I managed to bundle it safely away out of reach of the ripping branches overhead, and turned quickly to my oars. My raw, rope-burnt hands flinched on the timber of the oar handles, but I was in control again. Then, to my horror, I saw what lay ahead. At the further end of the tunnel of trees, a huge fallen pine tree lay clear across the channel from island to bank, seemingly damming the entire stream. I turned to row... oh so slowly... upstream, but the current was so strong that even straining at the oars with cracking muscles, I was still swept down like a leaf on the flood. Only at the very last minute I saw that the left-hand end of the felled trunk was actually submerged - there the waters sluiced through in a gleaming black-glass muscle of water. I paddled furiously to squeeze through the gap and by some miracle made it, without impaling myself on the wicked dead spikes that jutted out from the main trunk in every direction. With a dark hollow gurgle I was through.

But just as I was breathing a shaky sigh of relief I found I had relaxed too soon. The boat stopped with a jolt. After a second or two of violent heeling, there came an almighty crack from somewhere under the keel, and *Jack* drifted on once more.

The centreboard. I had left the damned centreboard down *again*, and now it sounded as though it might be damaged on yet another underwater obstacle.

I tried pulling it up, but it was stuck fast.

There was nothing for it. Just as I drifted clear of the lower end of the island a gently sloping shelf of mud and shingle appeared on the left bank. Moreover, the lights of a cottage shone out in the dusk a mere fifty yards up the hill. I turned towards the beach, rowed as far in as I could before I felt the centreboard grating on the river bed, and resigning myself to the fourth wetting in four days, hopped overboard into waist deep water. Tilting the whole boat over to see her keel, I could see the problem. The centreboard had clearly been smacked hard side-on and had split right across at the point where it protruded from the keel. Rather than breaking away completely, it still hung on by half its splintered thickness, but these splinters were preventing it being drawn up from inside.

A major amputation was called for. A few hefty heaves snapped the damaged centreboard completely in two, allowed me to beach the boat properly, and collapse sobbing onto the grassy bank in muddy despair. This whole boating idea really wasn't turning out quite as I had envisaged. I don't seem to remember Jerome K. Jerome leaving a trail of vital components in splintery heaps all the way down the Thames. Ratty had not spent all his summer days eschewing the delights of picnickery for yet another visit to Harry the Stoat's lumber yard. And in all the fairy tales I know chirpy little kingfishers do not lead innocent travellers into death traps and then vanish sniggering.

After lying soaked on the grass for ten minutes feeling thoroughly sorry for myself, I trudged up to the cottage I had spotted earlier, trying out different opening lines in my head:

Excuse me, do you have an open fire and require fuel? I have just delivered a whole stack of firewood to the bottom of your garden in the form of a small, useless dinghy. It will need chopping up, of course. Savagely.

Or...

Hello, you don't know me, I am a complete stranger and very possibly a raving lunatic. May I take my trousers off in your front room and drink your whisky? No? Oh. All right then.

Or...

Do you have a Bournemouth Telephone Directory by any chance? Thank you.

As it turned out, I knocked on the door and was greeted by a pleasant looking chap with greying hair.

"Er..." I began.

"Good Lord, it's Mackinnon, isn't it? Sandy Mackinnon?"

"Er...?" I continued. I'd never seen this man in my life.

"Yes, from Ellesmere College. Well, well. You don't know me, but I used to have sons there, and I've been back quite a bit and seen you around. Come in!"

"Er..."

"So what can I do for you? Lord, you're soaking, come in and take your trousers off. Whisky?"

"Er..."

"Excuse the mess, won't you. I've just been knocking together a few odds and ends in my workshop. Carpentry, you know. Bit of a hobby."

"Er... er... funny you should mention that, actually..."

Those of you who are sickened by this unfailing tendency to thrive on the kindness of complete strangers will be slightly mollified to hear that I did not in fact batten hungrily onto this particular stranger's kindness. Before I could work out the order in which I would take advantage of his various overwhelming offers of help I found out where I was - Wroxeter. Beneath this tiny hamlet lie buried the remains of the largest Roman city yet discovered in Britain. Recent archaeological finds even hint that this may well have been the stronghold of the Fifth Century *dux bellorum*, better known as King Arthur - the original Camelot in fact. It seemed that my Fisher King had led me true after all. Under normal circumstances, this fact alone would have accounted for the sudden surge of joy that now flooded over me, but on this night I had another reason for mild euphoria. Less than a mile from Wroxeter was the house of a family I knew well and it was to them that I could cheerfully turn my leech-like feelers for help and hospitality that night.

Jenny, a wonderful woman with a hugely warm heart and the energy to match, had been entertaining me for Sunday roasts over the years in her vast, chaotic household set in acres of orchard and vegetable gardens. In between running a business, driving children to three different schools, singing in choirs, sitting on committees and turning out an exquisite array of hand-painted silk goods, she had somehow found time to lend her talents to designing and making costumes for my drama productions over the years. A quick phone call, and I was soon ensconced on her sofa just up the road, sinking in a sea of silk cushions embroidered with pomegranates, tropical flowers and coral fish, and wolfing down a gin. Once my sorry tale was told, Jenny's husband Henry was dispatched to the work shed and emerged some time later with a brand new centreboard, which was then varnished and left to dry overnight.

As I continued to tell of the discomforts and trials of the voyage so far, Jenny kept getting up, banging about in various cupboards outside, and returning to hear the next bit. I was a little curious as to this intermittent attention but when I had finished, she brought in an array of goods for me to take with me on the morrow: gardening gloves for the prevention of blisters; plastic map case to prevent my already dilapidated map from crumbling further; large packed lunch of sausage sandwiches, cheese, home-grown apples and chocolate bars to sustain me all the way to Gloucester by the weight of it; a bottle of white wine in case I got tired of rowing in a straight line; a corkscrew; and, best of all, a big, soft cushion appliquéd with gaudy parakeets to sit on in comfort.

The next morning I learnt that there was to be an additional item to take with me; a crew member. Kate, Jenny's ten-year-old daughter, would accompany me for the next ten miles or so and be picked up at Buildwas Abbey downstream. A further surprise was in store when we all tripped down to where I'd left *Jack de Crow*, my new centreboard under one arm and the sack full of goodies under the other, and found another centreboard, newly made, leaning against the dinghy. A short note from my friendly cottager of the night before wished me well, was sorry to have missed me that morning, and hoped that his mock-up centreboard might be of some use. From some nearby willow came the thin tinkling sound of a kingfisher laughing...

Well, with my breakage record so far, I supposed, it would certainly be useful to have a spare.

Hastily, before anyone else popped out of the woods or hurried across the fields with newly made booms, gaffs, oars, rudders or the like, or just blank cheques and suggestions that I should simply upgrade to a yacht, Kate and I clambered aboard and *Jack de Crow* set off once more.

As the river approaches Buildwas Abbey above Ironbridge Gorge it runs in broad sweeps between flat green fields which lap against the dark solitary mass of the Wrekin, a steep conical hill dominating the whole plain from Staffordshire to the Welsh border. It came into being, says a Shropshire folk tale, when a giant carrying a shovelful of soil was setting out to bury the people of Shrewsbury in revenge for some unrecorded insult. Just six miles short of the town, he met a little cobbler and asked how far it was to Shrewsbury. The clever cobbler, divining the wicked giant's purpose, exclaimed, "Goodness me, you'll never get there today, nor tomorrow neither. It's more than a hundred leagues away!" When the giant showed signs of suspicious disbelief, the cobbler emptied his sack of broken boots and shoes onto the ground and said, "If you don't believe me, look at all the shoes I've worn out just walking from there!"

The stupid giant, so disheartened by this ruse, abandoned his plan there and then. He dropped the shovelful of soil where he stood, turned on his heel and went back home... and that is the Wrekin as it stands today.

Again, like the Breiddens, the Wrekin seemed to glide about in a most uncanny way as silently as a dark cloud mass, and it struck me for the first time how different such hills look from the river. They take on a new grandeur, a titanic loftiness viewed from one's lowly vantage point. They rear steep and solitary, rising almost pillar-like from the soft green reeds and sedges of the river basin. We mortals, most of us, live our lives in Middle-Earth, poised halfway between the heights and the depths, the low places and the hills, and neither river nor range seems to us remarkable. But take to your oars, become one with the muddy-footed fisherfolk, the water voles and moorhens, and the mountains take on the aspect of Asgard.

At one point, we sailed around a bend and straight into a flock of Canada geese, who all launched themselves into the air in a hurricane of wings. What a flurry and fury all about us, a whirring, wonderful snowstorm of beaks and bodies and wide, wide pinions. It was a phalanx of archangels ascending to the Throne. The gibble-gabble from a hundred outstretched necks, the creak and whoosh of two hundred wings, the spatter of water all around and our scarlet sail breezing along in the middle of it all; this is what I had dreamt of when I first thought of sailing the Severn. Ah! and the breezy air full of drifting grey goose-down afterwards.

After a little while the breeze died, but that didn't matter because I now had a galley slave. Kate, wearing my red and white spotty hanky pirate style on her dark head, manned the oars while I lay back dreaming in the noonday sun, dreaming of this and that, of giants and T.H. White's geese and golden days ahead, and wondering if I could perhaps purchase Kate for a fair price for the remainder of the journey. My idle happiness was tinged only by a very slight irritation that for a ten-year-old beginner at rowing, she was doing considerably better than me.

Alas, at Buildwas Abbey, my brief idyll came to a halt as Jenny appeared on the bridge, waving a huge Union Jack pillowcase flag and hooting like a schoolgirl. Once Kate was safely ashore again, and I'd had my ribs cracked by a last big hug from Jenny, I turned my nose downstream once more and prepared to face the Ironbridge Gorge.

Ironbridge, tucked away in its steep valley off the major roads, is not very big and I doubt if many people outside the Midlands are more than vaguely aware of its existence. Yet it holds the distinction of being the very birthplace of the Industrial Revolution. Here is where it all started: steelworks and foundries, factories and mills, smelting and iron casting, and all that that has led to over the last two centuries. An engraving of the Gorge done in the late 1700s looks like a vision by Hieronymus Bosch: the river banks crumble beneath the weight of factories, shanty-town houses, belching chimneys and sooty wharves. The river itself is clogged with ships and barges, cranes, derricks, steamers and wherries, and on every side are piles of filth: slag heaps, overflowing middens, effluent pipes and broken piles of rubble swarmed over by emaciated people, skeletal and hollow-eyed.

Today, mercifully, it has reverted largely to become a steep secluded gorge again, though rather too dank and sinister in the dark depths of its waters for my liking. Up the banks swarmed trees clad in thick creeper, a tangle of black bryony and bitter ivy. Autumn seemed more advanced here in this sunless vale, the leaves already rotting to dampness on the trees and clogging the stilly waters. Grim verses chased through my mind... *The shadows where the Mewlips dwell are dark and wet as ink...* and I found that I was singing faintly to myself the Twenty-third Psalm. Under the semicircular arch of Telford's Iron Bridge - the first to be constructed thus - I drifted ghost-like before the faintest of breezes, and was cheered to see a madcap figure standing high above me on the parapet waving that outsized Union Jack again - Jenny, who had raced down in her car for a last sweeping wave. On an impulse, I dug into my rucksack for my tin whistle and as the great curving framework drifted astern I played a rousing chorus of *Rule Britannia*. Thinly over the water came Jenny's lusty vocal accompaniment while Kate - no doubt - shrunk in horrid embarrassment at her mother's unabashed display.

But *Rule Britannia* gave way to the melancholy *Tom Bowling* and just before the bridge dwindled to a distant dot, I got in a couple bars of *Auld Lang Syne*, modulated to a minor key by the mournful echoes and the air of departure. For now, this was the start of another stage of the adventure. Once the waving figure of Jenny on the bridge had vanished astern, I knew that I really had said goodbye to my old life at Ellesmere. Up until this point I had been charting familiar territory, seeing old haunts and relying on friends, never more than a phone call and a ten minute drive away from some friendly face; but beyond the Gorge, all was new.

Final Farewell

I was not yet beyond the Gorge, however. At the bottom of the Gorge lie the Jackfield Rapids. These really are rapids, a welter of white water some two hundred yards long, thrashing over and between black boulders and jagged rocks. Every weekend the place is gay with kayaks and canoes and their various lycra-clad, fluorescent-helmeted owners, who spend happy afternoons doing impossible things in craft as slim and unstable as a French runner bean. But the point is that these boats are tough; the odd knock on a boulder at twenty knots is a mere scuff to the fibreglass, and as for flipping over - well, that's half the fun.

I, on the other hand, wanted merely to get beyond the rapids upright, dry and unscathed, and was none too confident about any of these three. '*Fortune Favours the Brave*' runs the Mackinnon motto - though I've always found that, be that as it may, she also favours the prudent, the discreet and the well heeled. I decided to opt for prudence. The plan was to adopt roughly the same method I'd used for the Shrewsbury Weir, though with protective gloves on this time. The problem, however, was that here there was no clear towpath for me to amble along, and there were large rocks midstream against which *Jack* might be crushed like an egg shell if she touched. Nevertheless, I tried.

I slipped and stumbled amongst the slimy black boulders on the bank, and attempted to control *Jack*'s progress on a short lead, but the current kept jamming her between rocks or spinning her into side eddies and I'd have to stumble back upstream a few yards to pull her free. Wiry and wickedly barbed brambles and the low sweep of ash branches jutted out over the banks, hampering my slow to-ing and fro-ing. This footling progress was not to last. *Jack*, an altogether more impulsive soul than myself, finally grew impatient with my caution, and took off with a sudden swoop down a small cascade. Taking me off guard, the rope tether pulled me from my precarious purchase on a wobbly boulder, and I dived head first into the river on the end of the line, towed along like an unsuccessful water-skier who refuses to let go. Here we go again. A rush and a roar of foam about my ears, a lungful of Severn water and a cracking blow on the ribs from a submerged boulder; none of these things could divert me from the sudden illuminating thought that if one is planning to take a boat down England's fiercest rapids, it makes more sense to be actually *in* the boat at the time.

Twenty yards downstream I surfaced spluttering in a side pool where *Jack* had fetched up on a black rock and was kindly waiting for me. When I had finished spluttering, I sighed. Day Five, fifth wetting. More worrying though was that when I went to pull *Jack* off the rock, there was a faint but unmistakable crunch of splitting wood from somewhere in her keel - and an ominously chunky smear of yellow paint left on the rock's black fang. As for my ribs, they were aching abominably. There were more than two thirds of the rapids still to negotiate below us. At that point, I lost my patience with this whole prudence lark and decided to take *Jack*'s lead. With a silent prayer, I simply hopped in, pushed off and rode the remaining two hundred yards of the rapids as though *Jack* were a Colorado inflatable raft. I believe I closed my eyes.

There were a rush and a roar, one or two sweeping ups and downs, several slow waltzing spins and I was through. The rush muted to a chatter, the chatter to a gentle chuckle, the chuckle to a murmur, and then dreaming silence stole in once more. I was through. The rapids were behind me, and I had survived the greatest hurdle of the journey to the sea.

But before I had reached Bridgnorth, after ten long miles of steady rowing downstream, I knew I was in trouble yet again. The gently rising tide of water in the bilges told its tale only too plainly. *Jack de Crow* had a hole.

Bridgnorth, approached by river in the slow golden sunset, is stunning. It is a fairy tale town, set on its high red bluff of rock above the deep winding river and topped by the red sandstone tower of St Leonard's and the more elegant green-domed cupola of St Mary's Church. That evening I walked up the steep winding Cartway that zigzags up between black and white timber cottages and four-square Georgian houses, each with lead-paned windows lamplit from within, looking indescribably homely in the blue dusk. I thought I was in Heaven... or at least some medieval Hamelin, waiting for its Piper.

A very good place, in fact to stop for two days of rest; letter writing, cups of tea, the Cryptic Crossword, and working out how on Earth one mends a hole in a wooden dinghy.

It wasn't actually a hole, I discovered the next morning; more just a dent or split in the timbers of the keel, which leaked water into the boat at the rate of six inches an hour. This was not enough to be alarming, of course, but jolly irritating all the same; enough to produce a permanent state of wetness in the shoe department and to soak the underside of my rucksack lying in the bilges.

I sought to solve this problem by visiting a hardware store, and looking at its vast range of sealants, varnishes, resins, fillers and glues. I picked up one likely looking packet off the shelf and carefully read the instructions:

(1) Ensure surface to be sealed is clean and dry.
(2) Use fine grade emery paper to sand surface of entire boat thoroughly.
(3) Apply Epoxy Urethane resin over ENTIRE boat, ensuring even thickness throughout. Uneven surface may cause later processes to fail.
(4) Leave to dry for ten hours in warm room-temperature conditions.
(5) Get sanding again. Go on...
(6) Repeat processes (3) to (5) four more times.

N.B. Ensure that Epoxy bonding Cement is mixed with Reagent in EXACT proportions of 57:13 by weight. Failure to mix in correct proportions may cause nasty explosion. Good luck...

Feeling this was a little beyond my capabilities, I took down another product. Ah, this was more like it. ZIP-O-SEAL, it proclaimed on its garish tube:

EASY TO USE!
INSTANT RESULTS!

ONE SQUEEZE and the JOB is DONE!
DRIES in SECONDS!
SETS like STONE!
SEALS ANYTHING.

My sort of product, I thought... until I read the fine print:

(*Not suitable for metal, plastics, porcelain, leather, bone, Bakelite, linoleum, paper, carbon fibre, graphite, glass, cloth, fibreglass or wood. Works just fine on titanium alloy though.*)

A third can of sealant I reached down off the shelf didn't seem to have room for instructions; the entire packet was taken up by a large skull-and-crossbones and the word HAZARD across it in red letters. Beneath this was the following message:

WARNING: Do not allow this product to come in contact with eyes, skin, hair, clothing, the food you eat, the air you breathe, or within 100 metres of loved ones. Toxic. Flammable. Volatile. Radio-active.

Finally I decided to tackle the problem without the help of the marvellous world of D.I.Y... I went to a lumber yard, bought some timber and some screws and found myself a riverside park bench. There sitting in the sunshine and to the curious glances of passers-by, I sawed myself four planks and two cross beams to act as bottom-boards. Bottom-boards are simply slats of wood that sit slightly raised in the curved bottom of a dinghy and allow any bilge water to slosh away beneath them, while supporting high and dry anything above, such as a rucksack.

As for the hole, I went for the amateur approach. Remember that glue, that advertises itself as 'setting harder than the wood itself'? Well, I reckoned that if I smeared enough of that in the dent on the outer side of the keel, and supplemented it with a few tightly packed shavings off a bit of old willow stick I found, it couldn't help but do the trick. So that's what I did.

A little while later a rather unnecessarily jocular young man with a spotty face passing by explained in somewhat smirking tones that yes, indeed, that brand of wood glue does set harder than the wood itself and is perfect for all sorts of carpentry jobs, big and small... except for the slight disadvantage that it dissolves in water, becoming, as he put it so amusingly, "wetter than the water itself, ha ha, snort, snort."

I thanked him politely, remarked that time would tell, and recommended a good acne remedy that he might find useful, for which he was clearly grateful, as he walked off rather quickly, presumably to find a pharmacy before they all closed. It's nice to share these little tips, I always think.

Time indeed would tell, and as I sailed away from Bridgnorth the next morning, I watched anxiously for any signs of leakage from the Jackfield bump. To be honest, although the wood glue and willow-chip method seemed to staunch the flow considerably, over the next seven months *Jack*'s bottom was never as dry as formerly, so perhaps my acned friend was right. Nevertheless I felt that compared with the radioactive poisoning, toxic gassing and major chemical burns that the official DIY methods were likely to induce, a slight filmy seeping about my shoes was a small price to pay. Besides, I had spent so much time in the water thus far that I had come to regard high-and-dryness as somewhat of a luxury, reserved only for timorous folk who stayed at home. It would save on baths, I reminded myself and, on that cheerful thought, set off once more down the green river to the sea.

Steam Trains and Smooth Sailing

'I must go down to the seas again, for the call of the running tide
Is a wild call and a clear call that may not be denied.'

John Masefield - *Sea-Fever*

Now my tale moves on a little more swiftly. Most of the disasters that can befall a small dinghy had queued up to occur in the first six days, and *Jack* and I had dealt with them one after another in quick succession. Having got them all out of the way, we proceeded on our journey with a considerably greater degree of stately calm, having time to enjoy the pleasures of river voyaging.

And pleasures there were aplenty. The day that I sailed away from Bridgnorth I remember as a splendid day of ruffled blue water, long straight stretches of river and high white clouds racing across a bright sky on a stiff northerly breeze. This took me in an almost unbroken run of twenty-six miles, the red sail out full, the water creaming under my bow and the glorious chuckling, rushing music of all sailing dinghies everywhere. Reach after reach I sailed, through deep valleys of beech forest, between cliffs of red sandstone, past dreaming meadows where cows grazed peacefully, and all the while deeply, gloriously happy.

At one point, an old black steam train burst from an oak wood beside the river in a chuffing cloud of white smoke. A glance at my map showed that this was the Severn Valley railway that takes trippers between Bridgnorth and Bewdley. For the next mile or so we raced together, train and I, down that long sunny stretch of water, red sails against white steam, while all the passengers leant from the carriage windows and waved and cheered. Then with a long drawn out hoot from the driver, the train drew ahead and vanished around a curve, and I was left blinking and wondering if I had dropped straight into an E. Nesbit story.

The Race

At another point that day, I encountered another rapid - one I had not been warned about. The valley here had deepened to such an extent that the wind had died to nothing, baffled by the curves of the gorge and the thick beech forest on either side, so I was rowing along but with the sail still set, idly flapping about my head, ready to catch the next breeze. As I rounded a bend and heard the telltale chatter of water over shallow stones I stiffened in alarm... but no. My experience in the Jackfield Rapids had taught me the wisdom of relying on the family motto; it was better to throw caution to the winds, and run straight down the middle. Besides, from the sound of them, this section of rapids was a mere trickle compared to the Niagaras I had faced already, a shallow chattering of water over golden dappled shingle.

There was one problem though. Strung out halfway across the river was a gaggle of kayaks, ten or so, occupied by small children and an instructor: clearly a school party of beginners learning that there was nothing to be afraid of on the river, that one was always in control, that even in a rapid such as this, one need never capsize...

As I have said, they were strung out only halfway across the river, leaving a good twenty yard gap for me to shoot through as long as I rowed hard across to the other bank starting *now*.

A heave at the oars, a slip of the hand, and suddenly my left oar somehow flew out of its rowlock and splashed overboard into the river. By the time I'd recovered an upright position it was twelve feet away and I was drifting broadside on, out of control, towards the happy novices in their frail craft. It was an aquatic game of skittles, and I was about to score a perfect strike.

I called out an apologetic "*Um... er... hello?*" and the instructor and his party looked upstream to see a large yellow dinghy in full sail hurtling sideways down the rapid at them. Newly learnt paddle techniques were abandoned as the pink kayaks struggled to splash out of the way in the turbulent waters and a dozen white-faced eight year olds suddenly decided to switch to Pony Trekking elective from now on.

There was nothing at all I could do, and, as it turned out, only three of the kayaks capsized, and of them only one child needed medical attention; an invaluable opportunity for the class to see some real First Aid in action, I thought. In fact, the instructor was even gracious enough to retrieve my truant oar and return it to me as I swept on down the next bend, bless him, though he need not have hurled it quite so vigorously in my direction. And for once, the pith helmet didn't raise even the faintest of smiles.

Stourport came and went - ever since my limping pensioner at Shrewsbury Weir had told me about his collision with a tanker at Stourport I had entertained uneasy doubts about the place. "*A tanker? What, an oil tanker?*" I had envisaged Stourport as being some sort of vast industrial dockland where liners and freighters jostled for position alongside huge concrete wharves - and a small dinghy was likely to come to an untimely end beneath seventy tons of misdirected scrap iron. I was relieved to find then that Stourport was nothing more alarming

than a little riverside town whose only pretension to the world of shipping was
that here the Severn became officially navigable. White cabin cruisers and motor
boats now became frequent sights along the river banks, as well as a whole host
of mysterious signs and noticeboards with alarming amounts of red-for-danger
symbols all over them. Ah well, no doubt I would find out what they all meant in
time...

I stopped that night in a place where there was a ramshackle riverside tavern
chiefly memorable for the fact that a large white goat had the freedom of the
main lounge and dining room. It would do the rounds of the tables, staring hard
with its pebbly goat eyes at the customers until they would nervously get up and
leave. Then with a deft nip, it would steal an empty crisp packet from the ashtray
and retire to chew it noisily in a corner until not a shred of silver foil remained.
It also seemed to favour paper serviettes and beer mats; these last were always
being rescued by the harassed bar staff in mid-mastication and returned to the
customers' tables with an exasperated *tut*. It was quite clear that beer ring stains
on the surfaces were an anathema to the establishment in a way that goat saliva
on the tables was not; a cheerful blow for freedom from the petty restrictions of
the EU Health and Safety Commission, I thought.

I can remember little of the next day's journey to Worcester... rowing mostly,
I think... and although Worcester is no doubt a charming town to its residents, it
appeared grimy and drab from the river when I moored up there in the late
afternoon. A tedious slog around the town eventually found me putting up for
the night in the Talbot, a hotel-pub on a busy road but cheerful enough. I had
intended only staying one night, but when I leapt out of bed the next morning
and gave a big hearty, yawny good-to-be-alive s-t-r-e-t-c-h, I suddenly collapsed
in whimpering agony as a vertebra went *click* and pinched a major nerve.

This sort of thing had never happened to me before; it was clearly the result
of all that unhealthy rowing exercise I'd been doing, and I had no idea what to
do. Wasn't there something called an 'osteopath' or a 'palaeontologist' who dealt
with bones and backaches? But where on earth would I find one?

I winced out of the Talbot into the main road and there across the street was a
rather dusty looking shop window displaying nothing but a skeleton. The
skeleton was dressed in a stripy blazer and a jaunty cap and was clutching a
cricket bat in a pose that suggested he had just scored a phantom six. On closer
inspection, the window display was advertising the premises behind: *Kenneth
Brookes, Osteopath.* Unfortunately, he was in fact out all that day, but a chat with
his receptionist (also known as Kenneth Brookes' mum) had me booked in for
8.30 that evening. I spent the day back in bed tucked up with a bottle of pain-
killers, a half-bottle of Scotch and the *Daily Telegraph* Cryptic Crossword; with
the combination of the pills and whisky, the resulting answers were even more
cryptic than the compiler had intended, I suspect.

That night, I dragged my whisky-sodden frame across the road and into the
clinic, nodded a fuzzy hello several times to a skinny chap just inside the door
before I realized it was the skeletal batsman, and went to meet my saviour.

I love clichés. I love those old Ealing comedies where the jokes are as predictable as a speaking clock. I love being able to mutter 'stupid boy' one second before Captain Mainwaring does in *Dad's Army*. I love it when the World lives up to its expectations, when Swiss clockmakers have bushy white eyebrows, when thrushes sing in starlit pear trees, when nuns look exactly like all those ones in *The Sound of Music*. And so I loved it when Mr Brookes did all those things like chatting away about the weather or gently rambling about the Test match and then suddenly surprising me with some necessary adjustment to my body.

Afterwards, when all the limbs were back in their right sockets and the back pain had fled into the night he took me next door to the Lamb and Flag for several pints of Guinness. I can cheerfully recommend this kind fellow for all your chiropractic needs, especially his post-clinical treatment. He even explained the difference between osteopathy and palaeontology - about three million years, I think.

And so the journey rolled on, mile after mile, day after day. Upton-upon-Severn was the next night's stop, a model village with a Roundhead history and an extraordinary tower called the Pepperpot, domed in green bronze and almost lighthouse-like in appearance. The next day came the abbey town of Tewkesbury where I lunched in a fish-and-chip shop whose proprietor stood amidst all the greasy bustle of his three harassed staff in the kitchen and practised gypsy tunes on his violin. Then full of battered fish and the Wraggle-Taggle Gypsies-O, I sailed on that afternoon to a tiny hamlet called Lower Lode where stands a wonderful riverside inn. Here the lawns sweep down to the broad river, horses champ in the cobbled yard behind, and an old ferryman passes the time of day over a mug of tea and talks of eel fishing and tides. For yes, even here, within hearing of the chimes of Tewkesbury Abbey, the river is tidal, though the landscape around looks as rural and land-locked as Shropshire - from this point on I must plan my days' journeying with the tides in mind. That night I sit and share my supper with the family Labrador, dine on blackberries picked that day by the innkeeper's wife and, because the inn is fully booked that night by fishermen down for a competition, I am put up on a camp bed in the skittle-alley. I cannot think of a much pleasanter place to stay, more homely, more relaxed and unconventional, and life takes on that Elysian tint that I had so looked for when I set out. Jerome K. Jerome is probably sitting at the next table.

In the morning seven fishermen and I sit down at a big scrubbed kitchen table for a breakfast out of a bygone age. There is milk in a big cream jug of blue and white china, steaming hot porridge and amber honey dripping through a comb, catching the morning sunlight in its golden net. There follows a cooked platter of fat sausages nearly bursting their skins, mushrooms dropped sizzling from the pan straight onto the plate, and fresh farm eggs poached on buttered toast, and after that more toast with dark, chunky Oxford marmalade and scalding coffee. The burly fishermen are amused and interested by my trip so far, and wish me luck on the remainder of the voyage. Only one thing my breakfast companions say depresses me. Gloucester is apparently only another day's journey downstream and, up until this moment, Gloucester has been the intended finishing point of my journey, the point at which I have been planning to leave *Jack de Crow* for Philip to pick up, and rejoin the 20th Century. Gloucester. One more day. A great despondency settles over me, and I push away a proffered second helping of toast. I didn't feel I was ending the voyage; I felt that I'd only just begun.

As it turned out I did not make it to Gloucester that night. The wind sprang up from the south-west and drove up the river in a steady head-on gale, so that I was forced to row or tack downstream. Here may be the time to explain briefly the process of tacking.

No sailing boat can sail straight into the wind any more than a twig can drift upstream. But with the sails pulled in hard and the centreboard down, a dinghy can sail diagonally into the wind; no more than 45 degrees. This is called being *close hauled* and when the boat zigzags from side to side like a bishop on a chessboard, it is said to be *tacking* or *beating*.

Out on the broad Atlantic, or even on a fair-sized lake, tacking is all part of the fun and challenge of sailing. On a river, I can tell you, only the challenge remains. Firstly, the relative narrowness of the river makes it necessary to be tacking every fifty seconds or so, with all the flurry and weight shifting and sail-flapping that this entails. Secondly, the wind is famously fickle, shifting direction every few yards depending on whether you are out in midriver or close in to a bank. When the wind is behind you, these slight shifts make no great difference, but when tacking, they are maddening. Three times on every tack I find myself pinching the wind because it has swung around a little, or clapped in irons under the lee of a cliffy bank, and must go through the whole tiller-waggling, sail-shaking process of starting up again.

At times that day the wind becomes so faint and flighty that I give up trying to sail and decide to row. So... Loosen the main halyard. Lower the gaff and mainsail into the boat, not into the water. Bundle gaff, boom and sail into a long wrapped red sausage. Hold together with two elastic straps. Hoist the whole furled bundle up the mast out of the way. Tie off halyard on the cleat. Haul up centreboard and stow it away on front deck. Pull up the rudder with the drawstring and cleat it. Ship the oars. Start rowing.

No sooner have I done this than the wind strengthens into a steady, silver gale, smurring the whole reach of the river with pewter ripples and making every oar stroke a futile attempt simply to hold my position and not be blown upstream.

So I decide to try sailing again. Then, of course, by the time I have reversed all the above process, the wind will have died to an idle, sail-teasing flibbertigibbet once more.

It was, frankly, heartbreaking.

Much was compensated for when I pulled in exhausted to a tiny hamlet called Ashlewort. Here a tiny riverside pub nestled next to an ancient grey-steepled church; inside it was cool and quiet, smelling of hassocks and furniture polish and old roses. On the lectern stood a huge spread-eagled Bible open, I discovered, to Psalm 107. There were the words, '*And those who go down to the sea in ships, And do business on the great waters, They too see the wonders of the Lord upon the deeps...*'

It's nice to have these Divine promptings occasionally but I was beginning to doubt if I would ever reach the Lord's great waters. After investigating the church, I found an old manor next door that was holding an open day. I spent a happy two hours exploring this charming 14th century gem - its dovecotes, tithe barn and walled garden, its mullioned windows and tower stairway and four-poster beds - putting off the moment when I'd have to return to the dinghy and slog on to Gloucester. Just as I was paying for my cream tea, however, I noticed a Bed and Breakfast sign by the door... at the cheapest price I'd seen since starting... and decided to stay the night. If this was to be my last evening before finishing at Gloucester, I would live like a lord. I slept that night in a bed that was possibly Elizabethan. Tapestries hung on the walls rich with hunting scenes or pomegranate trees - the moon that night made lozenges of faded silver on the counterpane where it shone through the diamond leaded glass. It was a scene from *The Eve of St Agnes* and I was slumbering Porphyro.

The next day, I rowed the remaining drab miles to Gloucester. Already the river was clearly tidal, as the mud banks dropped steeply into the turgid waters on either side and the roots of osier and willow hung bleached and scum-whitened above a tangle of debris: detergent bottles, polystyrene foam and hairy red waterweed. Beyond Gloucester the Severn, I had been warned, became utterly unnavigable, running out to sea in a series of wide estuarine loops that were at low tide a maze of mudbanks and shoals or in flood a raging torrent of whirlpools, eddies and maelstroms. In fact, it is the birthplace of one of the oddest tidal phenomena in the World, the Severn Bore. Every year at the Spring and Autumn tides, the inrush of water up the narrowing bottleneck of the estuary causes a single wave, four feet high, to race up the river, sometimes up to twenty-six miles inland. Spectators gather on the banks to watch this oddity, presumably well equipped with Wellington boots and perhaps even snorkelling gear. I read of one intrepid chap who took a surf-board down one year and rode the crest of this wave all the way up to Tewkesbury, arriving terrified and exhausted along with logs, smashed punts, a chicken shed and one or two human corpses that the wave had picked up along the way.

The imminence of the Severn Bore's arrival was one reason I could not even dream of going beyond Gloucester on the river. Besides, a large weir below Gloucester made the river impassable even for tiny craft, there being no lock or boat pass. It really did seem that Gloucester was the end of the line, and I would not even have the satisfaction of reaching the sea. So much for bumping into Africa...

I rather wished for a better terminus. True, the city's cathedral is a jewel of design, a glory of honey-coloured stone and fan-vaulted ceilings, and there are some pleasant walks about the Bishop's Court, but much of the town centre has gone the way of so many other English cities, spoilt by a rash of Sixties blocks built by the Public Lavatory School of Architecture. The old Wharves area has been resurrected, however - though whether designer clothes shops and hippy-hoppy burger bars are an improvement on the tarry bustle of cargo ships and barges, ocean-going yachts and busy tugboats, is a moot point.

But as I stood there gazing out over the wharves and warehouses, imagining the days when Gloucester was a busy maritime port, a question suddenly occurred to me: how, if the Severn River has been an impassable, unnavigable channel since the Pleistocene Age, did all these clippers and cutters, these barques and barges, these frigates and freighters ever get here in the first place?

The answer, I found, was a little thing called the Sharpness Canal, and I suddenly realised the voyage wasn't over yet. I might just be joining those Biblical seabound mariners after all.

High Tide to Bristol

'There is a tide in the affairs of men,
Which taken at the flood, leads on to fortune;
Omitted, all the voyage of their life
Is bound in shallows and in miseries.'

Shakespeare - *Julius Caesar*

The Sharpness Canal runs roughly parallel with the Severn Estuary for sixteen miles from Gloucester to the port of Sharpness on the Bristol Channel. The canal, I was to discover, cuts across flat, wind-bitten fields, featureless and rusty with dock and ragwort, enlivened only by the occasional lock-keeper's cottage which here are all incongruously decorated with classical Doric porticoes, each one resembling a miniature Greek temple. Once at Sharpness, you can be lowered to sea-level in an enormous lock and let loose on the Bristol Channel beyond the worst of the mud-flats and vagaries of the Bore. This then was clearly my route, if only to let *Jack de Crow* sniff the salt air and retire with the dignity of knowing she had reached the sea. Then... I told myself firmly... I really *would* have to stop. Definitely. No buts. For sure...

I set off out of Gloucester on a morning of grey skies and a strong wind that blew unwaveringly from the south-west. After a mile of slogging along through the usual dreary wasteland that fringes every town, between high brick walls, cyclone-wire fences, the backs of warehouses and supermarkets and multiplex cinemas, I had reached the edges of flat fields and pastures... and the point of exhaustion. The wind was simply too strong to row against. A brief attempt at hoisting sail had proved what I knew already - that it was far too narrow a canal to make tacking an option. I was on the point of deciding that Ellesmere to Gloucester was a perfectly respectable journey for a small Mirror Dinghy to make and wondering whether trains ran direct to London, when a booming hoot blasted out from astern.

There, steaming down the canal behind me was a huge vessel, a triple-decked party ship on her way down to Sharpness. As I rowed violently to the bank to avoid being run down by this Behemoth, the skipper called out:

"Ahoy! Doctor Livingstone! Need a tow, mate?"

Two minutes later I was aboard, a hot coffee was in my hands and *Jack de Crow* was bobbing astern riding the white wake like a champion surfer. It seemed we would reach the sea after all. The vessel was called *King Arthur* (which pleased me), and Terry, the captain, was a black-bearded, twinkly-eyed chap who, had his hair been whiter, would have been advertising Captain Birdseye fish fingers on the telly.

As we ploughed our way along the canal, he regaled me with tales of surly lock-keepers, dopey narrowboat owners and the one-hundred-and-one ways you can die on the inland waterways of Britain. One story he told had taken place at Ellesmere wharf, oddly enough. A motor launch skipper had arrived one night at

Ellesmere in the basin next to the old dairy in the days before it shut down. It was pitch dark and, unable to find a bollard, he cast around for something else to tie onto. Eventually he found a sturdy iron ladder welded to a white wall of some sort and, checking it briefly for stability and solidity, hitched his mooring line to it and went to bed. He was woken at four in the morning by an alarming lurch, and scrambled on deck to find himself and the boat hurtling at full speed along the canal before smacking resoundingly into the concrete wharf at the basin's end. As the water began to pour through the gaping hole smashed in his bows there was a tight thrumming quiver for a few seconds, followed by an almighty snapping *boingngng*, and fifty feet of recoiling rope came lashing back out of the dark to knock the hapless man into the canal. Poised in mid-air between deck and water, he noticed the large white shape trundling off up the road and realised his mistake: never tie your boat to the back ladder of an early morning milk-tanker.

Meanwhile, I was realising a few mistakes of my own. The first was not putting my centreboard down; the speed with which *Jack* was being towed behind was causing water to bubble up through the centreboard case at an alarming rate and already the dinghy was half full of water. The second mistake was not stowing the oars properly; I had been in such a hurry to clamber aboard the ship before Terry changed his mind that I had left the oars still in their rowlocks and merely balanced on the gunwales. The swooping and bucketing of the dinghy on the stern wash had dislodged the oars and now they were trailing precariously in the wake, threatening to drop overboard at any time. The third mistake was in being towed at all. Do not misunderstand me. I was very grateful for the lift and Terry's coffee and company were excellent, but I realised the dangers inherent in mixing large motorised steel boats with small unpowered wooden ones, when we suddenly struck a mudbank in mid canal.

The first thing that happened was that *King Arthur* stopped dead with a sticky slurp. *Jack*, not concentrating, carried merrily on at her former speed and nose-butted *King Arthur*'s stern with timber cracking force. Not only that, but the suddenly slackened towline drooped down into the water and threatened to wrap itself around the wildly churning propellers.

This somehow never happened, and *Jack* drifted around to a safer position snuggled up alongside her mother ship... safer, that is, until in an attempt to reverse off the mudbank, *King Arthur*'s stern swung heavily in to one side and looked like crushing *Jack*'s ribs between herself and the bank.

Terry seemed cheerfully unconcerned about all this potential damage to his ship or mine. He twiddled the wheel and shoved levers to and fro without abating the flow of amusing disaster stories from all corners of navigable Britain, and *King Arthur* churned and wallowed and swung about like a mother sow with *Jack* dangling from her tail. I began to wonder whether Terry had been merely a witness to all these tales of inland shipwreck, or in fact the prime agent. They were certainly told in the Third Person, but then so were Caesar's *Gallic Wars*.

I need not have been worried. Terry was as competent as he was kindly, and soon we were on our way again. However, the exercise had been a neat little demonstration in the Dangers of Being Towed, and had covered, I felt, all areas of concern. One other thing Terry did for me was to turn my two week jaunt into a year of major voyaging.

"You'll be going through the Channel then to Bristol I suppose?" he asked breezily.

"What?! Oh no... I mean... well, you can't, can you?"

"Don't see why not. Good little boat like that, no problem. You'd have to pick your tide of course, and your weather, but you'd be all right."

At first I thought he was joking. Then I wondered if this was how he had acquired so many hilarious boating disasters in his repertoire: by prompting gullible fools like myself to acts of idiocy and then standing back quietly to take notes. (*"Yes, the best way of opening the lock gates is to ram them hard. Standard practice, honestly... Right, now tie up to that white ladder there. That's right. Now off you go to bed, and don't worry about a thing... Bristol Channel in a Mirror Dinghy? Easy-peasy, lemon-squeezy! Let me get your name spelt correctly for the obituary column."*) Was he then a sort of Iago of the Waterways, encouraging all comers to rash acts of folly while he himself stood neutrally aside? But when we arrived at Sharpness and I said my thanks and farewells, he seemed so confident in my likelihood of going on, so matter-of-fact about the dangers and the ways to minimise them, that before I'd cast off and rowed three strokes, I knew my sights were now set on Bristol.

Sharpness is a place of contrasts. On the one hand there are the docks, a huge area of concrete basins, giant steel cranes, hangars and warehouses and ocean-going tankers, all as bleak and grey and businesslike as shipping ports the World over. But, just around the corner from all this, one branch of the canal ends in a secluded basin tucked beneath a gentle hill that shelters it from the salty winds off the Bristol Channel. Here in the clear depths grow waterlilies and globeflowers, and black moorhens dabble about the bankside reeds. A fleet of swans sails on the ruffled blue surface and a dilapidated row of pontoons holds a motley collection of small craft: old motor launches, small yachts, dinghies and punts with fading paintwork. The hillside above is a rich tangle of blackberry brambles and windswept trees with here and there a cottage nestled deep in a garden bright with autumn flowers: dahlias, marigolds, chrysanthemums, all in seasonal burgundies and golds.

At the head of this basin is a thick concrete pier wall, and stepping onto this I was surprised to find that the other side dropped a sheer forty feet onto the sands of the Severn Estuary. The tide was out. Standing there one could look out across a mile of tawny sandbanks and shoals and the curling silver ribbons of water to the opposite shore where rose the green pastures of Wales. To my right, the estuary narrowed into the blueness of distant hills and to the left, broadened into a sea of sandy waters stretching limitlessly to the southern horizon; a faint smudge of shadow down there was all that could be seen of the two Severn Bridges.

I stood for a while gazing at the purple weed tumbled against the foot of the wall forty feet below me, a pair of herring gulls wrangling over some fishy morsel on a nearby pontoon and at the vast glimmering hazy brightness of air and sea and sand before me... then turned to go and find someone to talk me out of my newly grown and perfectly idiotic ambition.

The running of an important shipping port like Sharpness is a serious business, demanding organisation, a military severity of discipline and an almost Teutonic respect for the Rules. And Captain Horatio Eggersley is just the man to do it. His short, plump figure and baby face with a wisp of red hair tufting out on top are belied by the steely-eyed manner in which he tackles his job as Harbour Master. Thousand-ton grain ships from the Argentine and rusting freighters from Russia are moved about with the tactical precision of chess pieces set before a Grand Master. Cranes and derricks swing to and fro in a balletic dance at his choreographic command, and the tides rise and fall to within a centimetre of his carefully computed calculations. The very gulls fly in formation within the precincts of Sharpness harbour.

His reaction to my tentative suggestion that I might take my Mirror dinghy down the Bristol Channel was not entirely unexpected. He fixed me with a long, cool stare to assess my mental state before reaching behind him and pulling from an orderly file a sheaf of documents. We were in his neat office perched high above the harbour basin; computer screens blinked and glowed, charts and timetables covered the walls stuck with little colour-coded pins and the afternoon sunlight glinted on the braid and brass buttons of his uniform. I found myself struggling not to address him as 'Admiral' each time.

"These may interest you," he said. "A few statistics about the Bristol Channel. Tide records. Information on currents. Position and depth of shoals. Prevalent weather conditions. And this," said he, hauling out a file as thick as a dictionary, "is a record of shipwrecks, lost vessels and fatalities in the Channel over the last decade alone. Do feel free to browse."

As he turned back to his desk and rapped out a few curt orders down the radio, I flicked through the pages. Numbers, figures, graphs swam before my eyes; the only thing that struck me was how many exclamation marks there seemed to be. As for the file of shipping disasters, well, they were all great big boats surely - huge, clumsy unwieldy vessels with deep keels that were just bound to catch on the bottom occasionally. Not nimble little craft like *Jack de Crow* with a four-inch draft and the buoyancy of a cork...

"Hmm, yes," said I, trying to sound thoughtful and wise. "So these tides...?"

"Second highest in the world," snapped Captain Eggersley. "They reach twelve metres or more."

"Hmm. I see. So that means the current is...?"

"Ten knots in most places. Fifteen under the bridges. Your outboard motor won't have a chance if you have to fight against it."

"'Ah." Was this a good time to confess that I didn't in fact have a motor?
I confessed.

Captain Eggersley's jaw sagged briefly and then snapped shut again.

"So the whole idea is, I'm sure you realize, out of the question."

"Um..."

He sighed. He took a deep breath, and then quite kindly and patiently said, "Look. Let me explain." Moving over to a wall chart and picking up a pointer, he continued:

"We are here, you see. Now every six and a half hours all this water *here*..." (he swept a hand over an area that embraced half the Atlantic...) "tries to race up the ever-narrowing channel of the Severn Estuary and rises TWELVE metres. It comes in at over ten miles an hour, which is four times faster than anything you've been on so far down the river. It is so fast that it actually forms ridges and bumps of water, standing waves in midstream big enough to swamp a boat twice your size. Six hours later the whole process reverses itself but with the added volume of water coming down the Severn itself. This is called 'flood tide and ebb tide'."

He was into the swing of it now. Sunlight, warm and strong, poured through the wide glass windows looking out onto the estuary under the late afternoon sky. The office was drowsy with the faint hum of computers - a bluebottle fly buzzed sluggishly on the window pane. So peaceful, such a tranquil place to sit awhile dreaming... Captain Eggersley moved irritably across to the window and dispatched the fly with a glossy copy of *Yachting World*, and I was wide awake once more...

"Now usually between the flooding and the ebbing there are tranquil periods known as high water and slack water. We here, however," he said proudly, as though he had personally invented the system, "have virtually no such periods. Ten minutes of still water at the most, and the whole lot is on the move again. Now to get to Bristol, which is nine miles inland, you will note here on the chart that a vessel needs to travel *down* the estuary on the ebbing tide for sixteen miles and *up* this other river, the Avon, on the flooding tide. You've got to time it exactly right. If you get swept past Avonmouth on the way down, you'll be in Madeira by tea time. If, on the other hand, you haven't made it down to the Avon before the tide starts racing in, you'll be in Tewkesbury again... that is, if you haven't sunk on the first shoal, sandbank or navigation buoy that you hit at ten miles an hour in the first five minutes. Now you can see why I'm advising you to give it a miss?"

I considered, frowning a little. It seemed to me that Captain Eggersley was being a trifle pessimistic. Didn't the South Sea Islanders reach New Zealand? Didn't the Vikings sail to Newfoundland? Didn't St. Brendan reach America? Didn't Doctor Dolittle bump into Africa?

"Er..." I said.

"*Look*," he said firmly, his voice regaining its hard edge. "I'm a busy man, I've got a lot to do, and when all's said and done, I can't actually stop you. However," he continued as he took the documents from my hands with a brisk snap, "I am here officially warning you, and most strongly advising you," (here he slipped the documents back into the filing cabinet and rammed it shut) "that to travel from here to Bristol in an unpowered Mirror Dinghy is, in my considered opinion, suicide."

He picked up the thick Shipwrecks and Fatality file and weighed it in his hand. "Still, high tide here tomorrow will be at 6.26 a.m. sharp. The lock gates will be open between then and 6.47 a.m. I very much hope I will NOT be seeing you then." He turned to replace the file on a shelf as I looked into his cornflower blue eyes. They were almost pleading. He sighed, glanced at the file in his hand, and replaced it on his desk. "No point in putting it away then. I expect I'll be adding another report tomorrow. Dismissed."

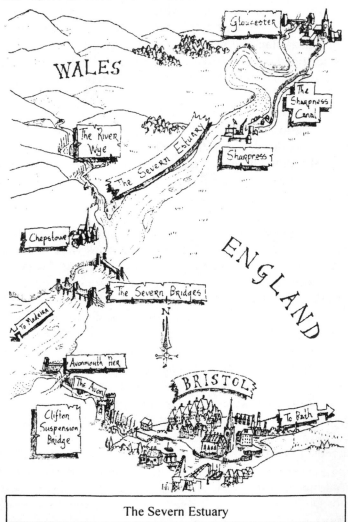

The Severn Estuary

I am not actually the reckless type. Nor am I a complete fool. I knew that one or two items of equipment were absolutely essential for this potentially hazardous trip on the tidal waters of the Bristol Channel, namely a chart and an anchor. The little chandlery down by the pontoons and the waterlilies had neither.

"All out of anchors, I'm afraid, Sir. We've got some more coming in at New Year if you'd like to pop back then. Now charts, Sir. We've got some nice Admiralty charts here. Let's see; Inner Hebrides, Outer Hebrides, New Hebrides, Isle of Man, Isle of Dogs, lets see now... Um, Solway, Moray, Medway, Steinway... Scilly Isles, Summer Isles, Skellig Isles... Black Sea, Red Sea, Dead Sea, Caspian... you could go all over the world with these charts, Sir, all over the world. Where was it exactly you wanted?... What? Oooh no, Sir. We don't stock the Severn Estuary, sir. Too dangerous. How about the Aleutian Islands, Sir, very nice at this time of the year, I believe."

So I got out my trusty Ordnance Survey map of the Bristol Channel area, my equally trusty fountain pen, and found a wall chart of the Estuary pinned up in the bar of the Sharpness Working Man's Club. There I copied as well as I could the buoys, the beacon posts, the leading marks and the major shoals onto my own map. As for an anchor, I found an old concrete besser-brick that no one seemed to be using, tied a length of rope around it, and voila... an emergency brake!

The next morning I woke early and hurried down from my Bed and Breakfast through the grey dawn to the harbour. I rowed from the little yacht basin around to the main port and into the lock that would lower me gently to the level of the sea. There Captain Eggersley was waiting with two other cronies, and all three greeted me with a mournful shaking of their heads.

"I can't dissuade you then?" asked the Captain. I hesitated. I did in fact have one main worry. For the past three days the wind had been blowing steadily from the south-west; even now I could see a green flag flapping out from the masthead of a grain ship lying next to the lock. This wind meant I would have to beat all the way down the Channel, and I had been warned that when the wind is blowing against the tide, the turbulence and chop is enormously exaggerated. In addition to this, I was concerned that my navigation skills were not up to keeping clear of the shoals while at the same time zigzagging about the Estuary. The centreboard would have to be down of course, and this increased my likelihood of sticking on the bottom - my experience with the barbed wire on the Severn above Shrewsbury had already shown me how disastrous that could be even in a mild current. In short, I was uneasy.

"Um... I think I'll be okay..."

"You've got a proper chart of course, haven't you?" asked one of the three. I proudly showed them my specially doctored Ordnance Survey Map. The early morning was damp and I wished I had used something a little more permanent than fountain pen ink. The headshaking increased.

"An anchor?" queried the other. I pointed out the besser-block lying on the foredeck and waggled the rope at them playfully. Their mutual glance between them spoke volumes. By this time the water level in the lock was dropping and I and the dinghy were gently descending with it. The three had to crane over the edge of the lock to see me. And still the questions came.

"Food and water? It's a long way to Madeira." Ah. I hadn't thought of this, but then remembered that somewhere in my bag, I had... ah yes, here it is. A Mars Bar. I held it up for inspection.

"Radio? Compass? Foghorn?" The words came dropping gloomily down the blackened well of the lock as the dinghy descended deeper and deeper, and my spirits dropped with it. "I've got a tin whistle," I called back brightly, but no reply came echoing down from the now invisible trio thirty feet above me. The only thing visible to me now was the rectangle of grey sky and that high green flag, still blowing from the south-west, but drooping even as I watched. The dank black walls and dripping gates rose sheer on every side as I continued to sink. It was like being lowered into a grave. Perhaps the three Fates up there were right. With the wind as it was... or even worse, if it dropped to nothing... I didn't think I could row the whole way.

One last call was coming hollowly down from above. The invisible Captain Eggersley was saying: "Look, I've just consulted the tide tables again. It's the Equinox. Today's tides are predicted to be the highest in thirty-six years. Leave it a week and they'll be back to normal. How about it?"

I stared up at the grey sky and that flag, thinking. I was certainly being offered a way out. It was arrogant of me after all to ignore the concerned and professional advice of these men who dealt with tides and shipping every day of their lives. It was all very well to play this hero game on quiet inland waters - to exaggerate the dangers of bulls and barbed wire, willow trees and weirs, and then laughingly go on my way regardless. It was fine to play the mythical wanderer, pretending that any goldfinch or bright star was an omen, a portent of good fortune to bless me on my way. But here there were no omens... and no belief anyway in any oracle save that of common sense. Was I really wise to venture out onto one of the most treacherous tidal channels in the world, in an unpowered and ill-equipped dinghy, and with a contrary wind to boot?

I glanced up once more at that drooping flag. And here, though no doubt I run the risk more than ever of incurring disbelief and drawing to me the name of Munchausen, I tell no lie. The wind had died completely, but as I watched, the inert flag twitched. It twitched again, then fluttered out faintly once more. Within a minute, it was bellying out in a fresh wind, a new wind, a wind blowing steadily... from the north.

"Well?" came that disembodied voice from the heavens again.

"Open the gates, thank you. I'm on my way."

And after all that, it was easy. I rowed out onto the estuary waters at the very top of the tide, a vast brown-silver stretch of calm waters almost a mile wide, and had my sail hoisted and rudder down in two swift easy moves. The northerly filled the scarlet sail as I reached across to the central channel and then turned south. My makeshift map was spread before me on the decking, the day was warming up, and I sluiced through the sand-coloured waters with enough speed to give me plenty of steerage.

Even once the tide had fully turned and started its long fierce ebb, the impression of tranquillity remained. Drifting with the water, of course, I was not aware of how fast I was actually travelling - only landmarks on the shore could tell me that, and these were so far away that they too crept minutely, serenely, by.

At times I would spot a distant buoy or beacon post and check my home-made map, ticking each one off as I passed it. Sometimes I would notice that two buoys, one behind the other, were shifting oddly in relation to one another and I would realise that the current was carrying me sideways across the main channel while my only apparent motion was forward.

The day grew so warm and the sailing was so easy - lying in the stern, steering with an idle elbow, watching the dreamy glide of the hazy land passing - I was in more danger of dozing off than anything. I was saved from this by a sudden air-shaking, ear-splitting roar at one point as five fighter jets went over, seemingly ten feet above the mast and setting the very timbers shaking with their thunder. As they turned and wheeled in formation, I saw the red wing tips and nose cones against the grey metal - the Red Arrow Flying Team, no less.

As the first of the two great Severn Bridges approached I sat up and took notice. I had been warned that the tidal current here was at its fiercest and that I would be reaching this point round about half-tide, the period of maximum flow. There was still a fair following wind, but I shipped the oars into their rowlocks in case I needed some extra power. It was only when I was virtually under the giant span, and too close to one of the upright piers for comfort, that I realized the strength and volume of water that was bearing me along. The brown water piled up in a foaming, bulging wave four feet higher on the upstream side of the piers than the surface downstream, and poured in an angry, tawny torrent beneath the mighty bridge. I was swept so swiftly along that the breeze no longer kept my sail bellied

Under the First Bridge

out, but let it flap idly as the current bore me quicker than the wind itself. Far, far overhead a trail of tiny vehicles were on their way to Swansea across that shining span.

The turbulence was worse under the second newer bridge - below the piers the water churned into a cauldron of eddies and back-currents and muddy coloured whirlpools that sucked at *Jack*'s keel and tugged alarmingly at the rudder. But so light and buoyant was she that the boiling race could never really get a grip on her shallow hull as it might have done on a larger boat. For all Captain Eggersley's experience and advice, I think I can now claim as true what I had guessed at before: a small dinghy with its lightness and shallow draught was in some ways safer from the shoals and tidal rips than many larger craft.

Not in all ways, however. By one o'clock the wind had died to nothing and I was rowing hard for the shore towards the enormous concrete pier at Avonmouth. The tide, swifter than I had calculated, actually swept me past the pier when I was a mere two hundred yards out from it, and yet it took me another hour of muscle-cracking, back-straining rowing to take me around the end of the pier and into still water. I tied up with shaking, sweaty hands to the rung of a ladder against the pier wall and regarded Captain Eggersley and his pet performing tides with new respect; I had very nearly made that predicted trip to Madeira after all.

The pier at Avonmouth is titanic in size. From where I moored up to a ladder rung I climbed a vertical eighty feet to the top of the pier. I knew I would have to wait here several hours for the last third of the ebbtide to run out before catching the incoming floodtide up the Avon to Bristol, and I was careful enough not to make the classic mistake of mooring *Jack de Crow* on a short line. If I did so, I would return in two hours to find her dangling down the wall from her painter, fifteen feet above the ebbing tide. No, I left her on a nice long line so that nothing could possibly go wrong. Then I clambered up the wet, barnacled iron ladder to the top of the pier.

There I was met by the Harbour Master of Avonmouth, a relaxed gangling fellow with amused eyes, clearly no relation to Captain Eggersley. "Ah, well done," he grinned, "I was wondering for a while if you'd ever make that last half mile. Come and have some lunch."

We repaired to his office on the end of the pier, a vast affair of glass and computer screens looking for all the world like a ship's bridge. Here, over sandwiches and coffee, he showed me the electronic instruments for measuring tides, currents and winds, the radio system, and the radar screen. "We've had our eye on you since you left Sharpness... or tried to at least. There's not a lot of metal on your boat, is there? You could sell the design to the Stealth project, no problem."

He had also rung the Coast Guard who had apparently been put on full alert, and Captain Eggersley to tell him that the black arm bands were no longer needed - then he turned the topic to football, his son's schooling and Life-in-General. A pleasant two hours passed until a green wavy line on a computer screen told us that the tide had just turned and it was time to be on my way.

"You did leave her on a long line, didn't you?" he asked.

"'Oh yes," I replied. "No worries there, no indeed."

And with that and a cheerful thanks for the sandwiches and coffee, I went back along the pier to the ladder-head. I leant cautiously over. Yes, there she was, more than eighty feet below like a tiny yellow toy duck at the foot of that vast wall. She was sitting on grey mud, but even as I watched a swirl of rising water was licking at her bows and soon she would be afloat again.

I clambered gingerly down the iron ladder that plunged away below me, but when I was still fifteen feet above the dinghy, my feeling foot met air. I glanced down, wondering why I could not find the next rung. Next rung? There wasn't one. The ladder stopped short right here, just where I had tied the painter two hours previously - between me and the boat there was nothing but a sheer drop of black, mud-slimed concrete wall. Clearly the designers of this gargantuan pier had only ever expected gargantuan ships to dock here, and had not seen the need for any ladder to descend fully to the muddy ooze.

Sigh...

I climbed all the way up the ladder again, marched off to the Harbour Master's office, and explained the problem. "Doesn't reach the bottom? Good Lord, I'd never noticed that before. Deary, deary me. You do have a problem, don't you?"

I marched back to the ladder head, and glanced around. Ah. Over there was a bundle of old nets and floats and... yes... a rope. Back again to the office.

"Yes, old boy. Take what you like. It's all old stuff."

With this great coil of hairy, slimy, coarse hemp rope over a shoulder, I made my way once more down the ladder. There, somehow, with one hand only (the other being used to cling on to a slippery rung) I managed to tie a bulky knot to the lowest rung and then steeled myself to abseil down into the dinghy. At the very last second, just as I'd taken a deep breath to swing into action, I remembered to untie *Jack*'s painter first. (Had I omitted to do this, I'd have had a further two-hour wait in the dinghy until we rose high enough to reach the ladder rung once more). Holding this painter in my teeth, tasting of barnacles and salty mud, I launched myself down the abseil rope. I would like at this point to be able to claim that the manoeuvre was executed with the ease and grace of a James Bond stunt, something ingenious using only a clean hanky, a safety pin and a dressing gown cord designed by Q. However, honesty compels me to admit that I went down that horrible rope like a bead on a string, serious rope burn only being prevented by the ancient sliminess of the mud that smeared its hairy length. I banged hard into the barnacle-encrusted wall three times as I descended, and believe that I actually let go of the rope entirely for the last six feet, falling in a muddy, shaky heap into the bottom of the dinghy. Luckily, she was now fully afloat. Had she been resting on the mud, my clumsy landing would have surely sent a foot straight through the thin hull. As it was, no damage was done and soon *Jack* and I, muddy but unbowed, made our way around the pier end, waved goodbye to the Harbour Master behind his glass walls, and turned our noses up the Avon for Bristol.

The next two hours were one of the pleasantest moments of the whole voyage. The incoming tide swept me up across mud-flats at a steady five knots and with barely an oar stroke needed from me except occasionally to ease the boat around a bend or keep her nose pointed upstream. In the dazzle of the afternoon sun, the mud-flats were no longer drab grey but silver-blue as they reflected the wide sky... and they were teeming with bird life. White gulls stood above their own reflections; redshanks and curlews picked daintily over the slabby mud, and flights of duck whirred into the air as I passed. As the channel narrowed and tussocky salt marsh closed in on either side the odd gaunt heron could be seen poised frozen on the margins - and as the marsh gave way to flat grassy pasture flocks of green lapwings shrilled and piped and flew with their big rounded wings flopping and rolling and pivoting in the air.

The Ladder Runs Out...

It was splendid. I was on a magic carpet, woven of soft greys and bright silvers, faded sea-greens and blues, a carpet that bore me silently along in the wide, empty afternoon sunshine, as much part of the landscape as the plovers and gulls that inhabited this bewitched no-man's land.

'Tell her to find me an acre of land' goes the song.

'(Parsley, sage, rosemary and thyme).

Between the salt-water and the sea-strand

(Then she'll be a true love of mine.)'

Here was that enchanted country at last, haunted by its own denizens: the web-foots, the cockle folk, the eel-people, the sand-fairies... and visited for too brief an hour by a passing Crow.

Soon the channel deepened and narrowed to a surprising degree. The teeming mud-flats gave way to mud-cliffs, and these in turn were replaced by black, kelp-covered cliffs of stone. Every now and then, I would pass a white house perched on the cliff tops, all curved walls and tiny windows in the manner of a lighthouse. When the tide is fully in they must squat right at the water's edge, their clean white and blue paintwork reflected in the river, but now they clung high up on the rocks like teeth on unhealthy black gums, thirty feet above the river. At intervals mud-filled creeks would cut down through the rock banks, littered with lopsided yachts all stranded high and dry, lolling on the gleaming mud like abandoned toys. Again, in three or four hours time they would all be dancing at their anchor chains once more alive and awake, little dreaming of the oozy depths below them.

Later the gorge becomes steeper and higher still - huge cliffs of orange sandstone above the river; and then there is the historical Clifton Suspension Bridge a hundred feet above me, soaring between its square stone towers; and finally the huge gates of the lock that will take me up forty feet to the floating harbour of Bristol Docks. I have made it, completed the journey from Colemere Woods to Bristol and finished on a note of success and inner contentment... and there is absolutely no question now of *Jack* and I parting company just yet.

"How about London?" says *Jack de Crow*.

"London it is," says I.

Wi' a Hundred Locks an' A' an' A'

'Vogue la galère.'
(*Row on whatever happens*)

Rabelais - *Gargantua.* 1.3.

Bristol is beautiful. Yes, approaching it by road or rail, your spirit sags under the unrelieved tedium of one-way systems, multi-storey car parks and the greyness of monolithic office blocks. But approaching by water, it is easy to believe that Bristol once rivalled all other places as the most elegant city in England.

The long harbour snakes for two miles between wharves busy with ships of every description, from tiny sailing dinghies to blunt-nosed tugs, from old schooners to *HMS Great Britain*, moored in splendid retirement. Everywhere you look, someone is doing something on, to or with a boat. Sails are being mended, awnings stitched, engines greased, ropes threaded, narrowboats restored, and a little black Puffing Billy steam engine runs up and down the quayside on narrow rails to give the place a further air of busy purpose. I was especially delighted to find one little ship there, high pooped and antique in design, painted laurel-green, but whose high prow was carved like a dragon's head in scarlet, a dragon whose tail curled onward down the green flanks. Here surely was Prince Caspian's *Dawn Treader* freshly returned from her voyage to the Uttermost East and Aslan's Country. The old tales were true after all...

On the north side of the harbour rises a long steep ridge, and up this climb the Georgian houses of 18th century Bristol in every elegant shade - cream, rose, pastel golds – the fashionable city of Jane Austen's novels. This too is the city of Isambard Kingdom Brunel, the great engineer of the nineteenth century who strode about the country with his cigar, knocking up railways and viaducts, tunnels and termini, as breezily as a boy playing at sand-castles on the seashore. I was rather hoping his flamboyant shade still haunted the place and would lend me some inspiration; I had a few engineering projects in mind myself.

I had decided that if I were to continue to London, (travelling overland via the Kennet & Avon Canal to the Thames) I would really need to conserve my funds by cutting down on accommodation prices. This I planned to do by converting *Jack de Crow* into a yacht, so that I could sleep aboard each night.

Well, no, not a yacht, but something more than an open dinghy. To this end, I hauled her ashore near a friendly boatyard and over the next three days, plunged once more into the baffling world of carpentry.

The idea was very simple actually, and lifted straight from *Coot Club*, one of the Swallows and Amazon books. In this, Tom Dudgeon equips his little dinghy *Titmouse* for sleeping aboard by making an awning that drapes over the boom at night and laces down either side like a tent. This I would do, but whereas Tom slept curled up in the bilges, I planned to make a sort of removable decking, allowing me to lie on a flat platform level with the thwarts. I hit on the idea of constructing some planks that by day would sit lengthways in the bilges under the thwart and replace my old bottom-boards, but by night would fit snugly across the dinghy side by side and create a temporary deck to lie on. The centreboard, trimmed to shape a little, could also lie across the dinghy in front of the thwart to be part of this deck.

The carpentry involved was basic, but it still took me three days to complete - three days under the open sky and a mercifully warm sun. I was lucky to have the aid of Dave, the taciturn young man who owned the boatyard and kindly lent me the tools and advice I needed... advice such as *"No, that's a screw you're holding. It needs to be inserted with a screwdriver, not a hammer,"* or *"Try using the toothed edge of the saw, it cuts better."*

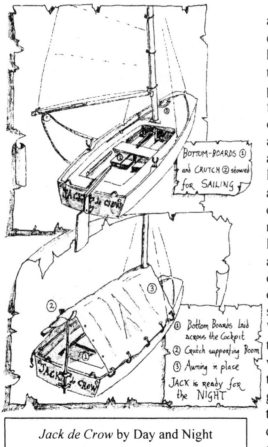

Jack de Crow by Day and Night

In the next door workshop was a blacksmith, and he made me a crutch, a thin pole of iron with a horseshoe-shaped piece of steel on the top. This slotted neatly into the pintel holes where the rudder fitted and would support the end of the boom; the boom then could act like a tent's ridgepole for the awning. The awning itself was a large blue tarpaulin that I took along to a sailmaker's loft overlooking the little Puffing Billy railway and the harbour wharf. Here a girl sewed a strip of velcro along the front edge and five eyeholes down each side. Through each of these protruded an elastic strap with a hook on the end. When the awning was draped over the boom, the front of the tent was velcroed shut around the mast and the five hooks clipped onto the gunwale, leaving a skirt of tarpaulin dangling outside the dinghy. The back end remained a clear triangle open to the air.

During my three days in Bristol, I stayed with an ex-student called Alex. He had only just left school and was in his first week of University there, an exciting time of new freedoms and throwing off the shackles of home and school... just when you want an old teacher turning up to stay on your sofa in fact and tell embarrassing school tales to all your new flatmates. Alex bore it with his usual exquisite manners and good grace. He is a tall, dreamy, flop-haired lad with all the aggression of a gazelle. Oddly enough, every character he had played in school drama productions over the last five years had demanded a cold and violent nature. A superb actor; nevertheless I had sometimes had a job to stir him to the necessary heights of bitter rage demanded by each part; his beloved goldfish pinned to the Drama noticeboard just before opening night usually did the trick.

When it came time to leave, Alex came down to the dockside, admired my new handiwork and presented me with a special bottle of something called Hobgoblin Ale - he knows my tastes in myth and magic quite well. Then I hoisted sail once more, and *Jack* and I tacked our way up the long harbour on our way to the unexplored mysteries of the Interior.

My love affair with Bristol faded as quickly as the afternoon wind died. Rowing out of the city was a grim business. On and on I rowed as darkness fell, but still I found myself behind Tesco supermarkets or derelict goods stations where wafts of sewage and pungent chemical odours rankled on the damp evening air and drove me on, looking for a mooring place where I would not be asphyxiated as I slept. I was also spurred onwards in my dreary rowing by a gang of youths who jeered and flung comments from a concrete stairwell. My temptation to stop and give them a short Baden-Powellesque lecture was stifled when they stopped flinging comments and started flinging half-bricks.

By the time I had left the suburbs behind and trees had crowded in on either side, it was pitch dark and I was cursing myself for breaking one of those Golden Rules - the one about never, ever continuing after dark.

Suddenly around a bend ahead there came the blare and tinkle of jazz trombones playing *New York, New York* at full volume and something resembling the Louisiana Belle came steaming down the river, decked out like a Christmas tree, all lit with fairy lights in orange, gold and red. I plunged out of the way to one dark bank and immediately tangled the mast and stays in an overhanging tree while the party boat swept by. Fifty merry sozzled passengers raised their glasses to the little yellow dingy crashing up and down in the wake, pinned to the bank by a spotlight beam that blinded the pith helmeted figure within.

" 'Allo, Doctor Livingstone," they happily cried. "Have a drink! Are you al'right there? Gawd, it's Michael Palin. Cheers! Bye..." and those vagabond shoes strayed off down the dark river and left me and *Jack de Crow* filling up with willow twigs and sploshes of water in the choppy wake.

Ten minutes later, eight of which had been spent carefully extricating myself from the twiggy clutches of my captor willow, back she came jazzing away like a full chorus of Seraphim and Cherubim but twice as glittery, and sent me ploughing into a mudbank to the brassy strains of *When I'm Sixty Four*. She turned out to be my saviour though. Half-an-hour later in a dark and bosky bend upstream, I found her moored against a section of river bank backed with steep woods, and her whole cargo of happy inebriates piling out into the little waterside gardens of a warmly lit house. In the light from the party boat's searchlight I could make out a sturdy pontoon with proper mooring rings and I decided that here was my best chance of a safe place to spend the night. As it turned out, this was the *only* place

I could have moored that night in safety. I did not realise until the following morning that this stretch of the river was in fact still tidal. Had I tied up to the bank anywhere else, I would have found myself high and dry by midnight, and as likely as not sitting on submerged rocks that would surely hole the dinghy. Mooring to the floating pontoon ensured that I stayed afloat whatever the tide level.

That night was the first spent sleeping aboard my newly converted dinghy. After a meal and a beer or two in the little pub, I crept outside, past a little tinkling fountain and a spotlit statue of Venus knee deep in ferns, and down to the dinghy. Here I set up the awning, put my decking planks in place and unrolled a thin foam mattress that I had purchased that morning in Bristol. Ten minutes later, to the gentle rocking of the stream and the small rippling night sound of the river, I was fast asleep in my new home.

The Avon River winds its way up to Bath to join the Kennet & Avon Canal that would take me over to the Thames. The two days up to Bath I remember little of - a winding stretch through broad parkland full of Sunday cyclists and families out walking the labrador and one or two busy locks by crowded beer gardens where parties come to sit and stare and make jocular remarks at the boats that bump and scrape their way through. I am surprised how rarely these beery commentators get thumped on the nose by irate skippers. *Jack* and I attracted more than our fair share of alcoholic witticism, but I put that down to the pith helmet rather than our erratic and oar-scraping progress through each lock.

I do remember that above one of these locks the river widened into a long sunny stretch where a whole fleet of sailing dinghies were holding a regatta, zigzagging about between reedy banks and wide pastures. There seemed to be two races going on, one between seven or so slim white Lasers but the other, to my delight, between a fleet of Mirror Dinghies, *Jack*'s red-sailed, snub-nosed sisters. I can see the puzzled faces of the other boatmen, frowning as they try to place me as I sail up the reach alongside the other racing Mirrors - *"We don't have anyone in the club with a pith helmet, do we? We'd have noticed, surely ..."*

And as we reach the buoy that marks the limit of the racing course, one by one my fellow Mirrors neatly round it to beat back up to the finish line. I keep sailing of course, rippling on towards a wooded bend upstream. Faint cries of alarm come from concerned skippers behind me. *"Er... yoo hoo! Hello! The course is ROUND the buoy and back to the Clubhouse... hello! You can't go that way... there's a bridge!"*

But what care I for rules and races, buoys and bridges? Let others compete for their tin trophies; I am on my way to the wide world beyond, leaving these tame sailors to shake their heads over the Clubhouse coleslaw and ask in wonder, *"Who WAS that pith helmeted stranger?"*

I should have listened about the bridge though. Unlike all the bridges encountered on the Severn, this one was a foot too low to allow my mast through, and I spent an awkward ten minutes in a welter of collapsed sail and tangled stays in an attempt to lower the mast and scrape my way upstream beneath the bridge's blackened arch. So much for the merry cavalier skimming away from the common herd to wide horizons and pastures new.

I should explain at this point that before ever I left Ellesmere I had rigged up an innovative contraption to allow for just this contingency. On a normal Mirror, the three wire stays holding up the mast are bolted firmly to the gunwale by shackles, useful screw devices for just such semi-permanent fixtures. However, I had rigged up the forestay to a running pulley system so that by simply releasing a rope, I could loosen it off and let it run free, thus allowing the whole mast to lean backwards and if needs be, lower completely to the deck. I could even haul the whole mast upright again using only one hand. I was really very proud of my Auto-Pulley-o-matic Ezy-hoist. It had therefore been a little disappointing that every bridge so far had proved to have enough headroom to render this ingenious invention unnecessary. So accustomed had I become to breezing under bridges that this one rather caught me by surprise, and my first use of the Ezy-hoist was less than elegant. I found however that the next ninety miles were to justify its presence to the very hilt - they are pretty niggardly in the south-west when it comes to bridge headroom, I discovered.

Rowing upstream, slight though the current was, proved to be tedious after a while; I had not realised how much I had been taking for granted the gentle onward flow of the Severn in the first few weeks. I found myself singing almost continually to keep up a steady rhythm - old folk-songs, hymns, musical numbers from various shows - anything at all to drive me onwards through the water. I soon found that the songs from *The Pirates of Penzance* were the most effective for this purpose; *Poor Wand'ring One* alone could take me a painless three miles upstream without me feeling a thing. But always there was something to catch my eye, something to cause me to rest on my oars for a few seconds and make the toil worthwhile - a pair of jays, blue-winged, flying out of an oak copse maybe; the discovery of some skullcap with its indigo flowers hidden beneath a grassy bank; or on one occasion a grass snake gliding across the stream just in front of the bows, so near that I could have leant out and scooped it into the dinghy. There on its greeny-bronze head was the yellow and black 'V' that T.H. White tells us of, the fatal mark that brands it falsely as a viper and leads to its indiscriminate slaughter, just as Mordred's soldier slew it long ago.

Finally I came to the City of Bath. Here the graceful curving horseshoe of the weir below the Pulteney Bridge prevents craft from proceeding further on the Avon River. They must instead join the western end of the Kennet & Avon Canal which rises sharply through six locks to continue its journey across the Wiltshire Downs and so to the east-flowing Thames a hundred miles away.

Bath is as beautiful as the postcards show it, a gem of Georgian elegance in honey-coloured stone. Avenues and arcades spread their amply respectable elbows as luxuriously as after-dinner smokers in a Hogarth painting. Graceful curved facades bask in the sun, tall windows conceal elegant drawing rooms behind rich brocade drapes and in the spacious squares about the Abbey buskers not playing Byrd, Purcell or Elgar are taken quietly away and shot.

The Abbey itself is famous for the vast windows of clear glass on every side - its epithet is the Lantern of the West - a light, airy building with none of the sombre heaviness of Gloucester and Tewkesbury. I visited also, of course, the famous Roman Baths - fascinating... or rather, that is what one is supposed to say. But Bath will remain in my mind not as the most important Roman site in Britain, nor the cultural and spiritual centre of the south-west, but as a place where I moored next to a bright garden where a pomegranate tree clambered up a sunny wall, its round fruit as glossy and magical looking as in an eastern folk tale. It needed a hoopoe or a pair of turtle doves in its William Morris branches of course, but was otherwise perfect. Bath will also be forever the place where I nearly died, dashed to death in the deepest lock in Britain.

Serious Inland Waterway enthusiasts will have been somewhat hurt and puzzled that I have not given some ink and space so far to the joys and terrors of locks. The fact is that even though I had been through twelve or so locks since halfway down the Severn, it was not until the start of the Kennet & Avon Canal that their presence began to loom large in my life: larger and more frequently than I would wish on my bitterest enemy. So let me tell you a little about locks, shall I?

Canals are artificial rivers but without the flow. Their sheer banks make them a death trap for any badgers or hedgehogs careless enough to topple into them, but otherwise they are charming and picturesque additions to the English countryside. They wind their way along the contours of the land - occasionally ducking through tunnels - on a flat placid level for miles on end; such flat sections of canals are called pounds. Inevitably, however, they must make their way uphill somehow and it is the locks that allow this 'Excelsior' ambition to become reality. A skipper of a boat approaching a lock from downstream finds himself facing a massive pair of black wooden gates, usually decked with hartstongue, moss and maidenhair ferns sprouting prettily from the woodwork. Once these are opened the boat glides forward into a narrow compound of concrete walls that rise up to twenty feet above him on either side. The gates behind him are closed, some sluices (called paddles) are winched open, and water pours into the lock, raising the boat higher and higher until he finds himself on the new upper level of the countryside with the next pound stretching away before him. Once the upper gates are opened, the boat can glide out and continue on its way.

Sounds simple, doesn't it?

"But who is doing all this paddle-opening and gate-shutting?" you may ask. "If the skipper is steering in and out of the lock, who is it operating the lock itself?"

Well the usual answer is the skipper's crew, commonly known as '*the wife*', or '*you silly moo, you've opened the wrong bloody sluice again*' - tempers on boats are generally shorter than those on dry land. But in cases such as my own, where the only crew consists of an earwig and a couple of stray woodlice that have somehow fallen aboard, the whole operation must be performed by Muggins, that's who. Going through a lock solo consists therefore of the following steps - especially when you find that the blasted lock is full and has to be emptied first to allow entry. So...

1) Moor up and climb ashore.
2) Step around nicotine-stained old tramp staggering about on towpath.
3) Go to bottom gates and wind paddles up.
4) Watch water level sink slowly... slowly...
5) Slowly...
6) Until level with bottom pound.
7) Politely agree with horrible tramp that yes, they ought to abolish all the ostriches (...?).
8) Heave and push and haul and strain against long, black-and-white painted beam to open lower gate.
9) Notice 'Wet Paint' sign.
10) Attempt to wipe hands and trousers clean of black and white paint.
11) Wonder where the blazes the lock-keeper is...
12) Assure tramp somewhat shortly that yes, I know I've got paint all over me. No, I don't want your hanky. Or your meths to remove it, thank you very much...
13) Return 100 yards to dinghy.
14) Row dinghy into dank, cavernous lock.
15) Bash around walls a bit, trying to bring dinghy alongside ladder.
16) Holding painter in teeth, start climbing slimy ladder to top of lock.
17) Realise painter is not long enough to reach more than halfway. Damn, damn, damn...
18) Cleverly tie painter to ladder rung with one hand while clinging on with other hand.
19) Finish climbing out of lock.
20) Heave lower gate shut, avoiding paintwork.
21) Winch open paddles in top gate.
22) Wait for water to rise.
23) Wait some more.
24) Realise that water is not rising and that I have committed the cardinal sin of lock operation; i.e. not closing bottom paddles before opening top paddles, thus turning the entire length of the Kennet & Avon canal into a freely flowing river.
25) Turn to find suddenly materialized lock-keeper returned from lunch-break.
26) Listen to irate lecture from lock-keeper about improper use of locks. Tramp nodding sagely over his shoulder, with occasional 'I-told-you-so' headshakes.
27) Hurry to close bottom paddles, bright red.
28) Watch water rise.
29) Quite quickly actually...
30) Suddenly realise that the ladder rung halfway down where my painter is tied is about to vanish under the rising water. Aagh!
31) Shin down ladder like steroid-addicted orang-utan and struggle to undo knot while water rises like flooded cellar to drown heroine in old black-

and-white silent movie.

32) Finally undo knot when it is a foot under churning brown-scummed water full of dead carp.

33) Scramble to top of ladder, soggy painter held in teeth, and tie it to bollard.

34) Borrow meths after all to rid mouth of dead-carp taste from soggy painter.

35) As waters rise level with upper pound, heave open top gates.

36) Row dinghy out. Moor up again. Close gates and paddles.

37) Repeat whole process SIX MORE TIMES.

Of course some of the above steps may be omitted if conditions allow, but *Jack* and I went through the whole gamut in that first of the Kennet & Avon locks in Bath: tramp, paintwork and all.

A LOCK and its environs

Actually this first one was the only lock so deep that the painter did not reach to the top of the lock wall, demanding that I hang halfway down the ladder above the churning maelstrom below, but each lock had its own little surprise to spring on an unwary *Crow*. Some would allow the prow or gaff to catch under a ladder rung as the dinghy ascended and I would have to make a flying leap to free her before she was dunked under and swamped by the rising waters. Others would fill, not by a steady welling up from below the surface but by a sudden horizontal gush of white water from the top-gates that threatened to fill poor *Jack* with half a ton of canal water and rotting badger if she ventured too close under the cascade. All in all, the one hundred and six locks of the K & A kept us very much on our toes.

Sometimes, the lock traversing experience was made delightful by the presence of passers-by and spectators who almost universally wanted to help. This often took the form of well meant but irritating advice (... *No, no, you'll strain your back if you do it like that. I had an uncle once...*) but I remember the very smart lady in a wide-brimmed hat, red as poppies, and a suit more fitted for Ascot than the rigours of lock operating, who insisted on performing the whole operation herself. I simply sat in the boat and called out instructions from below in the time-honoured phraseology of canal-boat skippers everywhere. (*No, no, you silly moo, et cetera*) This lady took me through not one lock, but three in a row, and after each lock produced a box of Belgian chocolates and rewarded me and herself with one each. She also kept up a constant bright chatter about how jolly it all was, and did I regard myself more as a Captain Hornblower or an Arthur Ransome hero. When she finally waved goodbye with a beautiful hand begrimed after the third lock, her smart suit crumpled, her hat askew, she called out "*Swallows and Amazons for ever!*" Such warm-hearted dottiness seems to haunt the waterways of Britain, and my voyage has been largely fuelled by the likes of these.

From Bath to Reading is ninety miles or so of narrow and often shallow canal, and mathematicians among you will have realised that those one-hundred-and-six locks will therefore occur at an average spacing of less than a mile apart. This makes for a dreary time of it, and I do not intend to take my readers through a blow-by-blow account of the next two weeks. Some highlights touched upon, and then moving lightly on, perhaps.

The journey from Bath to Bradford-upon-Avon was pretty enough as the canal wound along a hillside above a gentle valley, crossing it several times on aqueducts of mellow grey stone and running into deep, silent beechwoods beginning to turn red-gold as autumn waned. That day is only memorable for one long, easy stretch of steady rowing - so regular had my oar strokes become that I was idly dreaming of all sorts of things, including how I could perhaps string some old detergent bottles on a cord to make some much needed fenders, and admiring the smooth muscular way I was rowing her along in a dead straight line and how sunny and pleasant it all was when... WHAM!... I rowed straight into the stern of a big moored narrowboat. The owner, a very, *very* cross lady indeed, shot out of her hatch like an apoplectic cuckoo and screamed, "What the *hell* were you thinking of?"

"Er... fenders actually," I blurted out in a moment of tactless honesty. I'm not sure it was the most placatory thing to say, but five minutes later I'd managed to turn the subject to ceramics (a hobby of hers), bird watching (a hobby of mine) and away from paint-damage. I think we parted on amicable terms. The next day I bought some fenders.

Just below Devizes, there is a horrible thing known as the Caen Hill Flight. This I heard about from the friendly landlord of the Three Magpies Inn where I dined one night. The Flight is a stairway of twenty-nine locks, one after another, stretching over two miles of steady ascent. Narrowboats take about five hours to traverse the flight so must reach the first of the locks by ten o'clock in the morning. After that time, no more vessels are allowed through until the next day. Accordingly, I had carefully set my alarm clock that night to wake me at 7.30 the next morning. This would give me plenty of time to row the few miles to Caen Hill and be there for the ascent. What's more, there was bound to be a queue of narrowboats - I could slip in with one of them, concentrating on keeping *Jack* out from beneath the propellers of my leader vessel while her crew did all that tedious paddle-winding and gate-swinging above me. Thus, remora-like, I would batten myself onto an unwitting host, and save myself the heartbreak.

It was with a resigned sinking feeling that I woke that morning with the sun shining brightly on the blue awning, the birds chirruping in a suspiciously mid-morningish sort of way and my alarm clock inexplicably declaring that it was still half past two in the morning. It had stopped.

Not knowing the true time, I dressed, bundled the awning and mattress away and set off rowing up the canal like a demented windmill only to reach the Caen Hill Flight at five minutes past ten. The last boat had just entered the first lock. Not only was I not allowed through that day, but due to a water shortage the flight wouldn't be open again until Monday, two whole days away. I would just have to wait, explained the lock-keeper with an apologetic shrug. Sorry...

My Herculean feat of overland haulage at the Frankton Locks was not to be considered; not only was the distance just over two miles but it was uphill all the way. Unless I had some sort of trailer, I mused... Nearby was a farm, Foxhangers Farm, and off I trotted, disarming pith helmet in hand to see if they had such a thing as a boat trailer which I could borrow for a few hours. They did - and I could - for five pounds (*Deposit?* I enquired brightly. *No, rental fee*, they replied flatly). The trailer was mine for the day.

Even with a pair of wheels on this occasion, the haulage operation was no picnic. The dinghy had to be de-rigged, de-masted and emptied of its luggage, and even then seemed to weigh a ton; *Jack* had clearly been putting on weight since Frankton Locks. As I trudged up the long steady incline of the towpath, dragging *Jack* behind me, bystanders stopped and stared; they glanced from me to the canal beside the path and back to me again, and I could see the thought flitting across their worried brows - *Here is a chap on foot pulling a dinghy... NEXT to a canal. I wonder if I ought to point out the obvious?*

No one did however, so no one received a black eye, and I continued the long slog uphill, stopping every two minutes as a jellied wreck. It would be nice to boast that I got *Jack* all the way to the top unaided, but in fact before I was a quarter of the way up the towpath someone zoomed up on a quad-bike. I recognised him as a man I had encountered the day before, a lock-keeper who had given a very good impersonation of a clinically depressed Kodiak bear with toothache.

"*No,*" he had snapped yesterday, "*I couldn't bloody well go through his lock, who did I think I was, royalty or something? He had better things to do than attend to the needs of snooty-nosed boat owners with their yachting caps and gin-slings and goodness knows what else, even if he WAS paid by British Waterways to do so. Oh alright then, but I'd better be sure not to damage anything 'cos it was him who got the blame, and besides he had this terrible pain all down his left side AND his wife had run off with a Double Glazing salesman, AND there was rain coming, see if it didn't, which would ruin the new paintwork and... so on.*" Your average British Waterways employee in fact... or so my opinion had been at the time.

He had clearly had a frontal lobotomy since yesterday.

"Want a hand with that?" he chirruped. "Go on, hitch her on the back then, and I'll take her to the top for yer, Captain. Lovely day, innit?"

Off he whizzed and, musing to myself that the forehead scars had appeared to heal up very nicely, I went back down the hill to fetch the rigging. So heavy and bulky was this that it took two trips, but an hour later all this too was at the top, and I had only two more runs to make - one to return the trailer and then fetch my luggage to the top again. When I finally made it and reassembled the boat I was pleased to note that the overland route took just fifteen minutes less than the watery route; the last canal boat for the day was just chugging through the top gates. Besides, in walking eleven miles in all I'd lost two stone in weight.

Devizes was a grey little town, it seemed to me; the skies had clouded over after weeks of bright sunshine. I seem to remember being invited to a 50th birthday party for a chap called Ron, but how and why, I have no idea. That evening is lost for ever in a bright cider-tinted haze, I fear. The following morning I vaguely recall trying to install some fenders I had bought the afternoon before - hollow plastic sausages in blue and yellow with loops to be threaded on a length of cord. While I was doing this I was attacked by a swan.

I have not said much about swan encounters so far, despite the fact that from Frankton Locks onwards I had been baling them up, pursuing them, startling them, beating them off with oars or being hissed at by them every two hundred yards of the entire way. They had rapidly become my least favourite bird. Firstly, they have all the arrogance and empty-headedness of Public School prefects. This brainlessness sends them floundering off down the river ahead of one for miles and miles instead of simply moving to one side and letting one pass. Whole swan populations were shifted around from county to county in my two-month dinghy-sojourn in Britain. Genteel countrified Shropshire swans ended up sending out for fish'n'chips in sooty Midlands backwaters and Black Country birds with ghastly accents found themselves hobnobbing with Wiltshire farmyard fowl.

Secondly, they are needlessly aggressive. Every one grows up on those old stories told by parents to their tender offspring on trips to the park to feed the ducks: *Mind those swans, dear. They can break a limb, you know, swans can. They can drown an Alsatian!* I had always thought I was the only one to have received these dubious facts, but realised the widespread nature of these apocryphal warnings when one of my colleagues set a test in biology for his Third Form. One of the questions was 'What do swans live on?' and young Tommy Briggs wrote 'Dead wet Alsatians' - clearly my parents were better informed as to the dietary habits of British wildfowl than I ever suspected.

Thirdly, there are far too many of them. I was sorely tempted to compose a stiff letter to Her Majesty the Queen - who owns every swan in Britain apparently - and hinting that a little ruthless swan culling wouldn't be amiss, Ma'am.

To be attacked by an enraged swan when one is balancing low down in a dinghy, one's hands full of fenders and string, and suffering a throbbing, cider-induced hangover, is not an experience I wish to repeat. It is all a nightmare of hissing and huge wings, a nasty orange bill and mad little eyes - it is like being mugged by an enraged archangel. It was only when I managed to grab an oar and take a swipe at it that the wretched bird retired steaming and ruffled to the other bank. Pity poor Leda. I didn't hang around - the fenders could wait. I took off from Devizes and rowed east as fast as my oars could take me.

Out of Devizes the canal enters a quiet empty land of fields and flat pastures; sedges and bulrushes throng the banks and crowd even into the middle of the canal in places, making the rowing warm work at times. The grey skies have cleared once more. Nothing stirs in the hot afternoon glare but small flocks of birds - sparrows, chaffinches and a party of long-tailed tits, that flitter from hawthorn bush to hawthorn bush in chirruping excitement, or gorge themselves on the blackberries that hang in rich clusters along the bank.

So drowsy is the afternoon and so bountiful the brambles that I spend a happy hour picking blackberries from my dinghy pulled in close to the bank opposite the towpath. Here of course the crop has remained unharvested by passing picnickers, and the fruit hangs bright and heavy and ripe for the plucking. Soon my pith helmet is full to the brim and my fingers are stained with the sweet purple ink; my bare sun-browned arms too bear the evidence of blackberry picking, the odd white scratch or smear of blood from a thorn that has gone deep. It strikes me with an almost physical blow how lucky I am to be here. The rest of England is at work, pinched into suits and smart shoes in city offices or serving burgers in stifling motorway eateries; bathed in the pallid green glow of computer screens, or directing traffic in a haze of hot exhaust, or sitting in sweltering classrooms trying to lure back 3 B's attention from the bright world beyond the window to the dates of the Armada in front of them. And I...? I am standing in my shirtsleeves in the hot September sunshine, balancing aboard a buttercup-yellow dinghy, picking blackberries. I am Tom Sawyer playing hookey; Laurie Lee in his rich Slad valley; the boy Arthur in the Forest Sauvage, dreaming of giants. I am Sandy Mackinnon, in fact, aged twelve, picking blackberries in my own beloved valley above Adelaide and the holidays stretching away to the horizon.

I stopped for the night at Honey Street, which is worth mentioning. By the canal stands the imposing Barge Inn, which has been in its time a slaughterhouse, a brewery and a bakery. Having dealt with beef, beer and bread in the past, it now processes a new staple of the modern age - belief. In short, it is the Crop Circle Centre of the New Age. It is in the wide sweeping wheat fields that clothe the surrounding landscape and lap up on to the nearby downs that eighty percent of the crop circle phenomena has appeared, and if you wish to know anything whatsoever about the subject, then the back bar of the Barge Inn at Honey Street is the place to go.

Here the walls and ceiling are painted with a huge and beautifully executed fresco of a New Age landscape - spirals, standing stones, ley lines, moon-dazed hares, zodiacs formed in the ragged quilt of fields and pastures - and here too are noticeboards, bulletins, letters, magazines and files all pertaining to crop circles. Photos cut from newspapers jostle with petition forms to sign; complicated mathematical diagrams rub shoulders with letters that read like this:

WANTED. 10 acre wheat field in Honey Street area for Summer '98. Will pay. Contact Dept. of Cereology, University of Nurnberg, Germany. Ask for Mungo Sky-rider.

On first arriving, I passed through this room before entering the bustling, noisy, cheerful main saloon, jostled my way to the bar and ordered a pint of bitter. When it came, I shouted jocularly to the barman above the clatter,

"Interesting room out the back there. Is this where all the cranks come then?"

Well, you've all seen those old movies where an entire Western saloon full of cowboys goes instantly quiet when an incautious stranger mentions the old Harrison property down by Dead Dog Gulch? The reaction was similar here. The roar of voices and laughter died immediately, fifty pairs of eyes turned balefully in my direction and, had there been a piano bashing out a polka in the corner, it too would have stumbled to an ominous silence.

"Cranks, sir?" The barman coughed nervously and picked up a beer glass to wipe. "We don't actually use that word around here, sir." He glanced around at the waiting customers. "Leastways, not until October, by which time most of the bloody cranks 'ave gone off 'ome again. Isn't that right, gentlemen?" He finished on a roaring chuckle, and to my intense relief the whole pub started up again and the imaginary pianist in the corner launched into an uproarious can-can.

That evening, I chatted to a quiet chap with a close-shaven head who sat supping beer at the bar. He told me a little more about the crop circles.

"Of course, a lot of them are hoaxes," he said, flicking through a file of diagrams and photos. "This one..., this one..., probably this one though very neatly done...; this one of course, mere trashy rubbish, don't know why they bothered... but then we've got something like this."

Here he pulled out a photo and showed it to me. It was an aerial shot of a wheat field just bronzing to gold and there in the middle of it, formed by huge rings and discs of flattened wheat, was an elaborate double helix of gradated circles. The design was both beautiful and familiar, the classic DNA molecule twirl, and the lines were as neatly defined as though done with giant pastry cutters. Even assuming the work to be of human agency, the effect was extraordinary and must have taken days to achieve. But no, my companion told me; this one had appeared sometime in the space of four hours according to the farmer who had found it early one morning. It had certainly not been there at midnight, as he had been out checking some machinery nearby and would have noticed. Or so he claims.

Every summer hundreds of people descend on the area, said my informant - from curious tourists to serious scientists dubbing themselves 'cereologists' - from America, Germany, Sweden - and rent local wheatfields to record data and conduct experiments. Many try to reproduce documented crop formations, to see whether they could have been created by humans. Armed with stakes and balls of string and strapping giant paddles to their feet, they stamp about the fields in circles, calling like rabid corncrakes their claims and counter-claims across the golden seas of wheat. Meanwhile, headshaking farmers sit in the Barge Inn, count their wads of deutschmark and krona and order another pint.

I am left in two minds by this sort of thing. One part of me, the dreamy part that so happily accepts the role of mythic hero or relies on kingfishers as navigational aids, longs to accept the mystery of crop circles - not to mention crystals, pyramids, faeries and all that ilk. Another part of me, I'm afraid, is ruthlessly sceptical, wielding Occam's Razor like some philosophical winkle-pickered Teddy Boy. I know only too well how simple it is to fabricate stories in print, just how easily the printed word is taken as Gospel. It is the very strength of my desire to believe in mysteries that puts me on my guard against them. Perhaps that is why stories are so important - in that twilight world of fiction, magic can breathe alongside matter and neither can claim that kingdom solely for itself.

Still there was magic enough in that gentle vale for me to be going on with: the high bare grassy downs where barrow-stones brood and the great chalk white horse stands carved into the hillside; the rippling acres of young wheat ruffled into waves of silver-green by the wind, and skylarks singing in the empty blue... and foaming beer to be had of an evening in a homely inn.

From Honey Street, the Kennet & Avon Canal rises in a series of four more locks from Wootton Rivers to the watershed of the downs, and plunges through the Bruce Tunnel before beginning the long descent to Hungerford and the River Kennet. Here with England's genius for combining an appallingly soggy climate with annual water shortages, the canal had been declared desperately low over the tops. It would therefore be open only on alternate days. At Wootton Rivers I was told I must wait for two days before proceeding. This suited me fine as just a few miles away at Marlborough lived *Jack*'s godparents, Mary and David Du Croz. You will remember David Du Croz as the Headmaster of Ellesmere College in my first years there. He had since moved to Marlborough and it seemed appropriate to make a port of call and let the original Du Crozs know of their namesake's adventures so far.

David and Mary were as gracious and hospitable as ever. There is nothing remotely crow-like about David - if an avian comparison must be made, he resembles a benign stork more than anything, serious, tall and neat in a dark suit. Mary on the other hand is a slighter figure, an observant lady with a keen eye for any humbug or nonsense. In the years of playing the Headmaster's wife, she had maintained a professional discretion when it came to her private opinions about the mixed bag of characters in the Ellesmere community. Now that those days were behind her, it was entertaining to hear some wry observations about Minor Public School life. It was a pleasant respite for me from the rigours of life aboard and excellent company all the while, not to mention the much-needed use of a washing machine and a hot shower. When one is travelling alone, one never realises just how malodorous one has become until one is sitting amidst the chintz furnishings and cut-glass decanters of one's ex-Headmaster's drawing room. Then it hits one rather...

After several very relaxing days exploring Marlborough - the mysteriously named Merlin's Mount in the College grounds, the Chapel with its William Morris orange-tree window - Mary dropped me back at Wootton Rivers where I had left *Jack de Crow* two days earlier. There I found a narrowboat moored alongside, also waiting for the go-ahead to proceed through the locks. Her name was *Diana* and on board lived John and Di who within ten minutes of chatting had taken out adoption papers, got me to sign, and adopted me as the son they had always wanted.

They were wonderful. John was a shortish middle-aged chap with a capable manner and quiet eyes... and selective moments of deafness to Di's steady stream of Cockney badinage. Di herself was a woman with 'landlady' written right across her broad bosom and her hair the peroxide of barmaids everywhere - with the sharpness and boldness of wit to match.

Their offer to tow me through the first lock extended to the next three - then "why not the tunnel, luv, and since yore 'ere, yoo'l join us for sangwidges, wont 'e, John. John? JOHN? Gor blimey, 'e's switched right orf again, I dunno, 'e'll forget 'is own 'ead one day..."

Over thick, succulent tuna sandwiches eaten on a sunny lock side followed by homemade coffee cake and mugs of tea, Di expounded on Life.

"It's funny, Sandy, innit, but wot I fink is yer got to *make* time, ain'tcha, uvverwise wots it all abaht, eh?" Here she handed me a mug the size of a small barrel. "I mean, take kingfishers. *I* see kingfishers, *yoo* see kingfishers, even John 'ere sees kingfishers. But John's sister, now she dahn't see 'em, does she, does she John, even when there's one right under 'er nose? There's one, I says, right there, but she can't never see 'em cos, like, I don't fink she's got inner peace, if yoo know wot I mean."

She paused to let out a long sigh. "I fink inner peace is somefing yer got or somefing yer ain't - yoo got to be special to see kingfishers... sort of all quiet, like." Three seconds of inner peace would follow, and then we'd be off onto the next topic: Water Voles and the Art of Give-and-Take, for example. She was marvellous.

That evening at Little Bedwyn we moored up on a peaceful grassy bank where white geese grazed in a meadow. As I was setting up the awning for the night, Di came down the towpath and fixed me with a beady eye.

"Now look 'ere, Sandy. I'm not doing this out of charity like - and it's no good saying no 'cos I won't 'ear of it - but yore coming for supper tonight on board *and* yer'll eat wot yer given, and there's the shower there also to use as yer like, orlright? And 'ere's a glass of white to be getting on wiv, okay?"

Well, I'm a timid kind of chap and hardly dared refuse. Of course, I'd have preferred to wander off to a pub in the dark, spend an outrageous sum on a microwaved Chicken Kiev with French Fries and spend the evening reading beer mats - but one must make sacrifices at times. One mustn't be selfish. So I forced myself to have a scaldingly blissful hot shower aboard and ended up choking down Di's honey roast ham, the pease pudding, hot green beans and onion sauce, the chocolate sponge and the selection of fine liqueurs afterwards before deciding that I had been dutiful enough and retired to my little floating bed.

Next morning's awakening was one of those moments I look back on when things are dark and grey - something to fill me with a bubbling glow of contentment. Coming awake on *Jack de Crow* was always lovely anyway - to watch the golden-green reflections of reeds and morning sunshine rippling just half a yard from my feet through the open triangle of tent; to see the faint mist curling off the water, suffused with dawn light, and hear the ducks and coots dabbling at the river's edge; to smell wet grass and cows and the water mint crushed between *Jack*'s hull and the spiderwebbed bank an arm's length away: these are faint previsions of Heaven. But when on this particular morning it is supplemented by John standing barefooted on the dewy grass in his pyjamas and holding a breakfast tray, it is beyond the dreams of angels. There on the tray was a mug of aromatic coffee, piping hot; buttered toast with scrambled eggs, light as a cloud and sprinkled with black pepper; slices of toast with thick, dark marmalade - and a silver knife and fork winking in the bright sun, wrapped in a flowery napkin. And a note:

Bon appetit. Get your skates on. We sail in an hour. Di.

I don't remember exactly how many days *Jack* and I remained firmly attached as adopted waifs to Diana's motherly wing. From the sheer volume of information I learnt about John and Di's life history and philosophies and the amount of superb food pressed on me at every opportunity, I would guess six months, but my diaries seem to indicate two days at the most. Meanwhile on we glided, leaving the wide skies of Wiltshire and down into the thatched-cottage, chocolate-box villages of Berkshire.

And so we draw near to the end of the Kennet & Avon Canal where it joins the mighty Thames at Reading. Several days passed in sunny innocence, days in which I rowed beneath a warm sun through a gentle landscape, one feature of which was the little concrete pillboxes every mile or so along the northern bank of the canal - a relic, I believe, of the Napoleonic War but revived in the Second World War to act as a line of defence against any invasion from the south. It seemed odd at first to think of this quiet pastoral wiggle of water being any sort of military Maginot Line - why, it looked narrow enough to leap across - but I soon realised that to an advancing enemy it would certainly create an obstacle, especially when covered by firepower from these sturdy pillboxes. Nowadays each one is half covered in brambles and periwinkle and used to store fertiliser bags by local farmers ... or for less reputable purposes by the young folk of the area.

It was along one such section of the canal that I decided to go bathing. Here the River Kennet ran in and out of the canal at intervals so the water had largely lost its murky dead-rabbit colour and was relatively clean. It was a lonely, solitary spot so I decided that a bit of skinny-dipping would not go amiss. I enjoyed a happy ten seconds snorting and wallowing in the canal before deciding that in the interests of preserving my extremities, I would leave this sort of sub-zero bathing to the Finns. Just as I was hauling myself out of the depths however, there came a rustle from the hedgerow and out stepped an elderly gentleman with a brace of delightful beagles at his side. Clenching my teeth, I lowered myself back into the frigid waters.

Mr. Beagle did not seem perturbed by the sight of a blueish torso rising from the canal waters; in fact, he was inclined to chat. After some genial questions as to the presence of the nearby *Jack*, he told me of the annual rowing race that takes place in these parts, the longest of its type in the world. It runs from Devizes to Westminster along the canal with all its locks and then onto the Thames and down to London. The only stipulation is that the boats must be light enough to be carried over the locks, British Waterways not being geared up in temperament to cope with the sudden heated rush of a hundred or so excitable contestants. My beagle man went on to explain that many years before, when he had been working at the nearby paper mills, he and some colleagues had constructed a rowing boat out of corrugated cardboard. The resulting vessel had proven to be so portable and light that it had won the celebrated prize ... and then promptly sank after being holed by a small piece of driftwood.

"By golly, it was cold in the river as I remember," he reminisced, "and that was only June. Things must've got warmer since then. You certainly seem to be enjoying your dip," he added before raising his hat politely, calling his dogs and sauntering off down the towpath. That was the last time I tried skinny-dipping in the waterways of England - my extremities have never been quite the same.

And so on along an increasingly dreary canal to Aldermaston Wharf for a night, and then on to Reading. As one approaches Reading, even from miles away, a subtle drabness creeps over the landscape. There is nothing you can put you finger on - there are still fields and trees and hedges, birds and cows and fishermen, and all the trappings of rural England. But the trees seem somehow spindlier, their trunks sootier, their leaves more listlessly drooping. The fields seem scrubbier, the cows moodier and the birdsong is reduced to a dispirited fitful cheeping. As for the fishermen, well, it takes a practised eye to tell a normally morose angler from an especially morose angler, depressed by his proximity to Reading. The only thing that slightly cheered me up in those last two days was when I came around a corner of the canal just before a lock and found a concentration of fishermen staring glumly at the water, rods and lines in serried ranks along either bank. Knowing the temperament of your average canal side angler, I slowed right down and oared as gently and noiselessly as I could between the fish-eyed gauntlet of stares.

Dip, glide, slisshsh.

Dip, glide, slisshsh.

Dip, glide...

"Oh for God's sake, keep it down, would you?" snarled one green-wellied octogenarian. "There's a competition on, can't you see? Really..!"

"Sorry!" I called in a hoarse whisper.

"SHHH!" came back a sibilant chorus from both banks, which then subsided to a sour muttering about tomfools in blasted dinghies windmilling away selfishly scaring every fish for miles, no respect for rural traditions, youth of today, pah, in my day we'd have him horsewhipped, sirrah, et cetera.

I was nearing the lock gates, and considering I'd got off lightly - there are recorded cases of boat owners being lynched for their audacity in bringing boats onto the Kennet &Avon Ninety Mile Fish Pond - when a sharp-nosed reddish chap in tweeds called out in high nasal tones from the bank.

"Hey you! Boy! Yes, you. There *is* a competition on, you know. People ARE trying to fish, in case you hadn't noticed." He twitched his riding crop aggressively.

"Yes, sorry, but..."

"Well, 'sorry' won't catch that prize carp they're after, will it, boy? Hmm?"

"I really am trying to be..."

"You don't catch the seven-pound carp that's swimming about in there by being 'sorry' do you, boy? There's money on this, you know. We're not just wasting our time messing about in boats."

"Look I..." - but Colonel Fox-Snooty was already stumping away up the canal to tell off a boy flying a kite three fields away.

Gingerly, I filled the lock. Gingerly I pushed open the gates. Gingerly I rowed in, got out, closed the gates and emptied the lock of its swirling brown water and scummy debris. It was only as I was rowing out of the bottom end that I noticed something large, white and scaly floating in the lock alongside me - something that had clearly come down in the crushing, bruising cascade that fills the lock from the top pound. Hmm. I considered my options.

1) Climb up the bank, give a cheery wave and hold up the dead, white seven-pound thing in one hand, calling out: "Is this what you're looking for, gentlemen?..." before being cut up for bait.

or

2) Leave the moody buggers to carry on fishing fruitlessly for the prize carp that wasn't there anymore, the one that got away... in the most final sense of the phrase.

Option Two seemed a good idea. I turned my nose towards Reading and beyond that, Old Father Thames.

Death and the Dreaming Spires

'Slow let us trace the matchless vale of Thames;
Fair winding up to where the Muses haunt...'

Thomson - *Seasons. Summer. L.1425*

From Reading the Thames flows sixty miles south-eastwards to London, which meant that I could finish my journey in about four days. But as I rowed out onto the broad green river in glittering sunshine there was Caversham Bridge spanning gracefully over its reflected light and shadows, and I thought of all that lay upstream: Pangbourne and Goring with their willowy lawns and stately riverside manors; the old Roman town of Dorchester-upon-Thames; then Oxford, of course, and all its associations with my beloved Inklings and the like... and so on all the way to Lechlade in the Cotswolds where there lived a certain lady I had not seen for some years and thought I might surprise.

Besides, the breeze was blowing steadily from the south and like all those enviable heroes in every adventure story you've ever read, my time was my own - I was in no hurry to get to London. The decision was easy. I would go and chart the length of the Thames before turning around and making the final run down to London.

It was glorious to be out on a wide river again. I had barely been able to sail at all over the last eighty miles and my progress had been a fitful series of stops and starts. But here on the Thames it was different. With a good southerly breeze I was able to ripple along upstream at a pleasant pace, past the islands and outskirts of Reading, past the riverside houses with their velvety lawns, their elaborate Tudor boathouses and their monkey-puzzle trees and so onward to the Goring Gap. This was a very different river from the Severn. Here was wealth, here was prime real estate, here along the waterside fringes of each stripy-mown lawn was a coil of brand new razor-wire - a picturesque detail that does not appear in *The Wind in the Willows*. On the Severn, meandering down that wild Welsh border, people rely on the indefatigable brambles to secure their property from passing boaters - or vicious swans or mad bulls or the Severn Bore - but here in the broker belt trespassers are warned off by movement-sensor spotlights, Securicor personnel and the absolute certainty that one will be sued for damages by the family lawyer if so much as a croquet hoop is displaced.

Above Reading long hills rear on either side. These are the Chiltern Downs flanked with beech forests turning to red gold, and topped with grassy ridges seamed with bridleways and footpaths through the springy turf. At their feet, nestles the mellow-stoned manor house of Mapledurham, the model for Ernest Shephard's illustration of Toad Hall. Then comes Pangbourne crouching by its wide white weir. Here I stopped for the first afternoon and totally failed to appreciate its prettiness and charm due to the rain that had suddenly blown up from the south and settled into a steady soaking downpour.

I had, up until then, been extraordinarily lucky with the weather. Now however, the rain seemed set to stay so I moored up at the Swan Inn above the weir and trudged off to find my favourite of all places when in a strange town - a Laundromat. You can keep your tea shops and coffee houses, your pubs and shopping malls. On cold rainy days, there is nothing quite so cosy, quite so warm and womb-like as the local Laundromat. Outside the big plate glass windows, shoppers hurry past in the downpour, heads down, coat collars up, dancing along the kerbs between dirty puddles and ducking in front of steamy-windscreened buses. But here in the Laundromat there is the blast of warm air and the comforting hum and rumble of tumble-dryers, the clean smell of soap powder and endlessly fascinating articles in eight month old housewives' magazines about Forgiving His Nasal Hair problem or Attractive Christmas Wreaths You Can Knit Yourself.

Laundromats are also the best place, the *only* place in fact, to write letters. In pubs there are jukeboxes and beer slops; in cafés there are those cappuccino milk-frothing machines that sound like mating fire extinguishers. Even in Public Libraries nowadays there are generally the shrill tearful tones of the Assistant Librarian explaining to somebody that she can't get beyond RE-RUN PROG on the screen and it's been like that for five days now. But not in Laundromats. And on that account they are wonderful places for hours and hours of uninterrupted, toasty-warm letter writing, which is how I planned to spend my rainy afternoon in Pangbourne. A long, important letter to write and hours to do it in. But first, a quick phone call from the booth across the road...

Here's a good trick you can play if ever you're bored. Take a cigarette, half-smoke it, and then, without stubbing it out, place it in the Coin Return flap of a public telephone just seconds before some naive chap in a pith helmet arrives to use it. Then watch from a distance as said chap finishes his call and sticks a probing, change-searching finger straight into the flap and onto the still-burning cigarette butt. Wait for the yelp, appreciate the faint smell of scorching flesh and the loss of temper, and then run like blazes. This stunt is provided courtesy of the Pangbourne High School Student body and is guaranteed to prevent the victim from holding a pen comfortably for at least the next three days. So, while my washing went round and round, instead of writing letters I sat and read how to avoid unsightly ear wax build up instead.

The next few days saw the weather alternate between solid rain and bright skies with high white clouds hurrying westwards across the sky, but all the while a blustering knockabout wind drove me up the river in a succession of squalling blows. It was so swift and exhilarating that I remember very little of the countryside and landmarks that I passed. All my concentration was on where the next gust was coming from, and watching for a sudden gybe that could easily capsize me. So I remember the run up to Oxford as a time of hard sailing between banks where the dried sedges and rushes hissed like snakes before the wind's flail and the osiers turned their leaves in sweeping silver-green shadows; where the river showed slate-dark catspaws ruffling and patting the steely brightness of the water and where *Jack de Crow* surged and slackened, surged again and steadied her way up the long reaches.

I came to Oxford late one afternoon just as the purple skies opened once more. Before I could moor up, I was drenched to the skin and shivering with cold, flexing my cramped hands after long hours of holding the mainsheet hauled in. Abandoning any anthropomorphic fondness I may have previously displayed for *Jack de Crow*, I hurried up Headington Hill to find warmth, dryness and a large drink at the house of an old friend, Jo.

Jo, an energetic lady in her late forties, has the zip and crackle you get when you throw a bicycle into an electric substation. Over the last few decades, I had enjoyed the hospitality of her family in Yorkshire farmhouses, villas on Ithaca, cottages on the Cornish coast or in deep Devon woods, the Dordogne, the Highlands and by quiet Surrey golf courses - that easy brand of hospitality that points out where the coffee is kept, throws you a *Daily Telegraph* and makes it quite clear that sofas are for curling up on. I knew I was in for a comfortable stay then, when I arrived at Jo's front door.

The rain continued to blow in gusty waves over Oxford for the next four days, and Jo insisted that I stay until the weather cleared up again. This I was only too happy to do; four days of sleeping under a quilt the size and softness of a cloud, of writing letters (my scorched finger had healed), reading books and cooking exciting new meals with all the odd things to be found in Jo's cupboards that have not yet made it to the Ellesmere Supasave: sun-dried tomatoes and green peppercorns, tzatziki, pesto and ciabatta, Mocha coffee and Malaysian starfruit flavoured yoghurt - things like that. Four days also of dashing out between the showers to cycle on Jo's bike around Oxford: the Radcliffe Camera; the Eagle and Child pub where the Inklings met to read aloud their works in progress; the grounds of Magdalen College and its deer park; the wild, beautiful graveyard of the Church of the Holy Cross where Kenneth Grahame's tomb lies amidst a tangle of briar and seeding grasses; and a hundred and one other places with rich associations for anyone like myself with a long history of admiration for the group of Oxford dons and their friends who in the 1940s spun enchantment out of their dry scholarship like gold from dust and straw.

Lastly I cycled up the hill to Headington Church where the chief of these men is buried - C.S. Lewis. Standing by the simple grave beneath the yew trees, I offered a silent tribute for all that this man's work had meant to me over the years. Even as I stood there, I was conscious of the mawkishness of doing so, let alone writing about it. In all the months past and months to come no moment was as important to me as that one. In all the pages to come, no episode is more difficult to shoehorn into a narrative such as this. But so be it. Let it stand.

After four days then of ease and Jo's good company and sun-dried tomatoes on pumpkin-seed toast, the weather brightened again and I had no excuse to linger. After baling poor abandoned *Jack* of several bathtubs of rainwater, I set off once more to row upstream, through Oxford and beyond. For some reason I had always imagined the Thames (or River Isis as it is now mysteriously called in these parts) to flow past all the Colleges, the dreaming spires, the lawns with their wallflowers and ancient groundsmen, the honey-warm stonework and mullioned windows, and black-gowned academics cycling absent-mindedly to lectures cancelled in 1945. But it doesn't. Instead, it rather half-heartedly dives for one edge of the town, slips under a few bridges, skirts cautiously around the Head-of-the-River pub where rah-rah-ing Oxford Rowing Club types sit on sunny afternoons and drink themselves silly, and then makes a dash for the countryside again without so much as a glimpse of a College Quadrangle or a Porter's Lodge.

Nevertheless, a few miles above the town the river broadens into a lovely open stretch of water along the glorious Port Meadow. Here piebald horses graze on a vast flat pasture of common land that sits barely inches above the river level, an open unfenced area dotted with the odd gorse clump or furze still golden with late blooms. Yellowhammers tinkle in the hawthorn bushes on the left bank and young folk stroll up the earthy towpath arm in arm on their way to put in some serious study at the famous Trout Inn at Godstow, way over there at the head of the Meadow.

The wind had swung to the north after the days of rain, so I had to beat up this pleasant stretch, tacking to and fro and nearly grazing the low banks with each turn. People stopped and watched, marvelling at the scene - the red sail and the yellow hull gay against the clean new-washed colours of grass, water and sky. It was good to be on the move again and making people smile once more.

Once beyond the ruins of Godstow Abbey and the ancient Trout Inn by its foaming weir, the character of the river changes again. Suddenly the landscape seems to spread out, unroll into a wide carpet of empty fields, lonely farmhouses and thin spinneys and copses. There are no more villages for mile upon mile, only the iron giants of electricity pylons that march across the silent fields. The river narrows to a meandering lane of green, wandering like a lost child between flat meadows and reedy banks - sailing around these wiggly curves had the old excitement of playing at follow-my-leader where the leader twists and turns on his way and the children must follow every loop and sidestep. Then in a more serious mood the stream straightens out between row upon row of thin plantation trees whose paper-dry leaves whisper and rustle in the dying breeze. I too find myself whispering to *Jack* a few encouraging words under the blank stare of tall ashen trees and tall steel pylons as I take down the sail and set to the oars.

Long into the evening I row through a silent land, a land devoid of anything whatsoever. I have sometimes fancied in my dreamier moments that it is possible to detect those spots in a landscape that are faery-haunted. At times I have walked across fields and through woods around Ellesmere and stopped, touched by a certain... something, an indefinable air about where I stood that spelt enchantment. It is never anything as physical as a pricking on the nape or a sudden chilling in the bones - none of the classic symptoms of the ghost story genre. Indeed it is not physical at all. But it is as definite a change as a swimmer feels, who, snorkelling over a coral reef, glides from a cooler mass of water to a warmer one. Perhaps it is no more than an imaginative eye for a scene. I would hesitate to put it in stronger words than to say *If this were a story, it would be just here... this sun-warmed dell, this greying stone... that the hero would encounter Faery...*

But here on this stretch of the river and in the fields either side I felt not so much a presence as an absence - a nothingness of character and spirit, a Limbo where neither history nor Faery nor even plain modern living held sway. It seems odd looking back on it now. The fields about me were hardly Deepest Africa; in fact it would be hard to imagine a tamer region, more ordered and well tended a landscape. Yet I felt more than ever a sense of mounting unease, a desolation that at once unsettled and excited me. I had been wrong; there was Faery here of a kind... or if not Faery with its thronging presences, at least Myth. This was the Wasteland, Parsifal's Dream, the Plain of Carbonek whose barrenness hides the Grail at its heart. As I rowed into the featureless dusk, songs and stories and snatches of poetry ran through my mind in a steady litany to keep the weariness at bay - Father Brown and Flambeau rowing up the winding creek beneath a goblin moon to find Prince Saradine in his house of reeds and mirrors; Tolkien's errant mariner who '*wandered then through meadow lands to shadow-lands that dreary lay*'; Saki stories where a walk amongst English hedgerows and flat fields reveals wild beasts and casual death - a child taken by a hyena, a girl gored by a stag - and from *La Belle Dame Sans Merci* the mournful words:

'*O what can ail thee, knight-at-arms,*
Alone and palely loitering?
The sedge has withered from the Lake
And no birds sing.'

But as all these ebbed and flowed in my tired brain with the rhythmic oar strokes, one line kept snagging in my thoughts again and again, until it had crowded out all others with its ominous finality.

'*Childe Rolande to the Dark Tower came...*'

What can ail thee, Knight-at-arms? Lack of food, lack of beer and an over-vivid imagination, that's all. The twinkling yellow lights of the lonely Maybush Inn shining out through the darkness at last cured all three. An hour later, the gentle rocking of *Jack de Crow*, a cosy sleeping bag and deep dreamless sleep drove all the dark phantoms far, far away.

"And No Birds Sing…"

I had visited Lechlade many years ago when I first arrived in England. Before I had left Australia one of my students, a gentle girl called Emily, had said to me,

"Oh, when you get to England, you must go and visit my aunt. She's just lovely... AND single... her name is Daisy May and she lives at The Meadows, Lechlade. You'll get on so well."

Daisy May of The Meadows! Daisy May! With a name like that, how could I not get on well with her? In my year's travelling to England overland, I held a picture in my mind, a picture of a muslin-smocked Daisy May gathering forget-me-nots in her Cotswold cottage garden and just waiting for me to turn up. Oh yes, and singing madrigals. She was bound to sing madrigals, from merry morn to moonrise. Daisy May of The Meadows...

Well, when I finally arrived in England, I had found my footsteps meandering towards Lechlade and, just on the off-chance, just to be sociable, just really to say howdy from Emily, you understand, I found myself standing on the doorstep of a cottage whose name-plate had half vanished under a cloud of honeysuckle and yellow roses, and knocking on the old green door.

Silence, while I went through various explanatory opening lines.

"Hello, you don't know me but I was told by your niece Emily whom I taught in Australia which is where I'm from to come..."

No, too convoluted.

"Hi, Sandy's the name, you must be Aunt Daisy."

No, too familiar.

"Er... do you sing madrigals?"

Possibly, possibly...

My reverie was broken by the door being flung open and a voice snarling out of the gloom:

"Yes? Well?"

The figure before me was not quite what I had conjured up in my mind on those sleepless tropic nights. She stood before me, a gaunt, iron-grey woman with short-cropped hair, a hatchet face and aggressive eyes, swathed in a crumpled dressing-gown. Visions of forget-me-nots and muslin smocks dissolved in a hot sweat. She had something of the wolfhound about her, and if she sang madrigals at all, she would probably be taking the bass line.

"Oh... er... um," I stammered.

"Oh, er, um?" she echoed. "Hardly helpful. What do you want? Speech therapy?"

"Ah... I... oh," I continued.

"Oh, for God's sake!" she snapped. "Stop doing vocal warm-up exercises, and tell me what the devil you want! Well?"

I had decided flight was a better option than explanations. She had begun to bare her teeth.

"Look, I'm terribly sorry to have disturbed you, you don't know me, I was just calling on the off-chance but I see it's not a good time to call and I'll be off now..." I burbled, as I backed down the cottage path. But she fixed me with a flinty eye and rapped out:

"Oh, no you don't. You've woken me up. You've dragged me to the door. You'll explain to me right here and now who the blazes you are and what you want or I'm calling the police. You have thirty seconds. One. Two. Three..."

Well, somehow a tumbled explanation came out in a rush, and I suspect that hot tropical nights, my single status and forget-me-nots got included somewhere in the garbled, terrified babble that left me blushing to my hair roots and cursing young Emily for sending me to her tyrannical old crow of an aunt, Miss Daisy May.

From the doorway came a snort of grim amusement.

"Daisy? You want Daisy? She lives next door at The Meadows. This is actually Number Three, Meadowgate Cottage. People of low intellect like the postman are always muddling the two. Bell's the name, Frances Bell. Come and have a drink."

Relief and embarrassment swept over me in equal measure.

"Oh, look... no... I... er..."

"Oh for God's sake, don't start that again," she growled. "You'll come in and have a drink now that you've disturbed me, or I *will* call the police. Daisy's out but will be back in an hour. And if you stutter again, I'll have you shot."

And that is how I met Mrs. Frances Bell. Within minutes I was seated on a large shabby sofa with a gin and tonic in hand and deep into a conversation about T.H. White, C.S. Lewis, William Morris, the Pre-Raphaelite painters, The Anglo-Saxon Chronicle, the deplorable state of Eng. Lit. amongst Oxford graduates these days and terminal cancer... the last, by the way, which she had. Hence the mid-afternoon nap, the dressing-gown, the cropped hair and wolvish expression.

Her reaction to the condition was to give it extremely short shrift... along with anybody careless enough to offer sympathy or condolences. Bouquets of flowers left by well-wishers, I later learnt, were put immediately through the compost shredder, wrapper and all. Second offenders had the resulting mulch returned to them in small paper bags. 'Get Well' cards were cut up into individual letters and rearranged in the manner of a hostage note to spell rude anagrams. On Wednesdays, when the vicar called, it had been known for the front door to be booby-trapped with a small tub of over-ripe apricots and a trip wire.

When I questioned her reaction to this neighbourly goodwill she replied very firmly thus:

"Look, Sandy, to the whole village, goodwilled or not, I have suddenly become an object of interest, of tattle, of gossiping sympathy - a potential invalid with a satisfyingly dramatic disease that can handily become the focus for all their latent mothering instincts, all their charitable Sunday impulses and a boost for the bloody florist. If once I accept that role, the role of dying mother of two boys, the brave-but-cheerful-to-the-end victim, then I'm done for."

But aren't you anyway? I thought but could not of course say out loud. She read my mind.

"Of course I'm not done for. This is my body and my mind where I live, and I will not have things going on uninvited inside it, and I certainly will not pander to it by smiling wanly and building a tomb for myself out of flowers and bloody cellophane. No buts, Sandy. If it's a choice between playing the tragic but gracious invalid or staying alive until my boys are grown up, then I think I know which is the more important, don't you? I'm not fighting it, because there's nothing to fight. Unlike the Local Council... now there's a battle worth fighting!"

And her grey eyes sparkled with a steely glitter as she poured me another gin, lay on the sofa and told me about her on-going campaign against the idiocy and greed of various Council members who were planning to build a housing estate right across the quiet brook-bordered meadow common that lay beyond the window. Frances was conducting a one-woman war against the proposals and had so far, it seemed, been successful. All over the Cotswolds, members of the Lechlade Council were known for their nervous twitches and haggard eyes, and sales of hard spirits had soared at the local bottle-shop.

I saw Frances Bell again on several occasions. Before I'd departed that first afternoon, she had invited me back to dinner to meet the family the following Wednesday. When I explained that I would be in London then, she'd curtly handed me a train timetable and said,

"There *are* trains, you know. Big choofy things that get you from A to B. London is A, Lechlade B. Work it out, chum." I reckoned the Local Council didn't have a chance, not a chance.

While I was teaching for a term at Cheltenham College nearby, I was invited over once or twice and continued to come away exhausted, exhilarated and more admiring than ever. (I think on some of these occasions I did actually meet Daisy May, but she rather pales into the background in comparison with Frances' hatchet wit and indomitable spirit). The last I had heard from Lechlade was that the cancer had gone into remission - submission more likely - and had meekly sent a bouquet ready for mulching and a letter of apology for any inconvenience it might have caused - as had the Local Council who had finally given up the unequal struggle and left the meadows to the larks and dragonflies and forget-me-nots. These last remained for ever unpicked by my phantom image of Daisy May-As-She-Might-Have-Been.

It was four years since I had seen Frances and the family, and it was to Lechlade that I was now heading, toiling slowly up the Thames to knock unexpectedly on that honeysuckled door once more and be barked at by that gruff sardonic voice.

I pulled in eventually under the Ha'penny Bridge on an afternoon of blustery rain, three days after leaving Oxford. For the last few miles, the tall Cotswold-grey spire of St John's church had dominated the horizon ahead, wavering to and fro like a swinging compass needle as the river meandered and wound through gentle meads. At the last lock gate had lounged a giant greeny statue of Old Father Thames, with flowing curling beard and eely locks and a codfish expression. I knew that the official uppermost navigable point of the river was barely a mile upstream from here, though I intended to see how much further I could take *Jack*. But first, my long-awaited surprise call on Meadowgate Cottage.

I left the boat moored under a willow by the old woolpack bridge and made my way through the wet streets of Lechlade. Even under grey skies the Cotswold stone glowed with characteristic warmth, and the shops and houses on either side of the broad High Street looked prosperous and well proportioned. Antiques and old prints sat comfortably alongside Laura Ashley fabrics; second-hand books and William Morris tapestry cushions tempted me from shop windows but in vain. I found the narrow little lane between stone walls that led to Meadowgate and sauntered along it between late celandine and ivy-leaved toadflax, startling a blackbird bathing in a puddle. It flew off in a glitter of scattered raindrops and sat scolding from a nearby pear tree whose golden fruit hung over the wall as perfect as one of those Morris cushions.

But when I reached the gate of Frances' cottage, I suddenly knew that there would be no gruff bark or caustic quip after all. There was an indefinable air of dereliction about the place; something to do perhaps with a row of untended shrubs in terracotta pots, now greening over with mould... or the drab curtain that hung half shut and askew in the sitting room window... or the honeysuckle, a massed tangle of dead brown twigs and curled fading leaves at this autumn-tide which hung too heavily over windows and doors, like unruly brows drawn down in grief. There was silence of course when I knocked damply on the door. I didn't wait very long, but turned back up the little lane and made my way back to town. There on the High Street was the little art shop run by Daisy May, but when I pushed my way through the bell-tinkling door I saw a lady that I did not know standing behind the counter. Daisy, it seemed, had gone to Australia for a month to visit her relatives out there, Emily's family... and yes, I was told with a rueful shaking of the head, poor Mrs. Bell had died three months before. The cancer had returned suddenly, and the end had been really quite quick. Such a loss, she murmured. Such a very... *spirited* lady, she added, and I wondered briefly if this was one of the kind souls who would be picking shredded cellophane out of their garden beds for years to come. The family were away at the moment but was there a message?

"*No. No message, thank you,*" and I stepped back out into the dull afternoon, a little despondent and suddenly very tired. I stood for a while indecisively and then made up my mind - my main reason for coming to Lechlade had been chopped from under me, so I would follow my original idea. I returned to *Jack de Crow*, unmoored, donned my pith helmet (how Frances would have cut me to shreds over that) and set out to row upstream as far as I possibly could while the afternoon light lasted. The physical action of rowing soon cheered me a little... Kipling's cure for the camelious hump seems to work just as well for despondency... and I had resigned myself to the fact that she had had her wish after all; the two boys must be grown lads now, through school and out of the nest. And she had fought long and hard and with grim humour to save what she believed in... though I fully expected her to break through from the other side the moment I mouthed to myself those mawkish words... and besides, one cannot be soulful for long when there is a boat to row, and the light green and dark green of willows and water are melting and merging on the river's glassy palette and a golden wagtail has just flitted, chipping fitfully under the white span of the foot-bridge ahead. It was only when I rounded a bend half a mile above Lechlade and saw the big new board in a field on the bank that my new-found comfort deserted me.

THAMESMEAD ESTATE, it read. *50 ACRES OF PRIME RIVERSIDE PROPERTY TO BE DEVELOPED FOR HOUSING AND RECREATION.*
For details, contact Town Clerk, Lechlade Council, High Street.

Had there been an observer on the footbridge or by the curved walls of the curious Roundhouse there that afternoon, he may have wondered why the boatman in the little yellow dinghy was propelling his craft along with oar strokes of quite such needless and sudden savagery.

Frances Bell had died in July. By mid-August, after a seven-year stand off, the bulldozers had moved in, and work on the Dark Tower had begun.

My journey upstream was nasty, brutish and short. A few miles beyond the Roundhouse on its willowed island, the Thames had become little more than a brook between high banks. Ash and osier and willow closed in overhead, thick sedge and reeds clogged the river's course and where they did so the current trebled in strength, making it all but impossible to work my way upstream. Some sour remnants of anger and adrenalin drove me onwards, my oars catching in clumps of vegetation every few strokes and the low branches raking across my hair. Visions of the Morda Brook closed in around me. Finally, I came to Hannington Bridge, a lonely stone bridge half hidden in trees. Here the stream tumbled swiftly down over a shallow rocky bed beneath the arch, chattering between fallen lumps of rubble and masonry, and five attempts to propel *Jack* up and into the quieter pool beyond proved fruitless. As I rested on my oars after the fifth time, a kingfisher, dragonfly-blue, came skimming upstream, flashed past me and vanished through the darkened arch. An omen? A sign to struggle on through? A herald leading me beyond the Wasteland, beyond the Dark Tower, beyond the River Gate to the land of the Fisher King himself?

Possibly. But let some later Childe Roland do the finding. *Jack* and I were weary, and besides, it had begun to rain again. "Out oars for Narnia," I cried, turned *Jack*'s nose, and started the long haul downstream.

Hannington Bridge

Return to Reading

'I chatter, chatter as I flow
To join the brimming river,
For men may come and men may go,
But I go on forever.'

Tennyson - *The Brook*

Two days earlier, I had been sitting having a conversation with Mr. Michael Palin as I rowed up from Oxford.

"*Mr. Palin,*" I had said, "*I have a bone to pick with you. Every time I set off to do something mildly eccentric and adventurous in the travel line I find myself being eclipsed by you and your latest documentary. I arrive at some aunt's house after a year of wonderful adventures, full of stories about marrying Laotian princesses, or being eaten by Komodo Dragons or starving for a week on a becalmed yacht in the Arafura Sea, and am invariably greeted with the words 'Oh, Sandy, come in, come in. Shoosh now, there's a programme on you'll just love; Michael Palin's 'Diagonally Backwards Across the Great Deserts of the World.' He's so intrepid!'*

This, to be frank, irritates me enormously. Even on this latest venture, I have been mistaken for you on three occasions on account of the pith helmet - been approached by some warmly smiling stranger only to have him suddenly realize his mistake, turn abruptly away and mutter to his wife, 'I TOLD you it wasn't Michael Palin; just some loony in a pith hat.' And do people want to know about the adventures of Jack de Crow? The Battle of Frankton Locks? The Tidal Terrors of the Severn Estuary? The Native Customs of Kintbury? Do they? No, not without an entire BBC film crew and a well-loved actor to back up the commentary.

AND what is more, despite all the fame and adulation, everyone seems to think you've remained a perfectly nice, unspoilt chap all along. It's all a bit sickening, frankly, and I wish you'd stop it."

This conversation with Mr. Palin may have had more effect had he been actually present at the time. As it happened, I was alone in the dinghy staving off the boredom by conducting the above diatribe purely in my head. I did think of putting my thoughts down on paper and sending him a letter but had no idea of his address or how to obtain it, so eventually banished his phantom form overboard and turned my attention to giving the mast a lecture on 18th Century Augustan verse instead. (It really was a very dull stretch of river.)

The point of all the above is merely to lead to one of those coincidences that so irritate my friends and family. To cut it very short indeed, two days after this conversation with the imaginary Mr. Palin, I bumped into him at a nearby Town Hall where he was giving his celebrated lecture 'How Yet Again I Upstaged A.J. Mackinnon.' As it turned out, the lecture was booked solid, so I sat in the Town Hall café and wrote him that letter after all. After the talk, half of Gloucestershire lined up to have books signed by the poor man while I stood in the queue and talked quietly but persistently to anyone who would listen about how intrepid life could be in a Mirror Dinghy. Eventually at one o'clock in the morning, I reached the desk where he sat saying deliriously *"Crucifixion? Splendid. One cross each, on the left."* I slipped him the letter, he said *"I say, nice hat!"* I got all embarrassed and said *"mmnghngkyou"* in reply and that was that. I had met a celebrity. My voyage had reached a new status. Now, when over dinner tables around the world I was interrupted in the middle of my Komodo Dragon story by some relative enthusing, *"Oooh, Michael Palin went there! Did you see...?"* I would be able to say casually, *"Palin? Oh yes, met him once. Nice chap. He admired this very hat, actually. Now, where was I? Ah yes... So, as the Dragon lunged forward, its foul breath hot on my face..."*

I would never be eclipsed again.

The journey from Lechlade down to Oxford again was uneventful but pleasant. I have not mentioned Kelmscot Manor, the home of William Morris and Dante Gabriel Rossetti, a serene 16th Century house with mossy apple trees against a sombre background of dark yews and mellow stone and an old dovecote where white fantail doves and grey pigeons strutted and cooed. No doubt around the back somewhere there was a persimmon tree full of bullfinches and mistle thrushes and green woodpeckers overhanging a strawberry bed and a meadow full of hares. This manor was the headquarters of the whole Arts and Crafts Movement in the last century. Here began the revival of the Medieval style in painting and poetry and furnishings, those rich tapestries and carved rosewood bureaux and the marvellous paintings of Burne-Jones and Waterhouse, as a backlash against the devouring monotony of industry. The whole Movement ended in bitterness and division many years later fuelled by infidelity and illicit love amongst the prime movers, but not until it had produced a wealth of treasures that has remained unsurpassed by anything created since. I can't help feeling that the manner of the Movement's downfall would be thoroughly approved of in hindsight by Morris and his colleagues; it chimed through with echoes and re-echoes of the Arthurian tragedy they so loved to portray - the triangle of Arthur, Guinevere and Lancelot; the hopeless Grail-quest; the sinister ambitions of Thoroughly Modern Mordred.

For each landmark I saw and noted on my downward journey, a dozen I missed. Referring now to the indispensable Nicholson Guide (which I foolishly failed to obtain until the last ten miles of my trip to London) I see that those upper reaches are rich in history and folklore. Here at Radcot is the oldest bridge on the Thames; those woods over yonder are haunted by a headless sailor, Hampden Pye. In this village, Morris dancing originated; at that manor, Pope translated his celebrated *Iliad* in a tower.

But without a Guide, I rowed and sailed down the long empty miles ignorant of the ghosts of Time that crowd the land, aware only of a heron beating slowly downstream ahead of me or the quick rustle and clop of a diving water vole on the bank. It is here in these infant waters of the Upper Thames that one can most easily set *The Wind in the Willows*. There is the great meadow where Mole came running on that first morning; here is the bank where Ratty lives, his eyes twinkling like twin stars in the darkness of his hole. Over yonder is the Wild Wood, the menacing mass of Wytham Great Wood as mortals call it, where Oxford University scientists do ecological experiments on carol-singing dormice and foot-shuffling hedgehog urchins, and where you are NOT allowed to go unless you are a biologist or a personal friend of Mr. Badger's. And somewhere here surely in a reedy backwater by a foaming weir is that Island, Pan's Island, the setting for the most beautiful chapter in English prose ever written: *The Piper at the Gates of Dawn*.

I came after two days to Godstow again, and walked up the hill to Wolvercote Cemetery to pay my respects over another author's grave, that of J.R.R. Tolkien. He is a writer whom the world either loathes or adores, so I will not spend time eulogizing here. Those who, like me, have been touched by his magic will need no convincing - all others will never be persuaded. Many folk are put off by the very whiff of Fantasy fiction, with its lurid dust jackets, its role-playing, its fan clubs, its aura of spiky, sexy leather armour and skull-hilted swords, its pseudo histories and its characters striding around crying *The Rune of Shannaroth challenges the Dragon-Virgins of Lur!* Take comfort from the fact that all this repels me as much as it probably does them. My own love affair with Tolkien's works had more to do with the scholarly Oxford style - something redolent of bookish studies on peaceful afternoons, the distant clack of shears outside in a garden bright with nasturtiums and wallflowers, and the vinegar smell of ink, black and red, drying on the yellowed paper of end maps.

There was something of this atmosphere about the cemetery that morning and the plain grave where wild thyme and a red rose bush grew. The grave of Tolkien and his wife is inscribed simply 'Beren' and 'Luthien'. They were two of the central characters in his mythological opus 'The Silmarillion', a mortal man and an elven maid who won through many perils to be united at last – the usual irritating problems of these mixed mortal/immortal marriages: disapproving fathers, giant wolves, cursed jewels, how to sort out Life Insurance and Pension schemes and the like. The thyme and roses were still in full bloom, surprisingly for mid-October, so perhaps there are hints of immortality and enchantment there after all.

Rowing back through Oxford, I turned up the Cherwell River to see if I could find a more scholastic mooring place as befitted the bookish *Jack de Crow*. The Cherwell is a dark, quiet, tree-shadowed river that winds its dank and mossy way between the Botanic Gardens and various secluded College grounds up to the Magdalen Bridge. Here every year after the celebrated May Ball, a hundred or so honking students ruin an equal number of dinner suits by leaping from the ancient stone parapet into the slick-dark waters below... under the mistaken impression that being drunk, plastered with duck-slime and removing water-snails from their crannies for weeks to come will render them irresistible to the opposite sex.

Just below the bridge, I pulled *Jack de Crow* up onto a fine lawn of green-striped velvet beneath yellowing horse chestnut trees in a secluded - and very clearly private - arm of the Cherwell and set off with my rucksack to spend another night at Jo's place up the hill. Finding a way out onto the public streets was trickier than I thought, involving as it did crossing over several white wooden bridges, ducking through tunnels, edging along wall tops, traversing a couple of willowy islands and finally climbing over a low gate onto the Magdalen Bridge itself. I felt rather like a participant in the Konigsberg Bridges conundrum or some Lewis Carroll problem in topology. It was not far from this very spot in fact that *Alice in Wonderland* was written, with its wealth of logical and mathematical problems disguised as hallucinatory fantasy - as children's literature, it is nightmarish; as an array of philosophical paradoxes it is sheer brilliance. (How do you reassemble a chessboard to lose one square? Why does a mirror's reflection reverse from side to side but not top to bottom? Can one behead a Cheshire Cat if it is all head and no body?).

I had cause over the next twenty-four hours to ponder on a few Carrollian mysteries of my own. I seemed to have stumbled on a small patch of turf that displayed all the qualities of Wonderland; things vanished and reappeared like the Cat's grin, the paths beneath my feet twisted and turned like a nestful of Moebius eels and the willow-framed, tea party setting completed the Looking-glass imagery.

It started like this. Just as I was making my way through one of the tunnels, I noticed a satchel lying in the pathway spilling papers from its opened flap. I was hot, hungry and tired and my arms were full - the satchel besides looked rather grubby and damp - but I reached down, grabbed one sheet of official looking paper from the sheaf and stuck it in a pocket to peruse later. You never know, I thought, it might be important...

Later that evening, over a drink with Jo in her apartment, I remembered the paper and brought it out. It was a letter from some double glazing firm to a Dr. Kathleen McRae, and Jo, with her customary electric efficiency traced the name via computer to the Oxford Department of Biochemistry. Ah ha! A quest! The next day I would cycle down to the Magdalen Bridge, recover the dropped satchel and its no doubt vital academic contents and continue on to return it all to the good and grateful Doctor at her laboratory. It's nice to have the leisure to play the gallant knight errant once in a while...

It was with some exasperation therefore that on returning to the damp tunnel the next morning I found the satchel missing, papers and all. Nearby an imposing building frowned over the manicured lawns and riverbanks, and a sign proclaimed RECEPTION: VISITORS REPORT HERE. I wandered in and found my way through to what turned out to be the outer office of the College Dean. There I was confronted by the Dean's Secretary, a severe-looking lady with silver hair in a tight bun, small spectacles and a gimlet eye. She looked none too pleased at the apparition of a slightly soiled figure in a large hat rabbiting on about tunnels and biochemists and satchels that appeared and vanished mysteriously. On enquiring whether perhaps a groundsman or College student may have picked the satchel up and handed it in, I was told in a steely Edinburgh accent that:

a)   her duties as Secretary to the Dean of St. Oswin's College did not extend to keeping track of Lost Property,

and

b)   that students were excluded from those parts of the grounds to which I was referring, as indeed were members of the general public.

Here she glanced meaningfully at me over the bifocals and I felt it was time to confess that as well as trampling over the hallowed precincts of St. Oswin's, I had actually had the temerity to moor a small battered dinghy on one of their well-clipped lawns. This, to my surprise, broke the ice somewhat.

"A dinghy? How splendid," she chirruped. "From Shropshire? Well, gracious me! No, of course there's no problem leaving the dear little thing there. Had we known you were coming, St. Oswin's would have put on a welcoming tea and perhaps built a small boat shed. And what a simply marvellous hat! How kind of you to go to the trouble of rescuing a stranger's satchel, even if it has vanished again, and may we fetch you a cup of tea? Watercress sandwiches? Brandy and cigar? Oh never mind about him, that's just the Dean. Come and sit over here next to me and tell me ALL about your wonderful, wonderful travels..."

And this was before I'd told her about meeting Michael Palin.

Nevertheless, no satchel, so escaping from St. Oswin's, I had the odd task of cycling off to the Biochemistry Laboratories to explain in a neat paraphrasing of the Gospels that that which was lost, was... er... still lost, sorry.

Dr Kathleen McRae was a stunningly beautiful redhead, quite clearly just arrived from picking heather tips in the Highlands and singing airs from *Brigadoon*: fine-boned bonny cheeks, eyes like mountain streams over greeny-grey pebbles, just the sort of lass you don't want to have the following conversation with.

"*Ah, Doctor McRae, you've lost a satchel, I believe. Did it have anything important in it by any chance?*"

"*Well, APART from your whole thesis, I mean?*"

"*Uh-huh. Your purse, credit cards and car keys. I see. Anything else?*"

"*Oh really? Top secret research plans into a universal vaccine to cure all known ills? I see. And...?*"

"*Some unimportant and totally insignificant letters? Ah HA!! Well then, Doctor McRae, this must be your lucky day. May I proudly and happily return to you THIS, a valuable letter from... let's see... a double glazing firm, offering you some very exciting discounts as a valued customer, and as for all the other stuff, well I left that lying on the path and... er... sorry, it seems to have disappeared.*"

"*Still these Alu-steel window frame offers are NOT to be sneezed at, I think you'll agree.*"

(I exaggerate for effect of course, but it really did have her thesis in it.)

Doctor McRae was terribly nice about it and thanked me for going to all the trouble of letting her know that the thesis was well and truly lost and hadn't just slipped down the back of a sofa, but I must excuse her as she had some serious catching up to do such as five years' research to begin over again. As I backed apologetically out of the laboratory, I realised a further disaster: somewhere I seemed to have mislaid my hat. I thought for one brief moment that I might try to cheer up the despondent Doctor by sharing this loss with her - comrades in misfortune, that sort of thing - but she was already bent over a microscope and I thought better of it.

I am happy to report that the tale has a happy ending, however. On my way back to Jo's that evening I popped in again to visit the Dean's Secretary as I thought I may have left my hat there on the morning visit. No, she hadn't seen my hat, she replied, bringing out a cup of tea and some home-made shortbread she'd rustled up on the off-chance I might pop back, but the satchel had turned up! So I was able to cycle back, find once more the divine Doctor Kathleen McRae and say, "*Only joking! Here it is!*" and claim a kiss and half her kingdom as a reward... well, a hearty thank you and a warm glow in my breast for the successful completion of a good deed.

Good deeds are their own reward, they say. One certainly doesn't expect material riches to come tumbling after. But neither does one expect the smiling gods to throw the banana skins of misfortune in one's path and sit smirking into their ambrosia. After saying farewell to Jo the next morning and resigning myself to the loss of my beautiful hat, I sauntered down to the Magdalen Bridge, and threaded my way through the gates-bridge-tunnel-island maze once more to where *Jack* lay deep in horse chestnut leaves on the hidden lawn. I swept the leaves out of her, stowed my rucksack in the usual place just between the thwart and the foredeck, heaved her down the bank and into the water, clambered in and reached for the... oars?

The oars?

Where were the oars?

I must have left them on the bank. Quickly, before I drifted too far, I grabbed for a tree root, climbed ashore again, dragged *Jack* half up onto the lawn again, and stood scratching my head. No, I was sure I had stowed the oars neatly in the dinghy two days ago. Still, they might be here somewhere amidst all the fallen leaves. I spent an increasingly panicky fifteen minutes scrabbling in drifts of crackly leaves like a hyperactive squirrel and peering into the shrubbery only to come to the horrible conclusion - the oars were gorn!

Surely... possibly... maybe... a zealous groundsman had come across the dinghy and taken the oars to keep them safe – or, more likely, confiscated them to make the point that St. Oswin's College water garden was not a public marina. Nothing for it then...

I retraced my steps (island-tunnel-bridge-gate) to the Dean's office and popped my head around the door once more. The Dean's Secretary's face lit up with a schoolgirl blush.

"Ah, hello again, remember me? Lost the satchel, lost the hat, *found* the satchel, hat still missing? I appear now to have lost my oars. Any clues?"

But no, it seems that the vanishing oars were a mystery, despite several calls made to the head groundsman and his staff. The pith helmet had been found, however, and handed in if that was any help? Well, delighted as I was with its recovery (though mystified as to where it had spent its brief Sabbatical... pilfered for a while by the Mad Hatter perhaps?) I could hardly paddle to London using only a pith helmet, so, staving off the Dean's Secretary's offer of salmon sandwiches and a holiday for two in Majorca, I set off to buy myself a new pair of oars.

I suppose if one is going to lose oars, one cannot choose a better place than the rowing capital of Britain to do so. Nevertheless I had a long walk across town and up the river to Bossom's Boat Yard, halfway back to Godstow, before I found a suitable pair for a Mirror dinghy. A horribly large sum of money exchanged hands and I stumped rather crossly back the two sweaty miles to St. Oswin's, unmoved by the stares of the citizenry of Oxford at the pith helmeted figure striding along the Cornmarket with a pair of oars over his shoulder.

However my mood lightened a little as I came once more to the Magdalen Bridge, completed the exercise in advanced topology (through gate, under arch, over bridge, across island,) and stood once more ready for the off. Oars stowed, more recent leaf-fall swept off foredeck, heave and lift, and *Jack de Crow* slid easily down into the river and bobbed lightly on the dark waters of the Cherwell. Surprisingly lightly in fact. Almost as though...?

Oh for crying out loud. My bleeding rucksack was now missing!

What was this place, the Bermuda Triangle of Oxford? A secluded patch of green willows, hemmed in by walls and rivers and railings and virtually inaccessible without the maze skills of Ariadne, and yet things kept vanishing and reappearing like hankies at a Magic Circle Convention. I considered, for one wild moment, popping into the Dean's office yet again, and saying, "*Ah. Sorry to disturb you once more. Following in the tradition of the vanishing satchel, the reappearing pith helmet and the absconding oars, it seems that my rucksack containing everything that I own in the world has now done a bunk. I don't suppose... ? No?*"

But I was worried that:

a) I might not escape from the adoring Dean's Secretary a third time...

and

b) if I did, I would return to the river bank to find the dinghy itself spirited away, leaving only a faint feline grin fading away into the treetops.

I was on the point of raging despair, when I noticed sitting under a nearby holly bush my rucksack. To this day, I've no idea how it got there from its place in the boat. A kindly groundsman shifting it to a safer place? A mischievous student pulling a half-hearted prank? The work of the March Hare? Fairies at the bottom of the St. Oswin's garden? Whatever the facts, I now had all I needed to flee that glimorous place, so lost no time in launching *Jack* once more, flinging my rucksack wildly into the bows and rowing hard and fast down the inky

Cherwell and out into the broad glitter and sunshine of the Thames once more. By the time I had reached Iffley Lock my heartbeat had slowed to normal, my mind had cleared and the shadowy webs of dark enchantment had been blown away by the breezy normality of the outside world. But one strand of suspicion, of certainty almost, remains: those missing oars are even now criss-crossed on the wall above a certain silver-haired Secretary's bed, the last thing she sees before she drifts off into dreamland where she rows nightly on rivers of champagne with a bronzed and pith helmeted stranger pulling steadily away beside her.

Fleeing the Cherwell

The new oars were six inches shorter than the old ones. You have no idea how irritating this is. For six weeks and over two hundred and fifty miles, my arm muscles, my nerves, my shoulder blades, the very calluses on my hands, had become accustomed to the old oars, every fibre tuned to their rhythm and length. Now, with oars just six inches shorter, it was like learning to row all over again, and I splashed and jerked and caught crabs in a rare old temper long into the evening as I made my way down to Abingdon.

Abingdon passed uneventfully enough; it is the oldest inhabited town in Britain, claims the museum, which celebrates that fact somewhat surprisingly by displaying nothing more than a collection of paper doilies through the ages, watched over by a hawk-eyed lady hovering in case anyone is overcome by the sheer excitement of it all. I managed to stay upright and calm, and kept on downstream.

I came late in the afternoon to lovely Day's Lock nestling under the dramatic rise of ancient earthworks known as Wittenham Clumps, throwing a cold shadow over the river. It is a holy, haunted site and more than made up for the History of the Doily that morning. On a more homely level, it is at Day's Lock that the annual Poohsticks Championships are held, the contestants standing on the white painted bridge and dropping their twigs or pine cones ('*in a twitchy sort of way, if you know what I mean, Pooh*') into the weir stream below.

It was early evening when, a mile below Day's Lock, I turned into the narrow entrance of the River Thame and rowed up between high rushy banks, snaking my way to the ancient Roman town of Dorchester-upon-Thame. This quiet village lying amidst flat meadows and high earth dykes was once the cathedral capital of ancient Wessex and Mercia; the abbey was built in the 7th Century and boasts a unique window I wanted to see whose branching stonework imitates living trees. The rector, I had been told, was a certain John Crow - clearly a cousin of our own beloved *Jack*. It seemed a perfect place to stop for the night.

Yet as I moored in a little meadow under the shadow of the abbey where the little Thame had dwindled to a mere brook I felt all of a sudden terribly lonely and tired and dispirited. The sun had set like a frozen red blood-orange behind thorn trees ragged and bare. For the first time since leaving, the air was icy cold and already it seemed that a blue frost was crystallising on the bleached grass of the field. My breath came in white puffs on the evening air and as I struggled with the awning and the decking to prepare *Jack* for the night I noticed with dismay how wet with dew everything had suddenly become. I toyed feebly with the idea of treating myself to a Bed and Breakfast room that night, but told myself firmly that such extravagance was unwarranted; I certainly couldn't afford to keep staying in hotels and guest houses and besides, what was the point, I scolded, of making a beautiful awning and a lovely decking and setting off to have exciting adventures if I just kept bolting for hot baths and warm duvets and Full English Breakfasts every time it got a little dewy round the ears, hmm?

"*Oh, shut up, shut up, leave me alone,*" I whimpered. Then I savagely jerked the awning into place with a frozen hand and fell backwards into a clump of nettles.

"*See!*" said that other voice in Governess tones. "*That's what happens when you get all grumpy. Now stop making a fuss over a wet bottom and a few little nettle stings. Besides, the stings will keep you warm,*" it added with a tight-lipped smirk. I was on the point of mentally smacking that inner school-marm with a metaphorical brick, when a real voice intruded into the conversation. It sounded remarkably like the one I'd been about to silence, with its ringing tones of disapproval and command.

"You! What is that boat doing there?!"

A silvery-haired lady was looking over a gate above me, two black labradors panting frostily at her side. Green wellies, padded jacket, leather dog leads held like some mediaeval weapon; I recognised the formidable archetype of the English countrywoman. A little wearily I replied,

"Sorry, is this private property? I'd thought the river banks would be common land."

"I've simply no idea," she trumpeted back. "I'm simply curious why a Mirror Dinghy... it is a Mirror isn't it?... should be tying up in the middle of nowhere. And what on earth's that blue thing?"

I explained the purpose of the awning.

"Lord! You're not going to sleep on the thing, are you? It's freezing."

"I..."

"Nonsense!" she rapped. "I've got a spare room and half a chicken that needs eating up. Now come along!" she called briskly.

"Um... I..."

"Hurry up! The dogs are getting cold and need their supper. Chop chop!"

In ten seconds flat I had grabbed my hat and rucksack and without a backward glance at poor *Jack*, I was trotting to heel along the icy road endeavouring to keep up with this lady's vigorous strides. After fifty yards she turned to me and said,

"Now, I'm a widow, mind you, and alone in the house, so I'm taking a risk. Still, I'm trusting you. I don't think you're a madman." A pause. She stopped, glanced at me briefly, pith helmet and all and added, "Well actually I do think you're mad, but I don't think you're dangerous..." and strode onward into the dusk.

People are extraordinary. I set out on this voyage with no very clear aim in mind, no Northwest Passage to discover, no treasure to find. But one treasure I did find on the way was a wealth of kind hearts and courageous spirits; I discovered a strange world where, despite the daily assault on our fears by the media, people are still full of goodwill and take a positive delight in trusting each other; it seems the best way to get there is by Mirror dinghy.

The following morning after sincere and hearty thanks - it had been a delightful evening the night before; she had lived and sailed in New Zealand as I had, was a great gardener with a special love for medicinal herbs, and her chicken in leeks and white wine sauce was divine - I walked back to my abandoned *Jack* via the beautiful abbey, and rowed off to the Thames to continue south.

The day was yet again glorious, and it seemed that even in the fortnight since I had rowed up this stretch of river, the bright banners of autumn had unfurled on every tree and bush. The beeches by Shillingford Bridge were rich in copper-reds and golds, their sweeping canopies supported by green-grey trunks that looked like carved and fluted pillars of stone. Oaks and horse chestnuts were bronzing in the woods with here and there a maple luminous in primrose yellow glowing through the gloom. Along the banks, too, ash and willow were speckling with yellows and greys, and though the sun was shining in a bright sky there was a chill breeze over the water - when I rowed from sunshine to shadow, the air breathed icily on my bare neck.

As I rowed down past the Palladian water-steps of Rush Hall, past the busy, vulgar cheeriness of Benson's Boat Yard and round the river bend onto the long empty stretch down to Goring, I turned over in my mind a little idea that had been growing ever since Bath. Somewhere, somebody had told me of a man who had planned to take his narrowboat from the Black Country to the Black Sea, crossing the Channel to Calais and entering the French canal system. From there, I had heard, it was possible to navigate on inland waters all the way across Europe to the Danube Delta on the Black Sea. The idea sounded highly dubious to me. Weren't there some mountains called the Alps in the way? Wasn't the Rhine River full of rocks and rapids and Lorelei sirens luring sailors to their deaths? Wouldn't he have been shot by Slovakian Secret Police or brainwashed by Bulgarian Communists... if he ever made it beyond the Anglophobic, onion-hurling French, that is? And as for crossing the Channel in a narrowboat... well, that was plain suicide. Narrowboats are roly-poly, unwieldy vessels made of solid cast-iron and about as seaworthy as a tin pig. Ridiculous to even consider it...

But a Mirror Dinghy? Now there was an idea. The more I thought about it, the more the idea appealed. I had tentatively mentioned it to one or two people along the way and met with various reactions. The main difficulty would be the other traffic; the Channel is the busiest shipping lane in the World. Jo in Oxford had explained that to cross the Channel in a Mirror would be like trying to cross the M25 at peak hour on hands and knees. John and Di on *Diana* had been cautiously polite, clearly reluctant on so short an acquaintance to throw me to the ground, bind me hand and foot and slap me till I came to my senses. Several times Captain Eggersley had appeared in feverish dreams holding up shipping statistics and tide charts and threatening to shoot me with an emergency flare. Most worrying of all was the phantom appearance of Terry in those same dreams, standing on the bridge of *King Arthur* and giving me a cheery thumbs up and his *No worries, easy peasy* grin while skeletal figures danced a grim hornpipe on the decks behind.

But as I hoisted sail after Benson Lock to catch the fresh northerly breeze and felt the clean rippling rush of water under *Jack*'s keel, noted her sturdy buoyant frame and valiant scarlet sail, and the way she dipped and heeled under the following wind, the landscape melted in my mind's eye and became quite, quite different. The silvery osiers solidified, calcified to white and shot skywards. The cold blue waters softened to salt-green and swelled in gentle rolling waves - a pair of nearby swallows transformed into a couple of great gliding gulls, suspended on a mild sea breeze that sent me skimming along under the White Cliffs of Dover on my way to France.

Yes, I thought. One has to try these things...

I had such a steady breeze that day and so full were my thoughts of P&O Ferries out of Dover Harbour, Calais cockles and the salt tang of sea air on my lips that I swept past the undoubted delights of Wallingford and Moulsford all unseeing, rippled gaily beneath several fine Brunel railway bridges whose curving brickwork beneath the arches does odd Escher-ish things to the eyes and sense of perspective, kept up a shouted conversation with an elderly jogger on the river path for a mile or so (he thought a Channel crossing was a stupid idea as well) and found myself just downstream of the Whitchurch Bridge at Pangbourne, an elegant span of white iron and woodwork where herons roost, as the sun set in an apple-green sky.

With dusk, the wind died to nothing and a consultation of the map showed that I had two choices. I could either row back upstream the mile or so to Pangbourne or row the six miles down to Reading. Heaven knows why, but I chose the latter option. In fact, I found on my whole trip a deep, irrational reluctance ever to retrace my route, even by so much as half a mile and even when the benefits of doing so were manifestly clear. It stemmed, I think, from the feeling that this trip was in some ways a peregrinatio, the medieval practice whereby a monk or pilgrim would climb into a small coracle without oars or sail, push out to sea and go where the winds and waves took him. In this way, so the theory went, the holy traveller could be sure that he was going where God intended, undirected by fallible human agency. It was a way of putting oneself fairly and squarely into Divine hands and relinquishing that all-consuming desire to control one's destiny. The medieval tales are full of marvellous accounts of the results of such peregrinations - glassy isles, benign whales, dead nuns in gilded barges with silken sails, lands of fire and ice and the whole bright world of the Celtic West. St. Brendan on one such trip even discovered America, Divine Providence working on a particularly grand scale on that occasion... though the canny Saint had actually equipped himself with oars on that trip, contrary to the rules.

I, too, had oars of course, and a sail, but nevertheless I still felt that whenever the river current, the winds or my own lack of timekeeping skills took me further than was wise or swept me one way rather than another, I should take that as a cue. To ever go back, retrace my course, unwind the past was, I thought, to deny the designs of Providence... even if it did mean rowing six miles down a dark river to Reading of all places.

As it happened I had only rowed half a mile on my way when Divine Providence manifested itself in the shape of three thirteen-year-old lads in a dilapidated motor launch. At first when a young tousled head popped out of the cabin and asked if I'd like a tow, I was delighted and flung him a line saying, "Gosh, thanks, yes if you don't think Mum or Dad will mind," assuming the presence of some adults below... the normal family on a boating holiday in a hired cruiser.

The lad calmly tied my line on to his stern, replied over his shoulder, "Mum or Dad? They won't know nuffink about it. They're at 'ome. Hang on to yer 'at." Then he called below into the cabin, "Righto, Eric. Let 'er rip!"

"Okay, Rodney!" came the reply and the launch shot off on a spurt of foam into the darkness. A second later the towline went taut with a resounding drip-flinging '*twangngng!!!*', *Jack* shot forward like an excited puppy and I went over backwards from my standing position to a crumpled heap in the stern. Icy water welled up around my buttocks and for a heart-stopping minute I thought *Jack*'s bow had been pulled clear away from the rest of the dinghy by that mighty yank, leaving me to sink swiftly into the night-time Thames in the remaining half of the boat. And the life jacket was in the bows of course, keeping safely out of the action as usual.

On recovering myself I found that the dinghy was still intact - the impression of sinking was due to the sudden flood of water bubbling up through the centreboard case with the new spurt of speed, water which was continuing to fountain into the dinghy in excited sloshes. I jammed the centreboard down to quench the flow, edged nervously forward in the boat now skidding and surfing over the motor launch's wake and called out tentatively,

"Er... excuse me... thanks for the tow and all that but... um... could we take her a little slower please?"

"Wot? Can't 'ear yer!" came back the reply.

"Um... could we slow down? SLOW DOWN PLEASE!"

"Wot? 'Ang on. I'll cut the motor..."

"No, no!" I cried in alarm. "If you DO THAT you'll..."

Too late. The young skipper gave me a smiley thumbs up and shouted below "ERIC! Cut the motor!"

A half-second later, the roar of the engine died, the motor launch wallowed to a sudden stop and the lighter *Jack de Crow* surged forward on a great rolling wave of glimmering foam. She nose-butted the launch's stern with a resounding crack and sent me once more reeling into the watery bilges.

"So, wot was it you was saying?"

After this inauspicious start however, things proceeded a little more smoothly and soon I found myself gliding down the river under starlight at a safe and steady pace in the more capable hands of the skipper of the boat whom I'd not yet seen. This was Martin, another thirteen-year old boy, who had taken the control of the launch out of the enthusiastic hands of Eric and Rodney and shown a somewhat more seamanlike approach to the task.

"Sorry 'bout that," he confided to me. "They're me mates, but they're a bit thick sometimes. I'm tryin' to get 'em trained." A shake of the head and a deep sigh revealed a little of the difficulties of the training process.

Actually Eric and Rodney, when not in pivotal roles aboard ship, were thoroughly delightful... as was Martin. He had, he explained, inherited the boat as his very own from his grandfather and was planning to make a career of it somehow. Most evenings he was on the river with or without his crew, exploring the backwaters, getting to know correct procedures in locks and marinas and equipping himself with the experience to run a boating business as soon as he could leave school. He had an air of purpose and quiet confidence that I've rarely seen in one so young, and his practical skills were demonstrated to perfection as we negotiated Mapledurham Lock by moonlight unaided... no easy task when one is towing a small frail dinghy.

So I passed a very pleasant two hours towing steadily downstream to Reading chatting to the threesome and giving my own private thumbs up to Divine Providence for rewarding my faith in the art of peregrinatio.

Eventually the lights of Reading came into sight around a bend and just above Caversham Bridge Martin expertly cast me loose and turned his motor launch upstream. Just before he chugged away he called out,

" 'Ere! Wotcha gonna do when yer get to London?"

"I'm not sure yet," I replied. "Finish there, I suppose."

"Nah!" came back the reply in triple chorus. "Yer wanna keep goin'. Take 'er to France. Take 'er to the Med. Yer could go anywhere in that! Bye." And with those last encouraging words, off they went back up the river to their mums and dads and 'omework to do before tomorrer. It was nice to know there were some other sensible folk in the World.

Capsize and Colleges

'Then rose from sea to sky the wild farewell -
Then shriek'd the timid, and stood still the brave, -
Then some leap'd overboard with fearful yell,
As eager to anticipate their grave.'

Byron - *Don Juan, Canto II, St. 52.*

Henley-on-Thames glittered in the late afternoon sunlight, a thousand window panes flashing like diamonds along the riverfront - white painted inns and hotels; restaurants with awnings in lemon-yellow and bottle-green stripes; a large Mississippi-style showboat like a floating wedding cake. This impression of wealth and brilliance and whiteness may be completely mistaken, as I was concentrating hard, attempting to beat up the long wide Henley stretch while avoiding some boating race going on at the time. Not *the* Henley Regatta, I hasten to add... at least I think not... there'd have been more crowds surely and more people with megaphones shouting curt instructions than just the one.

Sailing dinghies confuse oarsmen. Oarsmen as a rule are a fairly limited and literal breed. You wish to proceed from Point A to Point B. You therefore aim the boat at Point B and row in a straight line between the two, stopping when you reach the latter. The vagaries of wind and tide do not allow themselves to intrude on their single-minded pursuit of a goal, and the world of *luffing* and *sail-curvature*, *gybing* and *wind apparent* is as a closed book to their simple minds. In short, they simply don't understand the need to tack upwind.

There were seven boats in this particular regatta. I had to tack thirteen times before I was clear of their course. Seven times thirteen is ninety-one, which is precisely how many times I was told "Make up your mind, can't you!" by an irate passing oarsman who clearly thought I just couldn't decide which bank I preferred to be on. As a matter of record, I did actually prefer the right bank - it was on the *left* bank that the increasingly murderous man with the megaphone was cycling up and down, threatening in short bursts what he would like to do to my rollocks. At least I *think* that was the word...

The rowing course... and the abuse... ended at Temple Island, one of the prettiest sights on the entire length of the Thames. Here at the end of the long Henley reach a mile below the town is a wooded island, burning with the golds and ambers of autumn trees, and on the upstream point of the islet is a perfect Classical Temple, a symbol of the Augustan Age in all its confident serenity.

Here Pope may well have penned a satiric verse in devastating couplets, or Swift sat and dreamed of Lilliput. Here, had I time, I could myself have stopped and composed something suitably 18th Century, with quaint spellings and indiscriminate capital letters entitled *An Imitation of Musick in Arcadia; being a poor Shew of Wit to Sylvia who Is Herselfe her owne Muse...* or something like that.

But the woods of Remenham Hill were showing long shadows and the red flame of the trees was soon quenched by the blue dusk. Once more the wind had died and half-an-hour later, I had moored up at a tiny wooden jetty green with goose and swan poop, walked up a wooded lane and was sitting down to an enormous steak pie in the wonderful Flowerpot Inn at Aston.

The relationship between rivers and roads is an odd one. Space and Time do odd things along the banks. Whichever of the two networks you are currently travelling on, it always seems to you the most direct and logical one, the shortest distance between two points, the defining line that gives the truest perspective of the land's topography. Travelling by boat down a river loop, the distance between Henley and Aston simply IS four weary miles. The fact that by road the two may be a mere mile and a half apart is regarded not so much as untrue but as simply irrelevant. What value can the blithe boatman find in terrestrial mileages? What recks he of the slashing straight lines of the tarmac highways? For him, they are curved in an unimaginable paradimensional space by the fluid gravity of the river's ribbon. By some Einsteinian law, the river itself straightens in compensation like a hose stream, pouring in a steady silver fall from village to village… and the gliding boat goes with it.

So too, for the happy boatman all bridges are alike – simple irrelevancies, mere passing shadows overhead no more to be regarded than the high summer clouds. Whether the bridge carries a farm track or a railway or the main highway from London into the west is neither here nor there – all alike to him appear as truncated wormcasts across the river's route, ending abruptly for all he cares at the first bend or crest on either bank. For him the meanest hamlet on the river is more real than the grandest city away from it - these are the Kingdom's capitals, toylike though they be - as to the rest, where are they? Nowhere.

And much of the river is bridgeless besides. Because of this, the world of the river traveller is a world of quaint dead ends, willowy cul-de-sacs, quiet lanes that wind down to the river's edge and drown themselves in kingcups like Ophelia. The frantic world of the motorist is busy choking itself on the distant uplands with every modern convenience to enable the Mr. Toads to go faster from centre to centre. But the Little Chefs and Happy Eaters, the Fun Pubs with their bouncy castles, the drive-in Tescos and handy-parking B&Q stores never make it down the little capillary lanes that go nowhere, leaving the river banks to the coots, the anglers and the loveliest pubs in Britain.

The Flowerpot Inn at Aston is one such pub. Given the whole two-dimensional spread of Britain's map to choose from, I suppose it is nothing special. But in the one-dimensional linear world of the river it assumes an importance beyond its humble pretensions. Why, to the boatman there isn't another place to spend an evening for three hours' travelling either direction. To put that in motorists' terms, that is like coming across the only pub in the centre of a vast bleak moor half the size of Scotland.

What I am really trying to say, I suppose, is… well… just how much I enjoyed the Flowerpot Inn, that's all. There were a log fire, good beer, a cheerful young barman, a gruff landlord, a humorous local drunk, that steak-and-ale pie - and walls and walls and walls of stuffed fish. The pub houses the largest, most comprehensive collection of freshwater species in Britain, I was told, including several record-breakers. Dozens and dozens of glass cases display salmon, perch, dace and chubb, grayling, trout, eels and pike, all beautifully mounted and carefully labelled. One tiny glass case no bigger than a tea caddy contains a solitary stuffed goldfish; another, an artfully presented old boot in the process of being caught.

That night it was bitterly cold. A quick peep out from under the awning at midnight showed stars flashing like crystals of ice against a blazing black sky, the Scorpion's sting poised, diamond-tipped, to strike the World into endless night with its cold fire. Despite that, I slept well under my downy sleeping bag and woke to the loveliest morning yet.

A thick white mist lay over the still river and my awning and decks were furred with frost. Swans ghosted in and out of sight, heraldic birds in a silver world, and the early sun spun the mist from the river in skeins of palest gold. Before it had fully lifted though there came from somewhere down the river a sweet whiffling chuff-chuff-chuff-chuff... not the harsh snarl of a petrol motor but the unmistakable sound of a steam-launch.

Soon it came into sight, a little affair of polished teak and gleaming brass, chugging upstream with a snowy plume of steam billowing from its shiny funnel. The waters furled cleanly away from its bow in a V that set the river mist swirling and *Jack* rocking gently against the pontoon... and the day had begun.

I dressed and sauntered up the little lane to the Flowerpot Inn again to see what they could do about breakfast. The lane was deeply rutted but the mud was frozen to iron; the frost had traced on every dead leaf in the hedge a delicate pattern of white veins that melted to nothing as I breathed my dragon's breath upon them. Above the sky was a pale wintry blue, and I was very hungry.

At first, a thin lady came to the door and said that no, they didn't do breakfasts... or at least only for overnight residents... but before I was a hundred yards back down the lane, I was hailed from the back door of the Inn and beckoned back. It was a young man with a frying pan in one hand standing at the kitchen door.

"You were here last night, weren't you?" he queried. "You had the steak-and-ale pie. Young Bob in the bar passed back to me how as you'd appreciated it. I heard the missus just now, but never mind her, I'll have a word. Come on in and I'll fix you a bite. Full cooked all right for you then?"

And ten minutes later in the front parlour, I was propped in a sunny corner tucking in to the glories of a Full English Brekker, and feeling like a hobbit in one of the earlier chapters of *The Fellowship of the Ring*. Of such small things are true adventures made, the sort of thing that has me punching the air and shouting "*Oh thank you God!*" at spontaneous intervals for the next three days. They make dull reading perhaps, but they are the very stuff of good travelling.

Part of the whole point of a peregrinatio is that you do NOT say, "I must get to Windsor Castle by tonight, come Hell or high water." This annoys the Deity and He is likely to produce both of the above elements in copious quantities just to make a point. Nevertheless, prompted by regular phone calls from my mother, that is exactly what I did do, the point being to reach Windsor that evening so that I could attend Sung Eucharist the next morning at St George's Chapel in the Castle. Here long ago my various uncles had been boy choristers and I had been assured that the service and setting were exceptionally beautiful. Thus I set out after my hobbit's breakfast with a good will to row the seventeen miles down to the royal seat of Windsor.

From the start, things conspired to slow me up. A rowlock (not the one mended by Alan Snell in Shrewsbury - the other one) had begun to weaken around the woodwork and at mid-morning I had to pull in to a waterside boatyard to see if I could fix it. This was a messy and time-consuming job, and left me with blistered hands and a heated brow... and the section of gunwale bristling with crooked screws and splinters. The boatyard staff, after one minute of watching how I handled a screwdriver, had been oddly reluctant to lend me a power drill. By the time this was over, I found myself rowing once more into a boat race, a rather more serious one this time, with motor-boats chugging up and down full of bossy men with megaphones telling me to creep slowly along the banks while the slim gulls-wing eights sped by, race after race.

This being a fine Saturday of sunshine and clear skies, every man and his dog was out on the river through Marlow and Cookham, two towns which I am told are splendid but barely saw for myself through the serried ranks of motor launches, cabin cruisers and narrowboats churning up and down and getting hot and bothered with one another in the true tradition of pleasure-boating. In addition the locks were busy so often there was a queue - this meant balancing on one's oars amidst the wake of much larger vessels charging in and out of the lock-cuts, ready to scramble for safety out from beneath a cruiser's bows or row like fury to make it through the lock gates before some happy holidaymaker slammed them shut under my very nose.

Thus it was that by five o'clock in the afternoon, I had only just descended Boulter's Lock and still had seven long miles and several more locks to go. Divine Providence all day had been throwing large hints at me not to continue this headlong rush downstream to Windsor, and in ignoring them I missed the rich literary heritage of gracious Marlow - *Frankenstein* was written here, *The Wind in the Willows* just nearby - and missed also the opportunity to call in at Cookham and speak sternly to a certain Mr. Barber who lives there. He holds the unique appointment of Her Majesty's Swan Keeper... I'd been keeping a running list of complaints about his charges and whiling away the lonely hours by thinking up some amusing swan culling ideas I felt Mr. Barber should consider.

I had rowed hard down the long, still stretch beneath the beechwoods of Cliveden, the home of the Astors and the setting for the Profumo scandal in 1963, with hardly a glance to left or right, and by the time I had crammed my way in and out of Boulter's Lock, I was shaky and sweaty with the effort and cross with the lateness of the hour. I was also suddenly aware that it had been three days since I had had a wash. My shirt was clinging stickily to my back, my skin was gritty with sawdust and I was thoroughly fed up.

Then just below the lock as I plunged crossly downriver, a narrowboat chugged up behind me. Sensing my urgency, the skipper called out,

"Want a tow? Where are you hurrying to?"

"Windsor!" I called.

"Windsor? We're going down beyond Windsor. Throw us a line."

Two minutes later I was sitting back in the dinghy, relaxing for the first time that day and apologising to the sky, the water, the trees for my bad temper. Quite unnecessary, I told myself firmly. Life is good, people are kind, the World is beautiful... and another night without a bath would do me no harm at all.

After another couple of minutes, Life got even better.

"Would you like a beer?" called the skipper, waving a brown bottle and a glass at me from the narrowboat's stern. Well, what a silly question...

His mate started hauling the twenty feet of towline in closer and closer to the narrowboat and soon I was riding the wash, *Jack*'s nose just half a foot from the stern, swaying and surfing playfully like a dolphin trailing a liner's wash.

"Here we are," said the mate, leaning over the stern rail as far as he could go. I strained forward to reach the glass and bottle... nearer... nearer... one knee on the foredeck... shift of weight a little more and... and...

And Life suddenly got a lot worse. *Jack*, creaming along at an unaccustomed speed swerved under the weight on her foredeck and slowly, gracefully, inexorably turned turtle.

I disappeared under the icy green water in a tangle of stays and ropes, and into the Netherworld.

The River is a person. I did not know that until now. Up there in the sun and air the river is a highway, a playground, an artist's landscape, pretty-as-a-picture in white and blue. But here, down below the surface, I make the acquaintance of the Lady. She is cold-limbed and amber-haired and her teeth are the colour of gravel. Her skin is stippled all with rose-moles and glassy shadows play upon it. She arrays herself in fresh and flowing weed; silver fish-scales hang in her ears. Her voice is too low for human ear but as she sucks and nudges she tells me her woes. I am seeking a new husband, says she, and if you stay another year down here, you shall be King, King of the River, blind as an eel.

Where is the sky?

Somehow, eleven months later, I kicked myself free of rope and stay in the waterish gloom and surfaced spluttering and wide-eyed, with the glass and the beer bottle still in either hand. My first reaction was to swim after the narrowboat (which had immediately cut its motor) and carefully place those two bibular items on the low stern deck. It is only in emergencies that ones priorities become clear, isn't it? The skipper and his mate hauled me dripping out of the river onto the boat, (in the process kicking the rescued bottle straight overboard where it sank like a stone - a sacrifice to the river-queen I suppose... rather it than me) and, with three pairs of eyes aghast, we surveyed the scene.

Jack de Crow lay completely upside down in the water, her yellow hull wallowing half submerged like a strange luminous turtle. On the broad bosom of the river floated various bits of debris - my parrot cushion, my pith helmet, my small rucksack that contained all my writing equipment, wallet and so forth. The oars were making a spirited bid for freedom some way down the river and only the Lord knows what had happened to the main baggage stowed in the dinghy - my rucksack, awning, mattress and sleeping bag - gone to join the beer bottle no doubt, and live it up with the Maidenhead mermaids at the bottom of the deep green Thames.

Fortunately a little motor launch was coming up behind us and spent a busy ten minutes circling with a boathook, hauling the flotsam from the river and returning it to the narrowboat. Meanwhile, I had immediately stripped to my underwear and dived back in to see if I could right the poor dinghy. The usual method of getting a capsized dinghy upright again is to stand on the lip of the hull and lever the whole boat over, putting all one's weight on the end of the protruding centreboard rather as one might roll a small portly whale onto its back by hauling on its dorsal fin.

The problem here, however, was that there was no fin - the centreboard had not been in place when she tipped and was now presumably floating somewhere under the upturned hull in a tangle of lines. Taking a deep breath, I duck-dived down under the water and started exploring under the hull where I soon found the centreboard jammed against the submerged gunwale. I surfaced again for air, dived once more and went through a slow motion blurry-visioned struggle to poke the board up through the centreboard case and out through the exposed hull. This done, I went through the routine of righting the boat - slippery clamber up onto the yellow woodwork; toes jammed against the gunwale lip; a steady haul on the fin, and the slow rolling of the boat onto its side, as I fell backwards into the river's icy green bosom once more.

An agile sailor will clamber onto the centreboard itself as the boat comes half over and continue the rolling motion by hauling on the upper gunwale, even nipping over this and into the dinghy as she fully rights herself in one continuous move like an acrobat staying atop a rolling barrel. This graceful manoeuvre I signally failed to execute; it was another twenty minutes of floundering and flopping before *Jack de Crow* was wallowing upright and I was sitting in her flooded bilges surveying the damage. Remarkably, there was hardly any loss. My rucksack had jammed tightly under the thwart and the various other items had been secured by straps which seemed all to have held. Indeed the only thing that had irretrievably gone was my tin whistle which had been lying loose on the decking and was easily replaceable. And at least I had had that much-needed and long wished-for bath.

Even more remarkably, the narrowboat had not simply cut loose and vanished whilst I was performing clumsy aquatic stunts in my underwear. They had hovered nearby and as soon as *Jack* was upright again and baled out, I was taken aboard, wrapped in a warm, dry dressing-gown and handed a large hot whisky and lemon. It all goes rather hazy after that. I remember protesting and the skipper's wife (whom I'd not noticed before) pushing me firmly into a bunk-seat and assuring me that I would be delivered to Windsor that evening. When I tried explaining through chattering teeth and whisky fumes that it didn't really matter, it was just Mum and St George's Chapel and the choir and Sunday mass and something-or-other, it all came out rather garbled - I think they got the impression that I was due to attend my mother's funeral service or something equally momentous. Whatever it was she held a hurried consultation with her husband up on deck and they both came down with a new steely look in their eyes, saying:

"Don't worry, son. You'll not miss that service, even if we have to burn every stick of furniture aboard."

Capsize!

The next three hours passed in a golden fog of warmth and vague contentment. Hot coffee followed the whisky, a light supper of cheese toast and poached eggs came somewhere along the line, and then more whisky again. Meanwhile all my clothes and half the contents of my sodden rucksack were drying in the engine room draped over hot pipes and valves and grills. To this day I regret that I cannot remember these people's names, though I do know that the skipper's wife was marvellously beautiful... also that when I asked the skipper what his profession was he rather shamefacedly admitted that he was a North Sea Rescue officer, more accustomed to pulling people *out* of sub-zero waters than tipping them in.

Eventually, several hours after dark when my clothes were merely damp, my head had stopped swimming and I had finally persuaded them that they would not be receiving a letter from my solicitor concerning damages due, we reached Romney Lock just below Windsor. They were planning to get down to Weybridge that night and I had delayed them enough, but they still took some convincing that I would be all right - this stretch of the river was after all dark and empty, and they really didn't like to abandon me. In the end to reassure them, I told them that I had a friend living here, right here, not five minutes walk from the river, a very old friend who would be simply delighted to see me and yes, had a large rucksack-drying machine and I was fine, honestly. I reloaded my dinghy, refused the offer of a bottle of whisky to take with me and rowed off to the bank while they chugged away downstream into the night.

Once their lights had disappeared, I climbed out onto the shelving bank beneath an ornamental willow and considered my position. As I did so my cheery optimism faded. I didn't of course have a friend near here - in fact, I wasn't exactly sure where 'here' was. It was unthinkable that I should sleep aboard the dinghy that night, with my sleeping bag soaked through and *Jack* still awash with water that I had been unable to bail or sponge away. It would have to be a Bed and Breakfast - it was to be hoped that they would accept soggy five pound notes. If I could find one, that is. I appeared to be on the fringes of some large, dark, empty park. The night was clear and starry but bitterly cold, and I was beginning to shiver. Grabbing my wet rucksack and hat, I strode off across smooth grass beneath stately trees towards a distant solitary light. This turned out to be a lamp post by a pair of high elaborate wrought iron gates flanked by pillars. On one of the pillars was a name carved into the stone and gilded with a crest above it, dimly lit by the sodium glare of the lamp. At last I knew where I had washed ashore: the hallowed grounds of possibly the World's most famous school - Eton College.

Oh terrific, I thought. The security even at Ellesmere had been fairly ferocious. What it would be like in the school where Prince William was sleeping in some nearby dormitory, not to mention the various young Honourables, Viscounts and Marquises dotted about the boarding-houses, I shuddered to think. Any minute now I would be arrested and shot as a deranged stalker of adolescent boys – or, more likely, a paparazzi photographer attempting a few sneak shots of the recently bereaved Prince. My dishevelled appearance would hardly reassure people as to my innocence. Eton College of all places. Eton College...

Eton...?

Slowly my mind clicked to a halt. By golly, I thought. I *did* know someone here after all. A Housemaster. Yes, I did. Not very well, mind. He had taught long ago at Ellesmere before my time but had remained good friends with some of my colleagues there, and I had dined with him on one or two occasions when he had been revisiting Shropshire.

But nevertheless, I thought that in my present soggy plight, this faint acquaintance might justifiably be taken up. One thing was for sure. If this was the town of Eton, guest house accommodation would not be had for under forty pounds a night, a sum my Scottish ancestry would not allow me even to consider. And it was faintly possible that my Housemaster might just welcome me with open arms; I seemed to remember from one of those dinner occasions that he had had an interest in sailing - might in fact acknowledge a fellow mariner in distress. Yes, Providence was again smiling faintly upon me.

I knew his name but not which House he ran; a ring on the first doorbell I came to elicited a hollow voice out of an electric door-phone set in the wall which sent me off to an imposing Georgian porch down the road. Here I stood, composed myself and considered how best to initiate proceedings.

"*Johnny-boy! Hi! Remember me? That night at Ellesmere three, no, four, years ago? Sure you do! We had some laughs, eh? Well here I am, so let the party roll...*"

Or perhaps,

"*Hello, I'm hypothermic, in desperate need of food and warmth and a bed for the night. We HAVE met but I wasn't blue then, I'll explain over breakfast in the morning. All right?*"

Or maybe I should...

"Yes, hello. Can I help you?"

I blinked. This wasn't the figure I remembered. John had been taller surely, had had a moustache and had brownish hair. This person before me was quite, quite different: short, silvery hair and wearing a skirt and blouse. A lady in fact.

"Oh... er... hello. Is Mr. Clarke here by any chance?"

"No, he's out this evening, I'm afraid."

Damn and blast it. My newly acquired visions of hot baths and soft sofas were fading even in their bright infancy.

"Oh... Oh, thank you. Um... fine, thanks. No, no message. Goodbye."

"Goodbye then," the lady replied and started to shut the door. But just before she closed it, she glanced at me, poked her hand out of the doorway outstretched palm up and asked,

"Is it raining? I thought it was fine."

"No, it's not raining," I replied. "It's quite clear."

"But you, you're soaking wet! How on Earth... ?"

"Ah, well, now that's a bit of a long story I'm afraid. I fell in the Thames at Maidenhead, you see, and I came ashore here and..."

"You SWAM seven miles from Maidenhead?!" she exclaimed, door wide open now and eyes wide with alarm.

"Oh no, no, no," I stuttered.

"I think you'd better come in, dear, and warm up. Are you a friend of Mr. Clarke's?"

"Yes... well, no... well, sort of."

"Dear me, I don't think you're well. Well, let's leave that and sort it out later. Now come in and tell me all about it..."

And that is how I came to be sitting in the cosy parlour of that saint among women, Dame Jenny Jennings, Eton Housekeeper and surrogate mother and nanny figure to the sixty-odd boys of John's house. She was a lady who combined cosy domesticity with an elegant gentility and a good measure of common sense, and before half-an-hour had passed, she had sorted things out. There was no question of sleeping on a sofa; there was a bed made up in the spare room. John was out late with a couple of friends who were also returning to stay the night, so one more down for breakfast would hardly matter. Meanwhile, a hot bath was running and if I dug out my pyjamas from the sodden rucksack she'd have them dried and toasty warm in a jiffy, and after that a light supper of boiled egg and buttery toast soldiers.

When it came to bedtime, I was fully expecting to be tucked up by the good Dame, say our bedtime prayers together and kiss Teddy goodnight, but she contented herself with simply letting me know that she would leave a note for John to advise him of my presence and would see me in the morning about getting the rest of my stuff dry. Meanwhile, if there was anything I required, anything at all, she was just down the hallway... Goodnight, my lamb. Sweet dreams, my poppet, and off I drifted into wondrous slumber rocked on the fleecy billows of Sleep on a drowsy voyage to the Land of Nod and capsizing all the way there.

I awoke early next morning with a start. The large House was very quiet - all the boys were off on Half-Term - and soon I would have to saunter downstairs in Mr Clarke's second best dressing-gown (my clothes were still damp), wander into the dining room and nod hello to the two other strangers there, and as I helped myself to the devilled kidneys and scrambled eggs from the sideboard, attempt to explain casually to Mr. Clarke why exactly I had presumed on our somewhat slim acquaintance.

Somehow what had seemed perfectly reasonable the night before viewed from the position of squelching hypothermia now seemed in the broad light of day the most preposterous cheek.

"Remember me? No? Ah well, never mind. I say, these grilled tomatoes are super, aren't they? Pass the pepper, would you...?"

So I lay staring at the high white ceiling as a lozenge of sunlight crept slowly across it and birdsong filtered in from the garden trees outside, my thoughts churning like butter, wondering what on Earth I was going to say.

I needn't have worried. That remarkable Providence that hovers over me and smiles so readily upon me was, as usual, three steps ahead. A tap came on the door, a jovial voice called out "Are you decent? Your morning tea, sir," and into the bedroom bearing a tray of tea things bustled, of all people, Keith Shuttleworth - Keith of the Ellesmere Common Room, Keith of the Morda Brook, dear and familiar Keith whose presence made suddenly everything all right.

An hour later, we were sitting down to that breakfast as sumptuous as I had imagined but without the awkwardness. Keith, hooting with amazed delight, was exclaiming about the coincidence that had washed me ashore here on the one weekend in the year when he was down visiting his old friend, John. And yes, of course John remembered me; in fact Keith had been telling him only last night in the restaurant how I had sailed away down the Vyrnwy and was last heard of somewhere near Bristol, and that he'd not expected to see me alive again... and now here I was devouring bacon before his very eyes. John, though a little bemused by the oddity of the coincidence, was kindness itself - in fact, Keith was staying on another night so I must too, of course. That would give me time to sort myself out, dry my things and explore Eton and Windsor across the river. And talking of which, here was a jacket and tie to borrow to attend that service at St George's Chapel in the Castle. The gods were keeping their promise; I'd had Hell and high water, but now the rewards were dropping into place one by one as neatly as alphabet blocks clocking into a box to spell a word - three words, in fact; a phrase: something along the lines of 'MACKINNON : LUCKY SOD.'

Ah, what bliss to be in Windsor on a bright October Sunday! The massive grey walls of the Castle rising above the town, the wide courtyard of pale gold gravel and the guards in their scarlet uniforms looking straight off the lid of a Quality Street chocolate tin; the exquisite Chapel with its heraldic finery emblazoned on every wall and pillar and pew - a riot of gules and azures, lions rampant and passant, chevrons sable, bends sinister, and acre upon acre of gilded fleur-de-lis.

From the battlements, the town below looked as a royal capital should look, a toy town of red roofs and cobbled streets curving up around the hill's foot, of golden weathercocks and starlings in swift squadrons and the river glimmering away in a silvery ribbon towards the south-east.

It was good to catch up with Ellesmere news again from Keith as we strolled back from the castle; in reality, only six weeks of College life had gone on without me, but with the nature and pace of dinghy travelling, I rather felt that I had met Keith in some far-flung land across several oceans and had three years of news to digest. The chat continued late into the evening back at John's house while my clothes and sleeping bag rumbled to cosy dryness in the House laundry. There I smiled wryly at a roster pinned to the laundry notice-board informing the world that it was the Hon. Lancelot St. John's turn to supervise bed-stripping and pillowcase-collecting that week while Viscount Darley (Third Form) would distribute fresh linen on Tuesdays and Fridays. Dame Jenny Jennings, by the way, had assured me that her title was not in the same league as that of Dame Barbara Cartland and so on. It was simply the name by which all Eton housekeepers are called, and does not involve the Queen's personal intervention. After that I stopped bowing and walking backwards in front of her.

So comforting and welcoming was that house that I could have cheerfully stayed a week, even offering to do pillowcase duty for my bed and board, but come Monday, I steeled myself to return to *Jack* and continue on my journey.

After attending the boys' morning service in the College chapel - Half-Term had ended - a marvellous affair where I was the only figure not clad in a high white collar and tails and where I tried not to stare too obviously at the future King of England sitting opposite me, I bade farewell to Keith and John and Dame Jennings and made my way through the grounds to where *Jack* was patiently waiting. To my surprise she had been neither stolen nor confiscated, not even by some titled under-gardener, and apart from several trees' worth of yellow willow leaves lying in her, she was fine and ready to go. I loaded her up, untied her and soon we were rowing steadily down the river watching Windsor Castle dwindle behind us into blue haze. We were heading once more for London.

London and the Law

'A mighty mass of brick, and smoke, and shipping,
Dirty and dusty, but as wide as eye
Could reach, with here and there a sail just skipping
In sight...'

Byron - *Don Juan*. Canto X. St. 82

The Home Park, Old Windsor; Runnymede and the island where the Magna Carta was signed in 1215 AD; a fleet of Harlequin ducks looking as ducks would look if they went in for Samurai dress code; the M25 motorway bridge in its grey pall of exhaust: these are dimly noted stages in the journey into London's outer suburbs. I remember coming across a sailing vessel even smaller than my own just above Staines, a three foot model yacht whose rudder and sheets were controlled by a tiny remote control motor. It was being operated from the bank by a young man utterly absorbed in the task who was sending it tacking to and fro across the river, a ship from Lilliput manned by a phantom crew racing me down the Thames.

I remember also watching with excitement the exotic flash of a bird flying off into some treetops, some rainbow coloured bird with a long tail and a piercing screech. It looked for all the world like a parakeet in vivid green, lemon yellow and azure with a red splash visible on its back as it flew. I was thrilled to think that I had spotted a rarity, obviously a naturalised escapee, and was busy composing a letter to the Times and the RSPB about it when several miles downstream I came round a bend to see an extraordinary sight. In the middle of the river was a tiny island bearing nothing but three maple trees. The ragged leaves had almost finished now, lying in crumpled brown swathes at the trees' roots, but every branch was full of a rustling and squawking and fluttering - two hundred similar parakeets as bright and glossy as tropical fruit, looking like one of Jenny's painted silk designs back in Shropshire.

Down through Staines and Chertsey the river bungalows crowd along the shore and fill the islands that punctuate the map with their intriguing names: Pharaoh's Island, D'Oyly Carte Island, Dumsey Eyot and Penton Hook. The wind had stiffened into a brisk south-easterly and even in the bright sunshine it was cold as I tacked my way downstream to Shepperton where I stopped that afternoon by a friendly pub whose name I now forget.

As I look at the map now, I see that the next day I did all of a magnificent six miles, though for the life of me I cannot remember what slowed me up so much. There was an awful lot of hard tacking against the same biting wind of yesterday under a cold clear sky, zigzagging to and fro past the waterworks of Sunbury and Hampton where my grandfather had been Chief Engineer during the War, and Mother and her brothers had spent their childhood playing amongst the filterbeds and gooseberry bushes and boating on the Thames. I moored that night opposite Hampton Court with its famous maze at a charming pub called Fox-on-the-River and, depressed perhaps by my pitiful progress that day or by the thought that my voyage was nearly over for the year, I decided to ring some friends.

I don't like telephones much at the best of times. Conversations are stilted and bloodless and certainly whenever I'd tried ringing Ellesmere friends, I would find that some crisis would be fulminating in the background, reducing my friend's conversation to a staccato "*Yep. Yep, great to hear you, yep, look, bit busy now, got to go, yep, yep, bye!*" But those special coin-phones in pubs, those chunky grey items generally placed in the main service hatchway in a direct pathway used by irate bar staff, are specifically designed to trick you out of all your spare change without actually connecting you at all. They do this by displaying a flashing screen that says "INSERT MONEY" once you've dialled. So you insert your 10p coin. Then the screen flashes up "NO, NO, NOT UNTIL THEY ANSWER, SORRY, DIDN'T WE MAKE OURSELVES CLEAR - TRY AGAIN." You hang up, you jiggle the coin-return button and insert a finger into the change-flap (cautiously checking for lit cigarettes this time). It is empty, and the 10p coin has clearly been irrevocably claimed by British Telecom.

So, try again. Dig out another 10p coin, dial, ignore the screen that is once more begging you to insert money, and you wait. The person on the other end answers, saying "Hello, can I help you?" so you drop the coin in the slot and start speaking.

"Hi, it's Sandy here! How are..."

" Hello? Hello? Are you there...?" says the voice again.

"Oh? Yes, sorry, it's Sandy here; I'm ringing from..."

"*Hello? Who is this? Hello? Hello?*" continues your friend in rising panic making it perfectly clear that they can't hear a word you're saying. All the while, the screen is flashing at you a new message:

POA... POA... POA... it says, while you pump more coins in the slot. The poor friend on the other end is by now convinced she's receiving an obscene phone call and saying things like "*Ron! Ron, it's that silent caller again, call the police, this is the third time this week, why us? Oh my God, my hives are breaking out again, I can't stand it, why this senseless persecution...*", and all the time you're trying to work out what the bloody hell 'POA' means.

Only too late do you realise that it might conceivably stand for 'Press On Answer' and refer to a grey button tucked anonymously down the bottom of the console which you press half a second after your distraught friend has hung up and gone to find some bottles of sleeping tablets. The phone is dead once more, with several fistfuls of change smugly swallowed in its depths and the screen display now reading HA HA... HA HA... HA HA...

You now only have a pound coin left and deciding to try once more, carefully go through the whole routine correctly this time, to be answered by someone who says "*Yep, Yep, great to hear from you, yep, look, bit busy, yep, bye!*" and hangs up leaving the screen displaying:

YOU *HAD* 97P WORTH OF CALL TO MAKE BUT I DONT GIVE CHANGE SO THAT 97P IS NOW MINE MINE ALL MINE... BYE.

So I retire defeated and spend what the phone has left me of my dinner money on half a pint of beer and a packet of crisps and write a letter instead.

I woke the next morning to find a thick frost on the banks and a gossamer mist lying over the river. The early sun was combing the vapour off in phantom strands, and the grounds of Hampton Court lay ice-blue and white on the opposite bank behind their high iron railings. It was going to be another glorious day, and I expected that night to have reached journey's end: Surrey Docks just above Greenwich. Here, living aboard a narrowboat, was a friend of mine, Tim, the brother of Rupert the vet who had brought me the original *Jack de Crow* all those years ago. Tim did not know I was coming, of course. The idea was to sail up alongside, tap on a porthole and, when asked, casually mention that yes, I'd just rowed from Shropshire, well, why not? I was also rather hoping that he and Babette, his girlfriend, would not mind boat-sitting for a few months while I wintered in Australia, ready to return in spring to attempt the crossing of Europe.

For this I had now decided to do, definitely. Why not? *Jack de Crow* had proven herself buoyant and stable and manoeuvrable in all weathers and conditions, tough enough to withstand the bumps and batterings sustained in locks and weirs, and it seemed that judging from the fine weather that had shone almost continuously about me, I was in fact a sun god upon whom it could rarely if ever rain.

With these happy thoughts revolving in my mind, I set off down the river on the last leg of the journey into the heart of London. The frosty morning was still as glass so I glided along with the oars paddling out their soothing rhythm on the silken surface, a *steady ONE and two-three, ONE and two-three* composed of soft creaks, splashes and clunks; it is exactly the same rhythm as the introduction to one of the famous arias from *Carmen* but lends itself equally well to any number of Latin dances, so I hummed my way through Sambas and Salsas, Rumbas and Tangos down those gentle suburban reaches towards Teddington and the tidal Thames.

Here at Teddington there is an enormous weir and the means to measure precisely how much water flows down the river each day - in times of flood up to fifteen billion gallons a day. There are three locks here, including the tiniest lock in Britain, a miniature skiff lock designed to hold just one little punt or rowing skiff... and down this I went. It was a peculiar experience; I relived those old forgotten nursery fears of going down the plug hole when the bathwater is let out. But when the lower gate opened, I looked out onto a dazzling window of river and was once more seeing tidal waters, the first since Bristol.

I had arrived just a little while before high tide so the current was running upstream but sluggishly, hardly perceptible in its movement, and I had little difficulty in rowing on down the river against it. Down through Twickenham I went and moored for a while to explore Eel Pie Island, finding it to be a jungly little eyot, with damp and fading bungalows crouched under thick foliage but with names redolent of a braver age, an age of exploration upon the World's high seas - Coromandel House, Mandalay, Admiral's Rest, Cape Cottage. There is something about all islands everywhere that is utterly enchanting, something wrapped up with weatherboard and whalebone, with seashells in dusty rows and thick pale green glass in the windows, with telescopes and hibiscus and haphazard footpaths: Madeira, Nantucket, Iona, Norfolk Island, Inish Mor... these by their geographical isolation are linked by invisible isthmuses each with another, and here too with Eel Pie Island on a sunny Wednesday morning in late October.

Richmond Bridge, glowing honey gold above the green river, I passed by, and then rounded the broad bend to Kew. Just above Kew Bridge, however, the gentle monotony was broken abruptly by a noisy motor launch driven by three youths who roared up the river on a tidal wave of wash, steered straight for me and ducked aside with three feet to spare, sending *Jack* and myself heaving madly on the wake and scarlet with fury. The mast swung wildly to and fro - the bundled sail, gaff and boom thumped savagely from side to side and a curling wave of filthy water bearing with it a debris of plastic bottles, polystyrene foam and frothy scum sloshed over the gunwale in a stinking tide. No sooner had I recovered my balance and picked the worst of the debris out of the bilges than I saw with dismay the motor launch returning. These youths were not in the same league as my three Reading lads; they were out for laughs and thrills and didn't give a damn who suffered. As they drew near, I could see one cause for their recklessness - a crate of shiny brown beer bottles in the cockpit and four or five lolling empty on the decks. Even as I watched, one of the crew picked up a pair of bottles, held one in each hand over the side and smashed them together, laughing at the sudden vicious tinkle of broken glass.

I tried rowing steadily on, ignoring the blare of the ghetto blaster propped in the cockpit and the shouted comments ricocheting over the water. The river seemed suddenly very wide and lonely and *Jack* horribly exposed to whatever these drunken louts might try. I steered in towards the Kew bank, but this too was empty of people as far as I could see in either direction. Before I could get close in, the launch shot between me and the bank on a snarling wave and started to describe a tight circle around me, a ring of savage foam and choppy water encircling the dinghy. Briefly half a dozen literary parallels ran through my mind - the sea serpent that drew its deadly coils around the *Dawn Treader*; the tactics of killer whales in some half-remembered and highly inaccurate adventure story; the Hullabaloos in *Coot Club* menacing the peaceful Norfolk Broads with their wash and radio blare and reckless disregard for others. But literary examples, so comforting and enhancing in times of peace, are sadly inadequate when faced with genuine 20th Century thuggishness, and I must confess to an uncertain mixture of apprehension, embarrassment and uneasy fear that the better story-book heroes never seem to feel in moments like these. There are no patterns or scripts for dealing with modern day loutishness. Faced with an 18th Century highwayman with a silver pistol and burgundy coat and lace at his chin, there are a dozen poems and folk tales and films to provide the appropriate responses. The same too had these youths been waving cutlasses and sporting parrots and eye-patches and quaffing Jamaican rum; I would have felt quite comfortable being terrified or defiant, taking my cue from a whole range of experts from Burt

Lancaster to Captain Pugwash. But stripped of all romance, of plumes and pistols and parakeets, I was horribly at a loss and floundering mentally as much as *Jack* was by now floundering in reality on the motor launch's wash.

Another thought struck me then – (it is astonishing how several brief seconds of time can be filled with several essays' worth of philosophy) - namely that such so-called romantic escapades in the past never were perhaps as brightly tinged as Time has painted them. The highwaymen who haunted Epping Forest in the 18th Century and waylaid travellers were not really the gentlemen adventurers of popular romance; they would surely be no more picturesque or romantic to their victims than the pitiful commonplace muggers of today. And the rum-swilling buccaneers of Drake's day were surely no more charming and gallant than these thoroughly obnoxious slobs who were watching with beer-fumed glee the effect of large waves on a small unpowered dinghy.

As I say, these reams of philosophical musings only occupied a couple of seconds of real time before my body took charge of things. Tired of waiting for my confused brain to sort out sea serpents, Arthur Ransome and 18th Century perceptions, it stood up in the violently rocking dinghy, held up my folded map case like an identity pass and to the amazement of my disbelieving ears shouted, "River Police! I have noted your vessel's name and registration number, and you are exceeding the speed limit!"

Before my horrified brain could catch up with what it had just heard my body say and hastily correct it ("*Er... no, sorry. Not true, actually. I'm just a helpless citizen and this is just a map case*"), the three thugs had blanched, straightened up, and cut their speed to a demure four knots before heading off up the river arguing in furious whispers. "W*hose stupid idea was it in the first place? ...Yer Dad'll KILL yer when the police get through to 'im ... Nah, 'COURSE 'e was river police like 'e said, cos 'oo else'd wear a silly hat like that, it must be part of the uniform...*"

As I waited for the waves to subside, I bailed the boat, set the oars back in place and wondered what the penalty was for impersonating a police officer - what's more, for bringing the Royal Thames River Constabulary into disrepute by carrying out the deception in a ridiculous hat. Ten years at least, I reckoned, as I took to the oars once more and rowed on somewhat shakily down the river.

On I slogged then through Fulham and Wandsworth, alternately drifting and rowing past the extraordinary Wagnerian fantasy of the Harrods Depository in red terracotta, past the smart modern flats of Chelsea Harbour and under the splendid iron tracery of the Albert Bridge where a thousand starlings rustled and cheeped and roosted in a cheerful, squabbling swarm. Soon the sun was westering and the sky was turning pink and gold beneath the clear cool blue. Night was coming on, and I decided to check the map. One glance confirmed what I had suspected - Southwark Docks were another eight miles downstream and quite unreachable that night. But where else could I go? As I rowed the sky deepened to crimson and scarlet, a blazing furnace of a sunset the like of which I have rarely seen. The black silhouettes of the Battersea Power Station stood like cut-out cardboard shapes against the vivid sky. I could feel also that the water beneath my keel was behaving in an uneasy manner. This was no longer the placid silk-cool Thames I had been used to; the outgoing tide had turned the river into a broad, wrangling churn of grey water that poured under the arches of the Grosvenor Bridge and on towards Vauxhall. Before I had reached Vauxhall Bridge, a new hazard was apparent. Huge ferries swept by, and their wake rolling against the current set the river waters sloshing and slapping in a racing chop. Between the sheer embankments of concrete, these waves rebounded magnified and sent *Jack de Crow* crashing and reeling from side to side in the deepening dusk.

Before I had reached Lambeth Bridge it was completely dark, the waves were sloshing over the gunwales and I was terrified. So choppy was the water that I could barely use the oars. Somehow I managed to steer myself inwards to the north bank, cursing the ferries as they churned up the river, lit up like Elijah's fiery chariot and all unseeing of the little lightless dinghy bobbing down on the racing tide. Ferries were not the only peril. A smaller motor launch went zooming upstream along the further bank, red and blue disco lights flashing and some incomprehensible garble issuing from speakers, a jet of spray flung up behind from its rocket-like speed. I remember shaking an angry fist at its vanishing form and cursing it for its reckless hooliganism; surely it was illegal to be travelling at such a pace, especially at night. Where were the police? Really...

In the midst of all the fear there came one moment of sheer magic as I bobbed down beneath the Houses of Parliament and the landmark tower of Big Ben, just as it was striking seven. From my dinghy I could see into the lit windows of the Palace above me: a brief glimpse of some fan-vaulted ceiling, high panelled shelves lined with books in green and maroon leather with the gilt glinting on their spines. Some sort of drinks party was in progress: an assembly of figures in dark suits and silver hair, each with a cut glass of amber sherry in hand. As I passed, one youngish looking man came to the window and stood staring out beyond the glass into the darkness over the Thames. He rested his forehead for a moment against the cool glass, looking tired and a little glum, I thought, as though he longed to be away from that lit room and its men of power, its secrets and its linenfold panelling - perhaps longing to be in a small sailing dinghy off to foreign parts on an outgoing tide under the stars.

For my part, I would have been quite happy to swap places right then. I had had enough. This was quite definitely the most dangerous and stupid thing I had ever done and was also quite likely to be the last thing I'd ever do. I was being swept along at eight knots in a roaring world of darkness and glaring sodium-lights, which dazzled the inky black water with liquid orange slashes that confused the eye. The pylons of Westminster Bridge surged by in a welter of rushing, echoing current not three feet from my left gunwale, and as I shot out from under the black arches, I pulled sharply in towards the floating pontoon of Westminster Pier. Just before I was swept past the end, a wave slammed me against the pontoon's steel rim and I grabbed a railing with both hands, determined to simply stop here before I was sunk by a passing ferry.

Night Tide

I, as I say, was determined to stop. *Jack*, however, was equally set on keeping going. The current swept her from under my feet, my arms were nearly wrenched from their sockets and half a second later I found myself with my hands still clinging to the railing but with my feet hooked over *Jack*'s stern trying to race away downstream. The rest of my intervening body acted as a badly sagging bridge 'twixt the two, hanging horizontally over the dark racing Thames and slipping slowly drinkwards.

An agonising period followed in which I attempted to drag *Jack* back upstream to a position under me, an exercise involving more stomach muscles than I customarily use and during which my mind absented itself and wandered away humming hymn tunes to itself until the crisis was over. Eventually, I had got *Jack* back beneath me, grabbed the painter and tied firmly... very firmly... onto the pontoon railing. "That certainly won't be coming undone again in a hurry," I told myself. "Here I am and here I stay," I added as I started to climb onto the pontoon to find someone official to let them know they had a guest mooring for the night.

Just then a resounding BOOOHHHM! shook the night, the sort of sound one associates with supertankers in foggy Atlantic sea lanes rather than inland river traffic, and I turned to see an enormous ferry crowded with passengers just swinging in to dock at the pontoon. In ten seconds flat, *Jack* would be crushed like a matchbox between ferry and pontoon. I took a flying leap back into the dinghy, fumbled furiously with the extra secure clove hitches and bowlines I had just spent a careful ten minutes tying and tightening and somehow managed to cast loose three seconds before the giant stern of the ferry swung in with a grinding thud against the railings where I had just been moored. Even so, the swirling kick of the propeller-wash sent me bucketing and spinning downstream once more into the darkness and before I'd recovered myself I was a hundred yards down the river, helplessly adrift once more. The white bulk of the Queen Mary swept by, the piers of Charing Cross Railway Bridge clanged overhead, Cleopatra's Needle floodlit in gold reared up and vanished and the vast edifice of the Savoy Hotel mocked my frustrated attempts to halt my swirling progress.

Beneath Waterloo Bridge, the echoing swell of oily black waves decided me. If I survived this night, I would not be going to Europe. It was sheer folly to dream of crossing the Channel in a rotten little tub like this. If the choppiness was this bad so far inland up the Thames, how it would be further down the estuary and out into the Channel was unthinkable. No. I had clearly been indulging in a fool's daydream, lulled by the exceptional conditions of the Bristol Channel that long-distant day and carried away with unrealistic visions of my own abilities. If I got the blasted boat to Southwark Docks or even simply somewhere safe tonight, that's where she would stay until she could be shipped back to Ellesmere to lie amongst the dandelions for another thirty years. As for me, well, I wasn't sure quite what I would do... possibly dedicate my life to God, join a monastery in a desert somewhere; anything as long as this heaving, bucking, swooping, blind nightmare stopped now.

As Waterloo Bridge spat me out from under its booming arches, another pontoon on the left bank swept into sight. A little more carefully this time, I somehow oared alongside, grabbed at the huge black tyres that lined its edge and let *Jack* thump slowly to a halt against the giant rings. I tied on, climbed shakily aboard and called out a cautious "Hello?"

The pontoon was about fifty feet long and consisted of a long decking facing the river backed by a row of four rooms, each one with its door opening onto the deck. Keeping an eye out for approaching ferries that might want suddenly to dock there, I ventured to call out a little louder. "Hello? Anyone there?"

No answer. Funny. Each room had lights on, and all the doors stood wide open... I went to investigate. The first room seemed to be a sort of mini-gym, with weights and training equipment and lockers along the walls. The second was a small television lounge; an old sofa and a few armchairs lined the walls and the television was on, the seven o'clock news quacking and flickering its bluish light over the shabby carpet. The next room was a small brightly-lit kitchen: a toaster, a small hot plate and a kettle, and on the bench-top two mugs of coffee steaming. Visions of the 'Marie Celeste', of abandoned ghost ships riding the ocean waves, of ancient brigs manned by phantom crews fluttered through my mind before I reminded myself that this was central London and not the still-vexed Bermoothes, and the existence of a haunted pontoon was unlikely to have gone unnoticed within fifty yards of Somerset House. The last room explained the nature of the place, if not the mystery of its sudden abandonment. It contained a large VHF radio, a computer, a desk and filing-cabinets... and over the back of two chairs hung a couple of uniforms; river-police uniforms, standard issue, not including the pith helmet.

As I stepped outside onto the decking again, a fast motor launch zoomed up alongside the pontoon nearly swamping *Jack de Crow*, and I recognised it as the reckless vessel with the disco lights I had seen blaring up the river in the dark a little earlier. On closer inspection, I also recognised it for what it was - a river-police boat, with two irate looking river-policemen just hopping onto the pontoon. One of them was speaking into a walkie-talkie, and I heard him say; "It's all right. We've found him. He's on our pontoon. Over." The other stepped up to me, stabbed a finger at my chest and said with some asperity, "We've been looking for you!"

Oh dear. I hadn't thought that the crime of impersonating a police officer would have come to light quite so soon.

"Ah, hello, officers... sorry, can I help you?"

"We've been looking," he repeated, "and I quote," (here he consulted his notebook) "for a lunatic in a pith helmet out of control in a small dinghy without navigation lights, as reported to us by no less than three ferry captains. Can we assume that you are said lunatic?"

"Um... well I do have a pith helmet, officer, but..."

"Right, yes, lunatic would seem to be an apt description then. Are you aware of the Rules of Navigation that demand adequate navigation lights on any vessel sailing between the hours of darkness on public shipping lanes, sir?"

"Ah, yes. Well, no. Well, I could make a stab at them... er..."

"Are you aware, sir, of the dangers to yourself and to others of proceeding in such a fashion on this waterway at a time of maximum tide-flow, thus causing us to be called out mere seconds before settling down to partake of a well earned cup of Nescafé Gold Blend?"

"Er... sorry about that..."

"And the penalties for needlessly distracting us from our more serious duties, sir?"

"Penalties? Um... no, I wasn't aware..."

"Where, may I ask, sir, have you come from in that vessel?"

"Er... Shropshire."

There was a pause. A glance between the two.

"Blimey. Need a cup of Nescafé Gold Blend then? We'll make some fresh."

Ten minutes later, I was steadying my nerves with a hot mug of much needed coffee while my two police officers quizzed me about the whole voyage so far - Ellesmere, the Morda Brook, the Shropshire Weir, the Ironbridge Gorge and the passage through the Bristol Channel. Both had been all over the waterways of Britain and were flatteringly interested in the trip, and though neither revised their first opinion of me when it came to lunacy, they seemed to forget the penalties and charges of dangerous navigational practices on the night-time Thames as I took them along the Kennet-Avon canal and up to Oxford and Lechlade and back.

They in their turn explained how having received a call from a concerned ferry captain, they had flung themselves into their launch and sped upstream along the south bank to look for me, not wasting a second to lock up, turn the television off or grab their jackets. Meanwhile I must have just crossed to the north bank and watched them speed by, mistaking them for another boatload of hooligans such as my tormentors up by Kew.

Finally, it came to the crunch. Could I leave *Jack* here tonight, and fetch her away tomorrow? Wilf, the sergeant, fixed me with a stony eye.

"Are you a member of the IRA?" he asked.

"Er... no!" I replied in some surprise.

"Is your vessel packed with Semtex or explosives of any kind?"

"No."

"Right, you can leave her here tonight. Where are you going to sleep then?"

I poked my head outside. With every wave, *Jack* was slamming up and down against the pontoon tyres with a vicious jerk, rising five feet and then plunging into a dark trough of racing water each time. Sleeping aboard was out of the question.

"Ah, I don't suppose you know a cheapish hotel or hostel nearby, do you?" I hazarded.

"You are, my son, about two hundred yards from the West End of London. Hotel prices start at about ninety pounds per night. How much have you got?"

"Um... forty pounds?"

"You ARE a lunatic, aren't you? Hold on, I'll see what I can do."

He turned to a telephone, stabbed the buttons and leaned back in his chair.

"Ah, Royal Adelphi Hotel? Good. Wilf here, Wilf of the River Police. Yes, yes. Look, got a room for tonight, have you?... Uh huh, yes, it's for one of our boys..." Here he eyed me up and down; pith helmet, faded shirt, khaki shorts. "Plain clothes division," he added, winking enormously. "Good, excellent" (thumbs up). "Now what are your rates?" (pause) "Now surely you can go lower than that... lower... lower. Okay, hang on." He covered the mouth-piece and whispered, "Is thirty pounds all right for you, sonny? It's as low as they'll go for the boys in blue..."

I gave a delighted thumbs up in return, Wilf confirmed the booking and hung up.

"Good little place, the Adelphi - just off Trafalgar Square. Should suit you nicely. And now, what are your plans from hereon?"

I sat and told him how ever since the Bristol Channel I had half-thought of attempting to sail across to Europe, but that he would no doubt be relieved to hear that the last two hours had cured me of any ambitions in that direction. I was going to go on and tell him that in the short space of time since passing under Lambeth Bridge, I had already mapped out several cosy options for a boat-less year ahead - settling down to produce an illustrated herbal of plants growing in arid regions of the world; taking up archaeology in the waterless wadis of Northern Africa; auditioning for a remake of 'Lawrence of Arabia' - joining that desert brotherhood even - anything as far removed from the soggy pursuits of nauticalia as possible. But to my surprise, Wilf hadn't adopted the same eyebrow-raising grimaces of my previous confidants in this scheme. Instead he pursed his lips, looked at me thoughtfully and said;

"Now why not, I wonder? Dover to Calais? I reckon you could do it if you had a mind to. Not now of course. Go home to Australia for Christmas, but next March, say, when the weather's getting warmer, there's no reason why you shouldn't."

I must have been gaping like a goldfish at him, because he continued:

"You'd need to pick your day, of course, and you'd want someone to accompany you in a larger boat, but no, I don't see any real objection."

"Ah yes," said I, thinking of the dark and swirling waters beyond the pontoon lights, the looming bulk of the ferries, the swamping waves and the fear I had felt so recently, "Yes," I repeated, clutching for once at straws of prudence, of caution, of excuses not to go, "but where on Earth would I find someone prepared to accompany me across? I don't exactly know anyone with a large boat, and..."

"Yes you do," interrupted Wilf. "Me. I have a trawler which I take across four or five times a year." (*My arid herbs crumbled to fragrant dust*) "I'll be going round about March." (*Archaeology died a sudden death*) "Here's my number. Give me a ring early next year and we'll arrange an escort for you." (*Lawrence galloped off and turned into the mirage he had always been*) "Don't worry," he added cheerfully, seeing my face fall "the voyage need not end here after all. There's nothing to stop you and little *Jack* sailing all the way to the Black Sea after all! Have another coffee..."

That night, although the bed in the Royal Adelphi was soft and comfortable, I may as well have been aboard *Jack*, bucking wildly on the Thames. All night the mattress seemed to sway and jolt on a tide of darkness; phantom ferries loomed out of the fogs of sleep, manned by politicians sipping sherry, and the giant figure of Wilf kept handing me a sheaf of secret documents and a toy boat and ordering me to sail to France in it, saying, "Don't worry, my lad. You're our man in Europe. Plain clothes division." And when I found the toy boat sinking beneath me, someone kept saying in a rich avuncular voice, "That's right... you can go lower than that... lower... lower... lower..." until I drowned in the soft, thundering billows of slumber.

And so I come to the last day of this long and winding tale of reeds and rivers, weirs and willow trees, swans and sails and sunlit days and the secret ways of Britain.

I did not hurry that morning. Wilf had told me that the tide would not begin running out until about one o'clock in the afternoon so that there was no point leaving until after then. Besides, Surrey Docks was only five miles down the river and there was no point in arriving at Tim and Babette's barge until they were both home from work. I spent a pleasant morning exploring the National Gallery, trotting around Covent Garden and then visiting Kelvin Hughes, one of the best suppliers of maritime goods and charts. Here I found what I was looking for, a large map of all Europe and a good deal of Russia showing every navigable waterway, river and canal from Ireland to the Caspian Sea, from Norway to Turkey. And there in plain blue was a route through, from the tangle of canals clustered like varicose veins around Calais to the long single thread of the Danube running out into the Black Sea. It was, after all, possible...

The last stretch down to Surrey Docks was largely straightforward. The day was dullish but warm, with no wind to speak of. Wilf had advised me to get straight across to the south bank and stay well over, thereby avoiding the faster shipping traffic that kept to the centre. In broad daylight and as the river widened I had more leisure to look about me and enjoy the novelty of being a spectacle on the river... and a spectator. Here was the newly rebuilt Globe Theatre, remodelled exactly as Shakespeare would have known it, and the only building in the City of London to be allowed a thatched roof since the Great Fire of 1666. Over there was the dome of St Paul's Cathedral rising above the more modern bankside buildings.

Tower Bridge passed by in its lofty blue and gilded splendour, and the Tower of London on the far bank, much cleaner and whiter than I had remembered from a visit twenty-five years earlier. Old songs from a production of *The Yeomen of the Guard* flooded back and I went rowing down the river singing *Tower Warders, Under Orders* with its fierce brisk rhythm - and my favourite of all Gilbert and Sullivan songs, *I have a song to sing, o!...* the sweet, simple rolling tune sung by the melancholy jester, Jack Point.

And so too, my own *Jack* was singing his own lap-lapping melody as we crept down the last dull-eyed miles between the warehouses of Wapping and Bermondsey to Greenland Pier and the lock entrance to Surrey Docks. There a young lock-keeper took me up the lock, opened a swing bridge between one compound and another and I rowed through into the placid waters of the Surrey Docks marina. There was *Ilanga Umfula*, Tim and Babette's smartly painted narrowboat in royal blue and yellow, and there was a warm yellow light pouring out into the greyness of late afternoon on this, the last day of October. I had arrived.

The journey had covered something approaching 481 miles, I had traversed 160 locks and had been travelling for 59 days,... statistics that to my mind seem meaningless. It had often struck me on the journey whenever I reached for a map to show 'where I really was' on some stretch of the river or canal, in what odd a sense we use the word *real*. There I would be, tucked in a reedy corner of the river, an alder tree scattering its golden coinage on the black waters, a heron oaring slowly across the meadow marsh opposite and a farmhouse drowning its warm red brick reflections in the river's stillness, and I would be reaching for a piece of printed paper to tell me something more real than the heron, the wet grasses and the rustle of reeds in an evening breeze. "Ah," I'd say, putting my finger on a squiggle of blue ink and red dots, "here we are!" And I'd read out a name - Crowmarsh, Bampton, Oakhill Down - an airy nothing of syllables and spit - and then, only then, would I confidently plant my banner of recognition and reality and turn away satisfied, no longer needing the cool bright air and the reedy curve and the red bricks fading into dusk.

So I put the figures and statistics above merely to pay a nodding homage to our map-god, and then turn to better things; to the colours seen as September flamed into October and rivers merged with the sea; to the aerated minty smells of rushing water in deep locks and woodsmoke in country pubs; to kingfishers and coots and cloud-palaces in the sky; and to the goodness of people met along the way whose numbers defy arithmetic. Not because there were so many (though there were), but because each one held in the mind fills it entirely, floods every cell, admitting no others to jostle into a merely countable rank. There are no queues here, not in the Courts of Heaven.

The last of these were, of course, Tim and Babette, who acted with all the pleased astonishment I had been rehearsing them for in my mind. We sat that evening under a dusky sky, chatting of this and that - one or two of the adventures on the way; their own forthcoming wedding in a Zimbabwe game park, my plans for the coming year, poring over the map I had bought that morning and tracing out possible routes to the Black Sea. Across the Thames, the great glass tower of Canary Wharf raised its gleaming pyramid high into steamy clouds of its own making, and flashed its brilliant white light to flicker on the sagging bellies of the dim night sky... a crystal volcano from a sci-fi novel signalling security or doom to the worshipping tribes below.

It was Hallowe'en. The sprites and boggles of the English countryside would be out in force tonight - the Peg Powlers and the Urisks and the Water Kelpies, the sea-sirens and the marsh-folk, the willow-men and alder-witches, and Ellesmere's own Jenny Greenteeth whom I'd left so very far away - all would be abroad tonight. But *Jack de Crow* had eluded them each and every one and was safe at last in the safe and soulless heart of the great city.

But even here there was perhaps a little magic. For with the talk of Hallowe'en and its attendant goblin-folk, I had remembered something. Hopping down into *Jack* where she lay snugly moored against *Ilanga Umfula*'s side, I rummaged deep into her front locker. Ah yes, here it was... that curious brown bottle of Hobgoblin Ale given to me in Bristol by my old student Alex. I had been keeping it for this moment.

Three glasses and a bottle-opener were fetched out onto the stern decking of the narrowboat where we sat watching the night sky, and just as Tim lifted his glass in a toast, a burst of pink fireworks flowered in the southern sky over the water. Again and again they came with a volley of distant thunder, giant chrysanthemums of rosy light blooming the city skyscape and dissolving into showers of fire - a display, Tim explained, put on by a nearby Tesco store. But the prosaic nature of the event could not spoil the beauty, the aptness, the sheer perfect timing of the spectacle, and perhaps I may be forgiven for mentally claiming them as my own special reward. I almost... almost... expected them to spell out *Well done, Sandy!* in letters of pink fire against the broad sky... and said as much to Tim.

"Yes, Sandy," he replied, but knowing me fairly well, was kind enough to add, "Clearly just a technical hitch, Sandy. They'll have ironed out the problems by the time you reach the Black Sea, you just wait and see. Cheers!"

Jack shifted comfortably beside us in the darkness, dreaming of foreign parts. She seemed happy enough with the idea and so, I realised, was I. "Cheers!" I replied, and drank up. "Cheers!"

End of Part One

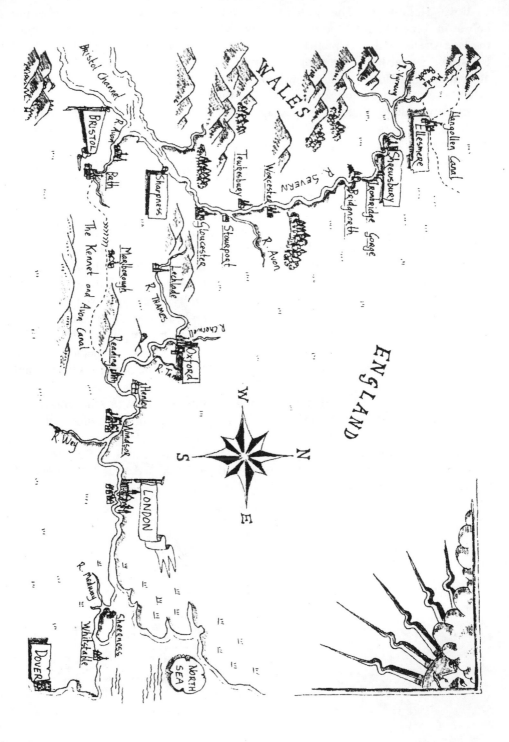

Part Two

Caution to the Winds

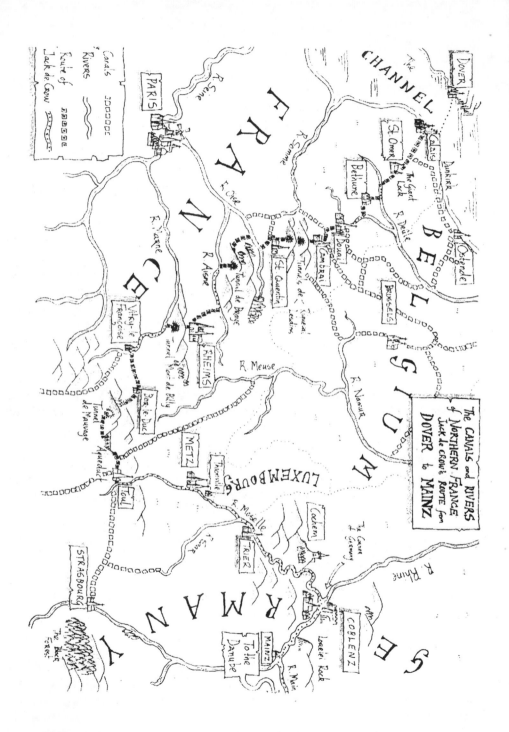

The CANALS and RIVERS of NORTHERN FRANCE Jack de Crow's Route from DOVER to MAINZ

Dooms and Delays

'Come, my friends,
'Tis not too late to seek a newer world.
Push off, and sitting well in order smite
The sounding furrows; for my purpose holds
To sail beyond the sunset, and the baths
Of all the Western stars...'

Tennyson, *Ulysses*

Let me tell you briefly about Fermat's last theorem, a clairvoyant and my bottom.

Many years ago, my mother took my sister and myself off to see a clairvoyant. We didn't tell my father that, of course, because he would have secretly worried that we were all getting enmeshed in some New Age Cult. No, we told him that we were going off to buy some herbs and shrubs for the new border and that was all. Which was true enough, because this particular clairvoyant owned just such a nursery in fact, and played the Delphic Oracle only as a sideline.

He was a giant of a man, sporting a jutting beard, frizzy eyebrows and a huge pair of boots, and his name was equally impressive: Mr. A.J. Mackenzie-Clay. He had – or so he claimed - been struck by lightning no less than three times, and it was after the third strike that he had woken up to find that he now had clairvoyant powers. These manifested themselves through the medium of Numerology, he explained. By adding up the numbers corresponding to your birthday, your age, and the letters in your name, he could predict your future, diagnose likely health problems and reveal the inner secrets of your soul. All this was accomplished while striding around his vast nursery, loading you up with another three pots of tradescantia, a tub of lemon verbena and a sack of organic compost to take home.

To my sister Margaret, his predictions were detailed, fascinating and unlikely... and mostly set so far in the future that by the time they came true... or failed to eventuate... he would be long underground and taking a more active role in the production of organic compost than ever before. Only one prediction was worth storing away, namely that after the next four years of considerable hardship my sister would find that the beginning of 1998 would bring a long-deserved reversal of fortunes. The long night would be over, and she would emerge victorious.

Meanwhile, what about *my* future? While Maggie and my mother went off to inspect some Iceland poppies I awaited my turn, half cynical, half curious. Mr. A.J. Mackenzie-Clay jotted down my name, birth date and other details on the back of an old seed packet.

"Hmmm," he intoned. "Interesting, very..."

I looked at the scribbled grid of numbers he was rapidly producing. He added up a column of numbers here, dashed down a total there, and drew a swift arrow to an earlier grid. Then he jotted down a hasty question mark, grabbed another seed packet and started again.

"Yes, odd, one doesn't often get such a... Ah, but wait a minute. Here's a double eight. Yes, that *is* interesting...With a preponderance of fives too. How very... sad." He finished on a sigh and shook his head.

My mother re-approached. "Well," she inquired, "and what about this one?"

"Ah, yes," said the prophet, gazing into the middle distance over the glass cloches to the eucalypt blue hills beyond. Then he announced my doom. "He will always have trouble with his bottom." And with that he strode away between the salvia beds and not another word would he utter.

Well, I ask you! In the long history of prophetic utterances, amongst the whole smoking, writhing, pale-mouthed league of Pythonesses, Cassandras, Weird Sisters, Sybils and Norns, has there ever been a forecast so undignified, so banal, so downright embarrassing as that particular piece of oracular lore? We drove home, sitting in an outraged silence amongst the verbena, Maggie smiling quietly to herself and my mother pondering out aloud the meaning of that last cryptic remark, saying, "Well, yes, you *have* always had a problem in that area, haven't you? Don't you remember that time...?" until I was forced to silence her musings with a fierce and heartfelt denial of *any* problem in that area *whatsoever* since the age of two. I did not give Mr. A.J. Mackenzie-Clay's numerological prognosis another thought until five years later when I was just ready to set sail in *Jack de Crow*, down the Thames to the open sea.

That is the tale of the Clairvoyant. Now let me tell you a little about Fermat's last theorem. Fermat was a renowned mathematician of the Eighteenth Century who is famous for his last theorem; that is, he proposed that no matter how far you looked, you could never find two cubes that would add up to make a third cube. What is more, he scribbled an airy comment in the margin of his notebook to the effect that he had found an elegant little proof of this fact which he *would* jot down here but there wasn't quite enough space, so another time perhaps.

Then he went and died.

For the last three hundred years that breezy assertion has been driving the whole world of mathematics to the brink of despair. It seems such a trivially easy thing to prove, especially as Fermat was so off-hand about it, but it has proved anything but simple, and has taxed the greatest brains of the last three centuries to no avail. The myth of Fermat's last theorem has held a fascination for mathematicians both professional and amateur down through the years, and there are probably hardly any students of mathematics since the 18th Century who have not idly tried to see if they can be the first to recapture whatever sudden insight led Fermat to make his claim.

For therein lies its fascination for the amateur; the idea that the proof, if it exists, does not rely on any complex supermaths, but probably in some very simple quirk in the way of seeing the problem, accessible to any curious puzzler. There are certain conundrums involving the cutting up of chess boards, or the movement of a knight around the board to visit all the squares once and once only, that are almost impossible to solve by any traditional mathematical means. However, take a child's set of crayons, colour in the squares in a certain pattern, and the solution comes leaping out at you with blinding clarity. The nature of the problem has not been altered by the colouring-in, but the filters through which we see the problem have rendered the answer transparent. It is just such a twist of perception that most likely lies at the root of Fermat's last theorem... and it is tempting to be the first in three hundred years to see just what it was that Fermat saw.

Or so, at least, think I. Thus it was that as I whiled away my days preparing *Jack de Crow* for the rigours of the journey ahead, my evenings were spent covering sheets of paper with formulae, diagrams of cubes, Pascal's triangle, Fibonacci's series, and a whole set of things that I dubbed '*Incompatible Numbers.*' (Don't ask.) And the fact is that I was onto something. I really was. I was working along lines that had just the right sort of quirkiness and amateur knowledge that seemed to be called for, and I had seen all sorts of odd and beautiful things about cubes that I had never heard anyone else mention. Yes, there were some really very promising insights emerging. By the time I had fully developed my theory I was writing in a sort of mathematical shorthand of my own invention, mysterious hieroglyphs as meaningless to the casual observer as Mr. A.J. Mackenzie-Clay's jottings all those years ago.

All terribly exciting, as you can imagine.

Or possibly *not*, if you have been looking forward to the continuation of the roving adventures of *Jack de Crow* upon the high seas, and are now a little bewildered by the absence of waves, dinghies and seagulls, and justifiably puzzled at the intrusion of clairvoyants, mathematical formulae and the author's bottom. There is a point to all this, I assure you, but before we get to it, let me turn swiftly to the details of *Jack* and the one or two preparations that had to be made before I set off on the second leg of my odyssey.

There was much to be done. The first thing on the list was to ring Wilf, the River Police Sergeant who last October had offered to accompany me across the Channel in his trawler on my return from my Australian Christmas break. As this was the only conceivable condition under which I could attempt the crossing to France in my ten-and-a-half foot Mirror dinghy, I had to phone to find out if the jovial Wilf had been quite well when he had made that extraordinary offer, or if, with the leisure to reflect since, he had wisely decided to claim temporary insanity at the time, and retract the suggestion.

When I got through to him, however, he was as blithe and cheery as ever, and said that if I could get myself round to Dover, then all I had to do was to give him a ring in mid-March and he would take a few days off to escort me across to Calais. So that was that.

Next thing to do was to make sure that *Jack de Crow* was fit to make the journey. Her adventures travelling down from North Shropshire had left her in a sorry state. Most of the bright buttercup-yellow paint had been scraped off her keel, her topsides were a leprous rash of peeling varnish, her prow and gunwales were battered by a hundred-and-thirty-two lock walls and she still had that slow but irritating leak in her hull that allowed a couple of inches of water to slosh about in her bilges.

I have written earlier about my cavalier attitude towards the world of varnish and woodshavings, polyurethane and paint strippers, and under the raw February skies of London, working away amongst the gravel and barbed wire of the Docklands, my enthusiasm for the tasks lacked a certain amount of professional oomph. Still, I managed to sand off all the worst patches of flaking paint from her hull and sides before heading off to a purveyor of marine paints and varnishes in Lincoln's Inn, there to discover that an edict had just been passed by some Environmental Board banning the sale and use of buttercup-yellow paint. It apparently has some sort of toxin in it not shared by paints of duller hue that poisons all the aquatic wildlife to come within its purlieus. When I think back to how much of the stuff I left in smears and scrapes along the docksides and locksides of England's waterways I am surprised that there is so much as a tadpole still surviving between London and the Irish Sea.

In default of yellow paint then, I bought several large tins of bright blue and a smaller can of gloss black, and spent a merry morning slathering on the paint, covering with bright blue all that part of *Jack*'s hull that would be below the waterline, and then, because I had already scraped away large patches around her prow, re-painting those bare parts with blue as well, trying my best to make the patches look elegantly deliberate and well designed rather than the hash-work of an inveterate botcher. Finally I repainted the name, *Jack de Crow*, in gloss black, and as a finishing flourish painted a set of coiling black spirals on her pram-nose that trailed backward along each flank to turn into black-feathered wings. When I had finished she looked as cheerfully eccentric a vessel as ever sailed. Her colour scheme was perfect – *Ho, Tom Bombadil was a merry fellow, Bright blue his jacket was, and his coat was yellow!* – and the jackdaw wings along either side lent her a brave air, rather like a jaunty Viking. She also, miraculously, stopped leaking. She was ready to fly once more.

Which is where Fermat's last theorem and my bottom come back into the story. As the grey March days progressed, two things started to develop rapidly. One was my work on Fermat's last theorem, and the other was a spot of discomfort in what the gentry of the 18th Century so charmingly called 'the fundament'. I thought at first that I had merely bruised my coccyx when sitting down too rapidly on a London bus stop seat, but as the days went by, instead of the tenderness subsiding, it grew worse and worse and was accompanied by a general feeling of nausea and lassitude.

The crisis came on the last and worst day of a blustery March, a foul day of heavy rain and strong winds, ushering a thunderstorm up the Thames and releasing it upon the city like a sullen buffalo. I dashed around the streets of Southwark dodging the rain showers and trying to accomplish a dozen different last minute errands; maps, charts of the Thames Estuary and the Channel, waterproof bags, a pot of varnish, and not least, a telephone call to Maggie in Edinburgh to find out how she was coping with the latest in a long line of battles at her workplace. As the day progressed and errand after errand failed, (the Chart

Shop closed, the waterproof bags too flimsy, the varnish tin leaking all through my bag,) the pain in my tail increased to an angry throbbing.

Eventually, just on the off-chance, I wandered into a doctor's surgery and an hour later was being admitted to the Kingston Hospital for emergency surgery. It transpired that I had a serious pilonidal abscess on my lower back... well, the very base of my spine really... well, all right, let's be honest, on my bottom. This had been merrily pumping poison into my bloodstream for a fortnight and needed to be operated on without delay. It was the last straw in a particularly frustrating day, not least because all that day while I had been busy getting soaked for no good reason, I had suddenly seen a way of getting those Incompatible Numbers to work for me, a neat little twist that could very possibly be what I had been looking for. All my notes and equations were back in the Docks covered in varnish however, and in all the rush I had had no time to try out my new idea. Now here I was lying in a hospital bed waiting to go under the general anaesthetic, and my chance to solve the greatest mathematical mystery of all time would have to wait until after the operation. That is, if I still remembered my new idea after the drowsy limbo of anaesthesia. Didn't funny things happen sometimes? Memory loss? A wiping clean of the mental slate? The irony of the situation struck me as grimly funny, the fact that the last person to make this breakthrough, namely Fermat himself, had died before he could share it with the world, and that now the only other person in three hundred years to do so was likely to lose his memory on the very brink of triumph.

Or die, even, I jested to myself.

Outside the hospital window, a blink of white lightning flared out in the late afternoon darkness and all the lights dimmed for a brief instant as the bolt struck home somewhere nearby. A second later the thunderclap shook the air, but a minute later it came as a re-echo from further off. Of course. The storm was moving swiftly westwards. Lightning never strikes twice in the same place, I mused.

Suddenly I sat upright.

Mr. A.J. Mackenzie-Clay, thrice-stricken...

His bearded face swum before me, his sad eyes on the distant hills. What was that ridiculous thing he had said all those years ago? My bottom? That my fate would come to me through my bottom?! Was this then the dread unravelling of Fate, this ignominious end?

No, I told myself firmly. This was nonsense. This was as nonsensical as I had thought it all those years ago and nothing had changed since then. I would stop feeling morbid, stop worrying about Fermat until after the operation and start thinking of something or somebody else... such as my dear sister whom I had still not managed to telephone. The time for the operation was not to be until just after midnight that night, so I had plenty of time to ring and hear about the latest act of petty sabotage perpetrated by her senior colleague, the chap who had been systematically destroying her confidence at work over the last three years.

So I did. A phone was brought to my bedside by a nurse, and I had a lovely chat and listened as Maggie told me the latest. The tide, it seemed, had turned.

He had gone, the persecutor, last Monday, and gone for good, his dark schemes all brought into the light, and the whole department had breathed a sigh of relief. From now on, things would be better... had already improved beyond measure in that last week, in fact, with an exciting breakthrough in one area of Maggie's research and a new grant slotting into place. It was all just peachy, just marvellous... and just, I slowly realised as I hung up, precisely as Mr. A.J. Mackenzie-Clay had predicted it five years ago. The year was 1998 and the fortunes of my sister had suddenly turned. So what did that say about my fatal bottom and the sad look in the prophet's eye? I clearly had mere hours to live, and what's more, Fermat's theorem still to solve. I gave the phone back to the nurse, requested pen and paper and set to work to make sure that mathematical posterity was not cheated a second time of its finest hour.

Well, I did it. At three minutes past midnight, just into the new month, I scribbled on a hospital notepad the final equation that proved beyond doubt that two perfect cubes could not be added to make a third perfect cube. It was simple really, and all depended on a certain insight into the fact that all cubes are actually composed of Incompatible Numbers in factors of six, and that these... well, never mind, there isn't quite the room here, but I'll get back to it later if you like...Anyway, I wrote across the top of the paper "*Fermat's last theorem... SOLVED!!*", added in big letters, "*PLEASE DO NOT THROW AWAY*" and added the date for posterity. Very important, that, the date. Then I flopped back exhausted, but very, very smug indeed – surprisingly smug for someone who was absolutely certain that he was not going to survive the forthcoming operation.

It was only as I was groggily melting under the anaesthetic in the operating theatre and the two young doctors were assuring me that yes, of course they knew which leg to amputate, ha, ha, only kidding, mate, that I realised what I had failed to take into account. Oh yes, the formula was fine, and yes, I had remembered to add in a translation of all those home-made hieroglyphics and explanations of how to generate Incompatible Numbers. But I knew for a certainty that Fermat's theorem had yet again been quashed by the tricksy hand of Fate. For of course no one finding the paper after my untimely demise would look twice at the document seriously... or at least not beyond the carefully dated title. It was April Fool's Day.

I survived of course. And on the bright morrow, with my blood no longer sloshing with septic substances and my brain cooling from its high fever, I saw within two minutes a major error in Line Eight of my marvellous theorem which rendered it quite, quite ridiculous. I laughed at myself, a little wanly, it must be admitted, and turned my mind back to the practical matters of life with a small sigh. The operation had left a gaping wound in my tail which needed daily dressing by a qualified nurse for the next month, a fact that made any thoughts of rowing away to France an impossibility. The first thing to do was to ring Wilf and let him know that the proposed crossing would be delayed. When he answered the phone and heard my voice, he immediately started talking.

"Sandy? Thank goodness you rang, I didn't know where to contact you. Bad news, I'm afraid."

"Oh yes?"

"Yes, I'm afraid that yesterday I broke my foot, duffer that I am. I'm out of action for at least a month. Sorry, old boy, but the crossing's off, or at least as far as my involvement goes. Unless you'd like to leave it till late April, of course. But I expect you're anxious to be off, aren't you?"

A pause...

"Ah, funny you should say that actually. Let me tell you about my bottom..."

I spent that month in Dorset in a tiny and remarkable village called Trent with some old friends of my mother. I could cheerfully write three glowing chapters about that single month of recuperation, such is the nature both of Trent village and Mike and Gill who nursed me back to health, but it is no part of this story – except to say that if I could have chosen anywhere and picked any month to spend my last weeks in England after my seven year love affair with that country, somewhere to savour it to the full, to distil all that I had grown to love about the land into one perfect, complete memory, then I would have chosen Trent in April, without a doubt. As it is, I returned to London four weeks later with my mind brimming full with last farewell presents: green hawthorn shoots in the hedgerows, long walks with black Labradors, church pews smelling of polish, shepherd's pie in Gill's kitchen, Mike's ash staff by the back door, the Rose and Crown, and Cadbury Castle's green summit floating like Camelot above the new burgeoning world.

And that long hiatus brings me at last to the dark and early hour when I finally stowed the last of my belongings, untied *Jack*'s painter, whispered a quiet farewell to Tim who had got out of his bunk to see me off, and set off down the Thames before dawn to see if I could find my way to Europe and beyond.

Tide on the Thames

The previous night it had poured with rain, lit in dazzling curtains by the camera-shutter flashes of lightning. Over the river from the Thai restaurant where we had sat enjoying a farewell meal, the dome of St. Paul's and the wedding-cake steeple of St. Mary-le-Bow had been momentarily etched against black like an old-fashioned silverpoint engraving of the City. As the rain came down in leaden sheets outside the huge plate glass windows, my resolve to leave on the morrow waned steadily until it was as limp as the coriander leaf salad on my side plate, as tepid as the cooling lemongrass and crab soup before me. But no, it had to be done. I had lingered long enough, seeking excuses to put off going, and I was feeling fat and discontented after too much idling around. Besides, with every extra day I waited the hour of high tide became earlier and earlier; another few days and I would be forced to leave at midnight, sailing five hours in darkness. As it was, I would be leaving at half-past four the next morning, an hour that I have hitherto regarded as sacrosanct to the purpose of knitting up the ravelled sleave of care.

Another flash stamped the nearby antennae and radar masts of *HMS Belfast* onto my retina, and thunder rolled like a tympanum over the river's ringed flood. I uttered a silent prayer that the elements would settle to at least a damp drizzle for my pre-dawn start, and turned to tackle the green Thai curry with fragrant black rice that had appeared before me. Tomorrow was another day.

Another day and, as it turned out, another weather pattern altogether. I woke to a sky watery with stars, big and soft and pale from recent washing. The air too was cool and fresh, and in the east there was the faintest hint of grey seeping into the sky downriver. My first miles of rowing filled me with a sudden joy, strong and fluid as the dark banks sluiced smoothly by: the dismal docks of Limehouse, the Canary Wharf Tower still steaming like a sci-fi diamond volcano, then Greenwich Palace fast asleep, the Royal Observatory, more warehouses and docklands, and somewhere far off but very loud and sweet, the melodious song of a solitary blackbird. It seemed such an incongruous sound for the dark hour and drab urban landscape, but, with my new sense of freedom and adventure just beginning, I found myself singing the old Paul Simon song:

"Blackbird singing in the dead of night,
Take my broken wings and learn to fly..."

And hard on the heels of that, with the grey suffusing to a pale primrose beyond the giant tracery of the Millennium Dome, there came to me that older song sung by David at the court of Saul:

"Yea, though I take the wings of the morning
And fly to the uttermost parts of the sea,
Even there shall Thy hand guide me,
Thy right hand shall hold me firm..."

I had my wings again and was off to the east at last, sailing into a new sunrise. I was extraordinarily happy again, and could not think why I had delayed my departure so long.

There is a thing called the Thames Barrier which everybody had been warning me about. "How are you going to get through the Thames Barrier then, eh?" they'd ask. "Didn't think of that one, did you?" they'd add, smiling knowingly. When I had endeavoured to find out exactly what the Thames Barrier was, people would go all vague and say, "Well, it's a barrier, innit, on the Thames, see. Huge great thing. Major obstacle if you're in a dinghy, mate, I can tell you!"

When I then tried to get them to be a little more specific about things like whether it opened and closed and if not, how did all those big ships get into the Thames because they certainly didn't come the way *I* did, they would look at me pityingly and say, "Look, it's a huge great bleedin' barrier, mush, to keep floods out. 'Course it shuts, wouldn't be much use otherwise, would it now?" and hastily change the subject.

So I was a wee bit relieved to discover that the mighty Thames Barrier, which I had imagined as looking something like a titanic version of the Shrewsbury Weir, looks instead like seven miniature Sydney Opera Houses all in tin, their shiny silver nautilus shells set on seven concrete blocks strung out across the river... but with enough room between each block to allow two aircraft carriers to pass abreast.

Or one Mirror dinghy with slightly wobbly steering.

I aimed for the centre gap, found myself swept by a mysterious submarine force towards the left bank, decided to compromise by rowing hard towards the *second* gap to the left, quickly decided that the tugboat currently chugging upstream through that one deserved the right of way, and squeaked through the gap nearest the bank under the very nose of the man in the control tower who was shouting what I like to think were words of cheer and encouragement. They were indistinct, but certainly energetic in their delivery. For the first time that morning, I really knew that I was on my way once more.

Below the Barrier, I found myself amongst the industrial docks where huge tankers and freighters were just coming to life, bossed and fussed into place by the little tugs like huge battle-grey cuckoos chivvied by mother wrens. The river was broad enough though and I was able to steer well away from the ponderous monsters as the channel swept on southwards to the flat sewage works of Gravesend. The landscape here should have been dreary with its loam fields and vast waterworks and empty wharves, but there was something clean and fresh about the air that early morning, a watercolour landscape still wet on the page, with pale yellow light and a clear sky and a blue breeze beginning to ripple out across the wide grey waters. This is what I had been waiting for, and as soon as I could I stowed the oars, loosened off the sail tyers and hauled the scarlet sail skywards.

I must mention in passing an odd architectural treasure that you are unlikely to see for yourselves unless you work the regular commuter ferry run as a stevedore or sewage plant operative on the lonely stretch of the Thames below Gravesend. This is a building which stands isolated amidst acres of dull grass and cyclone fencing, and looks like a long tall slab of silver and blue, all in chrome and glass and concrete… but a slab viewing itself in one of those distorting funfair mirrors. It waves and curves from stem to stern, as it were, so that it puts you in mind of a Salvador Dali painting - a surreal melting wall or a frozen flag of wind-billowed silk. I cannot guess its purpose, but I hope that it has won awards for sheer sinuous beauty.

By ten o'clock I was well on my way. London lay behind me with a thick smudge of soot-dark cloud over it, and the river had widened into a broad estuary, the land receding on either side to melt into blue smears along each horizon. Here for the first time I encountered the intriguing world of marine buoys and navigational markers. Every mile or so, I would skim by a channel marker, regular green bell shaped buoys on the northern side of the channel and red box shaped buoys occasionally coming up on the southern bank. These, I knew, mark the starboard and port edges of the deepwater channel, which sounds straightforward enough, but is that going downstream or coming upstream? I guessed the latter, and later proved to be correct. My brand new chart showed all the buoys and hazards, but I was soon bewildered by the discrepancy between the number of markers printed on the map and the number of markers scattered about the channel. One by one I tried ticking them off as I passed – the Tilbury South Cone, Ovens Bell, Mucking No. 7, Mucking No. 5 and so on – but what was that red box over yonder? Surely not the Lower Hope port buoy already? And if so, where was Mucking No. 3? And what was the West Blyth marker doing over yonder? The fact was that after having grown familiar with the large scale and meticulous detail of the Ordnance Survey maps through the waterways of England, I was finding the broad scope and blank spaces of nautical charts misleading. The estuary was far wider than it seemed from the chart. While I was looking for a steeple indicated on the north shore and expecting a clear needle of stone thrusting up from the low horizon, I would be lucky to spot the tiny speck floating above a distant glimmer that may or may not have been the Monkswick spire telling me I was off the Holehaven Sands. Strange monstrous towers and chimneys sprouted in the middle of perfectly blank swathes of the chart, and where the chart showed the entrance to some great tidal creek carving its way through the Essex flatlands the blue line of land on the horizon seemed to spread thin and unbroken as far as the eye could see. It was all thoroughly unsettling.

The day had started fine, but as I ventured down the estuary clouds came flying up from the east in extraordinary clumps and billows. As a boy, I had spent many a happy hour drawing treasure maps of exotic islands, richly bedecked with volcanoes, waterfalls, palm-fringed beaches and skull-shaped hills, and of course each and every map had sported a beaming golden sun in one top corner and a ferocious, puff-cheeked storm cloud in the other. Here, my childish drawing fantasies became fact. Each cloud that swept up the river to greet me was a perfect Pauline Baynes cloud-god, its lips pursed, its eyebrows curling and snowy, its chins and double chins indigo with shadow. They trailed cloaks of whipping rain and with pudgy fists they struck the water to slaty bruises. *Jack* would heel sharply beneath those swatting blows, the sails would crack and beat, and the tiller would hum and wrench beneath my tired hand until I could barely hold on another second. And then, suddenly, it would be over. The cloud would pass overhead, a giant cherub boy racing up the river to catch his playmates, and the decks would be steaming in the hot sunshine once more.

By mid-afternoon I was on the long stretch between Blyth Sand and Yantlet Flats, and the day had settled into fine weather once more. The estuary was so wide that the northern shore had reduced to a faint thread of silver and grey along the horizon, intermittent and sketchy. Along the nearer southern shore, wide empty fields and pastures crept by beyond the mud-flats, where nothing moved but the occasional crazy flight of lapwings rolling above the vacant green. Far, far to the south-east, a huge gradual hill of bright chrome yellow reared, unnaturally bright against the dim blue of distance, and for a long time I could not guess what it was. A vast heap of Kentish swedes covered over with several acres of yellow tarpaulin? An experimental station of some sort, its hectares of tin or glass roofing painted this luminous primrose? Only much later did I realise that it was a distant crop of oilseed rape, its acid bright blooms surely the most disturbing colour in Nature. Meanwhile, I was puzzled about a more pressing problem. All day, the heady pace I had been setting had astonished me. Since dawn I had rowed and sailed an extraordinary fifty miles or so, and had been congratulating myself on the swiftness of my oar strokes and the skill and balance of my sail setting. In fact, a few quick calculations at midday had me confidently expecting to pull into Dover harbour by suppertime. So it was with some frustration that I spent the long hours of the afternoon wondering why I seemed to have slowed to a snail's pace. The Tower of St. Mary's way over beyond the marshes inched to the stern by slow degrees and the long-looked-for Yantlet Creek mouth refused to crawl into view ahead. By four o'clock, I had barely made another few miles and realised that at present progress I would be lucky to make it to Sheerness which had just begun to emerge from the general flat silver as a solid line of houses above a long bar of tan shingle and a seawall. What is more, the afternoon breeze was dropping and I had to take to the oars again.

Now I'm not stupid. I know about tides. I've read as much as the next chap all those cautionary tales about rips and currents, small vessels being swept out to sea and the deceptive nature of coastal tides. But I want to get one thing very clear, and it is this. Of all the writers who have dealt with the subject of tides and small boats, no one has thought fit to point out one obvious – or not-so-obvious – aspect of the phenomenon: namely, its undetectable nature. You see, implied in the very phrase "*swept out to sea*" or "*in the grip of a fierce current*" there is a type of inbuilt image of swirling waters, racing buoys, receding jetties, helplessly spinning cockleboats and frantically waving pocket handkerchiefs. Given anyone of these cues or clichés, I will be the first to wisely nod and say, "*Ah, yes, tides, old boy*" and "*Got to expect 'em in these waters, of course,*" and "*Remember the Swallows, eh?*" and "*You should read Erskine Childers, old chap!*" ... and so on. But the fact is that these telltale hints and clues simply don't exist in the real situation. Let me bang on a bit about this because it's important that you realise that when we are all told that tides are deceptive, we are using the word *deceptive* in a sense that defies all normal usage.

Imagine, if you will indulge me for a moment, that you are sitting on a lawn one warm May day in the middle of... oh, I don't know... Worcestershire, for example. It is the lawn belonging to a gracious old manor, and is sprinkled with summer daisies. About you, but a little way off, are the borders and the flowerbeds and old, established trees that mark the boundaries of this thoroughly delightful garden. The sky is above, the grass is cool beneath your shoulderblades and very soon someone will come out of the house with a tray of afternoon tea and a bowl of strawberries and cream.

Are you going anywhere? Certainly not. It is far too comfortable here beneath the chestnut tree, and besides, a certain pleasant drowsiness is stealing softly upon our senses...

Are you going anywhere? No, we've already been through this, please leave us in peace. Somewhere a couple of wood pigeons are cooing high in an elm.

Are you going anywhere? Look, just what *is* your point, you irritating little man? Have a strawberry or go away...

The point is... the point IS... is that yes, you *are* going somewhere actually, you and your strawberries and your daisies and your wood pigeons with you. You are drifting out into a new region of space with every second that passes - imperceptibly, inconceivably, but... and this is the frightening bit... horribly, horribly fast.

That is what it is like in a dinghy, a mile off Sheerness on a golden late afternoon, rowing placidly through the glassy water to the welcoming row of whitewashed houses built atop the old sea wall. It is a beautiful afternoon, and twenty more minutes of rowing will bring us to the beach of orange shingle where the figures of two small boys are playing and an older gentleman is walking a cocker spaniel. It is pleasing to see the way that with every oar stroke, the gentle waters furl cleanly away from the prow, and a row of bubbles streams out in a tidy wake behind. I stop and rest on my oars for a brief minute, the dinghy gliding to a halt and hanging motionless on the broad mirror of the waters. The sun is warm on my shoulders, and the faintest of breezes cools the damp fringe of hair on my brow. Ten more minutes, and I will be sitting down to order a well deserved pint in the Sheerness Arms. Better start rowing again, I suppose, and bring this long and lovely day to an end.

There is a swirling, chuckling noise off to one side. A boat approaching quickly but quietly? No, not a boat chugging past, just an old upright beacon post, black with barnacles. steaming along up the estuary like the periscope on an antique wooden submarine. Its movement through the water is creating quite a bow wave – a jolly good thing it didn't hit me on its way to wherever it's heading. I wonder where it *is* going, by the way? I turn back to my oars, and continue rowing in to the shore.

Wait a minute?

I pause... think...

What do I mean '*Where is it going?*' ? It's not going anywhere, you fool, despite the quite obvious fact that it has just steamed past me at a good four knots. It's attached to the seabed, for crying out loud, as are the three large blackened posts with the red signboards on them that even now are hurrying up behind to overtake me at a similar rate. So if they are not going anywhere, then that means... then that means that I *am!*

Good grief, I'm drifting out to sea and I'm caught in a tide and I'm going to make the headlines because I'm going to get run down by a liner and what is the *point* in reading all that '*Swallows and Amazons*' stuff if you're just going to make the same classic idiotic mistakes and I really do *not* believe this is happening and my! isn't it getting dark all of a sudden?

And yes, sure enough, looking over my shoulder, Sheerness is now not a mile away, but two miles away and further west than it had been. The two boys on the beach are mere dots of brightness... before, I had been able to see the colour of their hair, for crying out loud. I set to the oars with a will, straining and heaving and driving myself mightily through the still glassy water, but those three gaunt posts, the rotting masts of some sunken ship I guess, saunter past me in an idle but inexorable glide. A pair of green buoys steam upstream, and all my efforts to catch them up are to no avail. Sheerness is fading into a gold blaze of westering light as I drift helplessly out into the North Sea. And still, that overwhelming feeling of calm stillness, the impression of being at rest upon a summer lawn awaiting the arrival of strawberries and tea.

There occur very rarely in the life of Man times and situations where he is utterly powerless to decide his fate. In almost any situation, no matter how desperate, there is something he can do, some last card to play – whether to make that one phone call to his solicitor, or try one last plea to his captors, or make one desperate attempt to trap an animal using a bootlace and an old safety-pin and so survive another day in the wilderness. But when a situation comes along where there is *nothing* to be done, no final trick, no last resource, no eleventh hour plea, then a great calm comes over him – in my experience, even a sort of glee. "*Crikey, I'm in for it now!*" goes a very tiny way towards expressing that mixture of exhilaration and curiosity and total abdication that I have felt on the three such occasions in my life. It is partly to do with the fact that whatever happens now, it is quite certainly out of our own hands... and this brings with it a strange certainty that therefore the hands in which the matter now resides are there, as they have always been, ready and sure, and infinitely more capable than ours. The Mind that keeps the sun spinning and the cells dividing and the green grass growing is ready to take the reins that we have at last been forced to drop. It is a sense of relief, really, like being a child on piggyback again.

Well, the sun spun, and the land cooled and the seas stayed warm, and there sprang up a breeze in the last hour of that long day, blowing steadily straight from the open sea to the little town of Sheerness, and I rode with it on my scarlet wings. Even now, the effect of the tide created a bizarre surrealism, for the opposite now was true. Whereas before I had seemed to sit on a glassy mirror at peace and in reality hurtled seawards, now with the wind in my sails and the foam curling at my prow and the rip-rip-ripple of water racing beneath the keel, I seemed to be flying across the sea as swiftly as a boy on a bike, and yet the beacon post twenty yards away stayed resolutely in its spot, refusing to draw an inch nearer despite my headlong approach.

But eventually as the tide slackened, that stand-off-ish beacon post deigned to draw near at last, allowed me to overtake it, and once more Sheerness assembled itself out of the gold and blue of the western horizon. Two hours after my first decision to row the half-mile to shore, I pulled in wearily to that long strand just as the sun dipped below the sea wall. My chart showed a proper harbour another mile back up the coast and round into the mouth of the Medway, but I was heartily weary of all things nautical. I had been aboard for fourteen hours, and had had neither a bite to eat nor a drop to drink in all that time. I had come sixty miles, and refused to row a stroke further.

Off Sheerness

Jutting out from the sea wall was a tall pier of solid concrete, which offered me the only chance to tether my dinghy along the whole length of ochre shingle. The seaward end of this pier was currently ten yards or so from the sea's edge, so I had to drag or lift *Jack de Crow* up over the shingle to place it at the pier's foot. This I did by recruiting the aid of the two urchins whom I had spotted earlier. On closer acquaintance, these turned out to be two eight-year-old lads called Matt and Luke, tow-haired, ruddy-cheeked and wellie-booted who said things like "Coo!" and "Cor!" and "'Ere, Mister, are youse a pirate then?" and generally acted straight out of "*Oliver*". They helped me bale the boat out and drag her up beyond what I fondly imagined to be the high tide limit, and after I had climbed up onto the top of the pier they threw the long painter up to me so that I could tie it onto a ring bolt in the pier top. All this while, they asked a million questions and finally, when they ground to a halt, offered to keep guard on the boat the *whole* night against "feeves 'n' robbers" of which, they earnestly assured me, Sheerness was full. "*And* pirates," they added solemnly. I declined their kind offer, but playing the amiable Captain Flint to their Death and Glories, tipped them a gold sovereign apiece for their help in stowing *Jack* so well. (Well, a pound, but you know what I mean…) Seeing me as a possible source of further wealth, they insisted on taking a bag apiece and accompanied me along the promenade to the Seaview Hotel, squabbling cheerfully over who got to wear my pith helmet. It was only once I'd checked in at the front bar, and suffered the baleful glare of a few old sea-salts who clearly regarded the front bar as a resolutely child-free domain that I managed to recover my hat and send them away with another fifty pence each, and many earnest promises on their behalf to keep an eye on the boat.

The Seaview Hotel was a grand edifice, built, I suspect, in the port's palmiest days. one lounge was called the Montgomery Room and had a plaque explaining that the Montgomery was a ship that had run aground and sunk during the Second World War. Its derelict masts protrude from the treacherous waters just off Sheerness (*Ah, that's what they were…*), but, as its hold still contains enough explosives to take the whole Island of Sheppey with it, all craft are expressly forbidden to go anywhere near the wreck. The only exception to this rule is small Mirror dinghies drifting uncontrollably on the tide, I believe.

I found a room on the second floor that had a view along the beach to where *Jack* lay in the distance, so I could keep half an eye out for the 'feeves 'n' robbers' I had been warned of. Much good this did me because in less than ten minutes I was sprawled on my bed, fully dressed and fast asleep. It had been a long day, I had come a long way, and even the promise of a hot bath and a cold beer could not prop my eyes open a moment longer. But I had made a start at last. The long journey had begun.

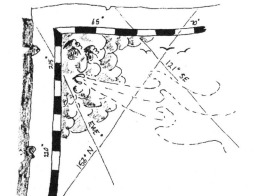

Of Shallows and Shipwreck

'They hadna sailed a league, a league,
A league but barely three,
When the lift grew dark, and the wind blew loud,
And gurly grew the sea.

The ankers brak, and the topmasts lap,
It was sic a deadly storm;
And the waves cam o'er the broken ship,
Till a' her sides were torn.'

Anonymous - *The Ballad of Sir Patrick Spens*

There is a thief in Sheerness Town on Sheppey Isle. He wears a grey cloak sewn with stars, he steals about in the darkness on silent feet and he sighs all night at his work. He shows no respect for the property or life of any man, and the only voice or law he heeds is that of his mistress, the Moon. And when I awoke the next morning, still in my rumpled clothes, and looked down the shingle shore, I saw at once that he had been at work on little *Jack de Crow*.

This kelp-handed robber had more than burgled her. He had taken her and trounced her and set her on her stern against the pier wall before rifling her pockets and leaving her petticoats and stays all in a dreadful tangle, seemingly broken and bent. To put it plainly, the first thing I saw from my bedroom window when I awoke at five that morning was that the tide had come in during the night and left *Jack* in a horribly precarious state.

When I hurried along the promenade to assess the damage I found that things were not quite as bad as they had first looked... but it had been a narrow escape. The painter had caught around a protruding iron bolt set in the concrete, probably when the tide was at its fullest and, when the tide had dropped away again it had left the poor dinghy hanging from her bow on the now-shortened tether. Only her stern rested against the shingle. With the angle she lay at and the battering she must have received half the night, one of the mast-stays had come loose so that her mast now leaned drunkenly to one side, the bundled gaff and sail unravelling in a tangle of ropes and tyers onto the sharp shingle. The front lockers too, being doorless, had been scoured out by the swill of the sea and their contents stolen away, leaving only a scrape of gritty sand and a few crabs scuttling in their recesses.

The greatest loss was the jib. This is the smaller triangular sail that runs from the prow up to the masthead, which allows a boat to sail much closer to the wind and assists in bringing the boat around onto a new course every time you tack. On the narrow rivers I had found that I was usually running downwind, a course where the jib is not useful enough to be worth the bother of setting in place, but here on the open waters I had been planning to use it regularly. To that end, I had just bought in London a set of brand new ropes to use with it, and these too were missing... an irritating loss. However, apart from that and a bottle of wood glue that I saw bobbing on the waves a little while later, nothing else was seriously missing or damaged, and I counted myself very lucky.

There followed an hour or so of re-rigging and scrubbing and emptying while Sheerness slowly woke to the new day and peered out their windows to see the foreigner at his task. At the end of that time I straightened up, stretched widely and realised suddenly that I was ravenous. I had neither eaten nor drunk a thing for thirty-four hours; the last food to pass my lips had been the Thai Green Curry on my last night in London with Tim. I stowed the last of my stuff, marched straight back to the Seaview Hotel and ordered the Full Cooked Breakfast and a gallon of coffee. I wolfed it down, and then ordered exactly the same again. When I sailed away from Sheerness an hour later any loss of ballast caused by that grey thief the Tide had been more than compensated for by the warm ballast settling comfortably into my belly.

I had been studying the chart carefully. Two possible routes lay open to me from Sheerness. I was at the westernmost point of the Isle of Sheppey which lies like a great green pancake off the north coast of Kent, separated from the mainland only by the thin muddy trickle that is the West Swale and the broader but shallower East Swale. I could either choose to continue along the northern coast of the Isle, remaining in the Thames Estuary proper, or I could duck back round up into the Medway and thread my way through the two Swales to emerge further along the coast at Whitstable. The outer route would be shorter, but more exposed to the wind and waves that even now were getting stronger; the inner route would be longer but provide a more sheltered route... and a more interesting one, I guessed, as I navigated my way through the tidal creeks and secret ways of the Swale. So before the wind grew any stronger, I made my choice. Pushing the dinghy out from the shingle, I hoisted the sail and ran down the strengthening nor'easter to the mouth of the Medway and into the calmer waters behind the Isle.

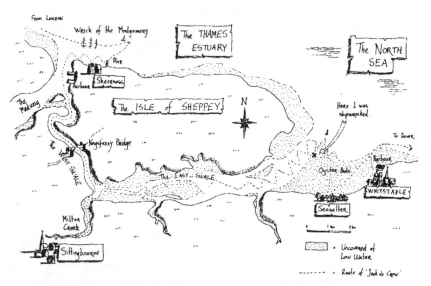

It was a pleasant run up the Medway to the narrow entrance of West Swale Creek, with mirror-grey waters and a following wind, and the bliss continued up the Swale as it snaked its way through the low grass pastures and mud-flats of this deserted landscape. Herons flapped slowly away across the waters, the odd knot of waders dibbled and pattered on the shore and the only cause for mild alarm was the sight of the Kingsferry swing bridge ahead, its red warning light telling all ships to stop and wait for the bridge to be lifted. All ships, that is, except the redoubtable *Jack de Crow* who pleases herself when it comes to these obstacles, who dips her tall gaff in stately salute to the goggle-eyed bridge-keeper and goes on her way unhindered.

I had been thinking that I would make it at least to Whitstable at the further end of the East Swale by that afternoon, but when I reached the point where the two Swales meet, I found that the incoming tide which had carried me so smoothly up the West Swale would now be against me if I tried to sail down the East Swale. The tidal waters rush up both arms at roughly the same time and meet in the middle, like the meeting of the waters in the Red Sea to drown Pharaoh and all his chariots. But as this fact dawned upon me I realised that there is a third way to take – the little grey serpent of Milton Creek which runs from this point up to a nearby town, and even now was filling fast with the combined floodwaters of the two Swales. With a nudge of the tiller, I had steered around into the narrow mouth of this baby creek and was being carried by my magic carpet of tide and a following wind up to the fair town of Sittingbourne. I would be there in an hour, and could spend the rest of a leisurely day devouring more Full Cooked Breakfasts.

Let us be honest. Sittingbourne cannot by any stretch of the imagination be accurately described as fair. Even the approach to it by dinghy along Milton Creek, which offers the most romantic route in, is depressingly dreary. As the creek wound inland, I passed the remains of derelict industrial wreckage at every turn, slowly rotting into the salt marsh. Here an abandoned factory, there an old rusting goods depot; now a snarl of cyclone-wire fencing protecting a compound of oildrums, and then a ruined farmhouse with boarded up windows and graffitied walls. Occasionally my heart would lift at the sight of a fellow vessel ahead... until I drew nearer and would find that it was merely the rotting skeleton of an ancient hulk decaying into the mud. Despite the very obviously modern nature of this industrial graveyard, there was something strangely Dickensian about the place. I half expected to see Magwitch come stumbling over the salt marshes or Pip escaping from murder in the ruined lime kilns, especially as the louring sky and the threat of rain had brought on a grimness appropriate to one of Dickens' bleaker novels.

I eventually moored up right at the head of the creek behind some sort of sheet metal factory, manoeuvred my way past barbed wire compounds where Alsatian guard dogs snarled in a frenzy and made my way into Sittingbourne. I suppose the residents of Sittingbourne entertain some sort of fondness and loyalty for the home of their forefathers, but honesty compels me to admit that I found it a sad and dismal place that afternoon. I found that the B&B's in town were fully booked (Lord knows why, a delegation of Industrial Archaeologists come to study prime examples of dereliction, I suspect), and I had to search further afield before I obtained accommodation in a large hotel that had prices inversely proportional to its charm. Nowhere did Full Cooked Breakfasts.

I knew that the next morning, I would have to time my departure to the minute. I must leave at the very top of the tide; any earlier and I would be fighting the in-sweeping current, but any later and I would find that there was not enough water beneath even *Jack*'s shallow keel to float her. The upper reaches of Milton Creek would reduce to a filmy rivulet within minutes of the tide turning. My tide tables informed me that high tide was at 4.30 the next morning - another pre-dawn start - so I would have to leave the hotel at 3.30 to walk down to the creek. As I was arranging to pay the exorbitant price that night for my early get away in the morning, I was asked if I'd be taking breakfast before I left.

"Breakfast? At that hour?"

"Certainly, sir, and we can bring it up to your room if you wish."

Determined to get my money's worth, I agreed, put in my order for a 3.15 wake-up call and a 3.30 room-service breakfast and went upstairs for an early night feeling that perhaps I had been a little harsh in my judgements on the good folk of Sittingbourne. Room service? Gosh!

At precisely 3.30 the next morning I came wide awake in that mysterious instinctive way that humans have despite the absence of alarm clocks, sunrise cues or, indeed, pre-arranged wake-up calls. I rang Reception.

"Hello, Hotel Reception, Jason speaking, can I help you?"

"Yes, I'm in Room 450, my name's Mackinnon, and I was expecting a wake-up call fifteen minutes ago."

"Certainly, sir, would you like me to make that call for you, sir?"

(A pause.)

"No," I said, speaking very slowly, "I'm awake now. That is how we are conversing at present."

"Yes, sir, what is your room number please? I'll just check that for you, sir, and we'll soon have the problem sorted."

(Another longer pause. This boy has clearly been ingesting mercury out of a nearby creek most of his life.)

"Look, don't worry about that now, my room is 450 and I ordered breakfast to be sent to this room at three-thirty. I'm on a bit of a tight schedule, you see, so I was wondering if it's on its way?"

"Certainly, sir, I have the order written here and it should be on the way up. Room number 330, yes?"

"*Four-fifty.*"

"Yes, sir, I'll just change that breakfast to 4.50, sir. You enjoy your lie-in, sir."

There followed some very clear, very crisp instructions from my end, and we finally established the correct room number and the fact that I needed the breakfast immediately. The crispness of my tone went no way to driving out the sing-song chirpiness of the youthful Jason's response.

"Yes, sir, enjoy your breakfast, sir."

At 3.45, I had washed, shaved and was ready and packed, awaiting my reviving hot brekker.

At 3.55, I rang downstairs to Reception again.

"Hello, Hotel Reception, Jason speaking, can I hel...?"

"Yes, it is *Mackinnon* in Room 450, anxious to eat that breakfast that hasn't yet arrived. Any hope of it arriving soon-ish? I should have left ten minutes ago."

"Certainly, sir, I'll just have it sent up, sir. Room number please?"

(A long sigh through flared nostrils)

"*FOUR-FIFTY*. It is on the fourth floor."

"Certainly, sir. Glad to be of service, sir."

At 4.00, the phone rang.

"Wake-up call for Mr. Mackinnon, wake-up call. Jason from reception, sir, just calling to wake you up, sir."

"I'm *awake* already, and I am *waiting* for my *breakfast!!*"

"Very good, sir, happy to be of service, sir. I'll send it up. Room number please..."

At 4.15, the breakfast finally arrived. It consisted of two triangles of leathery toast, a polystyrene cup of tepid coffee and an assortment of those stupid little plastic tubs of apricot jam that are completely impossible to open once your fingers have been made greasy by struggling with the foil-wrapped tiles of frozen butter. Somehow I managed to get a smear of conserve onto each triangle and wolfed it down, scraped the remaining three-quarters of the stuff off my trousers, and pelted downstairs to settle the bill, and, if possible, the chirpy receptionist as well.

While the acned Jason struggled to jam my Visa card into the machine the wrong way round, I realised that it was now too late to walk the distance and get to the boat in time for the tide, so I called an all-night taxi. When it arrived, I bundled into it and gave the order to the driver. "The derelict warehouse down on the old industrial estate please," and, considering the ungodly hour, may as well have added, "... just some unfinished business with Vinnie the Grass, the Dinsdale brothers, and a sack of quick-setting concrete." At any rate, the driver showed the whites of his eyes, paused on a question, thought better of it and drove me straight there, depositing me amidst rusting barbed wire and burnt out cars. Then he drove off rapidly, mentally erasing all memory of the trip, what trip, I don't remember any trip, and leaving me to my appointment with the Mob.

Well, there was still water in the creek... just... but not nearly as much as there was in the boat. She was yet again up to her gunwales in mud, crabs, stinking weed and salt-ooze; I can't think how, but there is the constant element of surprise when dealing with tides. She had clearly caught under some projecting ledge as she lifted higher and higher on the in-coming tide, or snagged on something similar as she dropped again, or a dozen other playful possibilities; whatever, the result was as though she had spent several centuries under the sea and had just now been brought to the surface like some miniature latter-day *Mary Rose*. In fact, there was so much water in her that as I climbed out of my long trousers and into some swimming trunks in order to bail I thought she may even have managed to hole herself, settling onto some underwater spike during the night. Only time would tell. By the time the boat was clean and dry again she had almost settled onto drying mud, but there was still a faintly glimmering eel of water winding down the creek and I set to the oars with a will, launching myself heartily into the day's journey. With the tide carrying me down the creek to the East Swale and thence to Whitstable, I reckoned, I would be well on my way by the time the morning was half done. Then perhaps an easy run down the coast to Margate, where perhaps I could stop for a spot of lunch, and then a jolly slosh round the coast to Dover perhaps, just in time for a six o'clock pint and a bash at the Cryptic Crossword before supper. Super. Just super.

So it was that, despite the darkness of the hour and the distressing odour of rotting crab still clinging about me, I set off in a jaunty frame of mind for what was to be, without a doubt, the worst day of my life.

April 27th, 1998

5 a.m. – 9 a.m. I row down the rapidly emptying creek, shaving mudbanks as I go, the dismal waste on either bank still mercifully hidden in the grey murk of a dark dawning. Soon a breeze springs up. It rapidly increases to a stiff wind, blowing directly on the nose from the north-east, and countering any effect the outgoing current might be having. A moment's respite to play with the idea of hoisting the sail has me two hundred yards back upstream grounded on a rapidly drying mudbank. A few Olympian heaves with an oar hauls me off into the stream again, but it now takes me half-an-hour to regain my former position. By nine o'clock I have only just reached the confluence of the Swales and can turn eastwards down the broad stretch of water lying behind the Isle of Sheppey. At last, I can hoist the sail and tack into the wind.

9 a.m. – 12 noon. After the four hour strain of rowing into the wind, it is delightful to be sailing. I must be careful though. Although the water stretches broadly away to either side, the navigable channel is quite narrow, and even I in my shallow little craft must not venture too far from it. Once or twice, in an attempt to lengthen a tack, I feel the centreboard drag stickily in the soft mud and must pull it up quickly before I ground completely. Navigation buoys mark the way, my old friends the green bells and red boxes, but I am also introduced to a new type of buoy, the cardinal markers, and these cause me some small confusion.

After several interesting encounters with mid-channel mudbanks, I have formulated a working theory on how to treat these cardinal buoys and am pleased to see that I am making good progress. I am actually rather enjoying myself. The landscape is exactly as I imagine the setting for Ransome's '*Secret Water*' – a huge sheet of water between low, featureless land, the tallest thing the old black beacon post rising out of the glass-grey mirror. To the left, the Isle of Sheppey rises gently in one vast green expanse, sloping up to a solitary farmhouse in a clump of trees and a windpump. To the right, the distant rises are painted in swathes of that artificial chrome yellow that I have seen from afar two days ago; the remote fields of oilseed rape beginning to glow radioactively under a darkening sky.

12 Noon - I have reached the end of the Isle, and the Swale has bent north-east and widened out into a great triangle to join the sea. The town of Whitstable lies visible across a wide expanse of lumpy grey and white water directly to the east, but now, at low tide, this is barred and broken by the oyster beds of Whitstable Flats. I must continue in the main channel as it runs straight into the nor'easter for several miles until I can finally bear away to starboard and head directly to the shelter of the harbour. The wind, now that I have emerged from the shelter of the Isle, has become stronger. It is an iron bar ruled straight across the sea from Holland, thrashing the waves to a savage chop of white horses, and already I am beginning to feel the strain of these heavy seas.

12.30 p.m. - This is dreadful. The waves are too big... Distinctly 'gurly' in fact, as Sir Patrick Spens would have it. Without a jib I am having a hard time tacking into the wind, and the main problem is trying to go about each time. With a jib, one needs only put the tiller across and the wind catches behind this little sail and pulls her nose around, readying her to shoot off on the next zigzag. But as I am, and with the waves large enough to be battering on *Jack*'s prow, each time that I try to change tack I lose way, am slapped sideways by the next grey fist of water and find myself blown back down the channel a hundred yards before I can regain control.

Another problem is that the vast triangular acres of Whitstable Flats are too shallow to allow me to sail directly across them to shore, but not yet so dry that they do not allow the vicious combers to come sweeping across them, driven before the wind like grey Furies. I am suffering the double disadvantage of being out on an exposed body of sea and yet hemmed in a narrow channel... and I am not coping.

After half-an-hour of weeping frustration battling with the wind and waves, I learn a trick when going about. At the very moment of changing course, I release the tiller for a perilous few seconds, grab an oar and haul *Jack* bodily around onto the next tack. There are a few seconds of jolting and sloshing and the frenzied flogging of the mainsheet, and then the wind fills the sail and the brave little dinghy kicks off towards the further bank of the channel. I then have a minute or two to bail the boat like a madman with my plastic half-milk-bottle, before repeating the process. Even this bailing is a precarious task. To balance the force of the wind in the sail, I must sit out as far as I dare go, my bottom right on the windward gunwale, my torso leaning out backwards over the sea and clinging onto the mainsheet for dear life. To bail, however, I must lean right in, stooping to scoop the water from the bilges, and then the dinghy, no longer balanced, threatens to tip right over. There are two occasions when the lee gunwale sluices right under and *Jack* is suddenly awash with the briny flood, and I decide that bailing is perhaps something that can wait a little.

Having said all this, I am, incredibly, enjoying myself. I am wet through, I am bone-cold and my tiller hand is cramped painfully to its task. I am also making a bare mile in the hour. But I am filled with adrenaline, I am singing '*When the Foeman Bares his Steel*' defiantly to the storm winds, and I am enjoying establishing a balance to counter the worst of the gusts. And besides, I am nearly to the open stretch and will soon be able to turn and reach smoothly down to Whitstable. Tee-hee and Taran-taraaa!

1.23 p.m. - I stop singing Gilbert and Sullivan and start singing '*For Those in Peril on the Sea*'. My boom has just broken.

Well, no, not my entire boom, just the vital bit. The mainsheet to control the mainsail is attached to the end of the boom by a large pulley. It is this pulley that suddenly decides that our chances of survival are actually not that high, and decides to make a break for it. One moment it is there - the next it has vanished with a splash overboard. The sail flogs uncontrollably. The loose mainsheet convulses into knots. I coolly re-attach sheet to boom with a special knot invented on the spot, and continue to sail. We have just blown back half a mile in the interval.

1.27 p.m. - I discover that my new knot is a rather clever sort of self-jamming knot. Although I can still haul the sail *in*, I cannot let it out again, it seems. This means that when gusts come, I can no longer spill the wind to balance the blow, but must instead lean out even further. This is only possible by actually *standing* on the gunwale, a stunt that Mirrors were not really designed for. I am now riding *Jack* like a windsurfer, and the rigging is emitting strange moanings and hummings. Astonished at just how fast a Mirror can go. I am going to die.

1.52 p.m. - Bailer blows overboard.

1.53 p.m. - I turn the dinghy sharply to retrieve it. This is a feat of utter stupidity, for in doing so, I run straight onto the eastern mudbank that here lurks a foot below the water. There is an almighty *CRRA-A-A-C-CK* from beneath the keel. Centreboard? Possibly...

1.59 p.m. - Bailer is back in Sittingbourne by now. Boat still sailing into the wind, oddly enough, so it can't have been the centreboard after all. Boat horribly full of water, so I use the pith helmet to bail. Marvellous! Much better than the old bailer, can't think why I didn't think of that before. Am beginning to get really rather cold and tired. Make slow but steady progress towards the corner spit just five hundred yards ahead, sloosh, slap, wallop, splash, thud, plosh, clunk. Thank God I don't get seasick.

Ever.

I think…

2.35 p.m. - Getting there. I am going to make it. I am actually going to make it. Decide to experiment tentatively with the centreboard. Gingerly try pulling it up a little. Stuck.

Tug harder.

Still stuck.

Another pull and… whoosh! Up she comes like a cork from a bottle… or rather half a cork from a bottle. I am left clutching just the top half of the bloody thing, broken off in a jagged line halfway down, while the lower half drops smoothly out of the bottom and reappears as a distant and useless bit of flotsam a hundred yards away. I'm sorry, but bugger, bugger, bugger, bugger, bugger. I *am* going to die.

2.40 p.m. - I have allowed myself to drift onto a nearby mudbank. I am two miles out to sea. Consider myself lucky that I am in a flat-bottomed dinghy and not in some deep keeled yacht at present. I take my anchor, newly bought in London, wade ankle-deep to the end of its warp and proudly stamp it home in the mud. I shall simply have to sit out here and wait for the tide to come in, cover the flats, and then drift or sail straight to the nearest bit of dry land when I'm ready. All shall be well and all shall be well and all manner of thing shall be well…

2.47 p.m. - No it won't. I am quickly freezing to death. Being soaked to the skin and sitting fully exposed to the North Sea gale is rendering me inexpressibly miserable. I need to be cool and resourceful yet again. I decide to rig my blue awning up over the boom, which is immediately and surprisingly effective in keeping the wind out; then I change out of my wringing wet clothes into some merely damp-through ones I find at the bottom of my bag. And then… and I think this is really the bit of my entire year's travelling that I am most proud of… I – listen to this – I make myself *a brand new centreboard* out of some matchsticks, a safety-pin and an old gull's wing. Well, no, sorry, carried away there a little by the whole Allan Quatermain-ish idea of it, not out of those materials, but, almost as ingeniously, out of one of the duckboards that I use for sleeping on at night. This is the right thickness, but needs trimming to size with my Leatherman Multi-Purpose Handy Saw Attachment, and then a hole drilling through the top so that I can jam a stout bit of rope through to make a handle. I also rig up a much better arrangement to allow the mainsheet to run freely to ease off the mainsail. By the time the tide comes in, my little ship will be properly equipped to sail to shore with dignity.

Those tasks done, I have nothing to do but wait. The tide is beginning to race in again but it will be another hour or more before the stretch of Flats downwind of me will be fully covered. As the waters race over the sands, they slap and jolt the sides of *Jack de Crow* and she crunches uneasily in the two inches of grey-tawny water. The wind is stronger than ever now, and I fear for *Jack*'s poor bottom. I am also, for the first time in my life, feeling distinctly nauseous, with the *crinch*, *slap*, *judder* of the boat beneath me. An hour or more to wait…

There is nothing for it. The usual solution. Hauling out my mattress and my sleeping bag, I think of another storm long ago over Galilee and fall fast asleep.

4.30 p.m. - I awake. *Jack* is fully afloat and there seems to be a clear run to the shore about two miles away to the south. In that direction I can just make out what seems to be a long line of cottages above a strip of shingle, but after my experience in Sheerness, I am reluctant to trust the dinghy to the vagaries of an exposed beach again. Besides, there will be no pubs or B&B's so far out of Whitstable which lies further off to the east. I stow my sleeping bag (damp), my mattress (damp), put on heavy-duty clothes (soaking), pack away the awning (sodden) and take in the anchor (damp but it doesn't matter). I then hoist the sail, and begin the four mile skim to Whitstable Harbour which I decide is a much better choice than the row of rather snooty cottages on the beach. All will be well, and all…

4.33 p.m. - Bugger Whitstable Harbour. In three minutes I have hit five oysterbeds and my Admiralty chart says quite distinctly that vessels grounding are liable to pay damages. Snooty cottages it is. I can get there without having to lower the centreboard, and more importantly, before I die of hypothermia. It has begun to rain.

5.07 p.m. - I have made it. I ground on the shingle with a rushing crunch, carried the last few yards by a sudden swoop of scum-topped wave. I am numb, exhausted and wetter than an incontinent walrus, and want to do nothing more than find a hot bath, a mug of Bovril and a warm dry bed.

But I can't, not yet.

The sea has dumped me on the steeply sloping beach only halfway up the tidal reach. I cannot leave the dinghy here, but nor can I lift it any further up the shingle unaided. There is nothing for it but to spend another weary hour crouched shivering by *Jack*'s side and with every wave that comes swirling in higher than the rest, to float her another foot or two uphill. An hour later, and it is nearly dark. The last and highest sea-wave takes her up with an almighty rush as though spitting her contemptuously from its mocking jaws, and she settles with a weary creak and scrape onto the dry shingle above the tide. She is safe now, and can wait for the morrow's day.

6.15 p.m. - I climb, bone-weary, out of my sodden clothes and find some relatively dry ones to wear. In doing so, I discover the final insult of the day. Somewhere between the early departure of the morning and this final staggering ashore, I have lost my wallet. Yes, I know, unbelievable. Credit cards, bank cards and seventy pounds in cash. This has happened almost certainly while I was thrashing my way in and out of dry-ish clothes while sitting out in mid-ocean. Therefore, the wallet is now in all probability at the bottom of the sea. Well, thank you very much, God. That is positively the last time I sing hymns to *you*, mate...I may as well just lie here and let the herring gulls finish me off.

6.20 p.m. - An angel appears. It is not in the form that I usually encounter, that of an elderly but sprightly lady bearing brandy, dog leads and good advice, but an anthropology student called Arif. He is a Moslem, and I am changing my religious allegiance forthwith. He takes me to his flat nearby, gives me two mugs of hot Bovril, lets me ring the Sittingbourne hotel to see if by chance I have left the wallet there... no, I haven't... and then loads up all my sodden luggage into his car and drives me into Whitstable to a Bed and Breakfast, pointing out the town laundromat and bank on the way. The B&B is, under normal circumstances, utterly charming. Tonight I bitterly resent the fact that it is located right on the seafront, as I never want to see salt water again in my life. Nor gulls, nor ships nor frilly shells, nor lighthouses nor lampreys, nor oilskins, oysters or compass-roses. In fact, for the next three hours, the pavement beneath my feet is going up and down, side to side, to and fro, and I cannot walk a straight line. I am dying for a drink to compensate for the wobbling, but my new-found religious beliefs will not allow it.

7.20 p.m. - 11.30 p.m. - This is all getting thoroughly tedious, but let me finish off briefly by saying that the day ends with:
1)   a visit to the Laundromat to put my clothes through the wash with a handful of borrowed change from Arif, blessed be he and his sons and his sons' sons for ever;
2)   a train ride back to Sittingbourne and a dreary walk to the derelict warehouse to see if I had dropped my wallet on the wharf-side when I had changed into boat-baling gear in the early hours that morning but all to no avail;
3)   a visit to the taxi office to see if the driver has found my wallet dropped anywhere in his cab as I paid him that morning, only to be told that that particular driver has gone home in a hurry and not been seen since, but has been overheard all day making enquiries about police protection schemes and emigration to New Zealand and muttering about concrete boots;
4)   a return by train to Whitstable to find that the laundry has closed for the night with all my washing still safely inside but me outside and still condemned to be walking the streets shedding small crustaceans with every step and smelling like a fishing net;
5)   a return to the B&B to find that the taxi company *have* managed to contact their driver and that, yes, (praise be to Allah and golly, it doesn't take long for *that* particular deity to kick in on the divine assistance front

for new converts, does it?) my wallet has been handed in and they would just like to assure me that nobody has taken a note of the name on the credit cards, my identity is quite, quite safe, sir, and please, we're just peaceful ordinary folk who don't want to get mixed up in whatever business I had down at the old docks that morning, that's my own affair and would I like to come in to the office to pick up the wallet, or would I prefer to arrange an anonymous drop somewhere?

6) Another train journey back to Sittingbourne, a joyful reunion with my credit cards, and an hour's wait sitting on the platform to catch the last train back to Whitstable, there to find that every bloody pub in town has just closed... except one: the Turk's Head, appropriately enough to my new loyalty, which serves possibly the nicest bowl of red-hot Hungarian Goulash the World has ever known.

7) Bed.

The human spirit is a funny old thing. The day has undeniably been a disaster. I am more tired than I knew it was possible to be. My left wrist, from thirteen hours of gripping the mainsheet in icy conditions, is hurting abominably; my little ship is lying on a distant stretch of inhospitable shingle with a faulty main-pulley, a jury-rig centreboard and no bailer. I have spent an entire day of suffering the strain of battling against wind and tide, the elements at their foulest, and have travelled all of seven miles. I have abandoned the faith of my childhood and grown to loathe the sea. And as I lie here between white linen sheets, and the rain drums on the windowpane and the old sea slap-slaps the wall beyond the darkness, I realise the oddest thing of all. I am happier than anybody else in the entire world.

Good night.

Cake and Carpentry

'Gae, fetch a web o' the silken claith,
Another o' the twine,
And wap them into our ship's side,
And let na the sea come in.'

Anonymous - *The Ballad of Sir Patrick Spens*

Whitstable is wonderful. It is a seaside town that has got left behind in the 1930s, the sort of place where Enid Blyton children still go to buy ginger pop and paper kites for a shilling, before cycling back to their secret camp on the downs to foil all those spies and ruffian smugglers. It is the sort of place where fishing boats come into harbour trailing the coconut flakes of sea-birds, and the huge orange crates of dead fish on the wharves are picked over by the squabbling, sardonic herring gulls. There are weatherboard houses in salty-white or tarry-black, all converted net-drying lofts or kipper-smoking rooms, and with names like '*Hove-To House*' or '*Sou'wester Cottage*' or '*The Oysterbed B&B,*' with large ginger cats and brass telescopes in the window. Along the seafront, there is a continual parade of headscarfed old housewives with shopping bags off to buy a bit of fresh 'addock for 'is Lordship's tea, or retired Colonels walking their tartan-jacketed Scotty dogs, or young mothers wheeling pushchairs with toddlers in them and their hair blown all over their faces... and everyone says, "'Allo, luv!" as you pass, except the Colonels who say, "Bit fresh, what?" as they march by into the gale. It is a peaceful, safe sort of place, the only danger being from the Famous Five if they think you look suspiciously foreign and spy-like.

Oh yes. And, before I finish, Whitstable is the Oyster Capital of England... and proud of it. Though I am not partial to oysters myself, especially when they are threatening to sink me out on the Flats, nevertheless I was made to promise to mention the fact by several publicity-minded citizens whom I got to know over the next five days, "you know, if you ever write that book, luv." So there we are.

The reason I was forced to stay in Whitstable for the next five days will soon become apparent. For now that we have wandered on this sunny breezy morning along the seafront, past the gaily striped beach huts (whose proud owners enjoy a day at the seaside by huddling together around a kettle and a transistor radio out of the sleet and drizzle of an English summer's day), we have come at last to the outlying village of Seasalter, the long strip of shingle backed by the cottages and strewn with driftwood - including the rather sorry sight of a small and sea-battered Mirror lying high up on the tideline of kelp.

With a spring in my step and hope in my heart, I have come armed with a new pulley, a packet of screws and a couple of bits of timber to fix all that went wrong yesterday. What I have *not* come prepared to do is fix the gaping hole in her keel. That last mocking wave of the night before that deposited *Jack de*

Crow above the tideline has dumped her fair and square on a wicked iron spike hidden in the black kelp, and this has punched a raw hole right through her hull. It is still there in fact, stabbing through the timbers from below. She is mortally wounded, and I possess neither the tools nor the skill to mend her. Nor, to be honest, the heart. The journey, it seems, ends here.

"Yoo-hoo!"

A lady has emerged from a nearby cottage. If she has come to ask me to remove my dinghy and myself from her property, I will drown her here and now. She is certainly walking towards me with a sense of busy purpose, and has the air of one who has come to be polite but firm to vagabonds.

"Yoo-hoo! Young man?! Is that your dinghy?" I resign myself to the lecture about trespassing.

"Look..." begin I, but am cut off by the torrent.

"If I'm being terribly nosy, do send me packing, but I couldn't help wondering if I could be of any use. And I'm simply dying to know who you are and where you've come from and what on earth you think you're doing. And whether you'd like a coffee? I'm Daphne, Daphne Dunster, by the way. What a dear little boat! *Can* I help? Or shall I just tiptoe away again?"

Daphne, says her husband Peter, is of the Mongoose Tribe - her motto is "*Go and find out.*" On further acquaintance, I found this to be indubitably true, but it would also appear to be backed by various other mottoes such as "*Offer Assistance to Possible Lunatics,*" "*Ruthlessly Organise Those Less Capable Than Oneself*" and "*Try my Date-and-Walnut Slice and Die.*" I experienced all these philosophies over the next five days in a giddy whirl of kindness and competence and good fortune unparalleled in the history of seafaring. From the moment when I first allowed myself to be chivvied inside by the ever-so-slightly bossy Daphne for a coffee and a good cry, she and her husband... and later her entire family... went into action to make sure that *Jack* and myself had no excuse for abandoning the voyage there and then. Blast them.

The first thing she told me over the morning coffee was that her husband was a keen yachtsman, and consequently his shed was full of equipment: power-tools, drills, varnish, marine ply, screws, fittings, paint; anything I might need, in fact, to rebuild a proper centreboard, fix the boom and generally sort out the problems that had arisen at sea in the storm. Meanwhile, although she couldn't put me up here in the house because the entire Dunster tribe were all arriving for the May Day Holiday Weekend, nevertheless, she expected me to join the family for lunch the following day and to start work on the boat. I mournfully pointed out that though I had at last acquired *some* sort of competence at carpentry, the gaping gash in the hull was quite beyond me; she countered by playing her trump card. One of her numerous sons-in-law who was coming down to visit was a boatbuilder.... and of course, he would be delighted to help and advise me in the mending of the dinghy. And now, if I had no more objections, the poor little thing couldn't stay there on the shingle any longer, so would have to be moved up onto their lawn at once... and look, there's a couple of joggers, such nice looking young men, who will be happy to help haul the boat up while she directed operations.

And off she trotted with a plate of that Date-and-Walnut Slice to bully the passing joggers into manhandling *Jack de Crow* up onto the grass outside the French windows to await the ministrations, expert and otherwise, that would fit her out for the crossing to France and beyond.

The next five days were utterly wonderful... and so make poor telling, alas. It would be nice to linger here over the carpentry and the coffee and the cake, the long, leisurely lunches with the Dunster tribe, and the bright May days spent passing screws and pliers to Paul the carpenter son-in-law lying on his back under the propped-up dinghy while he did clever and mysterious things to the hull and got varnish dripped in his eyes. It would be nice to be back there, in fact, forever in the limbo of that sunny pause, Odysseus entertained by the gracious Phaecians, able for a while to turn my back on the grey sea with plausible excuse.

Meanwhile, *Jack de Crow* was knocked into shape by the inestimable Paul. I must add that I didn't quite leave him to it entirely; I did at least see what was going on, and for those who are interested, I will explain briefly the process of fixing a hole in the keel. First we had to cut out the damaged section, leaving a neat rectangular hole in the bottom of the boat. The edges of the hole had to be bevelled slightly, like the sides of a plug hole in your bathtub. Then a plug had to be made to fit, a rectangular piece of wood with similarly bevelled edges, and this we made out of a stack of old marine ply from the shed, part of an older vessel. Lastly, a larger piece of ply had to be made as a sturdy plate. This plate would sit in the bottom of the bilges over the plug, and screw both to the hull proper from above and have the plug screwed to it from below. Finally, once everything was in place, the whole lot had to be slathered in a noxious red syrup whose name I now cannot recall, but which required exact mixing in ridiculous proportions, such as five parts to thirteen, and whose fumes stung the skin and eyes at fifty yards and induced interesting visions of purple dragons and singing lobsters in the sky when inhaled too heavily.

Personally, I've never found a need for solvents to promote mythical visions. Old stories seem to do the job for me, such as the fable by Aesop which tells of an upstart Crow who desires to become the king of the birds. Accordingly, he goes about the woods and fields and collects the cast-off feathers of birds more splendid than he, the kingfisher, the jay and the gaudy peacock. Dressed in his borrowed finery, he declares his new-found splendour, but his harsh voice betrays him and spiteful Juno, Queen of Heaven, orders all the birds to pull his Joseph's coat to pieces. I was interested to note, after all the repairs were finished on my poor *Crow*, that the new centreboard cut from that marine ply still bore the name of the yacht it had come from; *Pavo*, no less, Pavo the Peacock, the haughty one, sacred to the vengeful Juno. I just hoped that my new plumage would last until I had at least crossed the Channel. The moral was plain; keep my mouth shut and stay low.

After five days, it was time to be off again. As I wandered down the long shore to the Dunsters that morning I pondered again the good fortune that had driven me ashore at just this spot at just such a time. Are there many cottages along that stretch of the North Kent coast where boat building is provided at the drop of a hat, and, what is more, with five days of warmth and hospitality and good humour? I am fortunate enough to be accustomed to kindness in others, but this latest display had left even me a little bewildered. Was I suffering from amnesia? Was I actually a member of the Dunster family who had suffered a blow on the head and forgotten who he was? Would I suddenly come round, triggered by the fortieth slice of Date-and-Walnut Loaf in five days, look about me and cry, "*Mother? Father? What has happened? Where have I been? And whose is that ridiculous dinghy?*" and then trot upstairs to my old bedroom and start to piece together my old life as a native of Whitstable? There seemed no other likely solution as I humped my bags along the shingle to Seasalter for the last time.

After four days of wonderful May sunshine and blue seas, the weather had turned grey again. Though the winds were not as fierce as on the day I had sailed here, they were nevertheless strong enough to furl the sea into grey and scum-capped billows that hissed and rattled on the loose shingle and made Daphne look askance at me as I stowed my stuff away. But I reassured her. The wind was perfect. It was setting due west, just right to take me along the coast to Margate, and beyond that, the North Foreland Light and the heel of England. There the coast turned sharply southwards towards Ramsgate and Dover, and I could happily reach down that section, sailing across the wind which would in all likelihood be diminished by the bulk of high land blocking it from the West. Such was the theory.

Meanwhile, time to say my farewells and my thanks. Only Daphne was home then; I had said my farewells to Peter and the rest of the family the evening before, so it was just up to Daphne and me to carry *Jack de Crow* down to the sea's edge. There Daphne presented me with a new bailer, something I had completely forgotten to obtain, gave me a last big hug and a stern admonition to be jolly careful and to write when I reached France, and then steadied the dinghy in the waves while I climbed aboard.

Those first few seconds of launching are always a flurry and a fury, especially when there are waves attempting to spew you back onto the shore like a cat rejecting worm tablets. There is the sail to hoist, the rudder-string to release and the centreboard to jam down when one is confident of being out in deep enough water. Then there is the first alarming slop of a wave over the boughs, and the sudden awful fear that one is being driven back onto shore again, followed by the hand-over-hand hurry to haul in the mainsheet, already wringing wet and salty. But with that action, the wind takes hold, the little boat spurts forward, meets a wave, rides up and over it, and the tiller thrums more beneath the hand. Only then do we have the leisure to turn and wave to Daphne on the shore, and we are surprised to see how far we have come already. She is two hundred yards away and diminishing further with every second, her hand upheld in a last heartening wave. Another wave threatens us briefly, and we must turn our attention forwards again, so that is the last we see of her. Five minutes later, she has gone inside and the shore is empty.

But we are on our way again, and the *Crow* in her new and precious plumage is flying well. With our trap firmly closed, we sail on to Dover and the Channel crossing.

Dashing to Dover

'What matters it how far we go?' his scaly friend replied.
'There is another shore, you know, upon the other side.
The further off from England, the nearer is to France –
Then turn not pale, beloved snail, but come and join the dance.
'Will you, won't you, will you, won't you, will you join the dance?
'Will you, won't you, will you, won't you, wo'n't you join the dance?'

Lewis Carroll - *Alice's Adventures In Wonderland*

I have described at some length the discomfort and weariness of beating headlong into a brisk wind at sea – the strain of hauling on sodden ropes, the six-times-a-minute dousing with a pailful of cold salt water, the difficulties in hauling the boat about at each tack. But give me a choice between all that and the sailor's dream of a following wind and I will take the beating every time. Running downwind that day was utterly terrifying.

Most of the time, I was surfing down each wave into a green-grey valley of water, the blunt bow, never designed for these speeds, sending two great fans of spray up on either side like egret's wings. So highly powered was the boat with the sail out wide that the dinghy constantly threatened to nosedive into the waves and send the whole contraption somersaulting forward like a cyclist who has incautiously applied the front brakes too savagely on a steep descent. At times, the prow did dip under, and the sea would sluice over the foredeck in a shining torrent, filling the dinghy with another few gallons of Channel water. What is more, with the wind off to one side, one can always balance the boat by leaning out into the wind on the opposite side of the sail. But here, with the wind directly aft, the whole boat rocked and swayed alarmingly with every swell, and I was forced to sit crouched on my haunches in the middle of the dinghy, leaning from side to side to counteract each new wallow. An added danger was that of gibing, when the wind catches behind the sail and slams it across to the other side with murderous force. Had this happened, I could not have escaped capsizing, and breaking the mast at the very least.

Lastly, there is the sheer speed of travel. I was planing most of the time, a phenomenon usually associated with more hydrodynamic boats than a Mirror, skidding wildly down the face of each tremendous wave and setting every fibre of the old wooden hull straining and humming and vibrating until I thought she would simply disintegrate beneath me. All in all, the experience was rather like surfing on an elderly cello.

One thing can be said for that leg of the voyage. I covered the miles with a rapidity I had not yet experienced. Whitstable vanished astern, Herne Bay came and went, and in what seemed a mere ten minutes, the entrance to Margate Harbour opened in the shoreline. I badly needed a break. I zoomed in behind the old blackened pier wall... ah, that blissful relief of gliding out of the swell into calm waters... and there a crescent of sand the colour of Red Leicester welcomed me softly; an elderly and disreputable looking pigeon flapped down to perch on my mast which I chose to take as a nicely Biblical sign. I tied up, baled the boat, and trudged off to find some fish'n'chips and a hot mug of tea. As I walked, I wobbled like a jelly with nervous exhaustion and was yet again soaked to the skin.

I did consider stopping for the night in Margate, but the gilded town clock said that it was only two o'clock, and with the warm grease of fish'n'chips dribbling down my chin and the salt and vinegar tang in my nostrils I fooled myself into thinking that the recent emergence of a hot, bright sun would equate with gentler winds and smaller seas that afternoon. Besides, I have an appallingly short memory for terror, which is I suppose a blessing, but hardly a survival trait.

About ten seconds beyond the pier-end, I worked out that this was probably a mistake, but a few futile attempts to head back up into the wind to re-enter Margate soon had me resigned to continuing on to the North Foreland Cliffs. These aren't *the* White Cliffs, as I had been half expecting - they are in fact reddish in colour and not terribly high – but they are very much a landmark for mariners over the centuries. This is the Heel of England, the point beyond which you cannot even pretend that you are still in the Thames Estuary. You are now in the Channel. You are now officially at sea.

The Heel of England

All morning I had been praying hard for a chance to stop that precarious, headlong rush downwind, sometimes as many as three prayers a second, and as I rounded the Foreland, my prayers were answered. The wind changed in several ways: firstly, it doubled in speed and strength, and secondly, it now blew straight from the south, straight on the nose, and I was back to tacking. Two minutes later, I was thinking back with tearful nostalgia to all that glorious surfing downwind, and wondering how I could ever have thought that tacking was preferable.

But I have written enough about the discomforts of marine sailing in a boat built for the quiet inland waters of lake and mere. Let me record here that through all the drenchings, the haulings, the salt-slap-batterings of wave on bow, there was a great exhilaration, almost a lunatic hilarity, in my progress. There was an almost parental pride in the way that the rigging, as old-fashioned and Heath-Robinson-ish as those little model boats I once made out of corks and matchsticks, was standing up to the strain and buffet of the winds: not least those bits of rigging I had had to glue and screw and bind all by myself with whatever had been handy at the time. For a thing of shreds and patches, she was doing well.

So down that coast I tacked, at times drawing in close under the red cliffs where the wind lessened, and I glided between mats of slippery kelp before being forced by the black seething reefs to tack and turn out to sea once more. Then the wind would strengthen again, and the waves roll higher, and I would find myself in the dreadful quandary of fearing to tack, but knowing that as we drew further from the shore, the seas would grow fiercer and the winds gustier with every minute that passed. Then there would come the moment of courage, the thin cry of "Ready to Go About?" to my phantom crew, their white-faced nod of approval, and the pushing of the tiller to send us around. "Ready about!" I would cry. The waves would heave, the sail clap like thunder, the poor dinghy would pitch and toss like a rearing pony, and then we'd be round once more, running for the shore and wondering if it was worthwhile baling the boat yet again.

Eventually, at about six in the evening, I tacked in behind the huge pier of Ramsgate Harbour, right under the bows of a beautiful old Dutch sailing-schooner called the *Noordenlicht*, - timber, two-masted and with tan sails - which had kindly stopped to let me go first. Small wonder that havens and harbours are used so often in hymns and religious imagery - the still beauty of calm and windless waters behind a breakwater, the reassuring elegance and symbolism of a lighthouse, the security of tying up to a pontoon with shaking fingers and knowing that soon they will be shaking no more, that somewhere beyond the final stripping off of sodden clothes a hot bath is waiting - these are surely foretastes of Heaven.

The local branch of Heaven in Ramsgate is known as the Royal Temple Yacht Club. It sits perched halfway up the cliffs above the harbour, a huge redbrick Victorian edifice, and someone - I cannot remember who, but a blessing upon their name - directed my weary footsteps thither. Within the doors, I found an enormous and elegant saloon with deep leather armchairs, old marine oil-paintings of ships and seascapes, a gigantic trophy cabinet blazing with silver cups and pewter platters and mahogany shields, newspapers to read at one's elbow... and a bar. This bar was attended by a young man who had spent most of a very quiet afternoon watching in fascinated horror from his lofty vantage point my slow zigzag progress down the coast, his hand hovering over the phone for the Emergency Services every time a larger-than-usual wave had obscured me from sight. He admitted to me later that when he finally saw me slip in behind the harbour wall he had poured himself a large vodka and downed it in sheer vicarious relief. This barman then proceeded to introduce me to all the members of the Club who were now drifting in for a sundowner, and they in turn kept buying me drinks, impressed by what they saw as my intrepid courage, rather than recognising it for what it really was: the inability to read a weather forecast properly. I did not at the time see the need to disillusion them.

Best of all, the Royal Temple Yacht Club does bed-and-breakfast for the astonishingly reasonable price of twelve pounds a night, (though I suspect that potential guests, to be considered as such, must arrive in Ramsgate by boat, or at least soaked to the bone.) So after a hot bath, a trip to a laundrette and a phone call to the Dunsters to let them know of my safe arrival (Peter had in fact spent most of the afternoon driving around the coast to see if he could spot me), I settled down to a pleasant night in Ramsgate, much of which was spent in an excellent pub down the hill. There I met the sixteen crew members from the Dutch schooner which, it transpired, had just arrived from the Azores. I thanked them warmly for their courtesy in having stopped earlier that afternoon at the harbour mouth to let me in first. They informed me a little curtly that they hadn't stopped to let me through out of courtesy, they had steered to avoid my erratic course and run onto a sandbank, thank you very much. Still, they were actually quite jolly about it, and by the end of the evening, the skipper was sufficiently thawed to offer to put *Jack de Crow* and myself aboard the next day and take me across safely to Ostend – he possibly saw this as one way to remove a shipping hazard from the Channel, the major ports of Europe and from beneath the bows of his fellow skippers.

Now here was a quandary. The offer was certainly a good one, and seemed to be a gift on a plate, the hand of the gods again, playing me a chance-card just when I needed it. The offer, though fuelled by an evening of beer and good company, seemed genuine... and what an opportunity to see the graceful *Noordenlicht* up close! To be sure, I would find myself in Ostend rather than Calais, but my map showed that here too there were canal entrances whereby I might enter the waterways system of Europe. How about it? The Channel crossing made easy? Nay, the Channel crossing made *possible*?

I declined. I do not to this day know why. It was the sort of serendipitous opportunity I revel in, that I recount with delighted glee to friends weary of hearing just such good-luck stories added to the smug repertoire. But something stubborn in me won that evening, something wilful and daring, something that whispered that if I really *could* cross the Channel unaided in a Mirror, then there really would be a story worth telling. In fact, it urged, why even bother Wilf and his poorly foot?

I could probably do it alone.

The leg down to Dover was entirely pleasant. The wind had died right away by next morning, and the day was fair and warm with just a ghost of a breeze to carry me southwards. In such weather, I could cheerfully circumnavigate the British Isles in my faithful Mirror; indeed I spent most of that day idly dreaming of doing just that at some future date. The misery of the last section had dissolved into a dew, as shimmering and insubstantial as the mirage over there on the horizon, the glassy slurring of the sea that showed where the fabled Goodwin Sands were just drying out under the hot sun. To my right, the sweeping shoreline of Pegwell Bay receded into the distance, faded greens and sand-whites and ochre smudges. Beneath the bow, the water was clear blue-green, rippling happily as we footed forward at a gentle two miles an hour. So still and calm it was that I spent much of the day basking belly down on the foredeck, having rigged up the tiller in such a way that I could steer with a length of rope attached to an idle foot.

It was bliss. It was boring. Beyond the Sands, a yacht ghosted by, barely moving. To while away the long hours, I took compass bearings off distant landmarks and drew lines on my chart to pinpoint my exact position. I wrote a couple of postcards. I sunbathed again, until, at my head, a large fish suddenly jumped from the water, startling me awake, and I realised that I had, in fact, been snoozing.

By about four in the afternoon, I had reached the White Cliffs themselves, and the little breeze had died to nothing, so I took to my oars and set myself rowing the last stretch to Dover. The Cliffs themselves were beautiful, more so than I had somehow supposed from such a cliché. Most of the White Cliffs are topped by green pasture, vivid now in the late afternoon sun against the white chalk, but what architecture there is to be seen from below is varied and charming: a windmill, a row of fine gabled houses, a lighthouse, an obelisk and finally the grey ramparts and bastions of Dover Castle. They are the story-book structures from some Giant-child's toy box, all set out with loving hands amongst the folds of green counterpane and white fall of linen sheets at the edge of the nursery bed that is England.

But before your ever-ascending eye reaches this homely array, there are the cliffs themselves which still contrive to be as wild and giddying as Edgar, at the top, describes them to poor blind Gloucester in *King Lear.*
"...Stand still! How fearful
And dizzy 'tis to cast one's eyes so low!
The crows and choughs that wing the midway air
Show scarce so gross as beetles. Half way down
Hangs one that gathers samphire – dreadful trade!
Methinks he seems no bigger than his head...
...Look up a height; the shrill-gorged lark so far
Cannot be seen or heard. Do but look up..."

But finally, on the upward flight, ones gaze floats up beyond the chalk, beyond the green turf, beyond the last lofty cupola of tower or windmill and up into the sweet empyrean blue, the lark-singing English sky of a late afternoon, and the tune has changed to Vera Lynn and her bluebirds over... and the long day's journey is nearly done.

Nearly, but not quite. And now the music stops abruptly as I get my first taste of a Cross-Channel Ferry. Dover Harbour has two entrances, and I am approaching the northern one, rowing sluggishly against a turning tide. I am trying to creep in at the very foot of the strong-based promontory, and do not see the emerging ferry until it rounds the harbour wall with a throbbing roar and a mighty surge of wash – far bigger and more beetling, it seems to me then, than all the White Cliffs stacked on top of one another. At least the Cliffs stay still, give or take the odd tectonic shift every few million years. The ferry captain quite certainly does not see me far, far below his lofty bridge, so throwing the time-honoured dictum of *Steam Gives Way to Sail* overboard, I plunge wildly to one side and sit out the swell that threatens to swamp me.

Ten minutes later when the maelstrom has subsided, I try again, this time very sensibly checking carefully for the least sign of an outbound ferry. That is how I am caught completely unawares by the *in-bound* ferry that chooses that precise minute to steam up behind me, missing me by mere yards. This time, the tsunami-like wake flings me right up the harbour wall like a rejected lobster and nearly jolly well over it. A pity it didn't fully succeed in this feat, as it would have saved the patrol boat the bother of coming out to tow me in, as I'm sure they were very busy men and really didn't want to be bothered with a little nuisance like me, and all that tedious paperwork to fill in when they charged me *fifty pounds* for the privilege of their piloting skills. Yes, *fifty pounds* ... I think.

To be honest, I cannot actually now swear to that amount, but I do remember being extraordinarily indignant at the time and then making a conscious effort to forget the whole grubby little episode because Life is too short to be fretting about past expenses, and besides, it didn't really fit in with the whole image of the merry wanderer of song and legend, did it? Odysseus; Doctor Dolittle; Tom Bombadil; all that crowd, in whose entire histories, the words *chequebook*, *credit card* and *piloting fee* never get a single mention. So best to forget it really. Which is why I cannot now remember anything about it.

About what, in fact?

See? Easy...

I didn't like Dover as much as Ramsgate. It was all a little too big and impersonal, and besides, there was nobody buying me any drinks. It tries hard though. There is the Castle to visit, and the Roman Painted House and the Museum, but the whole place had about it the air of a doormat; useful, breezy, somewhere to wipe one's feet on entry to the country, but not a place to linger, to luxuriate. Like a doormat, there is something gritty and utilitarian about the place. I considered all the above tourist options, came across one called, thrillingly, The White Cliffs Experience, and at that point decided it was time to get out of Dover as quickly as might be.

Ay, there's the rub. For here I was finally, at the wire, the end of the spring-board, at Dover itself. No longer could I put off the decision, the call to Wilf or the choice to go solo. I had now to speak to the local people, the coastguard, the yacht club, the Harbour Master, everybody and anybody who could advise me about the Crossing. And it was here and now that I found an odd thing. For ever since I had first vaguely considered the idea, while I was still deep in the heart of Oxfordshire, people had been advising me in the strongest possible terms against such a course. Elderly couples cruising on the placid upper Thames in narrowboats called *Meadowlark* or *Buttercup* had warned me of the speed and size of oil tankers that ploughed the Channel day and night. Kindly landlords whose sole nautical experience had been regular weekly viewing of *The Onedin Line* twenty years previously seemed fully up-to-date on the casualty statistics pertaining to the North Sea. Whenever I had tried to introduce the idea of the gallant little ships of Dunkirk, *The Snowgoose* and all that, I had firmly been given more modern analogies, such as the one about attempting to cross the M25 at peak hour on your hands and knees. But strangely, as I had approached the actual sea, people had become less dire in their outlook. The Dunsters had thought it was possible... with an escort of course... and the Royal Temple Yacht Club members, at their most tanked-up, had been positively enthusiastic.

And here, now, in Dover itself, as I did the rounds, the attitude could best be described as blasé. When I tentatively said, *"Um... er... call it mad if you will, but I'm thinking of taking my Mirror dinghy across the Channel, ha, ha, I know, crazy, eh? Any advice?"* the response had ranged from bored to indifferent. The President of the Yacht Club said, "Yes, and...?" The Harbour Master said something along the lines of, "Really, yes, my seven-year old daughter sailed her Optimist across last July, got a pen-friend across there, you know what young girls are like, eh?" Various other seasoned sailors I met, picking up on the fact that I was after some reassuring advice, did manage to mumble something about, "Lovely weather for it. Wouldn't leave it too long, if I were you." When I finally rang the Coastguard and outlined my plan, I was relieved to hear a note of stern warning creeping into the voice on the other end. "Across to Calais, you say? In a Mirror? Right, now look here, I feel that I must most strongly advise you..."

"Yes, yes?" I asked, pencil in hand to take down some vital bit of marine wisdom.

"Are you writing this down? Good. Well, when you get into Calais Harbour..."

"*C-a-l-a-i-s H-a-r-b-o-u-r*" I wrote.

"And you turn to starboard..."

"*S-t-a-r-b-o-a-r-d*"

"There's a huge white building ahead that acts as a landmark, have you got that?"

"Yes, huge white building…"

"Good. Well, it's a restaurant, see, and whatever you do, *don't* have the mussels there. I did last August and I was as sick as a dog - anyway, it's overpriced. Apart from that, have a good crossing. Cheerio!"

And that was it, the sole piece of advice from the marine authorities about the crossing of the busiest shipping lane in the World in an unpowered Mirror dinghy. I went to bed that night singing to myself a jingle half-remembered from many years ago:

> "*Will I, won't I, will I, won't I, will I join the Dance?*
> *The further 'tis from England, the closer 'tis to France!*"

Interminably it revolves in my head as I try to place it. Isn't it something from Lewis Carroll, and something to do with a melancholy Mock Turtle? And isn't it a whiting or a Dover Sole making the invitation to the dance? Am I being invited by all the fishy, finny folk of the North Sea to join them under the briny blue, my bleached bones to dance to the tune of the tides in the salt and oozy depths?

> "*Full fathom five thy father lies.*
> *Of his bones are coral made.*
> *Those are pearls that were his eyes…*"

I'd have to check the weather forecast for the next week or so, find a 'window' as they say in nautical circles. I'd have a chance to visit the Castle tomorrow perhaps, brush up my knowledge about thirty-million-year-old chalk at that other place maybe…

It seems I was to be given no excuse. The next morning was fine, so I went.

Crossing to Calais

'*Wherefore my heart leaps within me,*
my mind roams with the waves
over the whale's domain, it wanders far and wide
across the face of the earth, returns again to me
eager and unsatisfied; the solitary bird screams,
irresistible, urges the heart to the whale's way
over the stretch of the seas.'

Anonymous Anglo-Saxon fragment - *The Seafarer*

It was on the tenth day of May that I made the crossing, a day in which the elements so combined that all the World could stand up and say, "This is the day to cross." I needed a wind strong and steady enough to allow me to move swiftly through the water and cover the twenty-two miles before nightfall, and yet not so strong that I would be in danger of capsizing. The day also needed to be warm and clear, to enable me to stay comfortably in the open and to see where I was going – poor visibility would spell disaster – and yet a blissful calm such as I had had from Ramsgate to Dover would be equally disastrous, leaving me idly adrift in mid-Channel with only my oars to propel me out of the way of the tankers and ferries that ply the waves with ferocious speed.

Just before I leave, I pay a last visit to the Harbour Master's office and they allow me to ring the local Coastguard. Despite their casual attitude of the day before, they give me a special number to ring and ask me to let them know when I reach Calais that evening, just so that they are not up all night worrying. With a final warning to watch out for the *moules au vin*, they ring off, and I have no more excuse to linger.

At about ten o'clock that morning, I untie from the sheltered pontoon beneath the harbour wall and row towards the harbour mouth. Before I am even halfway there, there is a sufficient breeze to warrant hauling up the sail and I glide smoothly across the gentle swell of water towards the entrance between its concrete moles. Even as I do so, I note that there is a swirling current around the northern mole, sweeping me towards it almost as fast as I am sailing forward, but I clear it with a good fifty yards to spare and am then out on the open sea. I have my compass lying on the central thwart, held in place by an elastic bungy-strap. The compass dial is set to the exact degree I must follow, 125 degrees, so all I have to do is steer in such a way as to ensure that the quivering red needle is kept pointing to the large red N on the dial and I know that *Jack* will be pointing her nose at Calais somewhere over there beyond the horizon. Of course, it is not quite as simple as that because with every wave, *Jack* veers about as she mounts the oblique slope of one comber and races down the further slope in a skidding sideways glide, but as long as the average of all her gyrations keeps the needle wavering about the red N, then nothing can be too amiss.

I am excited and elated and yet feel secure. I have learnt all my lessons over the past fortnight, so have started this leg properly prepared. I am clad snugly in my large green cagoule, my fleece and my waterproof trousers. I have gardening gloves on my hands... not exactly *de rigeur* for the Riviera yachting set, but adequate for the prevention of blisters and cramp, though still with a tendency to leak indelible navy-blue dye all over one's hands. Ship's provisions consist of two Mars Bars and an apple. My trusty and beloved pith helmet is on my head: warm, broad of brim to prevent sunstroke, and sturdy enough to ward off any sudden blows from the boom should they occur.

Not that such mishaps are likely today. The wind is what every sailor prays for, coming straight on the beam from the north-east, balancing the boat beautifully and sending her along with the optimum speed and security. Yes, there is the occasional gust that sends a fine arrow-flight of spray into my eyes and face, to be wiped laughingly away. Yes, there is the odd rogue wave that catches us unawares, and dollops into the bilges a lump of sea water, there to slosh and swish about my shoes until I can bale it out again. But these are no more than the spice on the adventure, reassuring, friendly knocks to remind me that this is intrepid stuff, this is real, this is remarkable.

It is difficult to keep watching behind me so that I cannot appreciate the White Cliffs dwindling astern. In fact, I miss the moment of their final fading. One minute they are there, faded blue and hazy white. The next time I turn around, they are gone. I am out of sight of all land, ringed by the wide horizon, and there is nothing to show where England has vanished to nor that before me lies the vast Continent. I am at the very centre of a huge green-grey plate about five miles wide, and licked clean and empty of every living morsel but myself.

My moment's reverie is broken by a particularly wet slap in the face by a passing wave and a threatening shake of the irritable sail. What can the matter be? A glance at the compass shows me that the needle is pointing wide of its mark, and that I have allowed the boat to swing too far north and into the wind. I hastily correct her course, and settle down to concentrate. Now that I am out of sight of land, my sense of direction is wholly dependent on this frail red needle in its clear perspex case and I must watch it like a hawk. Soon, however, I discover that the direction of waves and wind are so regular that I can steer on the whole by ensuring that I am angled into each new wave correctly. So too, to get the maximum speed out of the sail, I have eased it off to a point where, let out any further, it would lose its taut curve and start to flap. Thus if I start heading too far north and into the wind, the leading edge of the sail will start bellying fretfully and I will know to ease away a little. Less and less must I keep glancing at the compass; more and more I feel like some seafarer of the Ancient World, steering by wind and water and the flight of birds overhead. This is the whale's way, the haunt of scaly Fastitocalon, the wine-dark sea of Odysseus.

It soon occurs to me that the sea really *is* rather empty, especially as this particular stretch is supposed to be the busiest shipping lane in the World. Not only should there be all the traffic steaming up and down the Channel, but surely there should have been a few cross-Channel craft by now. But no. Far, far off to the south is a tiny dot on the horizon that might just be a ship and there is a vaguer smudge ahead that might even be land, but of all else the sea is empty.

There are just me, my compass and the thrumming rigging. Actually, this thrumming has begun to baffle me a little. It has distinctly grown louder in the last few minutes. I can see where the bottom edge of the sail is vibrating tautly in the wind, making a sharp buzzing rattle, but it would also appear that the whole ship is emitting a deep throbbing roar. Can wind and water on tightly stretched stays and hollow timber produce such a sound? A sound that one could now almost call a snarl? I glance around again, scanning the horizon and the skies for any sign of some other craft that could be responsible, but there is nothing, nothing at all.

The snarl has begun to crescendo, and every rope and stay seems to be vibrating like a manic set of harp strings, with the whining roar echoing from all about, sea and sky and wooden hull. I am just beginning to wonder if this is what victims of the Bermuda Triangle witness shortly before being carried to their dooms, when a panicky glance over my shoulder reveals its source. There, just a mile from my dinghy where there had been a blank horizon merely a minute before, is a Sea Cat. In two minutes flat, it has hurtled past in a snarling cloud of spray and disappeared over the horizon ahead, leaving the sea as empty as it was before, but still with that noise reverberating from the sky upon every side. It also leaves me in a state of wide-eyed, stiff-backed sobriety, realising for the first time that day just what a precarious position I am in. The speed of these Sea Cats is deadly, and had I been in its direct course, there would have been no chance of being spotted in time to avoid a collision. I doubt whether the captain of such a demonically fast vessel would even be aware of hitting anything. As far as I can remember, there are another four or five similar craft due to make the crossing today, quite apart from the ones returning to Dover or leaving out of Ramsgate, and suddenly I feel keenly the aptness of the M25 analogy.

Still, there is nothing to be done but to keep sailing onward, and the sooner I get to the other side, the better. Meanwhile, that faintest of specks on the southern horizon has materialised into a large orange tanker churning its way up Channel, and I am able to see first-hand just how fast these ships move as well. When I first identify it as a ship, it seems to be virtually straight off my starboard bow and about four miles away. It will quite clearly pass behind me. Ten minutes later, and I am not quite so sure of this; it now appears to be very much closer and heading straight for me. After another five minutes of willing *Jack* to skip along a little faster and cross its path well ahead of it, it becomes apparent that far from slipping under its bow, I will be crossing its wake only when it is halfway to Rotterdam.

Meanwhile, the wind is growing brisker and the waves bigger, but nothing that *Jack* and I cannot handle. An hour ago now we passed a large green buoy and I guessed that it might be one of the ones I had seen earlier on a chart marking the shipping channel. I estimate that fairly soon we should be passing a buoy marking the further side of the three-mile-wide highway, and then we can start reasonably looking for signs of Calais.

An hour later, and I am puzzled by the failure of any buoy to appear. I have just had to dodge yet another tanker, a large rusty freighter with Cyrillic lettering on its hull, close enough to feel the temper of its wash, so am probably still in the main channel. I do not really know how fast *Jack de Crow* travels, but I would estimate about three or four miles per hour in this wind. I have been travelling almost five hours, I guess, and I really am expecting to see some signs of Europe by now. It is quite a large place, I believe.

Eventually, I see a mile ahead a large buoy and breathe a sigh of relief. I am more than halfway across. Beyond and to the right of it, I can also see yet another large ship moving northwards. Something strikes me as a little odd about the ship's motion – it would almost appear to be sailing backward, blunt end first as it drifts along the far horizon past the buoy in the foreground. And then, like Tweety-Bird in the cartoons, I find myself exclaiming out loud, "It *is*! It *is*! It *is* moving stern-first, naughty puddy-tat!" and wonder at the sheer irresponsibility of these foreign Russian-type freighters that not only steer outside the main shipping channel but try clever stunts like sailing backwards, all tanked up on vodka, no doubt, tut, tut.

It is only when I have left the buoy behind me and am approaching the backwards freighter that I discover another anomaly. It has a large anchor chain sloping at an angle into the sea. It is, in fact, at rest. As was the buoy, presumably. Urr…? Brain cogs whirr slowly. Synapses feebly kick-start into sluggish life. Dimly remembered trigonometry lessons float out of the past to prompt me. *If a sailing boat passes a buoy at three knots and the angle between the buoy, the boat and an anchored vessel has increased by ten degrees in four minutes, how fast is the tide carrying the boat?*

Tide? Again? Not out here surely. But a few minutes later, I have worked it out. There is indeed a tide, a current carrying me northward almost as fast as I can sail east-south-eastward. Already the buoy that I have left a mile behind me is in fact nearly a mile south of me as well. Despite all my care with the compass and keeping angled consistently into the wind and the waves, nothing that I have done could compensate for the strong current carrying me all this time *up* the Channel. That is why it has taken me so long to cross the main channel, why ships have sailed backwards against buoys in the foreground, and why… mercifully, I now realise… I have not been mown down by every Sea Cat and Cross-Channel Ferry out of Dover that day. They have been plying their direct route straight across between Dover and Calais, unhindered by this petty piece of matchwood that has pursued its own diagonal course out of harm's way.

For this unwitting mercy, I am grateful… and alive today… but it still leaves me with the problem of being adrift I know not where in the English Channel, and the hours of daylight shortening. That I have drifted north, I am now sure… but how far? What course must I now take to reach Calais? If I turn south now, will I be battling with a current too strong to make any headway against? Would it be better, perhaps to keep struggling eastward in the hope that I will come at least to some land, any land? I try picturing the map in my head, trying to remember what lies north of Calais. Dunkirk? Ostend? Den Haag?

Norway?

Resolutely, I turn south and hope for the best.

After only half-an-hour of sailing, steering an uneasy course somewhere between due south and south-east, I am in luck. There ahead of me and off to the left is a long dark smudge on the horizon. It is indistinct, but there seem to be several tall chimneys and blocks that could well be factories or the skyscrapers of Calais. (Does Calais have skyscrapers?) I steer towards the long, low mass, a feeling of relief sweeping over me. That could have been a disaster, I tell myself firmly, and it's only due to your usual good luck that...

...that...

'Calais' is near enough for me to see it clearly and has revealed itself as not the gateway to a continent but as yet another tanker, anchored in mid-Channel. It is *enormous*, about the size of Luxembourg in fact, but it is not land. My heart falls. How far have I come off course to discover this phantasm? Where now is Europe? Apart from the vast bulk of the ship, the horizon is utterly empty. I might as well be in the middle of the Atlantic Ocean.

With a certain grim resolution, I turn southward once more. The light has begun to take on that faint golden tint of late afternoon, flushing each wave with a gilded crest and making my scarlet sail glow warmly in the levelling rays of strong sunlight. It is a classic light, the sort of light used by Edward Hopper in his Cape Cod seascapes, side-lighting solitary lighthouses and seaside houses of whitewashed weatherboard, or throwing the long violet shadows of abandoned sandcastles across emptying beaches where each breaking comber glows emerald and aquamarine in a caught curl of colour. It is a light that heralds in end-of-the-day happiness, plod-home tiredness, supper-on-the-table contentment... and the coming of the night. Of this last aspect I am acutely conscious.

Another ten minutes later ushers in a new and promising streak of towered grey on the horizon, this time off to the east. Half-an-hour later, this too has resolved itself into the shape of a vast tanker, and I am beginning to despair. The sun is really quite definitely westering, and I am zigzagging around the open sea in a ten foot dinghy like a blowfly on a windowpane. I have by now lost any real sense of where Europe should be, and I realise that very soon I am going to have to do something slightly absurd. I am going to have to approach one of these tankers - there are now two or three anchored all around me – sail my tiny vessel up to the beetling iron cliff of its hull (somehow avoiding being dashed to pieces by the swell of waves on steel), and knock on the side to try and attract the attention of someone aboard. I will probably have to knock quite hard. What I will do once I have someone's attention, I am not quite sure. They will, after all, be some sixty feet above me and possibly Russian. Will they understand me when I call up in a tremulous voice, "*Er... excuse me. Sorry to bother you, but could you tell me the way to Calais?*"

"Er… Is This The Way To Calais?"

I have just made up my mind that this, unlikely though it seems, is my best option, and am carefully choosing the friendliest looking tanker, when I change my plan. For at this point, a flock of seagulls comes flying by. They are the first birds I have seen all day, and even in my present circumstances I am carried away by how lovely they are. I have always had a fondness for gulls. They seem to me to be perfect symbols for human beings, with their squabbling, rackety rowdiness and their gutter-picking scavenging... and yet I am always haunted when I hear far off their yearning, keening cry. It speaks of sorrow and salt distance and unattainable lands, as though even gulls have some wild and cliff-girt Eden that has been lost to them. My deepest dreams and profoundest stirrings have been prompted by gulls.

And more to the point, these gulls look purposeful. They are all flying in a neat flock and heading due south, even a little westward, and have about them the air of gulls who, after a hard day's fishing, are heading home for a quiet beer and a night in front of the telly. They also look distinctly French to me... something about the beaks, perhaps, or the careless tilt of their wings. In fact, I am sure of it. They are Calais gulls, and they are going home right now. Without a single sensible thought in my head, I turn my back on the tankers, and follow the seagulls across the empty waves.

And ten minutes later, Calais, unmistakable Calais, heaves in sight on the southern horizon.

That last run into Calais is splendid. The wind is now behind me, but not so much on my tail as to be precarious. The Edward Hopper light I can now enjoy to the full, knowing that within the hour I will be safely in harbour. Off to my left are what seem to be long dunes and empty stretches of shore, and for a moment I am tempted to abandon the idea of Calais Harbour and run ashore on the wide sandy beaches re-enacting my own private Dunkirk...but common sense and a keen appetite for beer and omelette prevail, and I keep my course.

Eventually, just as I round the great northern wall of the harbour, precisely the same thing happens to me that happened when I tried to enter Dover. A monstrous Cross-Channel ferry is emerging at full speed from the harbour just as another ferry is arriving. For one awful moment, I am caught like a tiny cork between the two steel chasm-walls of either ship. There is barely twenty feet on either side, and one or the other must have seen me, because there comes a booming foghorn blast from on high that threatens to overwhelm me with its sheer volume. But the moment passes and, once the wake has stopped throwing me carelessly about, I lower sail and row hard for the far pier. A few minutes later, I have slipped into a smaller inner harbour and tied up to the foot of a black and barnacle-covered ladder. The tide is ebbing, so I make sure that *Jack* is tethered on a long painter, and then climb wearily up to the pier top. It is six o'clock, I have been sailing for eight hours, and I have made it. I am in France.

(I do want to add here a long parenthesis. A year after this crossing, I happened to be back in Ellesmere visiting my friends, two of whom had moved into my old flat. While I was there, the phone rang and I could hear Matt explaining to whoever it was that, no, Sandy Mackinnon didn't live here anymore, but by chance, happened to be sitting right here at this moment. When I went to the phone, it was Wilf, of the Thames River Police. "Ah, Sandy!" he said. "So you're alive, thank goodness. I was worried!"

This puzzled me a little, especially as I had written him several postcards from Europe, starting with an immediate one from Calais to let him know of my safe crossing... and besides, wasn't his concern coming a little late in the day, more than a year on from my crossing?

"No, I know what you're thinking, but I just got back from a holiday to find in my pigeonhole a report about a chap who set out to cross the Channel in a Mirror Dinghy. The thing is, he's missing. His boat was found upside down mid-Channel, but no sign of him, poor chap. I just couldn't think of anyone else who'd do such a thing, and I thought it might be you attempting to come back or something. Clearly it's not, thank goodness."

Thank goodness indeed. Quite apart from the coincidence of Wilf tracking me down at my old address just when I happened to be there, and the kindness and concern he showed more than a year on which I found touching, I add this in to deter any reader from attempting the same thing... or at least to deter anyone from approaching the possibility in the same cavalier and foolhardy manner that I did. I am not writing this with any sense of conceit. It is of course tempting to revel in one's own recklessness, to boast of getting away with a daring stunt... but not if it leads to the death of anyone who has gained a false impression from these pages. Having done the trip once, and been extraordinarily lucky, I would never attempt it again. The main danger... and it is a real one... is the speed of those Sea Cats, and I suspect that our poor anonymous Mirror sailor fell foul of one of them. It was through sheer incompetent good fortune that I drifted so far north as to be out of their way, but even that route could not be regarded as safe. I do urge readers not to take my stupidity as a model for some spurious Quixotic adventure of their own.)

Despite the overwhelming sense of relief and achievement on having made it to Calais, there were still many things to be done and the usual frustrations afforded by the tidal waters. I went first to find some accommodation, carrying only my small day sack and leaving the rest of my gear in the dinghy, but when I returned an hour later to fetch it all - fresh clothes, toiletries, dry shoes and so on - I found that the ebbing tide had deposited *Jack* onto the harbour bed, and worse, onto two sharp lumps of rubble lying at the foot of the wall. There didn't appear to be any damage yet - she had clearly settled gently enough - but I also found when I clambered down the slimy ladder that this ended four feet or so above where *Jack* now lay. Ordinarily, this was no great distance to jump, but lying as she was, I knew that any attempt to climb aboard would surely impale the dinghy's keel on those pointy rocks. My dreams of a hot shower followed by climbing into clean, dry clothes were on hold until the tide floated *Jack* off the harbour bottom again. A quick calculation told me that this would not be until about midnight.

The other problem was that the number I had been given with which to ring the Coastguard was also in the dinghy, and equally unattainable. I had promised to let them know of my safe arrival, and if I were to leave it until midnight, they would no doubt already have had the rescue helicopters out looking for me... or at least sent out that seven-year-old in her Optimist for a quick look around. In lieu of a better plan, when I rang my long-suffering sister Maggie to let her know of my safe arrival I asked if she wouldn't mind doing me a small favour and phoning the Dover Coastguard to pass on the news. For those of you not fortunate enough to know my sister, you must understand that amongst her many saintly qualities there is a strongly held belief that one should not bother complete strangers with odd messages. For someone of my sister's shy and retiring disposition, ringing a strange man out of the blue and saying "*I'm so sorry to bother you, my brother asked me to tell you that he managed to sail his Mirror dinghy across to Calais safely today, does that make any sense to you, this is the right number, isn't it?*" is as awesomely embarrassing as requesting most other people to walk in on a Matins service at their local church wearing nothing but a pink feather boa and shouting "*The Piglets are coming!! The Piglets are coming!!*" during one of the quiet bits.

Nevertheless, Maggie agreed to do this, bless her, as well as ringing various other concerned family members around the World, gave me a good ticking off when I told her about the ferries, chuckled gratifyingly at the bit about the seagulls, and rang off. I then had nothing else to do but squelch around Calais in soggy shoes, find myself some supper while avoiding mussel-poisoning, and write thirty promised postcards to everybody who had helped me along the way so far.

One of those postcards would be to the Master-in-Charge of Sailing at Ellesmere College. Readers with long memories may recall a certain conversation on the sunny banks of Whitemere in North Shropshire almost a year previously, something involving the phrases '*borrow a dinghy*' and '*pick it up from wherever you get it to*' and the possibility of Gloucester, say. I felt that by crossing the Channel, I had somewhat extended the concept of borrowing beyond its normal limits, and now an explanation was due. Consequently, one of the postcards read something like this:

Dear Phil,
Note the post mark and the picture on reverse! Arrived safely, both I and Jack de Crow cheerful and intact. Eight hours crossing in good NE wind, clear skies, but rotten navigation. Failure to take northerly current

into account nearly had me landing in Denmark.
Lost Europe for a while there, but saved by passing
gulls.
Er... about the dinghy? Can we now regard that loan
as more like, say, ... um... a theft? Or will a £200 bribe
do it? Please advise.

                              Best wishes,

                         Sandy & Jack de Crow

With a cheque dispatched along with the postcard, I knew that my request
was more in the nature of a *fait accompli*, but trusted that Phil would understand,
and buy the Sailing Club a new Laser or something a little more up-to-date.
Meanwhile, the fugitive *Jack* and I were at liberty to make our way across
Europe, our debts settled and our hearts footloose and fancy-free. But for tonight,
there were another twenty-nine postcards to be getting on with, and that was a
lot of writing. It was clearly time to find an all-night laundrette, somewhere to sit
and wait for the tide to come back in.

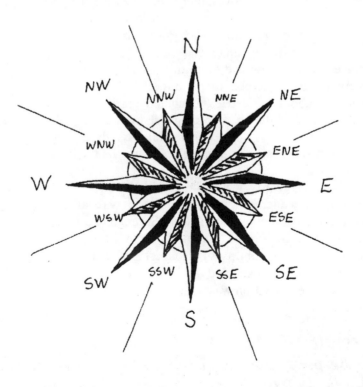

Dead Dogs and Englishmen...

'Spring, the sweet Spring, is the year's pleasant king;
Then blooms each thing, then maids dance in a ring,
Cold doth not sting, the pretty birds do sing,
Cuckoo, jug-jug, pu-we, to-witta-woo!

The palm and may make country houses gay,
Lambs frisk and play, the shepherds pipe all day,
And we hear aye birds tune this merry lay,
Cuckoo, jug-jug, pu-we, to-witta-woo!'

Thomas Nash – *Spring*

Now there starts a period of travelling that, as I look back upon it now, seems to be out of some enchanted story, some 18th Century Arcadian idyll, a heady mixture of Nymphs'n'Shepherds and Hey-Nonny-No, so much so that I fear to strain the reader's credulity. For it was May, the pleasant King of the Year, and I was in Picardy, whose very name conjures up for me - who can say why? - pictures of troubadours in patched coats, antique roses and dusty white roads, and the Queen of Flanders' daughter. And I was in a little boat, rowing by day and sleeping by night under warm stars, and living the life of a Scholar Gypsy.

It was not entirely a picnic, I must add. There were moments - whole days sometimes - of raw ugliness and back-straining frustration, but the transforming Philosopher's Stone of Memory has leached these things away and left only a sun-gilt tale with all the clarity and oddly tilted perspective of a mediaeval illuminated manuscript. How much is it now my duty to record the truth of those next few months, the routes taken, the mileage of the days, the locks ascended, the sights seen? Am I Baedeker or Thomas Cook? What is the reality of that strange voyage, gliding like a gilded barge through the woods and poppied fields of France? What will serve as a more telling landmark or fingerpost to the voyager who even now travels through the leafy echoes of these pages? That the distance from Cambrai to Douai is twenty-six kilometres? Or that the banks are lined with walnut trees and each one holds an echoing cuckoo amongst its broad and spicy leaves? I feel I must add to these notes the old maritime warning: *Not to be relied upon for navigational purposes.*

The first day out of Calais had me rowing through countryside in a surprisingly short space of time, out between banks frothing with cow-parsley in the hot May sunshine. Once clear of the last houses, a gentle breeze sprang up from behind and I was able to hoist my sail and ripple along sweetly, passing French fishermen, young and old, sitting on the banks dangling their lines in the green waters. French anglers seem to be more genial and complacent than their English counterparts; even when a momentary lapse in concentration sent me straight through a fishing line and had me dragging rod, stand and all into the canal, the owner merely grunted good humouredly, muttered 'De rien...'and set about retrieving his tackle. This went a long way to reassuring me of the friendliness of the natives – I had been assured at regular intervals from Shropshire to Kent that it was all very well relying on the goodwill of the English, but that anywhere beyond the Channel I was likely to meet with unabated hostility, surliness and unhealthy amounts of garlic. I was to find over the next few months that this was a pernicious lie... except about the garlic, and that I didn't mind at all.

As afternoon drew to evening I found myself rowing along an empty stretch of pastureland, where long rows of Monet poplars, mauve and smudgy and thin-stemmed, marched away in spindly avenues across the flat fields. I came at dusk to a small hamlet, tied up in a clump of nettles and went ashore to find that the nearest café was back in Calais. Just as I was standing there feeling a little cross with France for being so unhelpful, a man pulled up on his motorbike – middle-aged, pleasant-seeming and curious about the presence of *Jack*. In halting schoolboy French, I managed to explain what I was doing, and two minutes later found myself sitting on the back of his motorbike, arms wrapped around his chest, and tearing along a dirt track beside the canal. Soon we turned off into the courtyard of an airy, modern looking villa, the bike splutters to a halt, an ear-splitting scream rends the air and a magnificent peacock flaps to perch on a white railing. Alain, for that is the farmer's name, shows me inside and introduces me to Benedicte, his pretty wife, and their golden-haired three year old son, Aurelian. Is it just me, or is that the most beautiful name in the World?

It has not yet been made clear to me exactly why I am here. My poor level of French comprehension has led me to believe that Alain was taking me to a café where I could get supper. Now he explains that he has brought me home for supper and to stay the night if I wish. Which I do, yes, very much and merci, monsieur et madame... and God bless the snooty French, that's what I say. In discussion with Benedicte, I am able to say nothing that involves any more extensive vocabulary than *j'aime* and *beaucoup* and *bon*, and then a list of simple household goods remembered from Third Form French. At one stage, she asks me if I like ears, which has me floundering a little, until I remember that *oeufs* means eggs, not ears. (Yes, you see, that bad...) In my relief at sudden comprehension, I enthusiastically nod and gesticulate, admitting that, yes, I adore eggs, I love eggs, I have *un grand passion* for eggs... or at least compared to ears, to which I am largely indifferent. This results in a supper consisting of no less than five poached eggs for me alone, swimming in butter, lightly peppered and quite the best eggs I have ever tasted. They are all of different shapes and hues, ranging from bright sunny yellow to a bloody orange, and one of them has an alarmingly greenish tinge about the albumen. Hazarding a guess as to the origin of these wonderfully varied eggs, I dredge up some more vocabulary from *Parlez Français! Lesson Three: À la Campagne* and ask if these are eggs *de canard*, and eggs *d'oie*.

'*Oui*,' Alain and Benedicte respond, pleased with my progress. From outside in the dusk comes that ear-splitting scream, the scream of the foolish, jealous peacock in all his finery, angry that the Crow is here in the house being so well entertained.

Ah! I remember something. I may muddle eggs and ears, but I'm hot on French birds.

'*Et cet oeuf?*' I burble happily in my new-found tongue. '*Cet oeuf ,est-ce que c'est un oeuf du paôn?*' I ask, remembering with some pride the correct French word for peacock.

Alain and Benedicte glance at one another with some amused pity. '*Non, monsieur, ce n'est pas possible,*' Alain gently explains, and then mimes an instructive little biology lesson in the fact that peacocks, being male, are not generally relied upon for their egg-laying qualities. Outside, the cry of Pavo le Paôn has in it a note of derision. We change the subject.

In the morning, I am awakened from deep slumber by the smell and sizzle of breakfast being cooked, which turns out to be another three eggs, fried this time. What is the French word for 'cholesterol'? After breakfast, Alain offers to take me back on his bike to where I have left *Jack de Crow*, but just as I am leaving, Benedicte becomes terribly formal and presents me with a small red leather notebook. It is, she explains, for me to keep a journal of the voyage so that one day I might write a book, and it is this very notebook, much battered and travel-stained, that sits beside me now as I write.

Strange as it must seem, it had not occurred to me till then ever to write this trip up into an account. I suppose that, as I had originally intended merely to travel the length of the Severn in less than a fortnight, I had thought that a couple of letters home would suffice to cover the voyage. In fact, only now that I had actually crossed the Channel's Rubicon, was I committed to more than a few days ahead, and the possibility that such a trip might be worth eventually writing down. Whatever the case, I am immensely grateful to Alain and Benedicte for their spontaneous warmth and hospitality, my first taste of this in foreign parts, and one that was to set the pattern for the next three thousand miles... and their faith, as symbolised by their small gift, in the possibility of reaching the Black Sea.

The next four days were four days of blistering slog along canals made hideous by the hand of industry. For the most part, the Canal du Nord that I found myself joining runs between straight high banks of sloping concrete, often too high for me to see any of the surrounding countryside. What little view I did glimpse was of flat featureless fields, baking in the scorching sun, and, hazy in the distance, what at first I took to be the spires of some remote cathedral, but which turned out to be yet another pylon or factory chimney, the only lofty landmarks in all that wasteland.

Another interesting but disagreeable feature of the canals in that region was the number of drowned creatures bobbing in the murky waters. Many of these were small, anonymous creatures, unidentifiable in their distended forms - hairy, slimy balloons, bloated and swollen with gas - but there seemed to be an inordinate number of drowned dogs amongst the flotsam. I rowed gingerly through an ever increasing flotilla of these ghastly buoys - dachshunds, poodles, Alsatians, Rhodesian Ridgebacks - terrified that an incautious oar stroke might burst one of the carcasses and send it spurting and wheeee-ing foetidly about my head like a released balloon at some ghoulish party. At one stage my oar briefly scooped up what, to this day, I would swear was the corpse of a long dead platypus... though I do not pretend to guess how such a creature came to be in the Canal du Nord.

Another menace on the canals was the presence of the péniches, the large industrial barges that I here encountered for the first time, and was to become all too familiar with all the way to Romania. These are long grim barges of black iron, the freight-trains of the waterways, and ten times bigger than the little narrowboats of the English canals. Their speed was frightening, and there was no question of them slackening their pace for the likes of a little rowing boat. While on the major canals I was as out of place as a donkey cart on a motorway, and simply had to accept that here, the péniches had right of way at all times. As they steamed past, the wake, echoing and ricocheting from the steep concrete walls of the canal, would send my little dinghy pitching and tossing in a dredged-up stew of scummy water and dead spaniel, and leave me unable to row on for another ten minutes until the wash had subsided. It was slow progress I made in those four days, hot and frustrating and gritty for the most part.

Nevertheless, there were some memorable moments along the way. I remember passing a hot dusty field in which grazed, unmistakably, a zebra, calmly feeding amidst a ragged herd of brown horses. (How very French, I mused. Even the horses here wear black-and-white stripy tops.) A little while later, I pulled down a side arm into the sleepy town of Aire to find some lunch, and discovered that the town fountain runs a bright Curaçao blue, quite the least tasteful thing I have seen in a long time, but one that demonstrates the cheerfully independent thinking of the town's inhabitants. I siesta'd there beneath a shady willow tree in a park, setting the pattern for the next few months - it was simply too hot to row during the middle of the day.

Occasionally the concrete walls would give way to a pleasanter stretch of bank. One day, I rowed past an endless avenue of magnificent horse chestnut trees, each one laden with candles in pink and creamy-white, that threw welcome shadow over the waters. Here a man was exercising his German Shepherd by the novel method of pushing it into the canal, and whenever it tried to clamber out again pushing it back in with a stout stick. This continued unabated, despite the fact that after ten minutes the dog was clearly exhausted and beginning to founder. At one point the poor creature sensibly gave up on its master and swam after *Jack de Crow*, attempting to clamber aboard for a respite. I was on the point of hauling it into the dinghy and not releasing it until we had found it a new owner when the man whistled shrilly from beneath the chestnut trees and the dog launched itself loyally back into the water to swim to the bank. The last I saw of it, it was yet again being laughingly fended off from the bank by its master. Here perhaps was an explanation for the number of drowned dogs I had been bumping my way through, if this was standard French dog-exercising practice.

Other images I remember from that time. Several times I passed beneath high, ugly iron bridges which French youths climbed to dive and swim, naked or in tattered shorts, and as brown as gypsies. They lolled on the banks like young satyrs, smoking, laughing, or, perched casually upon some high platform, jeering and daring one another to clamber even higher amongst the grey girders, there to plummet into the soupy waters of the canal below. I envied them their hard brown bodies, their lean lack of shame, their careless bravado; they were the boys who ran mockingly away from me when I was ten, the ones I could not keep up with, who terrified and drew me but whose world of secret smoking-dens and swimming-holes was closed to me always. And even now they ignored me with that same enviable arrogance, or timed their plunging bomb-dives to miss my passing dinghy by inches, sending a fountain of stinking spray up behind me like a depth charge.

At St. Omer I encountered my first major lock. This is what is known as an *ascenseur* and was vast, unlike anything I had encountered in England. In fact, I thought for a minute that the canal had come to a dead end. Before me rose a giant wall of solid iron, black, riveted in plates and set between two vast concrete pillars on either side. Above this wall, three or four storeys up, was perched a little control tower office with green glass, far, far above me. I was just beginning to turn my dinghy around, thinking that perhaps I had missed the main turn off some miles back when the black water beneath me started welling and bubbling in alarming swirls, and I saw that the iron wall was beginning to rise. It was like something out of a James Bond movie where the arch-villain's hideout is revealed when a large section of the volcano side glides smoothly away. Once the gate had ascended fully, I found myself looking into a chasm between black walls, about three hundred metres long and sixty metres high. There was no sign of human life, nobody waving me in or shoo-ing me away, so I rowed gingerly into the canyon, my oar-clops setting up sinister echoes across the dark, slapping waters. Once I had rowed in about fifty yards, there was a low, loud humming all about me and I glanced back to see that the massive iron gate was sliding down in its grooves until the way was completely closed behind me. And before me. And on either side. This is the point where in all the best films, an Eastern European voice booms out over some hidden speaker, saying, *"Welcome, Mr. Bond! You have rowed into my little trap with less than your customary prudence. I am, I must confess, a little disappointed. Still, it will be all the more amusing to watch you die. Farewell, Mr. Bond."* Then water starts pouring in on all sides and the walls start closing in and James has to do something awfully clever with his watch, his belt and a shoelace to escape and go off and save the world.

Snapping back to reality, this is the point at which water *did* start pouring in on all sides... or at least began to well up from some unseen depths with frightening rapidity. After a first brief moment of panic, I was able to steady the boat and keep her balanced in the middle of the *ascenseur* and note that the massive bollards set in the walls at intervals were actually rising with the water. They were clearly not fixed, but attached to floating drums that rose or fell in long hollow vertical grooves in the lock walls. Thus a ship can tie up to a bollard and not fear being pulled under when the water rises, or left hanging when the water drops. I was soon to become extremely grateful to whomever devised these floating bollards; they made my experience in the biggest locks a safe and easy one, for, despite the vast quantities of water involved and the extraordinary rate of filling, there was actually very little turbulence in the lock itself and *Jack* rode up as sweetly as a gull on the tide. And each time the unseen evil mastermind apparently changed his mind and let me row out the other end unscathed.

For the first time since leaving London, I started sleeping aboard *Jack*. Now, each evening, I would take the planks from under the thwarts and lay them across the boat to form a flat platform or temporary decking. If the night was fine, that would be the full extent of my nightly preparations. If, however, I wished to protect myself from the dews and chills of the night, I would pull the tarpaulin tautly into place. A strip of Velcro at the mast end of the tarpaulin closed that end off completely. The stern end remained open to the night air, a triangle of starry darkness and river reflections beyond my muffled feet.

The whole idea was beautifully simple in design, but involved, I must admit, a clumsy set of manoeuvres to perform each night - several acres of tarpaulin and jamming planks having to be juggled into place within a tiny space without allowing any of it to drop overboard. At every possible opportunity, therefore, I took the much simpler option of finding a level piece of grass on the bank, spreading the tarpaulin out, and making my bed there, leaving *Jack* to her own devices.

It continued to be the right weather for sleeping out. Each day was hot and sunny, and the nights were cool, clear and starry. St. Omer one night, Bethune the next, and thence to Lens where I slept in a leafy park beneath an ash tree where a grey cuckoo chimed late into the starry evening, and recommenced at dawn. Then on to Douai after which I turned with some relief off the main Canal du Nord onto a quieter waterway that wriggled its way southwards to Cambrai and St. Quentin, and left behind the wash and churn of passing péniches and the stew of drowned canines.

Now there were pastures and woods and banks frothing over with cow-parsley and hawthorn and elder trees all in bloom, their umbels like heads of clotted cream on every bough. I pull into the pleasant little town of Cambrai later that afternoon and find to my surprise that there is another English boat there, a smart little narrowboat called *Oyster*, whose owners, Mike and Judy, kindly lend me a power drill to mend the pintel which yet again has begun to wobble loose. They also allow me to borrow their French waterways charts so that I can make a rough map of the canals for the next week or so. This is the barest sketch, a mere ink-black line with the names of locks, bridges, villages and towns, and the kilometres between them. Up until now I have been relying entirely on a map whose precise scale I cannot tell you, but if I point out that it shows the entire breadth of Europe from the West Coast of Ireland to the shores of the Caspian

Sea you will realise that it is hardly likely to mark post offices or canal side cafés popping up at about noonday for a spot of lunch.

Armed with my sketch map and a new confidence in my rowlocks, I wave goodbye to *Oyster* and set off mid-morning down the canal. The day is, yet again, horribly bright and cheery. Birds sing. May trees bloom. Frenchmen cycle by wearing berets and carrying bags of onions. Somewhere off to the left can be distinctly heard the ding-dong-hey-nonny-no of a country madrigal. There is nothing whatsoever, in fact, to prepare me for the uncanny and potentially fatal phenomenon that is about to ensue.

Somewhere south of Cambrai on that otherwise splendid May afternoon I came across the first lock on this stretch of the canal so far. Up until now, all the locks on the Canal du Nord had been fully manned giants but here, on this smaller pastoral waterway, the locks are quite homely, looking just like the little English locks I have been used to – willow-framed, fern-sprouting, sunny. I approached the lock gates with steady oar strokes, wondering as usual how long I would have to wait before the lock-keeper would spot me and start emptying the lock in order to permit my entry. The lights here, however, stayed resolutely red. I waited about fifteen minutes, idling on my oars, and then lost patience. I rowed up to the bank, tied up, and strode along to the lock to see what was happening. There was nobody there. Really! Typical French, I thought to myself without a shred of fairness. A small office stood on the sunny lock quay, but its door was locked and a glance through the windows showed me a rather dusty little room empty of all but an ancient swivel-chair, a stack of empty bottles and five or so dead flies on the sill. There was certainly no lock-keeper, and I did wonder rather hard about the bottles.

Puzzled, I explored the lock itself. This was empty, but the lower gates were fast shut and there seemed to be no winches or beams with which to open them. I found two iron rods that dangled down the sides of the lock, one blue, the other red, and obviously important. I tried to make out the signs painted in flaking paint on battered tin plates above them, but, apart from strongly suspecting that the red rod was there strictly for emergency purposes, I could not understand their function. Tentatively I jiggled the blue rod. Nothing happened. There was also nearby a large steel box with perforated holes in it and a few buttons which seemed to serve no obvious function apart from humming gently. It was all very puzzling.

I stood and pondered in the warm sunny stillness, wondering where the absent lock-keeper was. Suddenly a humming broke the silence, and I watched as the lower gates started to open of their own accord. Odd...And there downstream was my friendly *Oyster* chugging up the canal, approaching the lock in a steady glide. Hardly stopping to wonder where the phantom lock-keeper was that had spotted them coming, I raced back to my dinghy, cast off and rowed like a maddened windmill to follow *Oyster* into the cool moss-smelling depths of the lock. I was, I must confess, a little hurt by the fact that they chose to start closing the massive gates while I was still ten feet from them - it was not cool common sense but a little spurt of indignation that sent me driving forward between those black crushing jaws and allowed me to squeak through with mere inches to spare before they crunched shut with a damp and final thud.

Once in the lock, Mike and Judy were cordial enough, seeming to ignore the fact that the doors they had just attempted to slam in my face had come within a whisker of killing me; they seemed more anxious to talk about eyes and electronics and something else... to be honest, it was hard to hear as the water boomed and rushed in the echoing chasm of the filling lock.

Nevertheless, by the time the water level had risen to the top, there was now a splendid little breeze blowing from astern and I was in a forgiving mood. In fact, I was in a mood for a little showing-off. As we waited for the gates to open (where *was* that lock-keeper hidden?) I unbundled the sail and made ready to hoist it so that I could glide out of the lock in the wake of *Oyster* under full sail, a resplendent sight in anyone's book. The gates swung wide. *Oyster* churned out in a flurry of wake, and I hauled the sail to the masthead. The breeze blowing from behind caught the sail, swung it wide and *Jack de Crow* began to glide serenely along the lock, heading for the open gates. Mike and Judy, glancing back, applauded the fine sight and then turned their attention forward again to the bend ahead... so missed the next stage. The mainsheet, dragging along the quayside, neatly looped itself around a bollard and pulled the dinghy up with a jerk. She bumped heavily nose first into the concrete and was held fast for a minute while I tried to free her. By no means a disaster... but suddenly the gates ahead started swinging shut again. I was trapped in the lock, and yet again it seemed that a phantom lock-keeper was doing all he could to thwart my progress. By the time I had freed the straying loop of mainsheet from the bollard, the gates were firmly shut and I was locked in. *Oyster* had vanished around the bend ahead, and I was left alone cursing the momentary showing-off and the trap it had left me in.

Fortunately, just above the lock was a family of picnickers enjoying the warmth and the waterside, spread out on the grassy bank with bottles of wine and baguettes and lumps of white Brie. After a little while, I had worked out in my head enough French to go and ask for aid, and they were kindness itself in helping me unload *Jack*, de-rig her and drag her bodily over the gates and into the canal beyond... even feeling that after all that effort another glass of wine and a Brie sandwich all round would be in order. I rowed away from that lock feeling cheerily replete but still without the faintest clue as to the strange behaviour of the lock mechanism.

It took me four more similar experiences that day and the next before I finally understood. Let me explain.

The French locks are, as narrowboat owners throughout Europe will tell you, the best, the safest, the most convenient to be found anywhere between the North Sea and the Mediterranean. They all operate on a rather nifty electronic eye system. Any boat approaching a lock automatically activates an electronic eye set in the bank some fifty metres from the lock itself. Thus activated, the lock fills or empties (as appropriate) the gates open and the barge can glide serenely in, activating a second eye set near the gates as it does so. This second eye will, after a short time delay to allow safe entry, close the gates in a smooth and effortless glide, and it is at this point that the skipper of the boat must put down his morning paper and Sunday Supplement and actually do something to assist the process. This involves strolling along the deck to where those long iron rods run up the side of the lock wall. A quick tug on the blue one activates the whole next part of the process – the filling (or emptying) of the lock, the opening of the gates, and the stately glide out of the lock onto the next section of the canal. The departure of the barge serenely activates the eye at the open gates once more which closes both gates for safety and re-sets the whole system for the next boat to come along.

It is a system of the utmost simplicity, and should win several major design awards, possibly even a Nobel Peace Prize for nullifying the sort of bitter hatred that only canal-locks can engender in otherwise well adjusted couples. It was not, however, designed with *Jack de Crow* in mind. Being small and wooden, she was utterly unable to set off any of those electronic eyes so vital to the process, and that fact proved to be the source of a great deal of frustration and misery for me over the next three hundred miles.

It had been, of course, the steel bulk of *Oyster* that had activated the gate-opening-and-shutting of the last lock and not some secret spite on their part... nor the work of a hidden lock-keeper lurking in the loosestrife, and, though I felt a little better when I realised that, it didn't make my progress through the locks come any easier. I did find over the next few days that if I were very observant, I could detect the position of the electronic eye on the bank, and by rowing right up to it and waggling an oar in front of it for some time I was sometimes able to trigger it to open the gates for me and show a green come-along light. Then I would have to ensure that as I rowed into the lock itself, I triggered the second eye at the lock gates. Unfortunately, the only way of knowing whether one had triggered it off was to check that the lights had changed back to red. As the traffic lights were usually set ten feet or so back down the canal, I would have to row back to glance at the lights. If sure enough they *had* gone red, there would be only fifteen seconds before the gates started closing, and I would have to make a dash for the narrowly closing gap like some nautical version of Indiana Jones diving under the traditional tomb sliding door. It was all highly frustrating.

More often, however, all the oar waggling in the World would not trigger the eye, and I would be forced to land, climb up to the lock quay and make use of the large steel box with perforated holes that I had noticed earlier. This turned out to be a sort of phone. Into this, I would speak in very slow and painstaking French, and be countered by a babble of static-ridden, crackly French spoken extremely quickly of which I understood not one word. However, after a while, I learnt that such an exercise would invariably result in the appearance some fifteen minutes later of a small white Fiat hurtling along the narrow dusty track that verged the canal. Out of this would climb possibly the most patient man in the Solar System. This was the éclusier, the lock-keeper, whom over the next three days I disturbed some twenty-seven times in the same manner, and who seemed utterly unconcerned about having to yet again drive to yet another remote lock to manually operate for the thirteenth time that day the supposedly automated lock for the increasingly apologetic and grovelling Englishman in *le chapeau drôle*. He waved aside all my attempts to abase myself, smiled serenely into the middle distance, ushered me in and out of the lock at the appropriate moments and struck me altogether as an enormously contented soul.

None of this prepared me for the French canal tunnels, the first of which I encountered at Riqueval, lying halfway between Cambrai and St. Quentin. I had been told, for reasons that I did not fully understand at the time, that one could only go through at midday, so I spent the morning driving the dinghy along with oar strokes that made her skip across the water like that boat rowed by Obelix in the Asterix comics. To keep time, I sang *"Green Grow the Rashes, O!"* (*I'll sing you one, O!*) at full volume for five miles straight without stopping and arrived at the tunnel mouth ten minutes too late. The fact is that the Tunnel, at seven kilometres, is so long that boats must be towed through by a special electric tug, operating by hauling itself through along a submerged chain. As there is no ventilation in the tunnel, no combustion engines can be used. No, nor unpowered dinghies, so don't even ask... Or at least, that was the implication of the look that the guard gave me as I rowed up streaming with sweat and hoarse from singing. The next tow through? *A six heures et demi, m'sieur, ce soir.*

For the next six hours I sat in the shade of an old garden wall above the canal, dozing, writing letters and consuming a large hunk of strong salami and a bottle of beer that I had bought at the nearest shop some three kilometres away. Finally as the hot sun cooled to a fragrant afternoon, full of the smells of grass and horses and warm old brick, the electric tug hummed into sight and I joined the very tail of three other vessels all being towed through together. There had been much headshaking and Gallic muttering about the dangers of allowing such a small and frail boat to attempt the perils of the Riqueval Tunnel but, in the end, I had merrily flung my painter around the stern-post of the last boat and feigned smiling incomprehension at the serious talk going on above me. With a few even more Gallic shrugs, we were off.

There is a scene in *"The Voyage of the Dawn Treader"* where C.S. Lewis describes the children sailing into a mysterious island of darkness, which turns out to be the terrible land where dreams come true. Not daydreams, but dreams... and nightmares included. His description of the swift fading of the sunlit world, the draining away of colour and warmth and light, of sea-blues and sun-golds, to be replaced with chilly, black silence haunted me for many years. This was like that. Very soon, the arched end of the tunnel had dwindled to a tiny spot of greeny-white far behind, and then vanished altogether. Above me was the high curved roof of the tunnel, soot-black but smudged here and there with the dead white of some fungus or mould, and the odd glimmer of filmy water seeping through the brickwork. The passage of the boats through the tunnel was almost entirely silent, with only the swirl of water beneath the bows magnified and echoing into the darkness, and the steady hum of the electric boat some twenty yards ahead. After ten minutes of this chill and lonely voyage, strung on the end of a long line being towed through the darkness, I dug out my tin whistle and started playing. Sweet and pure the notes sounded as I played Crimond and 'Abide With Me', and all the hymns of sorrow and comfort that have ever been written. They echoed away on each quivering cadence and came ghostly back again from the curving walls in a mournful descant, and I understood why Orpheus took his lyre into the Underworld. In the darkness, music is the only light.

Two hours later we emerged into the waning light of day. The other vessels quickly detached themselves and hurried off down the canal, hoping, no doubt, to make St. Quentin before nightfall. The electric tug vanished back into the tunnel and I was left alone. I found that we had emerged into a steep defile where beech woods marched up on either bank in ominous ranks of grey pillars and interlacing boughs. Such beautiful trees usually, but here they closed in, crowding over the water, tangled blackberry brambles at their feet, and the sky a remote strip of primrose far above. So steep was that unnatural valley that no lingering light of day touched anything but the highest treetops on the further ridge; all was shadowed and chilly and beginning to grow damp with evening dew. My feelings of unease were confirmed when, mooring by the only bramble-free patch of canal side for the night, I discovered a large dead crow lying tumbled in the weeds. Its plumage was glossy still, shot with purple and green, but already there were white maggots in its empty eyes; both *Jack* and I slept ill that night under the satirical stars. It was the Valley of the Shadow of Death and I did not allow my thin piping to disturb the shadows that night.

Going through tunnels in a highly organised and well supervised way as described above is really quite safe, even for frail, unpowered dinghies. Where it gets intriguing is best illustrated by the sort of thing that happened the next morning. The steep beechwood defile continued unbroken for another five kilometres, an hour of windless rowing through a morning that promised to become stifling as the day wore on. There was a hint of thunder in the air and the sullen leaves hung lifeless on the beeches' coppery tracery. Then I came to the entrance of the next tunnel, the Tunnel de Lesdins. Here there was no sign of a tug, no guards, no notices – just a single set of lights showing green, and the small familiar grey box housing the electronic eye at the tunnel's mouth.

I stopped, pondering. What was meant to happen now? There was no evidence of a tug, so it seemed that one could not expect a tow. But how long was the tunnel? And what happened if I met another boat coming the other way? But no – surely if there was a green light at this end, there would be a red one at the other end? Of course it would be safe.

Two crows dropped heavily out of a nearby beech tree and flapped ponderously away down the gorge croaking. The water steamed in the hot morning sun. Flies danced.

...Unless...

Unless... that green light was simply left over from the last boat to go through from this end... and... think now... the system was now set equally biased to either end. It would wait for the first boat to enter in either direction, and only *then* trigger a red light at the other end to stop oncoming traffic. In which case... er?... I was still all right. I should stop shilly-shallying about and just go.

A large fish turned lazily in the scummy water, breaking the oppressive silence with a soft flop. The ripples spread sluggishly and died.

Yes.

Definitely.

...

Unless... hmmm. Unless, as was most likely from the experience of the past few days, my little wooden craft failed to trigger the electronic eye and so register my presence in the tunnel, in which case I was fair game to be turned to pâté by anything that came along in the next hour or so.

Hmmm. Still, humid silence.

There was nothing for it. I would just have to take a deep breath, trust to luck and row like blazes.

Cranking up Crimond, I entered the tunnel.

(*The Lord's my-y Shep-he-erd, I'll not want*;
He ma-akes me down to lie,
In pa-a-stures green, He lea-ea-deth me,
The qui-i-et wa-ters by.)

Black walls, white mould, seeping damp again, but this time, every hundred feet or so, a yellowing light bulb dimly illuminating the tunnel and, disconcertingly, the alarming state of the ceiling and rotting walls. I had preferred complete darkness. Every now and then there would sound above the hollow clop and creak of the oars the distant spatter of falling water. It would grow nearer and louder, and then suddenly I would be right under it, a freezing spate of water clattering in a chilly rope from some crack high above in the curved ceiling and drenching me for a second or two. Then the strong notes of Crimond or the Passion Chorale would go oddly squeaky for a brief moment and the lyrics would switch momentarily from the profound to the profane.

It was hard to estimate how long the tunnel was, or how fast I was moving through it. One of the major disadvantages of rowing as a means of propulsion is that one travels through life backwards, and I was for ever craning my neck around to see if in the darkness ahead there was that which I feared most – the steady light of an approaching barge. On the other hand, one of the major disadvantages of always craning one's neck around to look *ahead* in a rowing boat is that you never spot the barge rapidly approaching from *behind*.

Into The Darkness

Or at least I never spotted it until I heard it, and that, in my opinion, was jolly nearly too late. There it was, a yellow light coming up behind me and growing rapidly bigger all the time. I glanced around. The exit was in sight, but only just, a tiny half moon of daylight seemingly three hundred miles away. To my right was a concrete ledge that acted as a sort of rough towpath through the tunnel, but it had along it an ancient, rusted railing... and besides, was hardly wide enough to pull *Jack* onto even if I could have got her over the waist-high rail on my own. There was nothing for it but to row, and row, as they say, like buggery...

Sacred music of the more Lenten variety gave way to tunes considerably more robust. '*Onward, Christian Soldiers!*' was galloped through *accelerando*, Judas Maccabeus swelled its trumpet cadences in adrenaline-charged defiance of Death, but it was, I think, '*Tell out, my Soul!*' that finally sent me winging out of the darkness fifteen minutes later and into the welcome arms of the Day. I shot out of the tunnel mouth a mere ninety seconds ahead of the fifty foot barge that emerged at full, pâté-making speed behind me. A blast on its siren as it passed indicated that this was the first it had seen of me.

It did not look happy.

I, on the other hand, despite the shaking limbs, the sobbing breath and the sweat-stinging eyes, was just about ready for another verse of Crimond.

Et in Arcadia Ego

' *'Tis not through envy of thy happy lot,*
But being too happy in thy happiness, -
That thou, light-wingèd dryad of the trees,
In some melodious plot
Of beechen green and shadows numberless,
Singest of Summer in full-throated ease.'

John Keats – *Ode to a Nightingale*

In St. Quentin I visited a bookshop and the only two titles I could find were *The Tempest* and a book of Keats' poetry. These I bought, determined to defeat the boredom of rowing by learning some verse off by heart. As I rowed out of the town the next day, therefore, I had the Keats propped on the back thwart and started with *Ode to a Nightingale*. My heart aches, and a drowsy numbness pains my senses…

From St. Quentin onwards, the countryside becomes utterly lovely. I row through a Pre-Raphaelite landscape where the dog roses drop blushing petals on the water, where flag-irises stand in yellow fleur-de-lis along the banks, where elderflowers froth like heads of sparkling champagne on every bough and each new bend of the tranquil waterway cries out for a drowned Millais Ophelia or a Lady of Shalott swathed in tapestries aboard her tragic barge. The slow learning of the poem weaves its way into the landscape with an uncanny resonance. Here on either side are those very woods of 'beechen green and shadows numberless'; here sways 'Mid-May's eldest child, the coming musk rose, full of dewy wine, the murmurous haunts of flies on Summer's eves.' The woods on either side ring from morning to dusk with the maddening call of cuckoos and when I emerge from the cool shadows of the trees, I find fields scarlet with the silk of poppies, bright amongst the beards of green wheat as the blood of the millions who died here. For this is, of course, not far from the Somme, and Wilfred Owen whispers his sad anthems as a shadow to the jewelled colours of Keats.

I stopped at a village whose name I now forget the first night out of St. Quentin, and was met at the bank by two lads who were eager to help me tie up for the night and chat away in French. I responded to their friendliness by performing a few magic tricks. After the second trick, one of the boys muttered something to his companion and raced off into the village… a reaction that was a little disconcerting at first… until he returned some fifteen minutes later with seven other friends. Over the next half-hour, more and more people arrived, mostly young but a few adults as well, and I found myself doing more and more things with bits of rope, coins and my large red-and-white-spotty handkerchief, improvising the patter in appalling but vividly mimed French. The crowd on the bank, grown to about thirty, became so pressing that I had to retreat to the safe platform of my dinghy, standing there as it drifted on its mooring lines a few feet out into the canal, and thinking of Galilee. The comparison is arrogant in the extreme, I realise, but I will confess that nothing more miraculous occurred than the disappearance of a silk hanky - loaves and fishes were quite out of my league.

The next day I have marked down in my diary as Ascension Day, a public holiday in France, and I remember this as one of the pleasantest days of the whole trip. After a short sojourn on the Oise River, I turned onto the Canal de l'Oise à l'Aisne which started to rise rapidly through wooded hills and rolling vistas. Occasionally there was a distant glimpse of a turreted chateau through the trees, each tower topped with a dunce's cap of grey slate, and the locks I came to were set in immaculate gardens, walled entirely with neat stacks of firewood to waist height. To my great relief, the locks were permanently manned, and were calmly and quietly opened at my approach by the éclusier before he then went on with his firewood stacking or geranium potting. The world of electronic eyes had dropped behind, and I felt that I was rowing along the very borders of fairy tale – woodchoppers and white pigeons and little girls with baskets of goodies.

I remember seeing a huge brown hare lope slowly across an old bridge, where grass grew right across the crumbling arch and houndstongue sprouted in rich confusion from the yellow brickwork. At another stretch along the lonely canal, a trio of cyclists stood on the bank and waved cheerily as I glided past and an old fisherman suddenly hauled a great silver carp from the water in his fishing net. Each of these things seemed that day to have some hidden significance, as though they were the stages in some sort of treasure hunt or the figures in a Walter Crane illustration. I would not have been surprised to hear the hare speak or to find that the fish was offering three wishes for his release. The very air was fizzing.

At about midday, however, I failed to take the correct cue. Beneath yet another bridge, a figure hailed me from the shadows in rapid French as I rowed by. I could not make it out clearly at first as I passed from bright sunshine to cool darkness, but then I saw that it was an old man shabbily dressed and holding aloft a cider bottle. He was calling something indistinguishable and waving for me to pull into the bank beneath the bridge. A tramp asking for a light, perhaps? A merry tippler wishing to pass the time of day? Well, I was in the swing of rowing and had a good rhythm going so I called back something politely non-committal and kept oaring onwards. Again he called out something that sounded like a question, and waved his bottle and a plastic carrier bag in my direction, stumbling after me along the bank. I didn't understand the question, but I knew what my answer was, firm and dismissive. "*Non, non, monsieur. Merci, mais non! Au revoir!*"

At this, his face fell a little and he stopped chasing me along the towpath - only then did I see that he was accompanied by two other people, an old lady and a younger girl who had been standing out of sight on the bridge. All three had bikes, and the two women joined in a somewhat plaintive cry in my direction. Rather crossly, I resigned myself to Fate, slackened my strokes and turned the dinghy laboriously into the bank, guessing I was in for a tedious twenty minutes of halting questions and answers instead of getting the miles under my belt. My language skills are so poor that what would be a pleasure in England, I found an embarrassment here in France... and it is frustrating to have to stop and start all the time merely to satisfy the curiosity of idlers. It was only when I had crunched alongside the bank and waited for them all to come panting up did I recognise them as the cyclists I had seen two hours earlier. They proceeded to nod and smile and to my great embarrassment, handed me various items out of their carrier bag – two big packets of crisps, several long baguettes, a bag of bananas, a huge and smelly German sausage and four bottles of beer... and finally the bottle of cider that the old man had been waving at me. All this while, they were explaining in slow and pantomime French that they had seen me earlier, had been so enchanted by the sight of *Jack de Crow* that they had cycled off to a village some four miles away in order to buy me these items as a gift, and then spent the last hour trying to rediscover my whereabouts on the canal. How boorish I must have seemed trying to dismiss them with an irritated wave and a barely civil "*Non, non, merci!*" as I slogged on past. No wonder their kind and puzzled faces had fallen so. For the youngest-son-hero of my very own fairy tale, I had very nearly failed the first test of courtesy. That picnic kept me going for the next three days, but each mouthful was rightly flavoured with a tang of shame.

The kindness continued that night when I pulled into a little village in a clearing in a forest and moored up next to a tiny white cruiser. As I was preparing my awning for the night, the owner of the cruiser came down from his house across the grass and introduced himself as Jean-Philippe, and invited me to dinner with his wife Valerie and Lucat, their eleven year old son. Lucat – a keen naturalist – had been fascinated by my little flag depicting *Jack de Crow*, so in the course of the meal we discussed in halting French the differences between jackdaws and crows, ravens and rooks with the aid of a large and colourful bird-book. I have not mentioned this flag yet, though it was one of my prize possessions. It was sewn for me by my mother, and showed a heraldic crow on a yellow background holding in its bill a golden ruby ring, and it flew proudly from my stays to show the wind direction. The design was based on the Ellesmere College crest, depicting the Raven of St. Oswald holding his royal ring – the boat's home port was after all the Ellesmere College Sailing Club - but of course also represented the original Jack de Crow, my tame and thieving jackdaw of many years ago. So crow or raven or jackdaw, all these possibilities were earnestly explored over the steaming cassoulet and good red wine at Valerie's table.

At one point, my halting French caused some slight confusion. When asked by Jean-Philippe where or how I slept at night, I tried explaining about my sleeping arrangements and my mattress by replying, "*Ah, c'est bon! Ce n'est pas un problème. À nuit, je suis très confortable parce que... um... j'ai une ...what's the word!...une petite maîtresse.*"

It was only after hearing Valerie's stifled mirth that Jean-Philippe explained to me gently that the word I was probably looking for was *matelat*. My choice of '*maîtresse*' could well lead to some interesting questions. Where, for example, would she live during the day? (It was unfortunate that some weeks later, when I was asked the same question, I got it wrong again. Sure enough I remembered not to confuse *mattress* with *mistress*, but in casting around for that final key word I hit triumphantly upon '*matelot*'. The admission that what kept me happy and comfortable at night was the presence of my own little sailor boy left most people hurrying away determined not to enquire any further into my sleeping arrangements.)

Two days later, I sail into the city of Rheims, a long sought after goal. I arrive by chance right in the middle of a Waterways Festival, celebrating one hundred and fifty years of the French Canals. There are boats and barges of every description ploughing up and down the canal, banners hung out to welcome visitors from all over Europe and large marquees set up along the banks in the centre of the city by the little marina there. I am puzzled at first by the reaction of people to my little boat – cheers and waves from people all drinking champagne aboard a VIP ship, and blasts on the hooters and horns of each vessel that sails past. When I tie up at the marina, I am greeted by some chain-bedecked official who earnestly shakes my hand, kisses me on both cheeks and hands me a glass of champers, waving aside my questions about mooring fees. Proudly he calls some colleagues over and points excitedly at my two flags, the Union Jack and, oddly enough, the Jack de Crow pennant, and I explain that yes, I have come from England.

"Oui, oui, d'accord!" he cries, embracing me once more. "From England, oui, c'est vrai! And especially for our fête des canals, non? C'est magnifique!"

"Well, I didn't actually know about this festival but..." I start to reply.

"Non? Mais oui, monsieur, you play ze little jest on us, I zink. How can you not know about ze great festival of Rheims, and you wiz ze little flag of our great city flying oh so proud 'ere on ze brave little boat, non? Quel honneur, m'sieur, quel honneur!"

Only then do I look more carefully around me at the banners and pennants and flags that flutter and crack in the rising breeze. Every one of them bears a strangely familiar design: a heraldic black crow bearing in its bill a ruby ring. This, I find, is the ancient crest of the city, immortalised in Southey's poem, *The Jackdaw of Rheims*, telling the tale of the theft of the Cardinal's ruby ring by one of Jack de Crow's ancestors. It is clear that *Jack* and I are meant to be here.

In the next five days I sleep, eat crêpes, drink champagne, write letters, buy the *Daily Telegraph* to do the crossword, thoroughly spring clean the dinghy, re-varnish her flaking decks, enjoy the hospitality of various other skippers aboard their cruisers, and generally fail to visit any of the world-famous sights of the city.

I am a terrible tourist. I arrive in a place renowned for its architectural splendour, its mediaeval treasures, its fine food, its historic interest and all I want to do is sleep or read. I must admit that I did visit the cathedral, just out of a sense of loyalty to Jack's great-great-grandfather really, and rather enjoyed the great portal with its smiling angel, its gloomy angel, its rhinoceros and its goat gargoyles, and the beautiful jewelled Ship of St. Ursula in the Tau Palace. To be honest, the nicest thing that happened in Rheims occurred during a visit to a Chinese restaurant, actually. Many years ago I read a little known book by T.H.White called *The Master*, in which a Chinese gentleman called Blenkinsopp possesses an oriental tea set consisting of six cups and a jug. The little cups appear to be completely blank inside, but when water is poured into them the figure of a smiling lady appears in the bottom - the secret concerns a lens set in the bottom and relative refractive indices and so on; ask a physicist if you really want to know. The jug was even more extraordinary because when water was poured from it, it trilled and burbled and sang like a nightingale, again all to do with pipes and air-intake and vacuums. Now these two items sounded to me utterly enchanting and I had always wondered if such things were merely the creations of Mr. White's imagination or in fact really existed - and, if so, in what long-defunct museum of oriental curiosities. Imagine my delight when at the end of what was in fact a very good meal indeed the waiter brought out a small china cup and poured me a complimentary shot of saki. Suddenly there in the bottom of the cup a lady appeared, exquisitely painted, peeping coyly from behind a fan, and I nearly choked with excitement. To the astonished waiter, I poured out a babbled account of how for years I had been wondering about the existence of such a cup, and here was one at last. Before I knew it, he had whisked the cup away, returned with it clean, wrapped it in a napkin and presented it to me as a gift. Moreover, when I went to the counter to pay the bill, I noticed a highly decorated jug in green and blue and perched on the top a tiny ceramic nightingale.

"Is it...? Does it...?" I stuttered in excitement, and sure enough, it was and it did. The beaming manager filled it with water and let me pour it out into a glass and, just like the mythical Mr.Blenkinsopp's jug, it warbled and trilled and chug-chugged in rich, liquid tones while all the customers stopped and listened and smiled at the ecstatic Englishman in the hat and the big grin of sheer joy. Then, I tell you, more than ever seemed it rich to die, to cease upon the midnight with no pain while it was pouring forth its soul abroad...

The incident has a sequel. Several weeks later in Metz, in a shop specialising in oriental goods, I saw a set of four cups that looked suspiciously like the magical-vanishing-lady cups. I had in fact declined the waiter's kind offer of the gift back in Rheims – despite the seeming uniqueness of the present, the thought of transporting a delicate porcelain cup in my rucksack for the next six months had been too daunting – and I had been regretting my decision ever since. Now with the chance to obtain such cups again, I had an idea. It was my godson's birthday coming up shortly – Sam would be seven – and I thought that using that as an excuse, I could send him a cup in the post, a magical present from his magical (semi-) godfather. In fact, I would send a set of four cups, one for each of his family; himself, Mum, Dad and his ten-year-old sister Beth.

I hurried into the shop and asked the Chinese lady if the cups in the window were what I thought they were. *Yes*, I was assured, *nice lay-dee appear magic, chop chop, velly plittee lay-dee We have nice man too, he appear magic, velly han-som, velly proud.*

Ah, excellent, a lady each for Sam and his father, and two men for Beth and her mother then. They really were exquisite little things and so unusual. I could picture even now the first tea party in honour of Sam's birthday and it being explained to all the guests that Uncle Sandy always had *such* an interesting taste in presents, so magical, in fact, and that, oh look, there's the magic picture appearing now…

The Chinese lady was just about to wrap the fourth one in tissue paper when it struck me that I hadn't actually seen the hidden magical figures yet, and indeed was not likely to for some time, so I stopped her and asked whether she had any water to pour into the cups. With an audible sigh of impatience she bustled out to the back and returned with a teapot. Quickly she took two of the cups, placed them on the counter, poured in the water and the figures were revealed.

Fully.

Now I am no expert in oriental art, but it was immediately clear that these were not exactly willow pattern figures. In fact they were not delicate hand-painted figures at all but photographs, small but remarkably clear, and showed a well endowed young lady and an extremely excited young man concealing absolutely nothing from the camera. That the lady was 'velly prittee' was in no doubt, though her posture looked somewhat inelegant, and the young gentleman had every reason to be proud as the woman had claimed, but I suddenly felt that my reputation for sending unusual presents did not need this kind of support. Perhaps they could wait another fifteen years or so for Sam's stag night. I blushed like a beetroot, explained that I had changed my mind and, to the exasperated tutting of the Chinese woman behind me, I fled.

The next twelve days I must gallop through apace, or we will never reach our destination. On the navigational front, I travelled south-east out of Rheims on the Canal de l'Aisne à la Marne, passed through the Tunnel de Mont Billy and onwards to Châlon-sur-Marne, and from thence rowed up the Marne system to Vitry-le-Françoise. There I turned eastwards onto the narrow Saulx and rowed on through Sermaize, Bar-le-Duc and Ligny, climbing steeply to cross the last watershed before the long descent to the Rhine Valley. Here at the top of the range, I plunged through the last tunnel, that of Mauvage, and descended swiftly to Toul and… oh, sweet relief!… the head of the Moselle River. Those twelve days were spent almost entirely in rowing, entirely in fine weather, and entirely in a daze of beauty, Keats and birdsong. What else is there to say?

Well, the windmill I saw for starters, just outside Rheims, perched on a gentle rise striped with the green and golden rows of vines and cut through with the zigzag line of a white and dusty road.. Then there are the midday stops when the sun has grown too hot for rowing, and skinny-dipping in lonely bends of the River Saulx that runs alongside, just down the canal bank. Here the water is fast flowing and greeny-jade over amber gravel, and cool on the skin. I clamber out of the river naked and watchful, up banks of comfrey coarse as sandpaper on my bare skin, there to lie in deep beds of tickling vetch and loosestrife and dry out in the May sunshine. Sometimes on the outskirts of a village where I have just lunched on a metre-long sandwich and a bottle of beer I will pull my mattress out and spread it beneath a shady walnut tree and doze for an hour or so while the noonday sun declines to a tamer heat. There are tall poplars along the bank now, and every one of them is shedding a gentle snow-gale of drifting white down, making breathing a hazardous occupation. Soon the dinghy is full of fuzzy fluff and I am in danger of choking if I breathe incautiously. My lusty singing has to be muted to a close-lipped hum, but still the music continues to drive my oar strokes onwards.

There were days when I stopped rowing and rested, especially as in this part of the country the canals close on Sunday. Sundays also happened to be market-day in many of the little towns and villages, so I would spend a mildly irritable day moving from café to café in search of a quiet corner to sit and write letters while outside in the market squares there would burst a profusion of colour and noise and smells: roast chickens, flaky buttery pastries, barrows of peaches and nectarines and deep bloomy plums, racks of cheap gaudy clothes and everywhere the relentlessly cheery drone of accordion music over loudspeakers. Abba is very popular in that corner of France. They play it day and night, and any form of creative thought in the form of letter writing is effectively quashed. Add to this the presence of loud French youths in combination with those rattling, thumping table soccer games, and Sunday becomes the noisiest day of the week. I have become so accustomed to the silence and sweet birdsong of woods and meadows that my temper frays readily at the clatter of radio-tuned humanity enjoying itself. I have become a cantankerous hermit.

On the fourth day of June I come at last to the little town of Demanges, the last before the Tunnel de Mauvage. This will take me through the last great watershed before the land slopes gently away to the Moselle valley and thence to the Rhine. Here I am told, however that, 'le Directeur' will not permit me to row through the Tunnel... or be towed. Reluctantly, it is agreed that I may *walk* through the five kilometre tunnel hauling *Jack* behind me. How I will do this, I am not yet sure.

I go to sleep that night on the grass of a secluded bank by the canal, and watch a spider perfectly silhouetted shuttling to and fro between the mast-top and hoisted gaff. She is spinning an invisible web against the deepening blue sky, entrapping only the faint stars, diamonds in new constellations. Seeding grass stems nod above my head, likewise silhouetted, as delicate and finely drawn as a Chinese print. They stir and bend in the faintest of river breezes. In an ash tree nearby, there is a sudden rush and trill of song and with a jolt of my heart I realise that it is a nightingale. I have never heard one before, but my mind has been full of the very thought of them for years – not only the famed Keats but all the other niches in myth and literature that this beloved bird has held, not least that wisest of Hans Christian Andersen's tales, "The Emperor and the Nightingale." My heart, as I say, jolted, and for a few minutes I listened in rapture, carried away by the perfect poetry of the moment…

I must be honest though, and here I suppose is a good time to bring a few facts to the subject of nightingales and their song. The truth is, we've been had. I doubt very much whether Mr. Keats and company ever actually heard a specimen of the bird in full song, because if they had they would have searched around for some more suitable subject for their rapturous verses. True, the song starts off promisingly enough with a few very sweet, piercingly loud whistling notes, so loud in fact that it truly sounds as though the bird has been 'miked up', as they say in the world of theatre. But having got one's attention, so to speak, it then burbles into a hotchpotch of shrieks and shrill dithering, mixed with hisses, rusty creaks and catlike yowls, for all the world as though it is engaged in some life-and-death struggle with a tom cat and a couple of angry kettles. Just when you feel that the bird has lost the unequal struggle, out come a few rapidly-descending trills again, just to keep you from walking out and demanding a refund, but then it's straight back into the gravel-truck impersonations again. It is certainly not a beautiful, lyrical outpouring, a '*singing of Summer in full-throated ease,*' as Keats would have you believe. In fact, it is more like the Emperor's clockwork nightingale in the last stages of mechanical seizure. I suppose that it is the setting that lends the experience enchantment; the moonlit night and the '*melodious plot … Of beechen green and shadows numberless.*'

While we are in a mood for honesty let us dispel once and for all any fanciful notions we might be harbouring on the subject of dew. All very well bedecking with fairy jewels the morning cobwebs, glistening on cowslip leaves or lying in a pearly blanket over the back lawn, but no one ever seems to mention its chief quality, which is that it is simply damp. It is especially damp when you turn over at four in the morning and find that the other half of the pillow is sodden and clammy against your ear, that the foot of your sleeping bag is squelching with condensation and that the wretched nightingale is still hacking and wheezing away above you at full volume like an elderly squeeze box falling into a cement mixer.

The other thing about dew is that it comes accompanied by slugs. There was hardly a morning that I did not arise to find myself bedecked heavily with glistening black slugs, sitting stickily on my lower belly or insinuating themselves gently into my left ear, like some horrid moment out of a Peter Greenaway film. On one occasion I woke and was puzzled to find that despite all my attempts to open my eyes and greet the dawn they appeared to be gummed shut. A groping hand soon discovered the cause - a fat slug lying across each eyelid. Worse still were the snails which would crack with a soft and dreadful splitting noise if I inadvertently rolled over onto them in my sleep. The joys of outdoor sleeping, the stars, the night breezes, the smells of grass and water and cool air, were somewhat offset by these nature study details that rarely make it into the odes and sonnets of the Romantic Movement.

My morning routine falls into a steady pattern during this period of fine nights and hot days. I roll my mattress and sleeping bag - they are damp now, but will be dried later in the midday sun - I climb out of pyjamas and I slip into a comfortable old pair of bather shorts. I don't bother with a shirt or vest as already by seven o'clock it is warming up and I tend to row bare chested to show off the new tanned, demigod-like torso, having never had one before. I also make a point of shaving daily, sitting on an old stump by the canal. Why is shaving outdoors such a curiously intense pleasure? I always feel terribly colonial and adventurous when I do so, like some British officer in Zululand in the last century. Then to wake me up properly, a baler of river water over head and shoulders (bronzed, demigod-like shoulders, did I mention?) a last quick stow of odds and ends... and I'm off, gardening gloves on hands, stroking steadily through a light golden mist rising off the canal as the sun strengthens. All that is left to show that someone has spent the night there is a flattened patch of grass on the bank where even now, the crushed stems are slowly stretching and unbending and breathing again, and half-a-dozen bewildered slugs are heading slowly back to bed.

The Tunnel of Mauvage, through which I had been forbidden to row, proved to be only a minor challenge. The problem was to work out how to prevent *Jack* from bumping into the concrete tunnel wall as I hauled her on a rope along the walkway. I solved this after a short period of trial and error by attaching two lines to her, one to the bow and another to her stern. I then shipped her rudder, holding it at an angle with an elastic strap on the tiller so that she was constantly steering away from the towpath. Thus, though the bow rope was constantly pulling her *into* the bank, the rudder and the stern rope were urging her out again and between the two she kept a straight course about three feet out from the tunnel wall. All went more smoothly than I expected; I was able to set a reasonable pace, singing and whistling into the echoing, cavernous darkness while *Jack* glided along tamely beside me. I was going through a John Bunyan phase at the time, so I sang "To be a Pilgrim" heartily to the shadows to drive away the ghosts that inhabit such gloomy subterrains, seeing myself as a sort of Everyman trudging through an allegorical land. In those happy weeks Vales of Tears gave way to Meadows of Idleness, and Cities of Luxury offered tempting diversions to lead me off the Narrow Stony Way that was my one true path.

The other end of the Tunnel leads out into the green, warm, moist, grass-smelling world of daylight again, and I find myself at the head of a gentle valley, winding away into a blue distance. Beech and ash woods rise steeply on either side, but the valley floor is flat, consisting of sunny meadows and pastures, seeded with grasses and a thousand wildflowers – poppies, buttercups, scabious, lady's bedstraw, crosswort and valerian. Overhead, two crows flap heavily out of the wooded hillside and begin mobbing a large bird of prey soaring and tilting just above the treetops. Whatever is it? Too big for a kestrel, but not the heavy blunt build of a buzzard. Then I see the forked tail, the tapered scimitar wings, the glint of red bronze on its back... a red kite, no less. These are endangered in Britain and I have always longed to see one, and here right above me, mobbed by the rowdy crows is one at last, dodging and tilting and side-slipping to elude the thugs. In fact, for the next four hours I will have one or two of these princely birds above me, sometimes stooping to pluck something from the canal just behind me, sometimes circling effortlessly high over the valley; on one occasion staging an aerial battle with a rival kite for some morsel held in its talons.

I am falling in love with the dragonflies as well, miniature sun-fuelled helicopters. The females are bronze-green-gold with black stripes; the males are iridescent blue, kingfisher, sapphire, turquoise refracted in a glass splinter. There is a third type, though these may be damselflies; they are deep, deep satiny midnight-green, and their wings are of fine inky gauze. They look like rich jewelled assassins in mourning veils, and they are everywhere. And just as I am sitting idly dreaming in a lock, thinking about dragonflies and how helicopter-like they are, a real helicopter, blue as well, flies overhead, hovers, descends and lands just beyond the lock gates. What can they want? Could they be from the Voie Navigables de France sent to finally track down this pesky foreign dinghy and tell it just to stop it? Or perhaps some national news team come to interview this intrepid explorer for the nine o'clock news? Am I perhaps to be hauled away by the French Sûreté as a possible spy, attempting to sneak my way across France by the least likely route?

When I finally emerge from the emptied lock and paddle tentatively out, I am disappointed to find that they are simply a group of technicians from the Electricity Board and have no interest in me… although they all still make the usual noises of gruff French approval and admiration, such as '*Ooof*' and '*Bon Courage*' and '*Très fort, n'est-ce-pas?*', which indeed I get everywhere I go.

In the mid-afternoon a steady following wind springs up that clears all the canal to clean hard blue and silver. It is the first breeze in eight days, and the kite above me is making the most of it, angling and tilting on the wind's plane. Soon I too am tripping along with the sail out full, setting a wake rolling behind me, rocking the reeds and mats of crowsfoot and kingcups as I pass, and sending up the sandpipers in shrill panic at my approach. Mile after mile I sail as the valley widens out and flattens, past a small, ugly town, past a huge industrial quarry where no fewer than eight red kites wheel and squabble (I have become blasé about these birds now. Clearly if Mid-Wales wishes to re-establish this raptor as a common native species, it needs to create more industrial wasteland and rubbish dumps and do away with all that picturesque idyllic stuff, woods and unpronounceable valleys and so on), and so at last to a final three mile run along the curving flank of a hill high above a valley.

Here there is an aqueduct of grey stone and steel ahead, carrying the canal in one graceful span across the valley floor far below. I really should stop to take down my sail, but, throwing caution to the gods, I plough on regardless. As I sail onto the aqueduct the wind speed increases dramatically and I shoot across that dizzy height like a pea through a pea-shooter. Each side of the channel is nothing but a stone kerb, six inches high and less than a foot wide. This is all that separates me from a ninety foot drop to the river far below and I am ricocheting along this aerial watery tightrope at a speed sufficient to send my wake slopping over the rim in a great running wave. No sooner am I onto the aqueduct than I realise the folly of this sailing in the sky but can do nothing about it; I simply hang on and hold my breath. Two minutes later I am over, and am almost relieved to find myself in another wood, windless and still and safe. I cannot help wondering what a strange and splendid sight I must have made briefly to a distant watcher on the hillside: an aerial ship with scarlet sails, like *Skillibladir* in the old stories, sailing on the rainbow's bright arch to bring Frey home again from distant lands.

In Full Flight

And so at last to the end of this long day, the last hour spent rowing along a stifling stretch of canal to the little *halte fluviale* at Pagny. Here I discover that my funds have reduced to a few brassy centimes. It looks as though I may be going to bed supperless then, and I have not eaten all day. Overhead three kites are still wheeling, presumably scenting a potential dinner when they see one. If I faint from hunger now, I will wake up in small chewy morsels in some craggy nest somewhere. The evening air has become thundery and oppressive. I consider going for a cooling swim to take my mind off my hunger pangs, but seconds before plunging in I see two great pike floating on the surface and change my mind. With these reminders of the food chain in both water and sky, I will stick firmly to land and stay hungry. I am rescued, however, by a nice English couple on a gleaming white cruiser moored up to the pontoon. They invite me aboard for a long evening of pasta, garlic bread, red wine and talking about Buddhism, if I remember rightly. After the third bottle, having not eaten for twenty-four hours, I become a little hazy towards the end of the evening. The last thing I remember is falling asleep under a nearby apple tree while yet another bloody nightingale wheezes itself to death-by-emphysema overhead.

At three in the morning it begins to rain, a thin wetting drizzle, the first for almost three weeks now. The nightingale has fled, my head is thumping and tonight is my last night in the Arcadia of the French canal system. Farewell to ferny locks, to walnut trees, to midday snoozes on grassy banks. Farewell to cuckoo-echoing woods and elder-froth, to pleasant, sleepy *éclusiers*, to slugs and dew and the strange enchantment of Philomel beneath the stars.

Adieu! Adieu! Thy plaintive anthem fades
Past the near meadows, over the still stream,
Up the hill-side; and now 'tis buried deep
In the next valley-glades:
Was it a vision, or a waking dream?
Fled is that music: - Do I wake or sleep?

I sleep. And the next day I reach Toul and the start of the River Moselle.

Farewell to France

'Oh, sweet is thy current by town and by tower,
The green sunny vale and the dark linden bower;
Thy waves as they dimple smile back on the plain,
And Rhine, ancient river, thou'rt German again!'

Horace Wallace – *Ode on the Rhine's Returning into Germany from France.*

Toul is a pleasant town, ringed with wide grassy ramparts and a grey wall, a cathedral (closed), another tall-spired church with a name something like St. Gangrenous but it can't be, and a large central circle at the hub of the town which is bright with flowers and festive bunting for Mother's Day on the morrow. Here is where all the good folk of the town come to sit at pavement cafés and drink coffee or beer or drive around in circles honking madly at each other. There is a festival atmosphere about the place. There is cause to celebrate for me as well. From this point on, I will hopefully be doing less slogging along cramped and lock-ridden canals and more sailing on the broad and beautiful Moselle.

I spent a day in Toul catching up on letter writing, laundry and telephoning, and discovered several interesting things. One was that it is never a wise idea to attempt to wash any large waterproof item such as a mattress cover and then place it in a laundromat tumble-dryer and expect it or any of the accompanying garments to become even remotely dry. It retains several tons of water in its impermeable folds and simply sloshes around in the dryer like a cling-wrapped pond. The resulting lake on the laundromat floor resembled the Norfolk Broads after my third attempt to dry the mattress cover and would have hosted several small sailing regattas. Another interesting thing I discovered is that the French approach the sombre business of dispatching mortal remains with a cheerfully brutal sense of salesmanship. I noticed several funeral parlours in Toul and other French towns, but not a bit like those in England where a couple of faded lilies and a dusty urn comprise the full extent of window dressing. No, here the French seem to go all out to sell the idea of a snazzy funeral. These establishments all had huge plate glass windows, bold signs and customer parking. Some even had those gaudy plastic flags on string fluttering gaily over the pavement such as adorn used-car yards. Inside, they were set out like furniture showrooms, except that all the furniture here was of marble and granite, gleaming in black and gilt and marmoreal white. They came in all sizes and styles and each item bore an appropriate sign, usually with marked-down special-sales prices.

King-size Deluxe, Made to Last. 30% Off!!
Family Vault with Personalized Coffer Compartments. Buy Now, Save Later!
Economy Tomb with Revolving Wreath Accessories, Best Price in Town!
While-U-wait service. Gravestone Calligraphy!! You choose it, we hew it!!

If you weren't careful, you could be hustled into a suicide pact just to get the Twin Casket Special with extra cup-holders.

Another thing I discovered was how differently the French conduct their church services. I wandered into St. Gazelle's (or whatever) a third of the way through the mass to find some sort of special Confirmation Service taking place. At least, there were a lot of children processing, and all the girls were garlanded and dressed in spotless white with veils and bows and small white calfskin bibles clasped in their rosebud hands. In fact, through the clouds of incense and accompanied by the sweet ringing of silver bells, they all looked to my sober Anglican eyes as though they were going up to be sacrificed. At the back of the great church there was a constant coming and going of men and women who seemed quite happy to stand and chat and smoke behind the broad pillars. Occasionally they might stop to genuflect or join in one of the prayers offered by the diminutive priest a mile or so away in the sanctuary, but otherwise did not let the solemnities of the service interfere in any way with their animated conversation and sense of holiday jollity.

The next day I row the last mile of the canal system and onto the Moselle River, broad and blue and wind-ruffled, and am flying once more. I feel like a bird that has been cramped into a narrow cage for months whose very feathers are growing mouldy, suddenly released into the blue heavens. I pass various pretty villages, any of which would have given me a pleasant night's stop, but I am smitten with the need to make as much ground as I can possibly cover, so end up in a dreary industrial place called Dieulouard. Does *louard* mean "forsaken" by any chance? There is no cafeteria, no friendly bar, no riverside park but I sleep under a birch tree in a factory car park. There are no slugs that night, as even the slugs have taken against the town. The next day, however, I am more than compensated for by my arrival at Metz, possibly my favourite city on the entire journey.

Over the next few days, I was to find Metz utterly charming. This is due mainly I think to the mixture of architectures found nestling up to one another in the old town centre. From where the dinghy was moored, I could see up a pretty stretch of waterway beneath several low arched bridges of golden stone to a poplar'd island in midstream. Here stood the clustered steeples, towers and gables of the Temple Neuf, all in Germanic pencil-lead greys and steep lines rising out of the silver-point poplars that were set like lances about the isle. This was the first delight. But wandering up the steps into the centre of the town, I found myself in a maze of little alleys, shops and restaurants that suddenly opened into a broad square full of little tables, umbrellas, pigeons and tall gracious buildings in a wonderful honey-coloured stone.

Right at the top of the town dominating all below is the cathedral, nicknamed "The Lantern of God", as it claims to have more stained glass anywhere else in Europe… and surely that means the world as well, doesn't it? It too is built of this same lovely warm golden stone and is so clean in every pinnacled detail, every mullioned tracery, every honeycombed buttress, that it looks as though it were completed yesterday. The only clue to its age is that in places, beneath the innumerable gargoyles adorning its guttering or statues set high in their niches, a jade-green stain has seeped down, as pale and delicate as fern-shadow, from the bronze-green roof or the copper fittings, washing the stone in a blue-green blush.

I do not think I have ever seen a more beautiful building, inside and out. From within, the famous stained glass glows in rich, bright colours, "as are the tiger moth's deep damask'd wings... With twilight saints and dim emblazonings," each telling a legend or local story. The chief of these concerns a dragon, no less, that terrorised the town until it was tamed by St. Crispin, a 3rd Century bishop – (bishops clearly took a rather more militant role in the Diocese in those days. Which is worse, I wonder? Dragon-fire or Diocesan Sub-Committee minutes?) This same bishop also threw his episcopal ring away into the river (perhaps after a particularly tedious bout of chairing the Ecumenical Summit Advisory Board Meeting) but God returned it to him by the time-honoured delivery service employed by deities down through the ages – namely, in the stomach of a fish served up to the bishop for his supper.

There did not seem to be a corner of the city that was not transformed by a creative hand into something delightful, something surprising, something of quiet genius. Here a delicate wrought iron fountain played beneath a lime tree; there an unusual sundial of curving bronze and brass in a little plaza; down this alleyway, some art students were constructing a sculpture consisting simply of three hundred or so bentwood chairs rising in a vast and intricately tangled heap, and oddly beautiful with it. But best of all was an enormous trompe l'oeil mural painted on a great blank warehouse wall. This masterpiece depicted three muscular slaves in loin-cloths perched on a scaffolding plank right at the top of the wall hauling up with ropes a gigantic framed painting, a seascape of waves tumbling on a sandy shore with many gulls swooping and sweeping about the beach. It was a study in fresh sky-blues and sea-greens against the painted sandstone of the wall. However – a nice touch - some of the gulls were escaping out of the framed picture and gliding off against the wall and up past the heads of the three young Titans straining at the ropes above. So, a seascape? Or an e-scape? It was divine.

So beautiful was Metz – the locals pronounce it '*Mess*' by the way – that I broke a long-standing rule of mine and went and bought a camera. Now I never use a camera. I go off travelling, I come back with my head full of stories and pictures and all anybody asks me is whether I have any good photo shots. And if not, why not? The truth is, I have always been disappointed with photos, whether they are mine or those of more competent friends. I carry in my head such glowing pictures, such bright-limned memories, such marvels of colour and perspective and line that the reality of the photograph always comes as a rude shock. "*It was brighter than that, actually,*" I find myself explaining, "*and there weren't those power cables across the valley, as I remember.*" What seems to my memory the magical blue of distance turns to flat haze in a photo. Heights that seemed soaring, depths that seemed giddying, diminish to a confused lack of perspective in my palm. Besides, it is an attempt to sum up an experience in terms of a mere fifth of the senses available to us. I always realise with a jolt that where I thought I had been, say, revelling purely in the light dappling through beech leaves to fall in slanting shafts onto the copper-covered forest floor, in fact so much more had been going into making the experience – the cool air on a shirt damp with exertion, the plum-pudding smell of earth and deep leaf mould, the whine of evening gnats and the dying birdsong deeper into the woods… and the photo strips the experience of all these things, leaving only gloss and thumbprints.

There is also of course the dreadful effect of the camera's presence on the holiday itself. There is the old joke about the American couple who set off on a round-the-world trip toting their newest toy, a video camcorder. On returning three months later, they were asked by friends at the airport how the trip had been. Back came the reply, "We don't know, we haven't sat down to watch it yet." The lens is a little tyrannical god that quickly suppresses any spontaneous delight at a new sight in the interests of finding the best angle. The viewfinder becomes the cramped window into which all experience must fit to become valid. Is it possible to believe that we take Reality, select boxed moments and have them printed flat and miniaturised so that people can point to a fat folder of photos and say, in all earnestness, "This was my holiday"?

Nevertheless, I threw all these prejudices to one side, went and purchased a disposable camera and spent a miserable day walking around Metz all over again attempting to capture it on film. It was a day of indecision, frustration and futility and the eventual results confirmed all that I had ever thought about cameras and their value… or at least in the hands of an amateur like myself. I decided, not for the first time, that I would stick to recording my memories in writing, and let that suffice. No Gorgon's glassy eye would turn my living voyage to stone, not if I could help it.

The wind has changed into a stiff northerly straight on the nose, and I spend a weary day battling hard against it across the Messian plain before the breeze dies suddenly at dusk and I row on into a sunset like a furnace heaped with rubies, garnets, red gold and amethysts. I have exhausted most of the lesser odes and sonnets in my book of Keats, and have set myself to learn *The Eve of St. Agnes*, one of his more extravagant efforts. It will take me to Romania before I have all three-hundred-and-fifty-one lines down pat and abandon Keats forever more, but on this windless evening the rich words and jewelled imagery sustain me as I row.

And such times were, oddly enough, the happiest ones, the slow end-of-the-day rowing on the dark, mirrored water. My voice would suddenly sound out as resonant as polished cello wood as it sung the slow, steady songs that drove me onwards. The night air was cool, the river empty but for the herons and the plopping frogs and my old companions the stars glimmering out to listen to my music, and drown themselves in my liquid wake. We have not studied the causes of happiness enough, I suspect. It comes unawares, and treads on the shadow of toil and solitude, and has little to do with the tinny promises of pleasure. Or so the stars told me that night and many others to come on the long voyage downstream.

Thionville is the last city before leaving France. During the night a passing barge sends up such a heavy wash that my dinghy is violently thrown against the pontoon and the port rowlock is smashed into splinters… all this without waking me as I sleep aboard. The following morning, I fix it as best I can and set off once more before a good wind that allows me to sail rather than rely on my poor woodwork skills. As I draw near the border I think back with great fondness of the country I am about to leave; of its country villages shuttered and blistered against the noonday sun where pigeons peck and coo amongst scattered grain, and the yellow-dyed celandine grows up through rusting ploughs in deserted farmyards. Of the little bars where every single person to pass my table wishes me "Bon appetit!" in passing and the Gauloise-smoking, moustachioed, droopy-eyed patron offers me a glass of wine on the house for no apparent reason. Of the boucheries where can be purchased for a franc or two a freshly baked hot paté-en-croute to eat along with a cool furred peach in some shady park smelling of linden flowers. Of the boys who cycle alongside me on the towpath for miles and miles firing incomprehensible questions and then helping me to moor up at the day's end. Of the cuckoos and the nightingales and the poppies and the elderflowers and the kites and that zebra weeks ago... and even the moist company of the nightly bedtime slugs.

Of course, there are some negative aspects. Compared to your Full English Cooked, for example, the French *petit déjeuner* comes in a long way second. I could never really get used to those wretched breakfast croissants exploding into a thousand buttery flakes all over your lap and face and up your nostrils, and those little plastic tubs of bland jellied jam that you can never get your slippery, buttery fingers to peel open once you've dealt with the croissant grenade. And those huge bowls of tepid milky coffee forming a skin on it before you're a quarter way through it. And not a decent fried egg or cup of tea to be had for love or money, of course. And as for those ghastly French squat-toilets, how do people cope? Unless I am in any way anatomically abnormal, it would appear that you live in constant danger of toppling over backwards into the foetid pit.

It was in the midst of these musings on the strengths and weaknesses of French culture that I passed through the last lock in France and was promptly savaged by the only lock-keeper in the country who is not destined for canonisation. He came storming out of his cabin like an enraged minotaur, spitting with fury and saliva, and bellowing red-faced something of which I understood not one tiny bit. I started to explain that I was English and that my French was not frightfully good, and that if he would care to slow down a tad and stop spraying me with rabid spittle, I would do my best to fix whatever it was that was nettling him. I got as far as the word 'English' when he took a deep breath, turned a livid mulberry shade and notched up the fury to new heights. I still couldn't understand what I had done to upset him, but I'm sure I caught in there somewhere various references to B.S.E, Waterloo and the defeat at Agincourt, and the general theme of British arrogance and stupidity and rapaciousness down through the centuries. Just then, a big barge came along and so he had to let it through, and me along with it, and I rowed out the other side into Luxembourg with red-hot ears, shaking with tearful rage and suddenly happy to be leaving France behind me after all.

Luxembourg is just a nuisance really. With its own currency, its own stamps, its own telephone cards and a sort of Belgian dialect that didn't feature anywhere in Grade Eight French lessons, I spent the next two days fumbling with handfuls of the wrong sort of coins, attempting to unjam the wrong sort of telephone card from Luxembourgoise telephones, and failing to understand anything on the menu in several spotless, soulless restaurants where the prices, once converted mentally into French francs and then into pounds, left me reeling. Two days later I had to go through all the same rigmarole as I sailed out of Luxembourg and into Germany, while memories of that little country faded quickly away. All I was left with were impressions of neat, orderly towns, houses in a rather ugly pale grey and used-eraser pink, polite but worried people, and masses of paperwork to fill in at every turn. Oh! and, of course, a telephone card and a handful of Luxembourg coins useable nowhere else in the Solar System.

I sailed into Germany in a bad mood, due mainly to the fact that just as I passed under the massive Roman bridge at Trier a schoolboy spat from on high and scored a direct hit on my pith helmet. Due to the steepness and rockiness of the banks, I could not leap ashore and strangle him on the spot, so rowed furiously another two kilometres downstream to a mooring point, stomped around crankily for half-an-hour trying to find a sandwich and returned to the dinghy to find that my Union Jack had been stolen. Not a good introduction, I felt, to a country whose public relations with its neighbours in the past have been less than rosy.

Trier is the oldest town in Germany, and is famous for several Roman edifices, but I couldn't get terribly excited about Trier, I'm afraid. It rained hard while I was there, a warm greasy sort of rain, and the Porte Nigra, Trier's pride and joy when it comes to Roman remains, looked as sooty, dank and urine-stained as a Manchester railway viaduct. I ended up staying in the town for several days, but more out of a sense of listless boredom than for any other reason. I was cross and out-of-sorts, and eventually cheered myself up by digging out my tin whistle and doing what I had not done for seven years: street-busking. I added in some magic tricks, having to improvise the patter in a sort of pidgin German which I think was perhaps the most entertaining thing about the whole show, judging by the amused snorts from the passing Hausfraus and their kinder. Still, I managed to wring some sixty deutschmarks out of the local populace in a few hours, so began to feel that I was getting my own back for being robbed and spat upon on arrival. I played a good many old Vera Lynn favourites, and the theme from the Dambusters kept cropping up somehow…

Trier unsettled me somewhat, and I suppose I must confess to one extraordinary …for me at least… incident that in hindsight rather alarmed me. On my second night in Trier, flush with the takings from half a day's busking, I took myself off to an Irish pub for a few well earned pints of Guinness. I sat there attempting to look friendly and fascinating and the sort of chap that anyone would want to come over and chat to, and after an hour of utterly failing to attract any company at all, I fell back on an old pastime, which is to while away the hours solving maths problems; Fibonacci, this time, and the Golden Ratio, in case you're interested. As so often happens, within a minute of covering a paper napkin with equations and little triangles, half the bar were crowding around wanting to know what I was up to, and it turned out that all, including the barman, were keen amateur mathematicians and just dying to help out.

Well, one thing led to another, and an hour later I was deep in conversation with two Swedish chaps over yet another Guinness. I don't remember things too clearly, but I do remember that one of them looked exactly like a Scandinavian version of Oliver Hardy of Laurel and Hardy fame; twinkly little eyes in a dumpling face and a tiny toothbrush moustache of golden-white bristles - and a friendlier chap you cannot imagine. After a while, he pulled out a little tin of what looked like damp tea leaves, took a pinch, inserted it under his top lip, and carried on talking, though in slightly lisping tones. Fascinated, I asked what it was. He explained to me that it was *snus*, pronounced to rhyme with *moose*, and offered me some to try. Righty-ho, I thought, grabbed a wad and jammed it under my top lip, perfectly game to try anything so obviously cultural and 18th Century as this appeared to be. A minute later, my frontal lobes were tingling, my vision blurring in and out, and the room was doing a gentle dreamy dance around my grinning ears. Then there came an instantaneously sobering thought. I realised that I - I, Sandy Mackinnon – I, the cautious, clean-living, anti-drug schoolmaster who has never so much as put a cigarette within three feet of his mouth – had just made the classic error of ingesting some unknown substance offered to me by a bloke in a pub. There had been no element in my decision of risk or dare, no feeling of doing something out of character, no weighing up the rights and wrongs. I had just cheerfully accepted the proposal with rather less thought than if someone had said, "Go on, pick a card, any card." To this day I do not know what *snus* is, whether it is illegal or narcotic or hallucinogenic, or whether it is in fact a mild form of snuff partaken of by respectable Swedish grandpapas after supper in the midsummer twilight. But I am still frightened by how very easy it was for someone of my background and convictions to find themselves blithely trying substances of dubious provenance. I left Trier the next day with somewhat wider eyes than previously, and a slightly humbler opinion of my own boundless good sense. I had a feeling that as I continued into the heart of Germany and beyond I was going to need all the good sense I could get.

Temple Neuf, Metz

A Jollyboat in Germany

'Into the street the Piper stept,
Smiling first a little smile,
As if he knew what magic slept
In his quiet pipe the while;
Then, like a musical adept,
To blow his pipe his lips he wrinkled,
And green and blue his sharp eyes twinkled,
Like a candle-flame where salt is sprinkled...'

Robert Browning – *The Pied Piper of Hamelin*

From Trier onwards, the Moselle loops along its steep sided valley all the way down to Coblenz on the Rhine, and this stretch of river is perhaps the most beautiful part of the entire voyage from Wales to Romania. The gorge is so winding and sinuous here that often I find myself travelling twenty kilometres and ending up just one or two kilometres from where I had started, just across some high ridge or saddle. These valley walls are clothed on either side with terrace upon terrace of vineyards, all stripes of greeny-gold like young gooseberries, draped over the curves of each hill, and here and there in their midst a tiny shrine or chapel or crucifix, or a statue of the Virgin to bless the harvest. As the miles pass the hills become steeper and craggier, with great cliffs and buttresses of reddish sandstone breaking the terraces and looming over the water, but even here the vine rows straggle along the narrowest ledges, stringing along inaccessible ledges and filling gullies and ravines, so that it becomes impossible to guess at how the grapes are harvested without the aid of mountain-climbing equipment. At one point, in fact, I see flimsy ladders swarming up the cliff faces, seemingly as frail as willow sticks... and on some cliffs are painted giant sundials, presided over by yet another plaster Mary, watching the slow shadow tick around through the long summer days.

The very steepest crags are forested with pines and beechwoods and are invariably topped by a grim castle: sometimes complete and restored like a great gingerbread cuckoo clock, but more often just a ruinous tower like the stump of some black and rotting tooth. In the crook of each bend, a little fairytale town glides into sight - beamed houses, a tall onion-domed steeple, a gilded and painted Rathaus, a little pier for boats and a huddle of shops and high-gabled houses, all bright with window boxes of petunias and geraniums. Best of all though are the roses. Every house and café and gasthaus seems to cultivate these, great rambling trails and trellises of roses, usually deep carmine and smelling of heavenly wine, nodding over doorways, bending over cool stone archways, drooping down to kiss café tables, swarming up sunny walls. I keep stopping to smell them and thinking of all those Germanic fairy tales: Beauty and the Beast, Snow White and Rose Red, Rapunzel or a dozen other stories where to pluck the enchanted rose was to court disaster.

I didn't actually pick any, and disaster seemed to be steering clear on the whole. Unless you count of course the hailstorm that blew out of nowhere one afternoon, and in five seconds flat filled the world with a seething, icy, blinding roar. It stung my bare arms and legs, filled my boat with hailstones and sent me careering out of control down a river that had become a hissing white blistered maelstrom. I had just come out of a lock so fortunately had not yet raised my sail. Had I done so, I have no doubt that the suddenness and force of the wind would have snapped the mast like a matchstick. Even as it was, with the sail tightly furled, the wind was enough to drive me downstream for a few minutes as fast as though I were sailing in a good breeze under full sail. Then, as quickly as this vicious fist of hail and ice had struck, out came the sun and I spent a happy hour gently steaming and drying out as I sailed along in the warm afternoon.

Another near-disaster was due to the fact that the barrages on this stretch of the river were now serviced by two locks, one huge one for the great barges and pleasure cruisers, and one much smaller one for the likes of me. These narrow locks are plenty wide enough to take a rowing boat, but *not* a boat in the act of rowing; that is, with oars fully extended. This made rowing out of them a little tricky, and almost impossible when there was a strong breeze blowing in the opposite direction. In one particular lock, I spent a very messy, sweaty twenty minutes attempting with only one oar to scrabble my way out of the sheer-sided, slimy-walled lock against a contrary wind determined to keep me penned in for the night. I was terrified lest the automatic gates should begin to close after a particular time-interval and crush me like a flea in a closing encyclopaedia.

No disasters, as I say, but these challenges kept happening like a gentle tap on the shoulder by a smirking Fate, as if to say, "*Not getting too complacent, are we, dear boy, hmm? Good, good. Just checking. Carry on...*"

The fact is that, despite these minor hiccoughs, an astonishing question remains; namely, why isn't everyone else doing exactly as I am doing? For there is no doubt about it at all, that the very best, nay, the only way to be travelling down this particular river at this particular time of year is in a Mirror dinghy. It is the most perfect way of travelling known to mankind. When the sail is out full and I am propped up in the stern on cushions, feet up on the thwart, idly nudging the tiller with my elbow, why! I am the envy of the valley! Cyclists on dusty cycle tours clad in jaunty yellow baseball caps stumble to a halt and watch me breeze by, before wearily mounting their bone-hard saddles once more and attempting to catch up with their bronzed tour leader, thirty years younger and five miles ahead. Sweating workers high up on the terraced hillsides tying up vine tendrils suspend their twine and secateurs briefly to point and laugh and sigh. They are mere dots of bright colour on the green slopes, but I can tell even from here that they resume their hot work dreaming of sails and pith helmets and lands downstream. On gleaming cruise ships as they steam past, with their linen tablecloths and crystal souvenirs and scheduled stops for photo opportunities, wealthy American tourists from Detroit pause, a glass of overpriced Moselle to their lips; they loosen their collars a little as they contemplate diving in and joining me, to send later perhaps a brief postcard to their wives back home, saying, *"Gone to Black Sea. I'll explain later."* Or perhaps no note at all…

Some other nice details along the way – a trio of men in a little old boat catching eels in long stocking nets, all wriggly and silver and shining in the morning light; a moorhen's nest perched precariously on the anchor of a yellow work boat with seven speckled eggs inside it. One of the finest sights is of a curiously modern nature. At times small helicopters hover overhead, whizzing over the vine terraces and spraying them with pesticide. When they eject the spray, it curls up in streamers and curlicues and helices of gauzy mist, twirled by the turbulence of the rotors into something like those long flowing silky ribbons used by eastern dancing girls.

Approaching Cochem

I spent a night in a village purple with columbines and famous for an ancient stone carving of Romans rowing a ship full of wine barrels, and another in a weinkeller overhung by lime trees where nested a redstart, and so came to the jewel of the Moselle Valley – the fairytale town of Cochem. Here, Germanic fairytale architecture fountains into full flower. It is a mediaeval town of wood-carved gingerbread houses and steep alleyways o'ertopped by a castle from

Disneyland. In Cochem there is a little gilded town square where a fountain tinkles and a statue of St. Martin cuts his stone cloak in two for the beggar... who, incidentally is being somewhat carelessly trampled beneath the hooves of the good saint's horse. At certain hours, twenty bells in one of the carved gables chime out musical box tunes. The carvings on the gable ends of the Mayor's house are caricatures of the Mayor's chief rivals and tell an amusing story which I have now forgotten... as indeed I have forgotten the reason why in another part of the town, there is a statue of a goat being crushed in a wine-press. It cannot be an advertisement for the bouquet of the local wine, surely.

Cochem was so delightful that I decided to spend a few days here and, as in Trier, got out my little tin whistle, flung my pith helmet down in the main square by the fountain, and started playing. I half expected, as the sweet fluting notes echoed through the little gabled streets, to hear the patter and chatter, the squeaking and rustling and rumbling and roaring of half a million rats to come pouring out on every side, on their way down to the rolling river to perish. However, the only result was the occasional clink of a handful of deutschmarks being thrown hatward and, with that, I was content. There were many tourists in the town and at one stage, a large group of American tourists came panting into the town square following the strident voice and raised flag of a lady tour guide. Somewhat to my surprise, with the whole square to choose from, she strode over to within three feet of me and my tin whistle, and mustered her flock in ringing tones.

"Gazzer roundt, gazzer roundt, ladies und gentlemen, qvickly if you pleez. Here ve see ze marketplatz of Cochem viz ze byootiful fountain und all ze liddle carvings, ja?" As by this time I was pressed up to the fountain-coping by this lady's group and she was enunciating with vowels that would chop wood, I quickly brought my rendition of *Danny Boy* to an end and waited patiently for her to finish and move away. After some minutes in which I heard the amusing (but alas! now forgotten) story of the mayor and the gable ends, a further explanation of the significance of St. Martin and his cloak and various other tales rich in culture and history, the lady pointed at a far corner of the square and shooed her brood in that direction, urging them to "climb ze schteps und ve all meet at ze schloss, ja, gut!" Just as they were moving off, I decided to send them on their way with a few appropriate melodies, so struck up a medley consisting of *Yankee Doodle Dandy* and the *Dixie March*. There were a few smiles and some of the tourists threw some money my way, happy perhaps to hear something other than accordions and oom-pah-pah music, and played by someone who wasn't wearing lederhosen with a shaving brush stuck in his hat. Then, just as I was breaking into *The Yellow Rose of Texas*, back came the tour guide and over my playing, asked some rapid question in guttural German of which I only understood the word, 'deutschmarks.' Assuming that it was something like, "Oh, what beautiful playing, and how you enhance our little town with such sweet melodies, I'd like to reward you with some good German deutschmarks..." I nodded towards my pith helmet to indicate where she could throw a token of her appreciation. At that, she strode over to the hat, rummaged around in its depths, *extracted* three deutschmark coins and held them up to my nose before pocketing them.

"Zat," she explained sternly, "is for listening to my tour." And with a click of her heels and a curt nod, she strode off up the hill. Pipers still get short shrift in fairytale German towns, it would seem. Bring back the rats, I say...

The following day in Cochem was a Sunday, a blazing hot day of melted ice creams and red-faced Papas and cool tankards of beer... and the best pageant I have ever seen. This consisted of a mile-long parade of people, marching through the streets dressed in the costume of some bygone era in the town's history, from Rosenkavaliers to Little Tin Soldiers, from an entire Roman legion to a fat Bacchus twined in vine leaves and quaffing from a large goblet of wine. Unable to compete with all this splendour on the busking front, I took myself up to the fairytale castle on the hill, and on my way up saw running off down a side street ahead of me a naked man. That's all. I wish I could make something of this fact, turning it into some vital part of a story or drawing from it some fairytale connection... perhaps the poor fellow was a werewolf changed back to human form after a night's hunting before he could reach the safety of his home... or perhaps a pre-Bacchus member of the parade dressed as Homo Erectus who had lost his nerve when he realised exactly what costume - or lack of it - he was expected to appear in.

The castle was splendid, but somehow all the magic rubs off when you are following a guide who is carefully explaining everything as you go. I remember a lot of roses, balconies, carved wood and a lamp fashioned like a mermaid with a lucky red breastbone to rub and make a wish. I did so, wishing for a cooling breeze on the morrow to take me onward on the next stage of the voyage.

The following morning I wake to find that the mermaid's breastbone has granted me my wish. The sun is still bright but a cool breeze has sprung up from the south to bear me swiftly down stream to Coblenz and the mighty Rhine.

It takes me two more days to sail down to Coblenz. The scenery, though still pretty by any normal standards, has begun to fade a little in enchantment. I feel that I am sailing out of the Magic Kingdom and into the Twentieth Century again. Swifts scream in the sky, redstarts are quite common now and the riverside has become painted with the mauve of scabious and vetch, yellow St. John's Wort and the sinister greater celandine with its livid orange juice bleeding from snapped stems. These are the plants of high summer, of dusty dry highways, and the river itself is feeling like a country road drawing nearer and nearer to the big city of Coblenz and the highway of the Rhine.

In the last twenty miles or so, the wind gives out and the rowlock that was smashed by the wake of a passing barge in Thionville begins to present a serious problem. I will need to find a serious carpentry shop of some sort in Coblenz and get the whole thing mended. With almost every stroke of the oars, the timber of the gunwale is creaking and cracking, slowly working loose around the rowlock pin... and indeed as I look around, I realise how shabby poor *Jack de Crow* has become. Her foredeck is a mass of peeling blisters, the very prow has been battered into a crunch of splinters by some careless handling in a lock, and all in all she is looking a sorry sight.

I finally limped around the last bend, through a great grimy lock and beneath a blackened bridge thunderous with traffic and there a short way ahead lay the Rhine River. At this point I panicked. There on the right bank of the Moselle mouth was a sheer wall of concrete where huge white river cruisers were docking and departing with a flurry of propellers and hooters. On the left bank, however, seemed to be just a waste of black boulders and weeds fringing a wild sort of park. The chances of mooring a small dinghy safely seemed very small indeed. Furthermore, to carry on down and into the Rhine itself was out of the question. Not only was it impossibly busy with traffic, but it was also flowing in quite the wrong direction for me. I suspected that if I so much as ventured out into its main stream I would find myself in Holland by tea time.

The decision was taken out of my hands. A blast of a hooter behind me sent me scuttling across the Moselle to avoid the gleaming iceberg prow of a cruiser looming up behind me. A churning whirl of a reversing barge sent me zigzagging back to the left-hand bank of the river all too close to those black and bulky rocks. As I scooted along that inhospitable bank, I hauled desperately at the oars to avoid being washed onto the rocks by the wake of yet another passing leviathan... and the flimsy rowlock gave way with a splintery crunch. One heedless haul on the remaining oar sent me lurching towards the bank... just in time to see that here, blessed be to all the saints, there opened a narrow channel in the bank that led through to a quiet lagoon off the main river. With some relief I rowed gingerly in, and looked about me.

I was in a backwater, clearly by the regularity of its shape an artificial one, surrounded on almost four sides by steep banks topped by serious looking buildings. There was one pontoon on the northern bank where there was moored nothing but a rather rusty dredger. The whole place was rather dank and dark and was quite clearly not a public marina... but for now, it was the only place where I could moor with any degree of safety. Tying up alongside the dredger, I made myself presentable and climbed the steep flight of steps to the complex of buildings at the top. When I was halfway up my heart quailed. There at the top had appeared six or seven young men who were now staring down at me with grim and unfriendly expressions on their faces. They seemed to my eyes a somewhat rough crew, possibly inmates of a local Borstal, possibly crew members of a local stevedore gang. They all, to a man, seemed singularly unimpressed by the pith helmet and the jaunty little dinghy bobbing on their private pontoon. There were some unpleasant sounding jibes and jeers in my direction, and some consensus reached amongst them.

Just as they were preparing, I am sure, to charge down the steps and beat me senseless, a quiet voice floated down from above, and immediately the youths stopped, turned and skulked back off up the steps like a pack of hyenas that have been denied their carrion treat. They all vanished into a doorway and there was a figure approaching me down the steps, a quiet neat figure in a trim beard and grey eyes behind big glasses. Five minutes later I knew that yet again that strange brand of serendipity had come into play once more. For this was Peter Pohl, and I was in the grounds of the Coblenz Waterways Management Training College. Here trainee youths fresh from school were taught all the rudiments of commercial waterways maintenance, maritime law, river navigation, lock engineering, and, happily for me, boat repairs. Happier still was the fact that Peter was none other than the lecturer in boat building and himself a master carpenter. In fact, I had moored at the very brink of his workshop.

And yes, of course, he would be more than happy to help me fix that broken rowlock and, while he was about it, tidy up the varnish work and the prow and one or two other jobs that his practised eye immediately picked out as necessary. Meanwhile, I could moor here as long as I needed and use the staff shower at the top of the stairs if I so wished. And now, he had a class, so if I would excuse him...?

I was not terribly surprised actually. From the very first time that I had bumped fortuitously into Alan Snell at the very start of my voyage just in time to share a bottle of Chardonnay and have my rowlock fixed, I had got rather blasé about this sort of thing. The friendly boat shed in Bristol, the shipwreck at Whitstable and the wonderful Dunster family... it seemed that *Jack* no sooner had to snap off a vital part of her works than a friendly hand was reaching out of the sky with the offer of a drill, a bunch of screws and a load of expertise. My only concern was how to write all this home in letters to friends and family without stretching credulity to breaking point.

I stayed in Coblenz for four or five days, much of which is now a little blurry. I do remember seeing an elephant on a street corner, (honestly, I fed it a bun,) and having several overpriced crumbed things for dinner, but I failed to see any of the presumably marvellous things there are to see in Coblenz. On a more practical matter, I know that I managed to get a new Union Jack, or rather an ensign which is a red flag with the Union Jack in one corner. I also helped (or hindered) Peter as he went about mending *Jack* between his other duties; he not only fixed the rowlock but reinforced both rowlocks with metal strips. Then between us we sanded off all the peeling varnish and recoated the whole decking with several new coats, and did the same job for the rudder and centreboard. Finally, Peter replaced the little flat prow section that had been smashed earlier with a cut out sheet of perspex, screwing it tightly to the gunwales where they met to make the bow. By the time we had finished, *Jack de Crow* was looking as neat and shipshape as she had when we had sailed away from Whitstable. These repairs were to carry her all the way to the Black Sea without another hitch. Meanwhile, I explored Coblenz and, more importantly, investigated the possibility of getting up the Rhine to Mainz and the Main River.

I soon realised that I had made a fairly serious navigational error some weeks before. I could have continued along the French canals after Rheims and headed south-westward towards Strasbourg, hitting the Rhine further upstream. Then it would have been an easy matter to row with the current down to Mainz and the all important linking River Main that takes one over to the Danube. I had, however, been told that the prettiest section of the Rhine was the ninety or so kilometres *upstream* from Coblenz... and of course that the Moselle was not to be missed... so I had decided to come this way. What nobody had seen fit to add was that those scenic ninety kilometres of river were picturesque for a reason, namely that the waters poured between precipices and gorge walls with a ferocity against which even fully powered barges struggled to make headway.

Consequently, after my first glance at the rolling brown surge of the Rhine, I realised that I had to abandon any idle notion of making it under my own steam, and seek the aid of the local shipping. Peter had advised me that my best bet was to speak to Mick, the owner of the local *bunkerboot*, a sort of floating petrol and supply station for the industrial barges. He knew all the bargees and was in constant radio contact with them. The problem was finding him, as he moved around a lot, sometimes mooring in the Moselle mouth, but sometimes around in the main Rhine River. Once *Jack* was all fixed, I said my farewells and heartfelt thanks to Peter, and rowed off to find Mick on his *bunkerboot*. After some hot and fruitless oaring around in the Moselle mouth, I heard from a passing barge that he had moved over to the eastern bank of the Rhine and would be there for the next few days. There was nothing for it – I would have to risk the crossing of the Rhine. I confess I faced this challenge with considerably more trepidation than the crossing of the Channel, but I could see no way around it.

As soon as I hit the current of the Rhine, I knew that my fears were not ungrounded. Facing diagonally upstream, I pulled valiantly to haul myself across the five hundred yards or so to the opposite bank. Despite my cracking limbs and straining shoulders, I moved crabwise across and down the river so that eventually I ended up close under the eastern bank but some two hundred metres downstream from the confluence with the Moselle. Mercifully, I was not bothered with any major traffic. I think that every barge on the river was slewing wildly to avoid the idiot in midstream, but the effort and sweat in my eyes made me oblivious to all about me. Having reached the opposite bank, however, the real challenge began. I was now some seven hundred metres downstream from where the *bunkerboot* was moored, seven hundred metres of sheer bank fringed with large black breakwater rocks, with no place to tie up for a breather. Seven hundred metres does not sound very far... it didn't *look* very far... but I was now rowing full into the current of the largest river in Western Europe. Those seven hundred metres took me two hours. Much of the time, I seemed simply to be sitting perfectly still, just yards from the bank, gazing at the same park bench or litter bin for what seemed like an eternity. Then some extra effort on my part, or some mysterious slackening of the current would allow me to crawl forward a couple of yards, barely enough to be gazing at the upstream end of the same bench.

The only thing that kept me going through all this fruitless, neck-straining, heart-pounding exertion was the reaction of three old German men leaning on the riverside railing watching my agonies. I was, as ever, clad in my pith helmet, and along with the utter futility and lack of progress, was fully and happily conscious of the eccentric picture I was presenting. To this end, I kept grinning foolishly at the trio, and calling out things like, *Englische, ja!* and *Ich bin ein dumkopf, nein?* and other pidgin-German inanities, if only to let them realise that I was aware of my own folly and didn't mind if they wanted to break into howls of derisive laughter. They didn't. They didn't even flicker, not once in the whole hour I sat opposite them going nowhere. Their faces were set in a grim expression of stolid disapproval at the whole stupid enterprise. They radiated an unmistakable contempt for anyone inefficient enough, time wasting enough, to be engaged on such an un-Teutonic exercise. *Buy a motor, you stupid little foreigner*, they seemed to be saying. *Don't come here with your so-called charming English eccentricity and expect us to be impressed.* A sour glance at the hat. *Go home, in fact.*

I think it was as much a determination to see whether I could raise a smile in these three old cormorants as a desire not to be swept down to Rotterdam by nightfall that kept me straining away until I finally reached the *Bunkerboot*. There I introduced myself to Mick who immediately called the police. This threw me off my guard a little, until he explained that he had simply called them to give me a tow the remaining one hundred yards upstream to where there was a little pontoon at which I could safely moor for the night. For that, I was rather grateful, as indeed for the fact that he immediately got onto the radio to start organising a tow for me right up to Mainz. Before long he had contacted the owner of an industrial barge called *Barbara* who agreed to pick me up on Sunday morning and take me to Mainz. It was, with the help of Mick, that simple.

Meanwhile, the police had arrived and towed me up to the little bootshafn further upstream and handed me over to Wilhelm, the Hafnmeister. He, they assured me, would look after my every need. This I somewhat doubted. The grim unsmiling set of his jaw, the contemptuous iron in his eye and the loud sighs and tuts with which he accompanied every word of explanation by the police made my three aged friends from downstream look positively frisky and lambkin-like in their natures. I immediately decided that I was not going to sleep aboard *Jack* tonight... I made some excuse about the fumes of fresh varnish not being tolerable... and tentatively asked about any nearby accommodation. At this the Hafnmeister curtly rapped out, "Kom!" and strode off down the road without a further glance behind him. Fearing to disobey, I grabbed my pack and trotted off after him.

Soon my grim guide was charging up some steps cut into the cliff, and on reaching the top plunged into a tunnel carved into the rock. This looked nothing like a public thoroughfare – it seemed more like an abandoned mine working, dimly lit by a string of bare bulbs. Trying to catch my breath as I jogged after him, I was attempting to form in my mind a re-phrasing of my request for accommodation.

Nein, nein, mein Herr. Not the buried Nazi war treasures, please. Ein gasthaus, bitte.

But by the time I had worked this out, he was a distant silhouette further down the tunnel and I had perforce to hurry on after him. At times, this tunnel branched off in various directions and the Hafnmeister unerringly plunged down one or the other, calling back over his shoulder 'Kom! Raus! Raus!' while I stumbled on through the darkness after him, wondering where in Hades we were headed. Then it was up some more steps, round a few bends and out we emerged into a little wooded glade caught in a cleft of a hidden gorge. Here half hidden in hazel trees was the wheelhouse of an ancient chairlift – the cables soared up and out of sight overhead. My gloomy guide was engaged in some bad-tempered sounding altercation with the man in the wheelhouse.

"Um..." I started... "there seems to be some confusion, *mein Herr*. I was hoping to..." but he cut me off in mid-sentence.

" My English, it is not good. But here, my friend, are tickets for this gondola, and this will take you where it is you want. You will see, yes. Now, on the Sunday, this gondola it does not work so early, ja, so I come to pick you up in my car at six at the hour of the morning. This way, you will meet *Barbara* and be on your way."

When I started protesting at this unexpected display of generosity, he cut me short as curtly as ever.

"No, my friend. For me it is a great privilege. You, I think are some one special, no? I have been telling my friend here all about your travels. We are all very proud, ja?" At this the chairlift operator nodded vigorously. "So, I see you again on Sunday."

And at that he strode off into the tunnel and out of sight. As I took my seat on the chairlift, I reflected how badly I was doing at reading the Germanic manner... and, yet again, how extraordinarily kind people were.

I still didn't know where I was headed, but as the chair soared up and out of the little gorge, I saw that I was heading for the top of a very steep cliff surmounted by a vast wall of orangey-sandy stone. In this there was a great gate and it was at this gate that the chairlift gently deposited me. This was, it seemed, the local Youth Hostel. As I wandered a little awestruck in through the great arched gateway, I found myself on a huge terrace of reddish stone whose further edge was some fifty yards away. Here there was a low balustrade and beyond that, nothing could be seen but sky. On reaching the balustrade and looking over I found myself looking straight down to the Rhine far, far below and just beyond it the great equestrian statue that sits at the confluence of the Moselle and the Rhine, known as the Corner of Germany. From that vantage point, I was looking straight up the Moselle directly opposite, and could even fancy in my mind's eye seeing it winding away into its enchanted valley to Cochem and beyond. As a view, it was stunning.

The next day, I spent a final aimless day in Coblenz attempting to write and do a little busking. This was going splendidly until a small group of children arrived. This consisted of a seven year old girl and her three younger brothers. They were, I suppose, delightful in their own waif-like way, and I was at first rather touched when they started dancing to one of my livelier jigs and people stopped to look on and smile. It was like Browning's lines:

Out came the children running.
All the little boys and girls,
With rosy cheeks and flaxen curls,
And sparkling eyes and teeth like pearls,
Tripping and skipping, ran merrily after
The wonderful music with shouting and laughter.

When fifteen minutes later, however, they were still performing enthusiastically at each new tune, it started to become embarrassing. They took it upon themselves to pass the hat around to spectators despite my pleas not to, and when they all simultaneously started playing at being puppy dogs and sitting up and begging, the good folk of Coblenz shot me a collective dirty look and turned away. It looked for all the world as though I had my own children out humiliating themselves on the street performing - the fact that the urchins looked none too clean or well shod just served to outrage the passing populace further. In vain did I try to shoo them away in non-existent German. That excited their histrionic talents further, and the oldest of them actually came and hugged my knees and burst into tears, begging me, I think, not to send her back to the laboratory. Eventually, spotting a police officer who was strolling nearer with business in his eyes, I fled.

The next morning I am up early and row down a little way to meet *Barbara* and her crew at the *Bunkerboot*. After various trials, we finally de-rig *Jack*, hoist her up on such a short towline that her nose is resting right up against *Barbara*'s stern rail and only *Jack*'s transom is in the water. In other words, she is nearly vertical. Then, after heartfelt thanks to Wilhelm and Mick, we are off. The crew of *Barbara* consists of a German steersman, the Belgian skipper and his ox-like but amiable son, and a wretched black dog that keeps trying to bite me. I only know the name of the dog which is Wulf, appropriately. After it defecates in a mustard-coloured smear all over my bundled mast and sail, I take it by the collar and throw it overboard. Well, no, I don't, but I would very much like to. The Captain and crew are kind enough but my German and Belgian are not as polished as, say your average slug's, and as there are only a limited number of shades of meaning you can get across with a fixed grin and a nod I soon retire up to the bow of the barge and play my tin whistle. As the bow is several miles from the wheelhouse at the stern, I don't think I am in any danger of disturbing their concentration.

For this I am grateful. The current is so strong along this stretch of the river that steersmen have to be extremely skilled in their job. Barges approaching from upstream seem to hurtle towards you, slewing their way across the water, sometimes seeming to turn almost broadside on as they sweep downstream around a tight bend. On the other hand, barges like ours churning their way upstream hardly seem to move against the current, although it races by in torrents and frequently pours over the low gunwales. The scenery is itself pretty distracting. Here the river races through a broad gorge for mile after mile sprinkled with the usual Christmas decoration clutter of gilded castles and cuckoo-clock towers. Soon we passed beneath the fabled Lorelei Rock; not, as I had imagined, a siren-topped rock in midstream, but a tall promontory of cliffs around which the Rhine sweeps in a fierce bend. As we passed it I thought at first I was dreaming, or transported back into the Wagnerian legends, for it seemed that I could hear the low sexy song of the Lorelei herself. Then a further golden cadence fell from the high cliffs above me and glancing up I saw the sudden flash of sun on brass. It was a French horn player, who, I gathered later, goes there every Sunday to play on the pinnacle, busking, no doubt, far from the reach of urchin children intent on adoption.

This stretch of the Rhine is a sight that retired couples from all over the world pay a fortune to come and see, safely aboard one of the many gleaming river cruisers that ply their trade here. It is one of the great scenic trips of Europe. Unforgivably, once past the Lorelei Rock I slept through most of it. The ox-like son had shown me the forecabin right in the bows and indicated that I could make myself at home there if I wished. There is nothing quite so cosy as the forecabin of a Rhine barge. It is dim, it is warm, it is slightly stuffy and smelling of blankets and rope. The whole thing is vibrating and humming soporifically and the only other noise is the endlessly comforting swirl and chuckle of water sluicing by an inch from your ear. I kicked off my shoes, lay down for a few minutes and woke up seven hours later some ten miles up the River Main.

We had lost the German steersman somewhere along the way, but the skipper and his son calmly suggested I stay aboard for the night. It was too late to unhitch *Jack* now, and, besides, there would be nowhere to stay on the banks, the skipper explained in mime and gestures. Meanwhile, Young Albert, as the son was called, was cooking supper for us – a first, I was told - and he, Old Albert as he was known, would carry on steering. Perhaps I would like a beer?

And so it was settled. Supper was an extraordinary affair, consisting as it did of burnt fried potato, burnt fried egg, burnt fried bread and what I think was burnt fried liver which I usually hate but which had been rendered entirely edible by the simple expedient of reducing it to carbon. Nevertheless, we managed to communicate a little between us, and I found that the old magic tricks went down well... considerably better, suggested Old Albert with a scornful look at Young Albert, than the supper.

And then to bed, and then to bed, and another eight hours of warm, humming sleep while the Alberts took it in turn to steer the *Barbara* all through the summer night up the River Main and into the heartland of Old Germany.

In the morning I find that we have passed Frankfurt and are now some fifty-three kilometres up the Main (pronounced to sound like *mine*, by the way) approaching Mulheim Lock. Here Albert and Albert bid me farewell, wish me luck, refuse to take any payment and set me adrift. It is an overcast morning but there is a gentle breeze blowing from astern, so I re-rig the mast, set sail and am soon on my way upstream to Hanau. It is here that I intend to stop voyaging for a while. My sister Maggie has just completed her Ph.D. in Edinburgh and the Graduation Ceremony is coming up soon. To this end, my parents have flown all the way from Australia to Scotland, and it seems too good an opportunity to miss. Besides, I am tired. Tired of rowing, tired of Keats, tired of feeling foreign and inadequate about the history and architecture of the places I am passing through, but most of all, tired of my own company.

At Hanau there is a Waterways Maintenance Yard. It is without the slightest feelings of surprise that I find there three cheerful workmen who have clearly been sitting round waiting for me to turn up so that they can have the pleasure of hauling my boat out of the water on a little crane, empty her, store all the rigging in a dry shed, turn her upside down under a tarpaulin, and promise to keep her safely for whenever …if ever… I return.

I do what Odysseus could never do, what no great traveller permits himself. I catch a bus to Frankfurt, a train to Holland, a plane to Birmingham and I hitch to Ellesmere. Within thirty hours I am back to where the whole voyage began ten months before. And frankly, I'm ready for a break.

Contrary Currents and Kindness

'Does the road wind uphill all the way?
Yes, to the very end.
Will the journey take the whole long day?
From morn to night, my friend.'

Christina Rossetti – *Up-Hill*

"I have always relied on the kindness of strangers."

Tennessee Williams – *A Streetcar Named Desire*

After my three weeks back in Britain, the trip back to Frankfurt was beset by all the usual problems of modern travel, starting when I mistook the correct ferry terminal at Dover and missed the crossing. I had to stay an extra night there, realising that all the carefully arranged train connections through to Frankfurt would now be awry. As I sat in my cramped little B&B room in Dover that night, I couldn't help thinking how much easier the whole crossing is in a Mirror Dinghy of one's own.

Over the three weeks away, I had made some firm decisions. I had been appalled to note how much money I had been getting through as I travelled, but, when I stopped to consider, it was hardly surprising. Too many nights I had tied up, looked at the awning and the planks lying ready to be put into place. Then I had said to myself, "Not tonight, Josephine," and gone off guiltily to find myself a gasthaus or auberge for the night. The fact was that I was not doing this whole adventure lark properly.

But all that, I said to myself, was about to change. I vowed to myself that I would from now on sleep aboard *Jack* every night, no matter what the weather or how much the thought of hot showers and clean sheets appealed. Likewise, I would shun the lure of cafés and restaurants and discover the delights of a bread roll and a hunk of cheese eaten in the open air… and perhaps a bottle of beer as the occasional treat. As for money, the use of my Visa Card would be strictly rationed. From now on, I was on a budget.

It was a pity therefore that I arrived back just at the start of a stretch of grey rainy days, cold dripping nights, and dull scenery to boot. For three days I slogged up a river whose contrary current was far stronger than I had anticipated, sluggishly hauling between endless banks of silver-grey osiers and dreary willows that hemmed me in and blocked the view on either side. It rained most of the time, a thin wetting rain that soaked through my cagoule and trickled down my face so that, my hands occupied with the oars, I would have to keep licking the tickly drops off my face. At times when the rain cleared, it did so only to make way for strong contrary winds that had me hauling the sail up in hope, but taking it down again ten minutes later as I realised the impossibility of tacking into the wind against the current and without a jib. Finally, those three or four weeks in Britain had reduced me to flab again and I was hard pressed to travel more than fifteen kilometres a day... as compared to the fifty or so kilometres I had been making on the Moselle.

Still, I stuck doggedly to my new regime and my new budget, forcing myself to sleep aboard each night, although the rain seeped in under the awning and dampened my sleeping bag and pillow. So too I stuck to one meal a day, usually a bread roll and some salami that I bought from villages along the way... though on the dampest night, I confess to trudging off to a nearby bistro and drinking a very small bowl of hot minestrone. In a perverse sort of way, I actually enjoyed this Spartan life. I didn't sing as I rowed, I didn't recite poetry, I didn't think thoughts or talk to myself, or do anything. I just became all grim and morose and silent and dour. I went to bed, woke up, rowed, ate a bread roll, rowed some more and went to bed again. I don't think I actually spoke or exchanged glances with anyone else for three or four days... a bit of a record for me actually.

And then, just as I was settling into my role as curmudgeonly hermit, the World glanced around, noticed me, and said, "Oh, stop moping, Sandy!" and handed me about three hundred nice things on a plate to snap me out of it. Things like a red squirrel scampering along the bank, a spiral maze painted outside a village church, an elder hedge to dry my clothes on, a skinny-dip from a little secluded beach of red sand, a daffy girl called Meg with broken teeth who proposed marriage to me as she pursued me along the bank (unconnected, I think with the skinny-dipping), an ice cream bought as a special reward to myself for persevering with the stoicism and a whole host of other things. Those days... and in particular that ice cream... did teach me just how often we indulge ourselves purely out of habit before any real need or desire has arisen. We do this so often that, like the citizens of Huxley's *Brave New World*, we forget what it is even to feel a need... let alone the pleasure of satisfying it. We eat before we are hungry, we drink before we are thirsty, we amuse ourselves before we ever feel boredom... and slowly go numb inside. Our insides turn into the spiritual equivalent of pâté de foie gras.

The World has clearly also decided that I am no longer to be left on my own. Just after Miltenberg, at about two in the afternoon, two motor cruisers come by, *Mistral* and *Carpe Diem*. The skipper of *Mistral* offers me a tow, and, heartily sick as I am of rowing against the current, I accept with alacrity. This leads that evening to an invitation to dinner on the riverbank with the two families aboard each boat: Ute, Mannfried and their thirteen year old son Florian, and their friends from *Carpe Diem*, Claudia, Ralph and Mario, the same age as Florian. Florian is thin, jittery and slightly goofy with curiously topaz coloured hair while Mario is plump, dark and intellectual and I expect gets picked last in team sports. I am to get to know both quite well over the next few days. Also moored up along the bank at that village is *Barbara* and I am able to buy a bottle of wine to take to Big Albert and Little Albert as an overdue thank you present for the tow up the Rhine. They offer me supper... the smell of blackening fat is already in the air ... but I beat a hasty retreat to the company of my new friends and join them for their nightly custom. This is to drink one kirsch liqueur for every lock they have been through that day, calling out 'schleuse!' ('*lock!*') each time they down a drink. After my self-imposed abstinence from both drink and talk, my tongue is loosened as never before, and before long we are old friends. That night, poor Florian is turfed out of his bunk to go and sleep with Mario and I am given Florian's bunk. Outside, it has begun to drizzle again, but for tonight at least my pillow remains dry all night long.

As I went further and further up the Main, this kindness of strangers reached almost bizarre proportions. Take the village of Himmelstadt, for example. After watching me moor for the night at the lock, the fat lock-keeper comes down from his concrete tower personally to urge me to take myself along to a nearby bistro, the ancient and renowned Himmelkeller. I have finished the last of my somewhat dry bread, so off I trot, thinking that perhaps I might treat myself to a bowl of soup. The place is quite crowded but no sooner am I in the door than the kellermeister comes and welcomes me warmly, and starts introducing me around to all the other guests sitting at the long oak tables, proudly proclaiming me as a 'famous globetrotter.' It appears that the fat lock-keeper has rung ahead to warn the host of my imminent arrival. As I sit and eat my humble bread and soup, I am bombarded with questions by the other guests, which I try to answer as best I can. The soup finished, I am rising to go when the host appears with a huge plate of sausages swimming in leeks, carrots and white wine. Slightly alarmed, I try to explain that I did not order this and there must be some mistake. "No, no," pipe up a quiet couple sitting at a corner table a little distance away. "We did. We ordered it for you, and of course, we will pay for it. It is a speciality of this region. Do you like it?"

Well, yes, I do, thank you very much, how kind. But a lot later, when I go to pay the bill for the soup and the several beers I have had, the host says, "No, no. This is paid for."

"The sausages, yes, but surely not..."

"Yes, all of it," explain the couple in the corner. "You are our guest tonight. Perhaps if you reach the Black Sea, you will write us a letter." His name is Engelberht, which means 'bright angel', and as the village of Himmelstadt means 'heavenly place', I suppose I should have expected no less.

To top the whole evening off, the host presents me with a complimentary bottle of the local wine to take with me, a pale greeny-gold wine to remind me, as he said, of the good folk of Himmelstadt. I staggered back to the lock that night reeling with bemusement at all this unsolicited kindness.

The following day, several locks up the river, I am told firmly by the keeper there that I must stop there and wait. For what? But the keeper's English is not up to explaining the reason for my enforced wait. As I sit in my dinghy, a cold host of thoughts creep over me. Could it be that I had misunderstood the business with the bill last night? Had I walked away from the weinkeller wrongly assuming that the bottle of wine was a gift and now half of Himmelstadt were after me as a thieving opportunist? Had the German Waterways Authorities finally caught up with the fact that I was traversing their country without a licence? Did I actually need one?

Finally the mystery was solved. A very sweet young lady with clear grey eyes turned up with a microphone and a tape recorder, explained that she was from Radio Bavaria, and asked if I would mind giving an interview. She had been pursuing me all morning up the river but had kept missing me, until she had managed to get hold of the lock-keeper and arrange for me to be stopped. And how did she know of my existence? My jolly fat lock-keeper of the night before had been busy on the telephone proclaiming my exploits to the world.

That evening I find myself tying up at the pontoon of the Wurzburg Marina. There is a beautiful old bridge here with fourteen statues of various warrior bishops and florid princes perched along each balustrade as though about to leap off the bridge and end it all in the deep green waters below. *Mistral* and *Carpe Diem* are moored just up the river and I join them for a last 'schleusen-schnapps' session. As we have each been through a different number of locks that day, we resolve the difficulty of how many shots to down by the simple method of adding together the number of locks we've *both* been through that day… and so finish off the bottle. The local marina staff have heard the Radio Bavaria interview that afternoon, and give me free run of the clubhouse, so I sleep on the floor on my mattress that night after a welcome hot shower. The good fortune is holding, it seems.

The following day is spent shopping with the boys for a German edition of *The Hobbit* and a set of Tarot Cards (about which apparently last night's schnapps session has had me slurrily spouting forth) and, feeling that if I hang around any longer I will be invited to stay till Christmas, I force myself to part from these two families and their great kindness and row on up the river alone. They will turn back the next day and make the long winding trip down to Mainz. I set off just as the hot afternoon is dimming off to a cooler gold, and five or six miles up the river come to a little backwater set in the left-hand bank. The sun is just setting and *Jack* and I are nowhere near a town or village. This suits my mood; after the good company and generosity over the last few days, I feel that I want to re-capture the illusion at least of the wandering solitary life.

The place where I have stopped is pleasant enough, a sandy bay backed by a lonely field and a little promontory with a scattering of ash trees between the backwater and the main river. For an hour I have the place to myself, but after that a family arrive to camp. I am not sorry. My need for melancholy solitude has evaporated in about ten minutes since landing. Helmut, the skinny, dark-haired father lights a little campfire on the promontory while his three or four children play about in and out of the firelit shadows. There are three boys and a girl, a little pale thing quite unlike the other sturdy boys. Helmut invites me to join them around the fire and I do so gladly, sharing between us some sausages and cheese on toasted bread, chatting about hang-gliding and mountain-climbing. While we speak, some small creature, a water rat or vole, creeps right in about our boots and steals crumbs from the very edges of the embers. At some point, I ask the name of the children and Helmut tells me the three boys' names. "And the girl?" I ask.

"The girl?" replies Helmut in some surprise. "But she is not mine. I thought she was your little girl..."

When we call the children over out of the shadows, the girl has vanished. The boys have been playing with her but no, they do not know where she has come from or where she has gone to. Perhaps she is a wood-child or a river-daughter...

Later that night, after the others have gone off to their tents, I sit for a while by the glowing embers of the fire looking out over the river. The moon is full and makes little bright stabs of silver on the satin-black water with every fish-rise. The night is warm and the air full of white moths, and the dark night-river world seems suddenly full of enchantment. In fact it is a night for Wandering Aengus.

I went out to the hazel wood
Because a fire was in my head,
And cut and peeled a hazel wand
And hooked a berry to a thread.

And when white moths were on the wing
And moth-like stars were flickering out,
I threw the berry in the stream
And caught a little silver trout.

When I had laid it on the floor
I went to blow the fire a-flame,
But something rustled on the floor
And someone called me by my name.

It had become a glimmering girl
With apple blossom in her hair
She called me by my name and turned
And vanished in the brightening air...

The stars, the white moths, the fading fire, the little waif-like girl who belonged to nobody; all these were the elements of Yeats' poem here about me. Despite the warmth of the summer night, the fur on the back of my neck stood up and my heart pounded as I waited for the magic to manifest itself.

But no. The moon rose and set, the water vole rustled once or twice more in his foraging and the embers faded to nothing. I slept.

I woke early to clamorous birdsong to find that my boat had vanished. Clearly the glimmering girl had set it adrift in the night. It did not take long to find it; it had drifted across the backwater and caught in a tangle of black hazels beneath a steep bank. I had to swim for it, and when I hauled myself into it, dripping wet and naked, found it full of white moths' wings, thick as apple-blossom.

I set off early before Helmut and his family are up and row on through the morning, stopping briefly in Ochsenfurt to stock up on groceries and write postcards. My main diet has settled down now to the following: a couple of bread rolls, one with salami and mayonnaise, one with tomato and mayonnaise.

The tomato roll is always sprinkled liberally with black pepper and salt from a little cruet set purchased somewhere along the way and which seems to have survived the damp conditions. It reminds me of Sam Gamgee and his little cooking set in Ithilien every time I use it. After the main course, I usually finish up with an apple and down the whole lot with a glass of wine or a small bottle of beer. All this is prepared by simply placing the broad centreboard across my knees as a table, digging out the tupperware box and my Leatherman knife from the forelocker, chopping and cutting and spreading as necessary, and then… ah! this is the best bit!… simply scraping the crumbs and scraps over the side and wiping the centreboard down with the big sponge that lived in the bilges. In the next few months, this was almost my only diet and I never tired of it. Even today the making of a tomato sandwich can conjure up the lap-lap of water, the hot sunshine and the sheer happiness of that period of my life.

Later that afternoon a stiffish breeze springs up from upstream and after a little fruitless footling around with the sail, I have cause to be grateful to an unsmiling grandfather and his two grandchildren who chug by in a rubber Zodiac dinghy and offer me a tow. With their aid, I finally reach the outskirts of the little village of Schwarzach on the right-hand bank. Here there is a wide field flowering with yarrow and tansy and I find a corner of the field to lay out my tarpaulin and sleeping bag for the night. After a cooling swim in the river, I make myself a salami roll, devour it hungrily and prepare to go to sleep in the last fading light of the hot day.

But I cannot. I sit up five minutes later with an overwhelming craving for milk. That is all, a simple enough thing, not nicotine, not gin, not sex - just milk… but I must have some. I try water from my water bottle but this has nothing to do with thirst and the craving persists. This is ridiculous. I have never had a craving in my life. I try to turn over and go to sleep again but my thoughts are filled entirely with the smooth creaminess of cold milk in a tall glass. Eventually I get up, get dressed again and wander off into the blue dusk in search of milk. I find that the village of Schwarzach is a more interesting place than I had first supposed. A mile down the road there is a huge Benedictine monastery with grand gates and a sort of gatehouse with an exhibition inside. It all looks jolly fascinating, but, milk-free as it is, I wander on. Opposite the gatehouse is a restaurant, all heavy stone and coach lamps and vine leaves and diamond-paned windows. I waltz in, trying to ignore the fact that I am the only person there not dressed in evening wear. I breezily order a glass of milk. I am told quite firmly that they do not serve drinks only; I must purchase an entrée at the very least. My funds and my patience will not last, so I wander out again and find my way round to the back kitchen door. In vain I try to appeal to the sweating and over-worked chef on the other side of a fly screen door; he makes it quite clear with a wave of his cleaver that milk-begging mendicants will find no satisfaction here at the poshest restaurant in thirty miles.

The craving has now reached fever pitch. I remember with a fierce longing back to long, hot days spent up Brownhill Creek as a boy and coming home in the evening smelling of sweat and grass and mint and downing a long, cool glass of milk in the kitchen. I remember further back to when I was very little and guzzling milk out of half-pint bottles amidst the crayons and plasticine of primary school. I can't remember the last time I have drunk a glass of milk, but I know I need one now. Eventually, wandering back disconsolately to my flowery meadow and resigning myself to a night of cold turkey, I pass a house where a middle-aged man is digging onions in his tiny front garden. I am so desperate that I find myself stumbling out some incoherent pseudo-German in which the words 'milch' and 'tod' are predominant. Whether or not he thinks he is being threatened with death I don't really care. The important thing is that he retreats to the house and emerges with several pints of blessed milk, cold from the fridge, and I down the lot. Politely he asks whether he can fetch me a third pint, but no, the craving is gone and I am sane again. After a short chat about onions, I walk back contentedly to my field and fall asleep watching a weave of gnats above me against the deep blue sky.

I woke the next morning to a curious swish-swishing noise and something flashing regularly past my slumbering head. I sat up blurrily rubbing sleep and slug-dew from my eyes to make out an alarming figure looming over me. It was tall, dark and wielded the unmistakable silhouette of a scythe. For a few seconds I wondered if the odd craving of the night before for the things of infancy had presaged my death and here was the Reaper himself to gather me in. Then my eyes cleared and I saw that it was simply an old German farmer in dark overalls cutting the meadow with a scythe. He had clearly been up since dawn. The whole meadow was mown and the old fellow had courteously and carefully mown all around me without disturbing me. In another five minutes' time perhaps he would have had to prod me awake to finish off this last little square, but, as it was, I was packed and dressed and beating a hasty retreat to the dinghy before I lost an ear.

That was not the only surprise for me that morning. The couple of horses that had been at the far end of the field the night before seemed to have become curiously distended in the night. And spotted. And now surely there were more of them, though these newcomers had shrunk to the size of Great Danes. And the whole menagerie were being tended by the ugliest red-faced dwarf that could be imagined; even now he was shaking a fist at me and shouting across the field in some unearthly language of hoots and shrieks. It was only when I saw the striped red and yellow canvas of the Big Top that had sprouted overnight in the field like a giant gaudy mushroom did I realise that I was looking at the trappings of the celebrated Circus Trumf. Two llamas, five palominos, three Shetland ponies and a furious baboon... my enraged dwarf... were now tethered in the field. After such a bizarre and delightful start, I had high hopes that the day could only continue to enchant.

It didn't. A mile upstream I came to a large lock that refused to open. On climbing ashore and making my way up to the concrete tower where sat the lock-keeper I found out the lie of the land. Here, it seemed, the waterway split into two. The River Main above this point curved around in a great seven-mile bend like a capital C and a new stretch of canal had been constructed to short-circuit this bend in a straight cut of about four miles. It was this that I could see from the control tower where we stood, sheer-sided and concrete dwindling away into the heat-hazy north. The problem was that only powered vessels were permitted to use the Cut; all other craft had to go around by the old natural river route. The young lock-keeper explained this all to me very nicely and rather apologetically but assured me that the river route was terribly pretty and here, have these chocolate-coated energy muesli bars that his wife had packed for his lunch but he didn't want. Buoyed up by his obvious enthusiasm for the delights ahead of me, I accepted the snack bars, returned to the dinghy and set off into Hell.

Now here is an interesting exemplum, for those semantics students amongst you, of the difference between the two verbs *may* and *can*. Attend please.
1)   Unpowered boats *may* not use the canal-cut...
But
2)   Unpowered boats *can* not use the river loop.

Yet again, as on the Rhine, the lock-keeper's insistence on the scenic nature of the river loop failed to explain the very essence of that scenery; namely, rapids. Possibly on reflection, the gift of the energy muesli bars was a gesture from the wiser subconscious part of the man's brain knowing full well that I would need every ounce of extra energy I could muster for the hours ahead.

At first the going wasn't too bad. For the first few miles the river slipped away beneath me smooth and beer-brown as I hauled myself along, singing *Poor Wandering One* with gusto and tucking into one of the muesli bars. But by the fourth mile the current had become seriously strong and it was all I could do to make any headway at all. Then the nature of the river changed. All along the right-hand bank, tapering groins of loose stone projected about twenty feet into the river at right angles to the bank. These spits were set at intervals of about one hundred yards and formed calm stretches of water lying along the right-hand half of the river. Consequently, the left half of the river flowed all the more fiercely. Nevertheless, by sticking closely to the right bank, I could row in relative stillness for a hundred yards at a time. It was every hundred yards though that the problems arose. To get around the tip of each groin into the next backwater required a combination of hydrodynamics, trajectory motion and sheer brawn that would tax a ten pound salmon with a degree in Higher Physics. The trick was to get a good run up to the point, at the last minute emerge into the current that ran fiercely around each tip, and row like blazes. A moment's hesitation and the current would take the bow and swing me round to the left and broadside to the flow, waltzing me fifty yards downstream again. If I was very quick and very clever, I could so manoeuvre the boat that the current caught the stern instead and turned me neatly into the next backwater... there to sit shaking and sweaty and panting before setting out up the still stretch to try the whole thing again. (Remember in addition, dear reader, that all this fine calculation of distances and angles of approach had to be made while facing backwards in the boat. At least salmon get to face the way they are going.)

After several hours of this erratic progress, during which time I don't think I noticed the pretty scenery once, the current finally grew so strong that I simply couldn't get past one of these stony points. After three attempts, and three subsequent swirls downstream, I noticed an opening in the right hand bank that I had been too sweat-blind to notice before. This led through into what appeared to be a large shallow lagoon enclosed by high banks, and it curved away out of sight to the north... the direction I was heading. And sure enough, I could see further up the river beyond all the worst of the current what appeared to be another opening in the bank. The other end of this secret lagoon perhaps? A serene by-pass of this impassable rapid? This could well be my Northwest Passage. I abandoned any further attempt on rounding the rocky spit that had so mocked me and struck out for the gap into the lagoon.

As I rounded the corner, I found myself in what had possibly been an old clay pit. The broad and sluggish water shimmered with dragonflies and water boatmen and smelt of mud and weed and rotting vegetation. But there was still possibly a way through, though the water looked shallow in places. It was. Three strokes later, I had grounded on mud. I floundered for a little with the oars but this served only to settle us further onto the sticky grey bottom. There was nothing for it but to get out and haul *Jack* off by hand. With a resigned hey-ho, I climbed out and promptly disappeared to my waist in mud.

After the initial shock I laughed heartily to myself at the comic-book predicament I was in and set about extricating myself. Ten minutes later I was seriously panicking. The mud had a grip on me, a slow, slurping, sticky, porridge-like grip and nothing I could do seemed to make the slightest difference. To make matters worse, *Jack*, lightened by my disembarkation on her behalf had bobbed free, come off the bottom and drifted to sit a little way away, clearly not wanting to get involved. Without her gunwale to support me, I had no way of hauling myself out of that sucking grip. After another twenty minutes I was convinced that my early morning apparition had in fact been exactly as I thought: a presage of Death. It was such an ignominious way to go, I thought. I wasn't actually sinking further, but I was certainly not going anywhere. The sun was increasingly hot, the dragonflies had come to regard me as a fixture and were using me as a bridal suite, and being out of sight of the main river I had serious doubts as to whether I would be spotted by a passer-by. I rather thought that in a fortnight's time, some stray picnicker would find just a bloated, blackened corpse sticking stiffly out of the swamp, infested only with the swarming life of dragonfly larvae.

At last I stopped writhing, and as soon as I did a gentle breeze, the very faintest of zephyrs, ghosted up and sent a shimmer over the stagnant water. The relief it brought from the fierce heat was welcome, but it brought me something better, much better. *Jack*, having sat motionless on the glassy water above her painted reflection, drifted closer, closer... closer still, nudged by the ghost-breeze... until finally she was in reach. Two minutes later, I had hauled myself out and flopped shaking into her arms, smearing grey mud over everything, and kissing her all over in sheer idiotic gladness. Then carefully, ever so carefully, I poled her out of that dreadful lagoon and back into the main river.

Stuck Fast

My troubles were not yet over. I still had the rapids to face, and this I decided would require me to throw myself overboard again (after checking carefully that the riverbed was solid pebbles this time) and to stride up the stream chest deep hauling *Jack* behind me. Before doing this I dug in the very front of the forelocker for a pair of old sandshoes that I had last seen in Dover; these would protect my feet from the sharp, rocky bottom. They emerged from the darkness covered in something bright red and highly sticky which could only be blood. Appalled, I rooted around further, fully expecting to find a severed head or a disembodied limb that someone had stowed in there while my back was turned, but found only that the can of toxic red syrup used all those months ago in Whitstable to mend the hole in *Jack*'s hull had burst and was oozing through most of my limited possessions. Putting this firmly in the 'To Be Dealt With Later' category, I ate the second energy bar, climbed into the noxious sandshoes and once again jumped overboard.

I can say this for the next few hours; they were wonderfully cooling. The day had become really quite scorching and the chance to stand up to my chest in cold running water was one that I was thankful for. The next two hours were spent slipping and sliding over the submerged rocks, bodily hauling *Jack* up against an increasing current. Sometimes the stretches were shallow enough to allow a gentle wade upstream, with *Jack* tugging behind me on her leash like a fretful labrador that has sniffed an interesting lamp post two hundred yards back. At other times, however, the going underfoot became treacherous and I would find myself plunging chin-deep into some hole between the boulders while the racing water threatened to rip the painter from my hands and send *Jack* spinning downstream again. At one particularly tricky point the banks closed in steeply on either side and the river was too deep to wade except where the left-hand bank was overhung with low hazels. Here the current was steady and strong, a smooth amber muscle of water pouring down, and my progress here was a painful wade chest-deep amongst the spiky hindering branches of hazel. At one point, my foot slipped and I found myself borne away under the black water to end up in a submerged beaver's nest of roots and rotting boughs, held down for a few horrid seconds by the tangling net of vegetation before breaking through to the surface and the bright air.

Eventually I reached an impasse. The river ran in a fierce rapid over a relatively shallow bed of pebbles in midstream. This was only waist deep but the current was doing a fair impersonation of the Zambesi in monsoon season, and I simply couldn't budge *Jack* another inch. Every now and then I would try to shift my footing to gain a better purchase at which point the river would simply flip my feet from underneath me and *Jack* and I would end up fifty yards downstream again before I could re-surface. This happened four times. Each time I would spend another twenty minutes hauling *Jack* back up to the same rapid, and the whole thing would happen again. I didn't know what to do. There was nothing I could do. And, as so often happens in these moments, a sense of real enjoyment kicked in from nowhere and took me by surprise. I was reminded of times I had spent waist deep with a friend in the Crackenback River in the Snowy Mountains, trying vainly to fish for trout, half excited, half scared of the prospect of getting anything on our lines. The smell of water, the sunburn on our necks, the quiver and hum and scent of the ti tree bush around us... all this came back to me then as I stood frozen in the middle of that bloody river not daring to move.

At last, above the rush and swirl of water about my knees, I heard the faint drone of an outboard engine and, glory be!, around the downstream bend came the little rubber Zodiac of yesterday with the unsmiling grandpapa and the two boys. I had learnt by now not to judge a German by the expression he chooses to wear on his face, and this gentleman was no exception. Before very long he had thrown out a line, instructed me to tie my painter to his and then to swim over and hop in with him. Then, with the engine revving madly and a blue cloud of fumes ascending to the afternoon sky, the Zodiac inched forward and *Jack* slowly rode clear of the rapids into a broad pool upstream.

There were, it appeared, only a couple more kilometres before the weir and lock that would take me onto the main navigable river again just above the new Cut, so Papa Grim towed me the rest of the way, keeping a sensible silence above the buzz of the motor. Occasionally the propeller blades would clatter alarmingly on some submerged rock as we negotiated our way up another rapid, but finally we emerged into the wide and sandy pool below the weir and the struggle was over. I was bruised, battered and cut from a hundred collisions with underwater boulders, my hands were raw with straining on the thin painter, and my sandshoes appeared to have bonded onto my feet with an irreversible epoxy resin. But it was over. I had traversed the scenic section of the River Main and shown that not only *may* unpowered boats take the route but that they *can* as well. And very pretty it was too.

The last hour of that strange day was spent rowing in windless heat up a few more broad bends of the Main and stopping at a little sandy bay to give *Jack* a thorough spring clean. Epoxy resin, slimy mud, hazel leaves, bilge water and the sodden remains of my bread and salami were all slooshed out with the bailer and wiped away with the big sponge. At some point in this procedure another naked man trotted out of a nearby copse and vanished across a field. Perhaps he had been following me from Cochem. Perhaps the Germans do this sort of thing. Then with the boat as clean as I could make it I rounded one last bend, tied up in a little side-arm hidden deep under an overhanging willow, and marched off to find a beer and a meal. When I came back two hours later, some bastard had stolen my pith helmet.

That night, I really couldn't care. I watched a nightjar hawking over the starlit meadow and then I slept the sleep of the very, very tired indeed.

My pith helmet! Gorn! I really was very, very cross about this. It had been given to me by that same Rupert who had first brought me the original Jack de Crow, so the hat and the boat had, as it were, a common godparent. I had worn it poling a dugout canoe through the Okavango Swamp, rafting on the Zambesi, hitching across the Mogdagadi Desert and climbing in the Cuillin. I know that it has been, throughout this account, an affectation, an eccentricity deliberately adopted. But nevertheless it had become an important item for me in more ways than one. Yes, I know that every hero has his hat: Indiana Jones rolling back beneath the sliding stone door of the tomb to retrieve his old leather headpiece; Doctor Dolittle returning to the unpleasant Throgmorton Manor for his beloved topper; Sherlock Holmes striding around in his deerstalker. But the pith helmet had played a more practical part in the voyage as well. It had collected blackberries and deutschmarks in good measure, it had kept off the Picardy sun and the Oxfordshire rain; it had mollified suspicious lock-keepers and been admired by Michael Palin and Eton boys alike; it had done service as a splendid bailer during my shipwreck in the North Sea, and when on countless occasions an unexpected gybe had sent the boom swinging murderously at my head it had saved me from concussion and possible death.

And now it was gone, pinched I'm sure by some village urchin who had no idea of what a treasure he had purloined. May he get good use out of it, wherever he is now.

On a more practical note, I found myself missing it sorely the next day. The temperatures had soared to forty degrees in some parts of Germany; in fact I was shortly to read that Europe was experiencing the severest heat wave in a century of records. And it was through this that I was rowing hatless and sun-struck up the wide, windless highway of the Main. Perhaps 'drag strip' would be a better phrase. It seemed that every speedboat, every jet ski, every water-skier in Germany was out in force that Sunday on that particular stretch of the Main. They zoomed and snarled up and down, throwing great wakes behind them that sent the osiers swaying in panic along the river banks and the coots scuttling from their nests. Each time one passed, the wake was enough to rock me wildly to and fro, my oars slapping the water helplessly and disturbing the strong rhythm that is so vital to oarsmen in their craft. I hated the boats with a passion as they arrogantly churned by, their virile tanned crew, their reflective sunglasses, their bathing beauties draped over the sleek prows. And suddenly it seemed that without my hat, my wonderful hat, I was no longer a figure of mystery and adventure hailing from foreign lands, deserving a little awed respect from the locals, but just a rather hot and bothered middle-aged man who couldn't afford a speedboat and was turning a rather amusing shade of beetroot.

Then just as the scent of the lime trees was growing sweet and drowsy with the coming evening and the glare had gone off the molten river along with the powerboats, I came at late dusk to a village whose name I did not record. After tethering my boat, I wandered through the lanes of this place and found them utterly deserted. There were two inns, large dilapidated buildings both of them; one of them was closed, the other boarded up. The whole place smelt of straw and manure and was strangely quiet. The only living things I saw were three magnificent horses, dark chestnut, who cantered nervously and endlessly around a small field sloping to the river. They seemed terrified of something and their fear unnerved me. I sat somewhat uneasily in the next field and ate my salami and tomato supper, and then found growing in a thick bramble hedge around a lightless witch's cottage a single huge blackberry, almost as big as a small orange. That was my dessert, and exquisite it was. That night I woke suddenly to find a silent man standing over me with a torch. He didn't say anything. As I came awake, he snapped off the torch and strode off. In the gibbous moonlight I could see that under his arm he held a gun. In the next field, the three stallions were still circling restlessly. I could hear them in the night. An odd place altogether.

The next day took me without event to the little village of Eltmann, and there, through a series of bizarre events too tedious to relate here, a succession of complete strangers managed to turn my expected supper of half a stale bread roll and a lonely evening into... wait, I have a list here somewhere... four eggs, seven tomatoes, three bottles of beer, a large carton of chocolate milk, a bag of cookies, a further bag of iced pastries, five apples, a bottle of white wine, a corkscrew as a present and a bank-side rendition of *Lili Marlene* by an elderly grandmother, herself called Lili, who thought I was a good, good man.

Why, if I am such a good man, did I finally come to feel stifled and resentful of all this outpouring of generosity and interest? Why was I now anxious to get onto the canal and away from this enchanted river where a vagrant stranger could do no wrong, could come to no harm? Why, when I finally sailed away from Eltmann on a morning breeze with one of the many benefactors from the night before still there snapping photos of my departure, did it feel so like some sort of an escape?

The Kaiser's Canal

'The Bear went over the Mountain,
The Bear went over the Mountain,
The Bear went over the Mountain,
To see what he could see.'

Anonymous – *Nursery Rhyme*

The rose garden terrace of the New Bishop's residence in Bamberg is the loveliest place to sit and write letters between Calais and the Black Sea. A thousand blooms cense the air with perfume; petals of every shade, scarlet, crimson, white and yellow, pink and apricot, carmine, garnet, soft as velvet, cool as wine, fill the wide terrace with colour and fragrance. Fountains tinkle into round basins where fat goldfish nibble and dip, and here and there from the sea of flowers rises a marble cherub or a draped Venus. The whole terrace overlooks the red roofs and copper-green spires of old Bamberg, where the River Regnitz plaits its way in a number of channels, mill races and long still reaches through the heart of the finest town in Germany. It is also a nice place to have a cup of really excellent tea and pat oneself firmly on the back for having reached another milestone.

The fact is that Bamberg marks the end of the interminable River Main and the beginning of the Main-Rhine-Donau Canal, a long sought for goal (about which more in a little while.) I had heaved a heartfelt sigh of relief when the previous day I had rowed up the last thirty kilometres of the Main in stifling, thundery weather and come at last to the 384 kilometre mark ... 384 kilometres!...and the place where the current-less waters of the canal branched off to the right. Here I had stopped for lunch and a swim on the green spit between the two watercourses and discovered that my tuck-box still had an egg in it from the night before. Being raw, it was no use to me unless... ah, the very thing. A nearby children's playground had a slippery-dip in it, the shiny silver metal burning hot in the sun. An experimental dob of butter on the flattened end of the slide sizzled faintly, and a few minutes later I was scraping off a fried egg onto the bottom half of a buttered roll. True, it was a little runnier than I liked, but I rather enjoyed the intrepid nature of such bush cuisine. I also enjoyed finally turning my back on the meandering Main after fourteen days of upstream rowing and looked forward to the still waters of the canal ahead.

After fourteen days of sleeping on my boat or under the stars, I decided to treat myself to a hotel room my first night in Bamberg. My timing was perfect. The gods who control the weather, having been briefed to keep things nice for Sandy, took the opportunity while I was indoors for a night to really let rip with a bit of serious weather. That night, the heavens opened with a thunderstorm of Wagnerian proportions, the lightning striking the spires of the town all about me. Brilliant white flashes crackled in the window frame, and at one stage illumined a terrified cat pawing at the glass like Gallico's Thomasina back from the dead.

The poor ginger puss spent the rest of the night curled up damply on my chest clutched ever more tightly, I am afraid to confess, with each new crack of thunder overhead.

One thing that struck me though was how accustomed I had grown to the outdoors life. I found the confining walls of the hotel room that night unbearably claustrophobic and stuffy, the windows and doors and taps unnecessarily fiddly devices to fuss with. The water running from the taps to wash my face in seemed to me a thin and etiolated trickle compared with the fulsome emptying of a bailerful of cold water over the neck and shoulders each morning under a clearing sky. The hot bath for which I had so longed was a tepid, steamy, narrow, hip-pinching affair after skinny-dipping at noon in a wide, lonely bend of the river with cool mud squishing between the toes and the smell of green river-weed in one's nose and mouth. How clinging and marshmallow-like seemed my smothering quilt that night. How yellow and feeble glowed the lightbulb for shaving with the next morning. And the big plate of *puten-schnitzel mit butterknudeln unt grunesalat* I ordered for dinner was four times the amount I could happily eat, and took ten times longer in the preparation than my beloved daily tomato-and-mayonnaise roll. I rolled groaning from the table feeling that I had just consumed a vat of ambergris. I longed to be out of the city and on my way again.

But first Bamberg. I diligently played the tourist that morning as the rain came down in a fine and cooling mist; the churches, the bridges, the palaces and the tea rooms; once again feeling utterly inadequate when it came to understanding the historical or political significance of each place. To my eyes it was all pure Narnia, from the rose terrace and its tinkling fountains where princes walked and talked of love to the arched bridges over the green and foaming weirs that made of the town a maze... or that Seven Bridges of Konigsberg problem in topology. In the cathedral there is the Bamberg Rider, a sculptured horseman on a steed, with smooth curves, angular limbs, stylised features and powerful lines, somewhat like the cave paintings of France. Then there is the altarpiece, a magnificent sculpture in dusky gold dimly silhouetted against the window behind, creating a sort of dark brilliance to the piece. This shows Christ apparently umpiring a cricket match, with an angel batsman to one side and an apostle going for a dramatic catch. Christ holds a finger aloft and looks ruefully at the angel, who is clearly out. Mary and sundry spectators hover in the background ready to hand out afternoon tea. It is a remarkable work of art and, as one who has spent several aeons on the cricket field umpiring school matches, perfectly sums up for me the twin ideas of sorrowing judgement and perfect self-sacrifice. Here we see the pinnacle of human suffering in the figure of Christ the Willing Umpire, doing the job so that I might never have to again.

And now that promised word about the Rhine-Main-Donau Canal. This canal links the top of the Main River with the Danube, and so serves as the passageway between the two great river systems of Europe. Its existence allows ships to travel all the way from the North Sea to the Black Sea without ever touching the

Mediterranean. I had first learnt about its existence from my mother who had informed me with a great deal of enthusiasm and a total disregard for accuracy that there was this wonderful canal, Sandy, that crosses the Alps, just think of it, built by none other than King Ludwig, you remember all those fairy tale castles such as Neuschwanstein we visited when you were eight, Mad Ludwig they called him, and anyway, this canal is one of the great feats of engineering, there's a book, it's all terribly old, you realise, and it follows the Crusaders' route to the Holy Land, or perhaps that's something else, but yes, there is, a canal that is, I read all about it in a book. With this introduction, I had high hopes of the Rhine-Main-Donau Canal. I pictured in my mind's eye some extraordinary engineering marvel, a waterway that wound its dizzy way through the heart of the Alps, edging along precipices, scaling in flights of locks, a hundred at a time, the knife-edge ridges of glacial peaks, spanning the vast abyss of blue valleys via aqueducts of spidery slenderness a thousand feet above the swollen rivers below. I also imagined that being built by the infamous Mad Ludwig, each lock-house would be constructed in a cluster of turrets and needle-spires, dove-grey and icing-sugar-white, each possibly equipped with its own troop of red-jacketed soldiers in cock hats. The style would certainly be gingerbread, but... a cold thought struck me... if Ludwig was as mad as they said, would the construction materials be gingerbread also? (I remembered hearing years ago of a famous bridge in India which was discovered, after its disastrous collapse, to have all its main pylons full not of concrete as supposed, but of shoe polish.)The main danger, I supposed, would be getting entangled in the belay-line of some mountaineering party climbing up over the ice on their way to the Jungfrau... or avalanches possibly, set off by the high bleat of a passing chamois or the distant thunder of an alpenhorn quartet. Would I be shooing curious ibex off the foredeck? Plucking mountain gentians and edelweiss to stick in my hatband? I was certainly looking forward to finding out.

As it turned out, my impressions were somewhat fanciful. The Rhine-Main-Donau Canal has as much eccentric charm and baroque splendour as the M25. It does not, for one, pass remotely near the Alps, though it does of course cross a major watershed. This watershed consists of a vast flat plateau of farmland interspersed by pine plantations, small patches of heathland and medium sized towns of little character. Secondly, it was not built by Mad Ludwig but by quite a different Ludwig who was by all accounts a man of great industry, practicality and efficiency, and had no time for gingerbread at all, tending more to the sauerkraut school of architecture. It was he, presumably who chose to drive the canal across the practicable emptiness of the Bavarian Plateau rather than swing southwards through the ski-resorts of Switzerland. In fact, there wasn't a gingerbread aqueduct or a yodeller in sight.

The Author Dreams of Gingerbread

The six days rowing and sailing along the canal follow much the same pattern as the last few weeks and there is little memorable to report. The locks on this canal were, however, to prove increasingly troublesome as I progressed. These were not the mossy beamed devices of the English waterways with geraniums spilling gaily along the lock sides. These resembled your average-sized Soviet hydroelectric plant, with vast walls of white concrete and towers six storeys high topped with control rooms paned in green-tinted glass. Each of these offices held in its high and remote fastnesses a *schleusemeister* of a severity and efficiency to match the mighty complex under his care. It was his job as a modern day Moses to send the waters hither and thither through his titanic pondage at the push of a button and the flick of a switch. It was *not* his job, as was soon made clear to me, to swill thousands of tons of water about for the sake of every passing boatman who happened to be out for a Sunday jolly on the waterways. Such frivolous insects were pointed wordlessly in the direction of a distant noticeboard and expected to get on with following instructions. It took me a while to fathom the German, but eventually I worked out that near each board there was a device like a bicycle rack and locked to this by a coin-release system was a natty aluminium trolley or *bootwagen*. The idea was that skippers of unpowered pleasurecraft could release such a trolley, roll it down a ramp into the canal and haul their little craft out of the water. Then it could be wheeled with relative ease along past the lock and lowered again into the next section of the canal; on returning the trolley to its frame and clicking the lock shut, the coin would be recovered and the merry mariner could continue on his way... and all without disturbing the gods in their Olympian heights.

This was the theory at least. In practice I found that a little feigned ignorance and whimsical pleading with the schleusemeister would usually get me through at the tail end of an industrial barge that happened to be passing through at the time.

I came to the city of Nuremberg late one afternoon and a kind boatman called Claus drove me into the city the following day. Nuremberg is the home of the artist Dürer whose crouching hare must be the finest pencil sketch the world has seen. It is also, more infamously, the home of the Nuremberg Rallies and later the War Trials, and I found that there was an almost eager shame about the place, a desire to remind visitors at every turn of its recent history. The cathedral is a monument to justice and reconciliation, and that should be applauded, but I found myself longing to get away again. I knew someone once who would carry on apologising long after his first peace overtures had been accepted until one was forced to get cross all over again in telling him to drop the subject. This would be the source for a whole new set of ever-renewed apologies, and he eventually became someone I tried to avoid. Nuremberg, I felt, was like that... and I show my own crass insensitivity even to think thus.

After I leave Nuremberg a good wind springs up and, most unusually, rather than being directly on the nose or tail, comes from side on which makes for the very best sailing. This is because here the canal is travelling along its own high causeway above the landscape, rather as a railway travels along the top of an embankment. It feels unnatural but exhilarating to be travelling thus so high across the fields and woods. One evening I come to a lonely stretch of heathland and scattered pine forests. Here there is a strange monument on the right-hand bank, nothing more than a modern austere obelisk of white cement, a thin upright wedge oddly curved and pointed. It is to mark the highest point of the canal... that is, the watershed of the whole of Europe. Behind me the land falls invisibly away into the Black Forest, the valleys of the Main, the Rhine, the Rhone, the Moselle all the way down to the grey shores of the North Sea and the old Atlantic. Ahead of me a mass of land falls away to the Danube, which tumbles endlessly down through Austria, through Hungary, across the vast Magyar Plain, cuts beyond the Carpathian mountains and peters out into the wide wetlands of the Danube Delta. That night I check my maps and figures. I am not only at the highest point of my travels but I am almost exactly halfway between North Wales and the Black Sea. It is all downhill from here.

The usual routine – a swim in the green waters of the canal, applying a bar of soap to hair and skin with great vigour, then clambering out onto the sweet grass to dry off. The towel is hung to dry on the boom; it will still be wet tomorrow from the dew but an hour into tomorrow it will be stiff and dry with sunlight. Then as the light fades I pull out my tupperware box and make a sandwich, salami and tomato this time with the ever welcome mayonnaise squeezed from a tube. I worry slightly, as I do every night, that surely mayonnaise is one of those things that goes off terribly easily and brings whole wedding parties to their knees with salmonella poisoning and I now have had this tube for seventeen days in the unrefrigerated foredeck and am still cheerfully consuming it without any side-effects – but decide to stick to my policy of reserving any worries until the moment stomach cramps actually set in.

Behind me, as I sit facing out over the canal, a steep bank drops away to a pine forest. The bank is covered in mullein, their tall spires of sulphur flowers luminescing faintly in the dusk against the British Racing Green of the forest. There is a high shrill shriek from somewhere in the trees and a quick rustle – some small animal meeting its death at the claws of an owl perhaps? The stars are coming out, wavering in white S's and ?'s in the deep blue of the canal. I am suddenly desperately, hungrily, cravingly in need of company. It is as fierce and persistent a desire as my thirst for milk a few weeks ago. I remember that I have a bottle of white wine in the hold, that present from one of my various benefactors in Eltmann. I open it with the new corkscrew and fill a glass. Then I very solemnly raise the glass to the night and say out loud a toast of thanks to all the people of Wales and England and France, of Luxembourg and Germany, that have sped *Jack* and myself on our slow ascent to this height. I make a foolish little speech and drink the wine. It is excellent. Whatever it is in the wood kills again and I think, just for a fraction of a second, about such things as the Surrey Puma and the Dartmoor Panther. Is there a... check map... a Hilpoltstein Tiger perhaps?

After a third glass of wine, I am just about to climb into my sleeping bag which I have spread on the soft grass of the bank when in the gloom of the opposite bank I see the shadow of someone moving. He is directly across from me. After a little while, there is the flare of a match and a little fire is lit. The shadow is a man, about my age I guess, and he settles down to make himself some supper. He too has a bottle... beer, I think... and I soon make out a rucksack by his side. He is setting up camp for the night. I doubt if he can see me in the darkness across the width of the canal, though perhaps he has seen the pale yellow lines and mast of *Jack* snuggled up to the bank. I am tempted to call out to him, but what would be the use? The canal is too wide for easy conversing and there is nowhere to cross for miles. Besides, he is almost certainly German and what if he doesn't speak English or understand why someone is calling out of the darkness to him? I am snug in my sleeping bag now, and the craving for company has been drowned in the wine. I let it go and sleep, and when I wake the next morning he is gone.

I like to think even now that perhaps he was a fellow traveller, someone walking from the Black Sea to North Wales, that we passed all unawares in the darkness and perhaps shall never know the truth of it. I like to think so, that's all...

Now that I was going downhill, the lock-keepers suddenly refused to succumb to my whimsical reliance on foreign eccentricity and utterly forbade me to enter the locks as I had been doing. They pointed sternly to the *bootwagens* and insisted I use them. In vain did I plead that *Jack* was a seasoned traveller, well accustomed to the perils of every variety of lock between here and the North Sea. *Not zis vun*, they would crackle through their intercoms. *Use ze bootwagen. Iss fur ze kleine booten. Click.*

This was all very well, but *Jack* was no kayak. At one lock I came to the lock-keeper had been particularly abrupt down the intercom, and I had had to return three times to explain that the coin-release mechanism on the trolley was jammed. He clearly did not believe me, and after the third attempt to talk with him, he simply hung up and refused to answer. Eventually I managed to clear the dust and grit out of the slot with my knife and hauled the trolley all the way up to the top pound where *Jack* was waiting. Hot and bothered, I lowered the trolley on the end of a rope down the ramp into the water. Then waist deep in the canal, I manoeuvred *Jack* over the top of the trolley frame and tied her bow rope onto the upright 'prow' that made the handle. Then, gripping the rope tightly, I started to walk slowly up the ramp, hauling *Jack* behind me. The effort needed was tremendous. The boat, heavy with rigging and luggage, was nearly impossible to pull up the slope, and I strained and strained with all my might to inch *Jack* up out of the water. Then suddenly my feet slipped from beneath me on the green slime of the concrete ramp. This was not just a stumble or a skid – it was a perfectly executed Buster Keaton stunt. Picture it. Both feet shoot from under me in synchronisation, ending up perfectly level with my head. My horizontal body hangs there for a good three seconds, three artistic seconds that allow my head to turn to face the camera, and the brief glance over my shoulder to see where the ground has got to. Then the eyes close in resignation and there follows the swift plummet onto the concrete slab below. This is accompanied by a comic whistling noise and a loud splat as I land flat as a pancake in the stinking slime. The routine is not yet over. Somehow in the course of my aerial acrobatics, the towrope has entangled around my neck, and now as the laden trolley rolls gracefully back into the canal, I go with it, drawn headfirst down the ramp on the end of the rope like a trussed walrus. I am so stunned that I actually disappear completely under the water, my position marked only by a line of bubbles breaking the surface. I do wish I had been in a better position to appreciate the whole thing. As it is, the slapstick cheered me up no end, and despite the fact that I was covered in green slime and had a ringing head, my bad mood was dispelled for the day. That day ended with the canal descending into the valley of the Altmuhl, and my grateful entry onto that beautiful and little-known river. The Rhine-Main-Donau Canal was behind me, and I was launched on a current that would take me two and a half thousand miles to the Black Sea.

When I finally emerged onto the Danube a day later, I could not at first believe it. The water beneath me was sluggish and black and the banks were industrial and bare. I think that I had expected a swift and sweeping current in a gorge similar to the Altmuhl, and my first sight in the fading light of a dreary day was sorely disappointing. However, one small incident gave me cause for hope. Pulling through the oily waters in the dusk, *Jack*'s bow went *clunk* on something and I saw that I had hit a floating bottle. A second glance showed that it had in it a piece of orange paper, and on an impulse I dragged it out of the water. It was as I had thought. It was that classic mariner's find, a message in a bottle. I struggled to remove the cork and extract the piece of orange paper, and found that it was scrawled in a childish hand in coloured crayon. It was in German, but I later had it translated. It read:

"Good luck on your adventure, dear Captain. I hope I will meet you one day when I too have a ship."

It could not have been more clearly intended for me. I was no scavenger picking through debris on the shore. I was no boatman out just for the afternoon. Of all the people on the river, surely I was that same dear Captain off on an adventure that the child had seen in the mind's eye while setting out the coloured crayons. The childish writing, the aptness of the find, and above all the tremendous optimism implicit in the very act of throwing such a message to the elements, all conspired to lift me out of my dreary mood and sent me singing on my way through the darkening dusk. I had been wished good fortune and fair sailing by an anonymous child yet to learn the sneering laws of chance, and I look forward to the day when, as surely as the meeting of the bottle and my bows, I shall shake hands with the author of that fortunate note. Meanwhile here was a marina, here was light and company and food, and here was rest for the night. I had reached the Danube and it was surely all easy going from here.

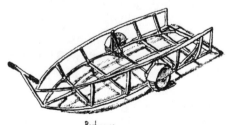

Bootwagen

Pigeons and Palaces

*'Much have I travell'd in the realms of gold
And many goodly states and kingdoms seen...'*

John Keats – *On First Looking Into Chapman's Homer*

'He who does not know his way to the sea should take a river for his guide'

Plautus – *Poenulus. III. 3. 14.*

I needed to make a phone call. The marina didn't have a phone, so I found myself wandering along a country road at night heading for the town of Kelheim about two miles away. Half a mile down the road, I came across a building, cheerful and lamplit, standing all by itself with bare fields on either side. Along with the warm light that poured from its windows into the night, there came the homely buzz of voices and the odd clink of glasses that betokened a pub of sorts. In fact as I peered at the building's frontage, there did seem to be a sign of sorts, and a name in German. This was clearly the German equivalent of the Red Lion or the Fox and Hounds... though here perhaps it would be the Two-Headed Eagle or the King of Prussia. At any rate, it would surely have a phone and I could follow it up with a pint or two of good German beer to celebrate my arrival on the Danube.

I pushed my way through the doors into the congenial smoky atmosphere of the interior and there were the customers all sitting around several long tables drinking and chatting with animation. The look of slight surprise they gave me as I entered was soon accounted for; they were clearly in the middle of some form of pub quiz night, as was attested by the paper and pencils scattered about the place between the beer mugs and coasters. I was a late arrival perhaps, having mis-read the starting time. Did I want to join in? I assume that was the question, because at my first halting words of greeting one of the men said, "Ah, English, ja?" and the question of my joining the quiz seemed to be dropped. Tentatively I asked if there was a phone I could use, and after some headshaking a large man pulled out his mobile phone and handed it to me. I protested, but he was insistent so after I had made my call I handed the phone back and offered to pay. At this there was much discussion amongst the jovial group and an older man was dispatched to fetch out from behind the bar a large plastic pigeon. This was shaken under my nose, which mystified me a little until I noticed that there was a slit in the top of the bird's head. It was in fact a piggy bank... or rather a pidgy bank, I suppose. I dropped a couple of deutschmark into the pigeon, and now that the business of the phone call was concluded turned my attention to the bar.

"Um...ein bier, bitte," I said "...er... if that's okay..."

The barman looked momentarily taken aback, (even I myself flinched at the mangled attempt to speak German) but soon the beer was produced and I dug into my pocket again to pay. To my surprise, out came the plastic pigeon again and I was invited once more to insert my deutschmarks in the creature's head as I pondered on the eccentric cash-till procedures of the otherwise efficient Germans. Soon I was invited to sit down at a table with the other customers – they seemed happy enough to suspend the quiz for a while out of courtesy to a stranger – and my life story was cheerfully dragged out of me. There were the usual exclamations of admiration and disbelief, and for the next half-hour we conversed in a broken mixture of English and bad German. After my second drink, paid for by a donation to the pigeon once more, I relaxed enough to take stock of my surroundings. It began to strike me as a rather odd sort of pub actually. There was very little coming and going – in fact, nobody had arrived or left since I'd been there – and everyone seemed to be taking turns behind the bar, helping themselves as they pleased, with the sole proviso that each time, the pigeon appeared like the Holy Spirit to claim its toll. And as I looked around, I noticed that there was a definite theme to the décor of the place. A series of shining silver trophies along one wall were topped by little winged hats like that of the Roman Mercury. Various pennants hanging from the rafters each displayed, as a symbol of peace, the winged dove fluttering upwards. Lastly I focused on a large faded poster on the far wall, which showed all the breeds of pigeons, wild and domestic, from around the world: fantails, pouters, wood pigeons, rock-doves, bronzewings, turtles, and of course, racing pigeons. A horrid doubt crept into my mind as I sipped my second beer. The quiz still hadn't recommenced... if it was a quiz, that is. A long pause had opened in the conversation and there was the indefinable air of well-bred patience wondering how to be frank.

"Er... excuse me... sorry. This *is* a pub, isn't it?" I asked.

Shuffles of embarrassed feet. Then one of my hosts spoke up. He spoke very kindly.

"Well, now zat you ask, nein, zis isn't ze pub actually. It's ze Kelheim Racing Pigeon Club, and zis is our Annual General Meeting. But please..." he added hastily, "it has been a pleasure to have you here..." (hasty nods all round)... "But now..." (as he picked up paper and pen)... "if you haf had enough beer, perhaps ve get on with ze meeting, ja?"

Just down the river from Kelheim, the Danube... or Donau as we must now call it...bisects the ancient University town of Regensburg. I had been told many things about Regensburg, and planned to stop there but the river, on entering the city, suddenly narrowed to a fierce channel that swept beneath the stone bridges, past the spires, and flung me out the other side before I could draw breath. Upon leaving Regensburg, the Donau flows across a wide plain in a meandering course between flat green fields and low dykes. The countryside reminded me a little of Norfolk, with reedbeds rattling in brakes and a pair of marsh harriers hawking low over the marshes. The main bulk of the hills had been left behind, but here and there rising out of the plain were solitary steep hills, as abrupt as loaves of bread, and each of these was the seat of some schloss or kloster with red roofs, perched high above the flat expanse and looking over a watery vista of silver and blue and flooded green stretching to the horizon.

I had continued my learning of Keats poetry all this while – I was only four verses off knowing the whole tedious length of *The Eve of St. Agnes* by heart but had also been concentrating on his *Ode to Psyche* as a break from Madeline and her vague regardless eyes. I was just revelling in the last stanza of *Psyche* when I rounded a broad bend of the river and saw a sight that made me quite literally gasp with astonishment. There ahead of me was one of these great isolated hills, and it looked as though it had fallen there from the gilded frames of a neo-classical painting, a Gainsborough perhaps. Flanking its steep slopes were groves of pine trees, luxurious in their dark fur, and great cedar trees soaring like scented green thunderclouds supported on redwood pillars. Beneath and between these stately trees, the grass grew fine and vivid, so that there came to me pat the lines:

"Far, far around shall those dark cluster'd trees
Fledge the wild-ridged mountain steep by steep;
And there by zephyrs, streams, and birds, and bees
The moss-lain Dryads shall be lull'd to sleep."

But the main feature of the hill was that sitting on its crest was the Parthenon. Not, you understand, that flaking ruin baked in the blinding glare and taxi fumes of Athens; no, this was the real Parthenon, a gleaming temple in white marble, every pillar and cornice intact, and looking as though it had just been completed last week. A great flight of stairs swept up the hill beneath the cedars to the portico with its familiar colonnade of pillars and shallow-pitched roof, displaying the perfect proportions of the Golden Ratio. The background of dark pines and verdant grass, and the vista it commanded of meandering river and wide, wide skies, made it the very embodiment of Arcadia.

At the foot of the hill there was a wooden jetty so pulling in, I moored up and climbed the three hundred steps, from terrace to terrace to terrace, with a sense of awe:

Who are these coming to the sacrifice?
...What little town by river or sea-shore
Or mountain built with peaceful citadel
Is emptied of this folk this pious morn?
Thy streets for ever more shall silent be...

As I approached the top, the sheer size of the place struck me. I was to find out that it was an exact full-scale copy of the original Parthenon but it struck me then as three times bigger than the dusty Athenian ruin I remembered. Inside I found a spacious hall, a splendour of gilding and mosaic and carved capitals, and on pedestals ranged right around the four walls countless busts and statues just as there must have been in Ancient Greece. But here at last there was a difference. For where the ancient statues would have been of gods and goddesses, divine youths and mighty Olympians, smooth-limbed and lissom, or thunder-browed and haughty, the statues here were of famous German statesmen of the last few centuries: chancellors, generals, philosophers, writers and economists, and there was hardly a single divine feature between them. Balding heads, stout tums, ridiculous whiskers, bulging eyes, double chins, full-fed faces – they looked as commonplace and suburban as any modern day meeting of town councillors. The temple was clearly devoted to celebrating the inner virtues of German greatness rather than the external aesthetics, and the sculptor had gone for realism rather than flattery.

The other fact that I discovered was that the whole marvellous fantasy was commissioned by none other than King Ludwig the Sane, the man who had built the Rhine-Main-Donau Canal. I was pleased to find that he seemed to have inherited some small streak of madness from his namesake after all. The only detail that I jibbed at was that in an appalling clash of cultures, this archetypal symbol of all things Arcadian, all things warm and southern and Attic, had been christened "Valhalla." An edifice less Norse it would be difficult to conceive. Nevertheless, as I stood there in the portico, gazing out across the wide and sunlit plain under an afternoon sky borrowed from Canaletto, I couldn't help thinking that this was the finest building between here and North Wales. It had been built of course "*...too late for antique vows, / Too, too late for the fond believing lyre*"

...but had captured again the times "*When holy were the haunted forest-boughs, / Holy the air, the water and the fire...*"

Had Ludwig turned aside briefly from his economists and his engineers to read the young English poet and then made the dreamer's vow a reality?

"*And in the midst of that wide quietness,*
A rosy sanctuary will I dress...
With buds and bells and stars without a name...
And there shall be for thee all soft delight
That shadowy thought can win;
A bright torch and a casement ope at night
To let the warm Love in."

Valhalla

    The next few days take me along the lazy river between grassy dykes and shingle beaches under a sky where high white clouds, sunlit and snowy, sail like galleons. At dusk a thin new moon, faint and curved as a nail paring, ghosts out of the blue and I fall asleep to the creaking of a million frogs. After Deggendorf the river quickens its pace once more, sluicing down at a merry speed between banks of osier and willow, occasionally passing through a town or village, but I have caught the river's mood, and I too am hurrying, reluctant to stop until the fifty miles a day is under my belt. The rowing is easy – I can slot into an automatic rhythm which will take me for hours, sometimes so dreamily that I will wake with a start to wonder where the miles have gone. A new feature of the river now is the presence of channel marker buoys, red for port and green for starboard. These are large hollow cylinders of tin with conical noses, and surmounted by a fin-like flag rising out of their rounded backs. With the current racing past them, they give the appearance of forging through the water upstream, the water spurting from beneath their tin noses and their bodies skidding and swaying with their apparent velocity. They look for all the world like squat antique torpedoes, launched by Dick Dastardly in an attempt to scupper me. It is just while I am musing on this that there is an almighty clang and I am propelled out of my seat into the bilges. I clamber up just in time to see that one of these missiles has struck me a glancing blow on the bows – even from here I can see the smear of yellow paint against the green. I check *Jack*'s woodwork but apart from a crunching dent in the prow, there seems to be no damage done... but I wake up after that. It would be a pity to sink now, torpedoed by these tin sharks.

I came at last to Passau, another one of the great medieval cities of Germany, and, I think, surpassing all that I had seen so far. It sits on the junction of three rivers, as here the River Inn and the minor River Ilz flow into the Donau from either side. This fact is much lauded in the tourist brochures of the town. *Passau! Witness the Natural Miracle of Three Rivers Conjoining!* they cry in a passion of exclamation marks, possibly unaware of other features in the world that might have a better claim to be natural miracles: Angel Falls, the Great Barrier Reef, the Grand Canyon, to name but a few. It is odd that they get so excited about this, because frankly, Passau is not short of sights worth seeing. The Stephansdom with its twin bronze-green onion-domes has inside a giant gilded pulpit, every inch of which is carved with figures of the four Evangelists and their fabulous menagerie, lions and bulls, eagles and winged spirits, rioting in a baroque tangle of allegory and allusion. Outside, the narrow shops are predominantly full of old musical instruments, antique manuscripts and fine glassware. The location of the town, perched on a narrow spit between the deep green of the Donau and the milky turbulence of the Inn gives the town the charm of an island fortress. Quiet walkways amble between the river and gracious waterside residences, where weeping ornamental trees uncoil their foliage down walls of warm buff stone. Twisting wisteria hangs from trellises, dropping its purple confetti into the stream, and small archways duck up into some courtyard where a bronze fountain plays to an empty house.

Rowing away from Passau the next day, I passed the point off the southern end of the town's spit where the Inn flows in from the west. Here the milky waters of that fierce river, laden with chalk sediment from the far off Alps, mixed with the bottle-deep Donau, and from that point on, the river beneath me was never clear again. It remained a murky hue, like paintwater at the end of the art lesson, sometimes a delicate grey-blue, sometimes a choppy fawn, but never again the limpid clarity of old glass. And a few miles downstream the river in its new khaki marched briskly out of Germany and into the fair land of Austria.

There is an elfin piper who haunts the steep woods below Schoning. "*Tweet-toot!*" I would pipe on my tin whistle, and a perfect two beats later, back would come from the cliffy woods, "*tweet-toot!*"

'*Tiddle–iddle-tweet-toot*" my pipe would play...

and...

"*tiddle-iddle-tweet-toot*" would come the reply.

The hidden faun or satyr and I played this game of echoing melodies for a full blissful hour as I swanned along in morning sunshine through the gorge. Here, a day's sailing from Passau, the Donau curves around in a series of sharp hairpin bends between U-shaped valley walls clothed with thick forest. This, like everything else in Austria, looks neatly brushed: dark pine and fir mostly, with the odd swathe of silvery-green ash streaked up the hillside or the lime-gold splash of maple here and there. The forest comes right down to the river's edge but every now and then I sail past a little flat open meadow where stands perhaps a single inn, primrose yellow or clean white, with carved window boxes of scarlet geraniums and a white cat. Between the house and the steep forest marge there might be a tiny orchard of apple trees rosy with fruit, or a huge neatly stacked pile of wood, three caramel horses grazing and sometimes a little church with square white tower and bronze-green onion dome. The inn or farmhouse looks newly painted, the horses freshly groomed, the grass new-cut and the cat just fed. The innkeeper's wife has been out that morning polishing the apples to a gloss on each old tree. This is Austria.

Little wooden ferries zigzag between these hamlets; these are curious affairs, narrow-beamed, with high square prows and elaborately carved and gabled "houses" on the stern. I am under the impression that these top heavy craft are the only means of transport in and out of these tiny community pockets. Any roads, if roads there are, are invisible.

And oh, so silent, so peaceful, so tranquil in the bright morning sun. No noise... no noise that is, except for the pure high notes of a tin whistle echoing down from upriver where a chap in a little red-sailed dinghy is rippling downstream before a light wind, steering with an idle elbow as he plays. And somewhere high up in the sylvan darkness, in a sweet Purcellian contrapunto, the teasing echo of the faun.

The night before, I had heard folk speak in the highest terms of the Winterhafn at Linz, glowing about the hospitality of the Hafnmeister, the luxurious nature of the facilities, and the never ceasing rounds of elegant soirées that made the Winterhafn the social epicentre of the Donau. At least, that is the impression I received, and was therefore determined to reach the fabled marina of Linz that night. The fact that it was sixty kilometres downstream didn't discourage me one jot.

This determination sent me oaring steadily through the afternoon, past pretty hamlets where horses grazed, past the lovely schloss-dominated village of Ottensheim at sunset, where cheerful café lights begged me to tie up for the night and halt my headlong slog... and so eventually at ten o'clock, arms aching, shivering with cold and exhaustion, illegally rowing through the darkness, to arrive at the much lauded Winterhafn of Linz. Here I looked around me in some dismay. Where was the brightly lit clubhouse winking gold and copper out into the frosty night? The lively bar breathing warm gusts of beer and tobacco and chatter from its welcoming doorway? I looked around in vain for the spotless bathrooms and hot showers I had been striving towards all day, the Swedish sauna perhaps, the fellow yachties waiting to applaud the valiant *Jack de Crow* and offer her skipper hot toddies, free life membership and the hands of their daughters in marriage.

There was not the faintest sign of these bright dreams. I found myself rowing instead into a dank industrial arm of the river, the sole amenities consisting of a small portacabin of toilets (locked) and lots of cyclone wire fencing. The only other craft there were three speedboats, all battened down for the season under tarpaulins. The nearest lights, orange sodium lights with their ugly glare, were a mile away along a windswept road between warehouses and wasteland. Thinking of the cosy villages I had spurned all that afternoon, I could have wept.

Starving and cranky, I trudged off down the road towards the distant lights and found, surprisingly, a huge hotel just as the cyclone wire ends. It was a vast and soulless affair, rather like an airport hotel, and there was absolutely no way I was going to allow myself to be tempted to book in to one of their overpriced, over-amenitied rooms, not an intrepid adventurer like me, but they did allow me to buy a bowl of warming soup... and a beer... and another beer... and a warming whisky... and before I knew it, I had succumbed. A hot power shower, sachets of complimentary shampoo, soft white towels, lots of them, a hair-dryer, a remote control TV, a digital alarm clock radio, a minibar with salted peanuts and cans of Heineken, and crackly sheets and stiff pillows. I am, for one night at least, back in the late Twentieth Century, an anonymous businessman on a routine trip to sound out possibilities in the expanding European market. As for the owner of that ridiculous little dinghy abandoned down in the deserted Winterhafn, he has stepped off the world for a little while, and cannot be contacted.

The next morning, I decided to assuage some of my guilt by spending the day busking in Linz, trying to recover some of my losses and dignity as a bona fide traveller. But first, a permit. For to busk in Austria, I had found out, one must first acquire a permit from the relevant authority. This, in the case of Linz, was to be found in the bowels of a vast and soulless building beyond the river which resembled nothing less than Orwell's Ministry of Truth. Once there, I found my way through a labyrinth of ill lit, low-ceilinged corridors to Room 2035 on the third floor, where I was relieved of my passport, given a form to fill in, and sent off to find Room 1037 on the second floor to have it processed. There, a stern lady told me that without my passport, she could do nothing about processing my B13 form, and, besides, I needed a CX 25 docket from Accounts on the fourth floor before she could possibly do anything useful. Returning to Room 2035, I found that the chap with my passport had vanished, but a secretary thought that he had probably taken it down to Registration in Room 1067 to have it ratified with a blue P300, and I'd best trot off after him if I didn't want to lose my passport for ever. After several hours of this sort of thing, and just when I was thinking that perhaps taking out Austrian citizenship might be the easier course of action, I found myself back with my passport, a licence to busk for an entire year, and a map of the city on an A4 sheet of paper with a single street on it highlighted in green. This street, the man explained, was the only area in Linz where buskers were permitted to perform. And good luck! And welcome to our warm and beautiful country, not to be in any way confused with our cold and humourless neighbours, the Germans.

The street where buskers were allowed to perform turned out to be a pedestrian precinct, but so chilly and draughty that few people lingered long enough to be entertained. When they did, they tended to be knocked down by a passing trolley car, running along the tramlines that someone had carelessly placed there... a curious design feature of a pedestrian mall, I thought. After three fatalities and the princely sum of two hundred Austrian schillings (enough to buy a bread roll) I decided to retire, threw my hard won busking licence into a nearby bin, and set off to find a laundromat. Here too I was frustrated in my efforts. Having sorted all my dirty laundry and hauled it into town that morning, I could find no laundromat at all. Eventually, I was informed by the faintly sneering official in the Tourist Office that most Austrians possessed their own washing machines so that public laundromats were hardly necessary, and probably a danger to public health no doubt and just one of the many reasons why Austria was a superior country to all others.

I found it hard to warm to Linz. It was grandiose in a wedding cake sort of way, with lots of monumental public buildings and white marble everywhere but it lacked the cobbled-together charm of the German towns. The weather matched the city: a bright but chilly sky, and a brisk policeman of a breeze keeping the blood tingling and the shoppers from loitering in the streets. I chose to loiter no longer, and rowed on.

The next three days I struggled on down the river, sometimes rowing but more often sailing against a wind that steadily increased day by day, ushering in grey louring clouds and cold rain. The days were empty of companionship and colour, but even at this point my journal records the odd delight. Golden wagtails, I note, are common around locks. They look as though they are trying to lever off their own wingcases with their tails. Then there was the distinctive flying cigar shape of a red-throated diver torpedoing out of an industrial boatyard, when I had always assumed that their only habitat was some remote and pristine sea loch in the Outer Hebrides. It seems that what with the Red Kites and the Marsh Harriers and, I am almost sure, a lone osprey four days before, I have met most of Britain's endangered species happily mucking in with common humanity over the last few weeks. European birds are clearly less particular about habitat than their British counterparts. Then there was the lunch stop where a waitress brought me fried eggs and bacon and sausages, but instead of serving it on a plate, just brought a knife, a fork and the whole frying pan to guzzle from, a splendid idea that I would rather like to see adopted back home. My journal reminds me too just how exciting Austrian bread is – it comes studded with crystals of rock salt, or peppered with poppy seeds, or tasting divinely of caraway or smothered in sesame – but cafés rather sneakily charge per piece without first informing you of the fact.

September has arrived, and the plum trees and vines are hung with fruit, bloomy purple or translucent green. Wasps are a nuisance, and I am grateful when the grey wind drives them away. On the second day of the month I realise that it is in fact exactly a year ago that I set out from Colemere Woods. I find a deserted industrial boatyard that night, so crowded with rusting dredgers, gravel-boats, half-sunken hulks and abandoned barges that I cannot tie up to the bank but must moor up alongside an old tug. My only route from the dinghy to the shore is a labyrinthine clamber over railings, along gangplanks, up onto iron decks, under gantries, down ladders and across pontoons, negotiating at least seven different craft along the way, and involving several giddy leaps across gulfs of rust-stained water. A light drizzle has started and the nearest village is a mile away. Thinking of all my friends waving me goodbye from the bridge a year ago, I become horribly maudlin. I am sick of rowing, sick of being alone, sick of travelling, sick of never getting any mail via Poste Restante, and sick of the drizzle and the damp and the whole damn dinghy. I am too tired even to bother making supper, and, besides, I think I am out of groceries. I will just go to sleep and blot out the miserable world for a brief time.

In this black mood, I am rummaging in my rucksack for something when by the feeble light of my torch I notice something for the first time. Before I left Ellesmere, the school matron, a very beautiful and gentle woman called Mair, had asked to borrow my old rucksack. When she had returned it, I saw that as a present she had sewn onto one end the Ellesmere College crest, a particularly appropriate design as it depicts a crow with a ring in its bill – my own ship's flag, in fact. This I had known about and thanked Mair for, as well as for the large red and white spotty hanky that she had presented me with exactly a year before. But what I have never noticed until this dreary night is that on the inside of the rucksack, on the reverse side of the school badge, she has embroidered in golden thread a message. By the dim light of my little torch I examine it curiously. It reads: *Sandy, may all that is good watch over you and keep you safe. God bless.*

The discovery was timely. With those simple words, my mood lifted, suddenly, soaringly. I had carried that secret blessing with me for a year, and as I thought back over the last twelve months I realised how much I had indeed been blessed by all that is good – by friends and strangers, by birds and stars and clouds, by fine winds and the world's poetry, and by adventure and song. With that sudden lifting, I remembered that deep in the bows there was a bottle of red wine to finish off, and that there was some of that Austrian salt-bread to be eaten and… why… here's a little cheese I had forgotten about. I slept that night in my iron labyrinth more soundly, more sweetly than at any other time of the journey, and sent a silent blessing back to Mair in Shropshire, over all the sleeping leagues of Europe that lay between.

The wind is a contrary gale as I set off the next morning downriver. The skies are grey and Wagnerian with bluster and flung rain. This is in fact the Wachau region, the land of the Nibelung, and the Valkyries on their storm-steeds ride me down like a fleeing warrior. The current here is strong, but the wind is stronger still; without a jib to turn her nose, if I fumble the turn even for a second or so I find that I am blown a good twenty yards back up the river. If I think about it, the experience is miserable. If I allow myself to settle into a grim businesslike numbness, the hours pass.

I come in the early afternoon to the town of Melk, famous for its great abbey. This occupies the whole flat top of a loaf-shaped hill overlooking the river, and is possibly the finest example of Baroque architecture in the world. A tour leaves one feeling as though one has just devoured several crates full of caramel meringues. Each individual room, sure enough, each chamber, each ceiling, each nave, taken one by one with good doses of plain fare in between, is admittedly splendid. But all together, piled one upon the other like some toppling confectionery extravaganza, well, to be honest, it left me wanting to lie down in a darkened room for several weeks afterwards.

Inside, the most impressive sight amongst many was that of the two great ceilings, of the Hall and the Library respectively. Each of these great rooms, parallel twins of one another, presents to the crick-necked viewer a vast domed ceiling, painted with a sweeping panorama of angels and cherubim. Here against a duck-egg and sky-blue-pink heaven upheld by marble pillars, Prudence and Justice, Fortitude and Temperance swirl in giddy dance with their lions and ever-pouring urns, their wreaths and ribbons and swords, all soaring to the zenith of the high dome. What is so extraordinary is that whereas the ceiling of the Hall is indeed deeply domed, that of the Library is in fact not. It is flat. It is impossible to believe this when one is first told it; the supporting pillars far above surely curve in great arches to that distant dove centrally outspread. It is only when you go and stand close up against one of the walls that the perspective betrays the painter's art, and you see for the first time that the marble pillars are simply painted illusions on a flat ceiling. The skill involved in such a heady deception must be immense. Could such an illusion on such a scale be reproduced today? Or is it, like the lost secret of the blue glass in Chartres, an art that has been forgotten, no less than the secret of the building of Stonehenge or the cutting of the Inca stonework in Peru?

The last great sight of Melk Abbey is the baroque chapel where the gilding and ornamentation reaches a magnificence, an opulence and a tastelessness to last a lifetime. Here the two most striking features are a pair of skeletons preserved in glass cases on either side of the main aisle. Instead of reclining decently in the usual manner of the dead, draped in mouldering shrouds, these two have been dressed and posed in a ghastly imitation of Life. One is reclining coyly propped on one elbow, his skeletal hand tucked under his chin, and one leg crooked as though he is posing for a fashion shot for *Cleo* magazine, pouting invisible lips at the camera. The other is clad in beetle-green silk pantaloons and is sitting clasping in his bony hand a quill pen and a little diary, recording the day's excitements:

Friday, September 4th (Quarter Moon)
Weather: *Cloudy. Intermittent showers.*
Appointments: *None.*
To do: *Moulder a little*
Comments: *Still dead...*

Several days after leaving Melk, I came at last to the Wienerwald, the famous Vienna Woods, and on an afternoon of sunshine and rain in equal measure, slid over green-silver rapids like a yellow willow leaf and came to the marble splendour of Vienna itself, greatest of all the Danubian cities.

My last visit to Vienna was memorable for the fact that I had encountered a ghost there. I had been only nineteen at the time, and had taken myself off on a penniless tour of Europe. I arrived on that occasion in Vienna late one evening, set out to buy some nourishing and filling bread and like some naughty boy buying some magic beans instead of selling the cow, ended up buying a single piece of Viennese chocolate for all the remaining schillings in my pocket. Then I set off for a large dark park to find a comfortable bench on which to spend the night.

I found one near the Prater which I knew vaguely about from *The Third Man*, and settled down on a bench in a shadier corner of the park. I knew instinctively even back then that the Austrians were not likely to allow riff-raff to clutter up their public gardens, so I was well back from the lighted avenue and away from the brightly lit fountain that I could just make out splashing noisily to itself off through the trees. Despite my famished belly, I was wide awake that night, alert to every sound, every waft of the warmish breeze that blew gently through the darkened park, every gust of noise that drifted in snatches from the avenue. Perhaps it was the strong effects of rich chocolate on a starved belly or the balminess of the breeze, too warm for October surely, but I was all at once acutely aware of the history of the city about me. Over there, rising above the trees I could make out the great Ferris wheel still turning its golden lights high into the sky; from somewhere closer at hand there came the sweet, swinging strains of a waltz, the Blue Danube no less, setting my hands conducting to the darkness with a one-two-three, one-two-three, one...From some nearby concert-hall on the main avenue spilled out a late night audience, dressed in elegant black and white or evening dresses, chatting and hailing cabs or heading off to some smart Viennese coffee shop or bar, and oblivious of the young vagrant sitting a hundred yards away under the darkness of the trees. It was all so very much what I had expected of Vienna; the meeting of culture and history and elegance and music, there on the lit stage of the distant street.

It was then that I noticed that one of the actors had left the golden-lit stage... or rather an actress. A figure had slipped away, it seemed, from the crowd and was making her way through the park, weaving an erratic course towards me. The more I looked at the figure, the odder it seemed. In the darkness under the trees, I could see that she was dressed in white, and what is more, a dress of some antique style, pinched in at the waist, and flaring out in a great bell, supported no doubt by hoops of whalebone and acres of crinoline. The whole thing looked insubstantial and filmy, white tulle or lace, as she swung towards me across the grass. It was obviously some young woman making her way homewards from a costume ball – had she not been on her own, I would have sworn she was a newly-wed bride in her wedding gown. That she was also drunk was plain. She was dancing and pirouetting across the park in giddy swirls, possibly so entranced by the distant waltz music that she was unable to slow her progress to a sober gait. And, although her tapered torso leant drunkenly to this side and that as she danced, I was entranced by the sheer grace of her movements. She seemed to my peering eyes veritably to glide across the grass, zigzagging her way through the trees as lightly as the breeze... and all the while drawing ever nearer to where I sat.

When she was fifty yards off, I began to wonder if I had been right in thinking she was merely a late night stray. The shape of her dress and bodice were clear, but her head was little more than a pale blob, too pale by far, her mouth and eyes mere shadowy sockets in that almost luminescent whiteness. A feeling of unease stole upon me. My slightly patronising smile at the girl's eccentric solitary waltzing faded from my face as the figure pirouetted closer and closer. Now she was dancing in deepest shadow, off the main paths and between the tree trunks. She appeared to blunder into a thicket and emerged more drunkenly than before, leaving a rag of white caught in the branches behind her. And now, although she was approaching the darkest part of the park, I could tell that she was skimming – how so lightly? – towards one of those low fences of bent iron hoops that are edged with knee-high hedges which one sees in municipal parks the world over. Nearer, nearer, nearer she approached it in a spinning waltz and then without the slightest pause was through it and gliding nearer still to me. In that instant, I knew for certain that I was seeing no mortal woman, for although anyone, man, child, or woman, could have hurdled the fence with ease, no one could have done it in the way she had - there had not been the slightest upward leap in her motion at all. She had simply glided through it as you or I might wade through a low-lying bank of morning mist.

She was now only ten yards from me, and my spine was attempting to escape backwards through the wooden slats of the bench-back behind me. To my horror, as the phantom figure swooped even nearer, her head leant coquettishly on one side, but more and more and more, until I realised that her neck was surely broken. Her torso too was growing thinner, and leaning over like that of a broken doll, so that the graceful dancer's figure was breaking up before my eyes. In my ears the distant waltz music seemed to swell louder and louder and the treetops rattled with the passing breeze – by this time, my eyes were closed shut in anguished prayer as the horrid decaying thing swept the last few yards towards me. I flung up flailing arms as I fought to keep off whatever it was approaching in the darkness. In fact, I think I let out a low moaning scream of sheer terror. Then there was a sudden fine wetness upon my face, the softest of kisses, and something tingling and cool clinging to my hands and hair before passing away into the park behind me.

I opened my eyes to see... what? So this was ectoplasm, was it? These airy bubbles, these strangely familiar clinging clots of froth, silver-white in the darkness, all that was left of the phantom dancer, being blown by the breeze about the park? As, trembling, I gathered up my rucksack and fled out of the park, I passed by the large fountain and saw the source of the mystery. Someone with a jolly sense of fun had poured into the agitated waters earlier a whole bottleful of dishwashing detergent, and now covering the surface of the pool were great cumulus clouds of bubblebath foam. These tall islands of froth were at intervals being skimmed off the waist-high parapet of the pool by the warm breeze, to be sent dancing about the park in bell shaped gouts of soap bubbles. Now that I looked closer, there were other characters to join my hanged bride: a light-footed pale hunchback dissolving over there, a phantom albino hippo gliding and bobbing between the trees over yonder, a disintegrating flock of misshapen geese floating skywards to be shredded by the bare boughs of the treetops.

My heart still thumping, my mouth dry with recent terror, I made my way back to the railway station and spent a wakeful night in the glaring discomfort of the railway waiting rooms. No lying on the benches, of course... this was Austria, after all...but no ghosts either.

Vienna was an important stop for me. Beyond it, I would be travelling into lands relatively unknown, leaving behind Western Europe and sailing into the former Eastern Bloc countries: Slovakia, Hungary, Croatia, Serbia, Bulgaria and Romania. For all of these countries, I needed visas. In fact, so much so were those former Balkan nations in a state of flux at that time that it was difficult to ascertain exactly which countries bordered on the Danube and which didn't. The Yugoslavian Embassy was a nightmare especially. There were queues of angry young women with squalling children, and older headscarfed women standing despondently, and as far as I could gather, they were one and all being refused their requests by the official behind the grille. I struck up a conversation with the young woman behind me in the queue and gathered from her that the country was in such a state that even long-term resident citizens of the country were being refused entry. She herself had her Yugoslavian passport, she had lived all but the last year of her life there, and now was unable to return to Dubrovnik to visit her sick father. The mood in the waiting hall was one of resentment and despair, and I am almost embarrassed to admit that, in order to distract the woman's little girl from her fretful tears at the delay, I pulled out my magic hanky and started doing some tricks. Soon the whole queue were watching in grave silence, and some were beginning to smile – more at the little girl's wide-eyed reaction than the childish tricks, I must add – but the mood lightened a little as we all made our way up the line. By the time I got to the window, I was convinced that if all these good folk were being refused visas into their own country, then I would not stand a chance. And indeed, on tentatively putting in my request to the hard-faced man behind the grille, his first reaction was a curt refusal. The borders were closed. The Bosnian situation had made things impossible. It would be better to travel elsewhere.

Ah, said I, taking a deep breath, and launching into an explanation about *Jack de Crow* and the Black Sea and rowing and how very tricky it would be to row elsewhere across the Carpathian Mountains and... and off he went, vanishing through a doorway to consult with a superior office about how the rules applied to dinghy sailors. To my astonishment, he returned a few minutes later with a visa application form, a tight smile, and an expression in his eyes that spoke volumes about the stupidity of the regulations, before turning back to the far more straightforward task of keeping apart a sick man in Dubrovnik and his daughter.

All this while, I stayed in a big, impersonal Youth Hostel and realised over those three days just how un-youthful I had become in terms of the sort of pitch and volume at which I wished my fellow dorm-mates would hold conversations, how much of other people's pubic hair I was prepared to accept in the wash-basin, and how late at night was an acceptable time to come in and turn all the lights on and conduct hilarious toothpaste fights an inch from the ear of the cranky, middle-aged sleeper on the bottom bunk. After three days, I was rescued from this pit of youthful high spirits by Alfons and Uli, two old friends from a walking tour years ago. I had arranged to meet them for dinner but when they found out that I was staying in the Youth Hostel they did not even let me return there that night. I was taken home to their elegant flat, pushed into a hot shower, gently but firmly told that I was staying there until further notice, and fell asleep on the most comfortable sofa bed in the known Universe.

For the next few days, it was rather like being entertained by two slim, immaculate, well-bred Siamese cats. Alfons made it clear with a demure insistence that anything I needed was at my disposal: the new racing bike for getting around Vienna, the contents of the fridge, the slimline phone for making international calls ("That is what it is *for*," he explained when I started to wave aside his offer)… in fact, everything. In return, I would have to help him sample the latest acquisitions in his collection of fine malt whiskies, and there was to be no more argument.

I responded to this extraordinary kindness by managing to clod-hop my way through the next three days, demonstrating in person the utter boorishness of all non-Austrians. When I applauded loudly the fact that Vienna had seen fit to provide free travel on all the trams I had been riding over the last few days and what a jolly good thing that was, Alfons and Uli pointed out quietly that no, this was not the case, but that they worked on an honesty system which no right-minded citizen would dream of abusing; tickets were available at all those booths I had failed to notice on every street corner. When we went off to a nearby pub in a rainstorm and Alfons lent me an old plastic mac, the only item of clothing in their possession that didn't look as though it had been tailor-made, I slung it onto a coat hook in the vestibule of the pub before charging ahead into the bar to buy a round of beers…and only found later that Alfons had discreetly sneaked back to re-hang it properly on a proper coat hanger provided by the establishment for the proper care of one's vestments. Lastly, I had been warned about the lift in the apartment block. This was one of those alarming contraptions of brass and mahogany and wire cables with iron grille doors that scissor back to open and shut. They appear in old hotels in Hitchcock movies in the last three minutes where the heroine is waiting for Cary Grant to come and deal with the one-armed murderer and as the lift descends to the lobby from an upper floor, the counterweight can be seen rising through a grid of shadows in the background with dangling from it the silhouette of a hanged corpse, which soon becomes all too clearly recognisable as that of a one-armed man, leaving the girl to suddenly work out that if the supposed murderer has himself just been killed, then that means that… no, it can't be!…and still the lift is descending and the lobby door is locked and… well, I'm sure you get the picture. Anyway, I had been carefully shown with a careful little demonstration that the lift was fine, just fine, as long as you didn't open the grille doors too soon, in which case the lift would jam irrevocably unless Cary Grant or Katherine Hepburn were around to let you out or murder you or whatever was most appropriate in the circumstances. It was therefore embarrassing to come home one day from touring the city on the bike, and find myself waiting on the ground floor for the lift with a breathless and slightly worried young lady who had just rushed in from outside. Partly to be friendly, partly to put her at her ease, I introduced myself as an English visitor and made comic running and panting gestures to show that I understood she was in a hurry. As we climbed into the lift, she relaxed a little and smiled at me, explaining in quite good English that yes, she had left her two-year old infant in the car in the street with the engine running while she just rushed upstairs to retrieve her forgotten purse. But all was well, she would take only thirty seconds, and what could happen in that interval, ja? We laughed merrily at her groundless worry, and as we approached her floor, I,

ever the gallant gentleman, stepped forward to pull back the doors to speed her
on her way.

Too soon.

The lift jerked to a halt, just six inches short of the fifth floor, there was a
clash of distant gears, and the grille doors stuck fast. I tugged at them. There was
no movement. I tugged again, but as this only produced an alarming creak from
the cables, I quickly desisted. We were stuck, stuck in a metal cage halfway up a
deserted midday apartment block, and it was remarkable how all our recent
international bonhomie and bridge-building suddenly evaporated. The next twenty
minutes are minutes I, for one, would really rather forget. In a very short time,
the emotional temperature in the lift became arctic, relieved only sporadically by
the woman being distracted from her contempt for the stupid foreigner by her
vivid images of how young Hans in the car had probably by now found the
handbrake-release and was even now taking his first, and possibly last, joyride
along the Frederikstrasse. I, in the meantime, was jabbing at buttons, rattling the
grille, tentatively jumping up and down to try and dislodge something, anything,
but to no avail. I did consider trying to lighten the atmosphere with a few choice
anecdotes from the voyage so far, as that usually managed to raise a few
chuckles, but in the end decided on balance that a better course to pursue would
be alternately to apologise and soothe in my very limited German. All those old
war movies and Stalag Fifteen escape movies had not really provided me with
the vocabulary for either apology or soothing comfort (*Raus! Raus! Achtung!*
and *Schweinhunt!*) but I think I can fairly claim that I gave it my best shot.

We were rescued after several ice ages by an elderly cleaning lady who had
come in to wash down the stairwell, and my now near-hysterical companion
raced out to hurtle down the stairs to check on the infant. She forgot to say
goodbye, now I come to think of it. I am quite sure she meant to.

Avoiding the apartment block after that gave me a chance to explore the
wonders of Vienna fully and I spent several days dutifully admiring them: the
tree-clad Hundertwasser House, the Belvedere Gallery, the great holy gloom of
St. Stephensdom with its crimson and azure Western Window blazing like a
chrysanthemum of fire on high; the blueberry-yoghurt-and-chocolate-Nutella-
flavoured ice cream that was worth the two-thousand mile row any day; and the
sheer marmoreal splendour of the city buildings themselves. I had never seen
such a wealth of marble, of gilding, of civic statuary - fountains swimming with
Tritons, monuments scrambling with horse-hooves and manes, squares, columns
and palisades, architraves and porticoes, each doorway upheld by a pair of giant,
muscular caryatids, and in every little town square or park or courtyard, a statue
of yet another famous person: Liszt, Mozart, Freud, Klimt, Bruckner, Strauss.
There seems to be a statue of simply everyone that ever existed. There is
probably one of me somewhere, though I never found it.

The last thing to love in Vienna is the cafés. I spent long, blissful hours in a
gloomy coffee house all in dark brown with an immense gilt mirror soaring up
into the darkness of the ceiling; the largest mirror in Europe, I was told. Another
favourite was Santo Spirito – this was tucked down a little side alley and was

furnished simply with polished bentwood chairs, lit only by candles and playing nothing but classical choral works; Pergolesi, Vittoria, Tallis, Byrd, Scarlatti, pure as candleflames themselves, flowered into the darkness as the rain poured down outside and yet another rich coffee appeared at my elbow as I wrote.

And what of poor *Jack de Crow* all this time, you may ask. How was she included in all this idle tripping about galleries and coffee shops? Well, to tell you the truth, she wasn't. I had abandoned her in a modern little marina on the shores of the main Danube which runs, as tourists are so disappointed to discover, some miles from the city centre and isn't even faintly blue. In my week in Vienna, I went out to visit her only once, and trusted that she was being well-looked after by the gods and the Hafnmeister who, since he was charging me a stiff number of schillings per day as mooring fee, was hopefully doing his job. But I was not completely idle. My thin foam mattress had been encased ever since Bristol with a waterproof mattress cover that was actually a stroke of genius on the part of a helpful lady in a Marks and Spencer store (and for the record, aren't they always so helpful in Marks & Sparks? Always middle-aged, always motherly, always helpful. Where do they get them from?) You see, most waterproof mattress covers that you'd find in camping shops are brittle, slippery, crackly things that make a night's sleep like lying in a box of after-dinner-mint-wrappers. But this kind lady had suggested the sort of cover they use to cover mattresses in old folks' homes for... well, she was too delicate to suggest what for... and so provided me with a large white zip-up cover that was fleecy and soft and warm on the outside, but fully rubberised on the inside. This had provided me with the best nine months' sleeping of my life. The only problem was that it was twice as big as it needed to be. This, however, fitted in very neatly with my other problem which was that my two pillows, a large slab of sponge-foam pinched from a dump outside Oxford and the parrot-embroidered cushion given to me by Jenny in Wroxeter were far from waterproof. What I wanted to find was a clever seamstress who could trim the mattress cover to a single bed size and turn the remains into a couple of zip-up pillow cases. Where I would find such a person who could do the job in a hurry, I had no... but tinkle-tinkle-tinkle, in came the usual magic and there, three doors down from Alfons and Uli's apartment door, was just such a shop and just such a girl. Just opposite it was the one other shop that I needed, an old-fashioned cobbler who could punch two more holes in my belt to cope with my ever decreasing girth and fix the straps of my deteriorating rucksack. The cobbler was an old man called Herr Wulf who had retired some years ago, become so bored that he had re-opened his dusty little shop, and now spent his days happily inventing a new type of pin-hole camera that would really work. We spent a joyful hour together in his back room over a mug of tea looking at surprisingly good photos of Viennese street life taken on his invention and admiring his home-made lathe. Such things sound trivial when one is meant to be extolling the wonders of the greatest city in Europe, but it was these little moments that made Vienna for me more than just a huge art gallery or museum.

Finally, I had run out of excuses to linger any longer. A week of blustery weather and squalls had begun to clear, all my jobs were done, my visas in order, my letters written, and the whisky collection of Alfons was looking distinctly thinnish. It was time to move on. I was, to be honest, nervous. Ahead of me, and only half a day's sail, was the border of Slovakia and the end of Western Europe. I knew nothing about the lands ahead, apart from vague apprehensions engendered by the fact that every evil mastermind in any thriller always talked to his pet cacti or piranha tank with an Eastern European accent. I had also heard something vaguely about trouble brewing in Serbia, wherever that was? No doubt I would find out soon enough.

Alfons and Uli came down to the marina to see me off, accompanied by Peter and Ingrid, two other good friends from that walking tour years ago. When they first saw just how little *Jack de Crow* was, they all visibly blanched; being accustomed to my stories, they had assumed that I had exaggerated her littleness and they were in fact expecting a small yacht. Nevertheless, they soon rallied and between them they produced a large bottle of wine, some stores of salami, bread, fruit and cheese, and a mysterious little package that clinked. This last item Peter told me to keep closed until I was in need of some serious cheering up. Then before a gentle breeze, I hoisted sail, moved out onto the broad grey river and set off into the east and the Unknown.

Into the East

'Oh, East is East and West is West, and never the twain shall meet,
Till Earth and Sky stand presently at God's great Judgement Seat;'

Kipling – *The Ballad of East and West.*

Jack did not lightly forgive me for my callous abandonment in Vienna. The next day she abandoned me and like naughty Albert at the Zoo, was nearly eaten by lions. It happened like this.

The first night spent out of Vienna was spent in a grim shipyard outside Bratislava, a cheerless place full of rusting tankers and oily water. Without any desire to footslog through industrial wasteland into Bratislava, I stayed on my dinghy that night, not even getting off to stretch my legs. After an early night, I woke at dawn and set off early down the river. As the morning progressed the day became wilder in all respects. The light early breeze stiffened to a following wind that sent me churning down the river at a cracking speed. The river too was fierce here; even in the early morning stillness, the placid seeming mirror of the surface would sometimes boil up in a great lazy swell, suck at my oars, and spin me insolently in a couple of circles before sending me on my way with a little pat on the behind like some multi-national magnate teasing a very junior typist. Such moments just served to remind me uneasily of the power of this cold-handed god with whom I was consorting.

As the miles passed, so the river widened until the banks blurred into the distance. Where I could still see them, they were as straight as a die, shelving parapets of rust-dark gravel and beyond them a landscape so featureless and bleak that it is difficult now to recall. Was it bare earth? No, for that would imply some richness, some potential for fertility. Flat fields? But no, there was no living thing, no hint of softness, nor the bleak beauty of dead winter pasture. An expanse of concrete perhaps? But that would suggest some mighty purpose, some monumental work of Man. No, the landscape was like one seen in a dreary dream, unimportant so not sketched in by the dreaming mind... or like the unfinished background of a poor painting not worth the finishing.

Such thoughts are not in my mind at the time, of course. All my attention is now concentrated on controlling the dinghy as she rockets along before what has now become a gale. The wind blows straight from the north out of a sky that is as raw as frozen iron, and the river has widened until I am now clearly on a vast lake. I cannot in the increasing murk actually see any banks at all – occasionally I see a lonely beacon post standing high out of the water, and then another, and then another, and these I follow for want of any other guidance. Sometimes far, far away, I catch sight of what might be a series of low bunkers or an electricity pylon, but otherwise I feel that I have stumbled onto a vast lagoon just off the North Sea... or the North Bering Strait for all I know. I certainly have nothing like this marked on my map. In fact, from this point on, my precious map of Europe's waterways is pretty well useless.

Nevertheless, as always happens when the conditions grow rough, I find I am unexpectedly enjoying myself. I am well rugged up and waterproofed and the dinghy is certainly moving almost as fast as I have ever known it. The wind has rolled up the water into big smooth waves, as big as those on the open sea, and I am riding each one in smooth, powerful succession. *Jack* is doing well, and has a spurt of foam at her prow, a bone in her teeth as the sailors say. But I still feel as though I am sailing in a grey limbo, neither foggy nor clear, neither sea nor river. It is oddly like that phenomenon in Lord Dunsany's tale, "*The Queen of Elfland's Daughter*", where there is a nothingness creeping across the land. And ahead, there really is nothing. The vast lake or lagoon seems to stop in mid-air, and an uncanny nothingness lies beyond.

Finally, I draw near enough to see the explanation for this sudden cessation of landscape. The lake laps right up against a low parapet that stretches from east to west across my whole forward horizon; this is just the top foot or so of a great reservoir wall. I am later to see that it drops a hundred feet on the other side to a flat plain, but the appearance from a small boat on the lake is that the water simply ends in a grey sky, and that this low concrete rim is the dreary World's End. Along to the eastern end of the dam wall is a concrete tower now familiar as the control tower of a lock, and before I can be blown right over the edge, I turn and reach across the wind towards the tower. Now that the waves are side-on, the sailing is less comfortable, but we bear up well, *Jack* and I, as we approach the concrete complex of piers and wharves directing shipping into the huge double locks that will let us continue on the river far below. It is only once we sail around into the relatively narrow jaws of the lock approach that the waves go berserk. Up until now, as I have said, they have been big enough but regular and rolling. Between the sheer concrete walls of the piers, however, the waves shoot up in savage vertical turrets of water, rebounding and interfering with one another to make a vicious chop the like of which I have never encountered. Even in the Thames Estuary, even in the Channel, the water didn't behave like this; in fact, I have only seen anything similar on film footage of underwater mines being detonated. All about me, explosions of water shoot up in six foot high towers, now here, now there, as though a hundred depth charges have been triggered beneath me by my arrival.

It is with a great deal of difficulty that we make it to the pier and an iron ladder up the side. Stowing the sails in their usual wrapped bundle about the gaff and boom, I hoist them up out of the way where they swing murderously from side to side. The rudder too is banging about viciously in the chop, so I hastily secure the tiller into a central position with a piece of elastic cord to stop it swinging around, and lower the blade into the water. If left wagging at the back in an upright position, it will snap at the first contact with the concrete pier. Attempting to clamber out of the bucketing *Jack* and onto the ladder while six foot waves are swooshing up my trouser-legs is no easy feat, but I make it to the top and tie *Jack* firmly to a bollard. She is still battering helplessly against the concrete wall with every new wave, but there is little I can do about that, so set off to see the lock-keeper about getting into the shelter of the lock proper as soon as possible.

The Jaws of Gabcikovo

The lock-keeper is less than happy. This, he explains in a mixture of Slovakian and German, is the notorious Gabçikovo Lock, and the very presence of small craft on the reservoir or in the lock is strictly *verboten*. He tells me that a yacht had arrived here two years back. It had been around the World several times. It had survived storms off Cape Horn; it had weathered typhoons in the Caribbean; it had run the gauntlet of the Torres Strait reefs... but here, *here*, he smirks with a sort of perverse pride, here at the Gabçikovo Lock, it had sunk with all hands. One of the crew they never found. Nevertheless, as I have presented him with a *fait accompli* by my arrival, he grudgingly agrees to allow me through along with a barge that is due in the next half-hour. I am to wait until it has passed in to the further of the two parallel locks, and row in afterwards. This is the procedure I have been following between here and Calais, so presents no problems. Meanwhile, *ja*, I am welcome to wait here out of the Slovakian wind until it is time to go.

Eventually through the murk we see the barge approaching down the lake and I button up warmly again and trudge the five hundred metres back down to the end of the pier ready to cast off and follow the barge in. She is half a mile away and approaching steadily. It is only when I am close by *Jack* that I think to myself how odd it is that she is no longer lying facing into the wind, as all boats do when tethered at the bow. Three dim seconds later I realise that, in fact, she is no longer tethered at all. The blue painter is still tied firmly around the bollard but with the sawing of *Jack* up and down against the pier in the dreadful waves, it has frayed right through. *Jack* is adrift!

Now normally this would not be too disastrous a problem. A dinghy adrift tends to blow aimlessly and quite slowly directly down wind, and this would bring *Jack* bumping along the pier wall until she fetched up against the closed lock gates of the nearer lock, in a sort of cul-de-sac. At the worst, I might need to fetch a boathook to reclaim her, and so miss the chance to go through with the approaching barge. But I had underestimated the free spirit of *Jack de Crow*. She needed no skipper aboard to guide her on a properly steered and purposeful course. The rudder was down, the tiller was held firmly by an elastic cord, and the hoisted bundle of canvas and gaff was enough of a sail in this wind to send her skipping across the waves on a course all of her own. She was sailing solo. The only problem with this jaunty show of independence was that the course she had set herself was on a direct collision course with the open lock gates and the approaching barge. She was, in fact, racing to get there first, and from the look of it, would arrive at the lock gates at precisely the same time her rival did.

Now let us be quite clear about one thing. Mention the word 'lock' in England, and one conjures up quaint pictures of mossy chambers where wagtails chip, waters pour in silver curtains and the hartstongue fern grows freely over mellow stonework. Mention the word 'barge' and similar pictures arise of narrowboats with names like 'Halcyon Daze' or 'Meadow Lark' or 'Buttercup Lass', gaily festooned with painted kettles full of geraniums. But here in the serious world of Slovakian industrial river transport, the locks are the size of hydro-electric schemes, and the barges would sit squarely in the middle of two football pitches end to end and not leave a lot of room for the players around the edge. These iron giants have names like 'Bratislava Hulk Haulage' or 'ΡΥΜΣΚΙ ΒΟΛΕΣΛΑϛ' and are not to be trifled with. You do not, for example, breeze merrily across their bows in a spirit of mischievous fun, or blithely bob along in the wake of their churning propellers playing a cheery hornpipe on the tin whistle hoping to raise a smile from the kindly bargees thereon. In fact, 'kindly' and 'bargees' is something of an oxymoron in this context. These behemoths are captained and crewed by grim-eyed, unshaven Romanians in grimy overalls who live on vodka, deep-fried pig's blood sausages and any dinghy sailors they can run down and gut. Get the picture? Good.

Another thing about these barges and the locks is that the one fits into the other like a truncheon into a sheath. There is barely any room between the iron precipice of the barge's hull and the concrete precipice of the lock's walls. There is certainly no room for a wooden dinghy off on a bid for freedom. In other words, in about three minutes time, there is going to be an almighty keel-crunching, hull-splitting collision between a two-thousand-ton, unstoppable industrial barge the size of Wolverhampton, a small thirty-year-old plywood dinghy, and the concrete mouth of a lock that has been there for the last thirty years and isn't going elsewhere on a whim at this juncture in time. Guess who's going to come out third?

I am quite helpless to do anything. For three daft seconds, I consider diving into the freezing choppy soup, clad as I am in waterproof over-trousers, cagoule, fleece, and several more layers of heavy winter clothing, in order to swim after the truant *Jack* and steer her to safety. Cowardice and sanity prevail, however, and I stay on land. I set off haring down the pier in a vain attempt to reach the collision point before *Jack* does, but the effort is futile.

I arrived blinded with sweat and too late. The giant barge was halfway into the lock, and there was no sign of *Jack*, not even a yellow smear of paint on the ironwork of the barge's hull. I stood numb with shock. Not only was all that I owned, passport, wallet, rucksack, now at the bottom of the lock, but the great journey had come to an abrupt end. The Gabçikovo Lock had claimed another gallant vessel. There would be no going to the Black Sea after all. The voyage ended here in this awful, awful place.

I sat down on a bollard and watched the last metres of the barge creep inexorably into the lock. The gates were closing. The crew were busy with mooring lines, and sure enough, appeared to be the rough Romanian crew I had envisaged. They seemed so unconcerned that it was clear that they hadn't even seen *Jack*, let alone noticed her demise. At least I would not have their angry recriminations to face.

Or would I? One of them was calling out and beckoning roughly in my direction. Ah well, time to face the music. I rose from my perch and trudged numbly down to the stern of the huge ship... and there, bobbing at the back, jaunty as ever, was *Jack de Crow*. I gaped. I gawped. I could not possibly imagine how she had been saved. Some crew were tying a towline to her; others were leaning over the stern examining her carefully for damage. Somehow, I gathered afterwards, the sharp-eyed crew had seen the imminent collision while I was running blindly down the lock, had deftly nipped forward to the bows and hooked *Jack* with a boathook, dragging her to the stern as the barge churned in through the lock gates.

Dazed with relief, I climbed down onto the barge into the midst of the unsmiling crew and, ignoring the stink of unwashed bodies and black teeth, went into my usual mime-routine, explaining that I had come from England. Beneath their grim, unblinking gaze, I then faltered into stammering thanks and apologies, and more apologies, and thanks, and apologies, and went to untie the bowline and disappear as quickly out of their lives as possible. At this point the grimmest of them all said, "Nyet! No! Kom!" and pointed down into the bowels of the ship.

Ah. Why? Was this the reckoning? Was I to face the stern Romanian *kapitan* and an angry, incomprehensible lecture on the folly of mixing footling pleasure craft with the serious Romanian barge industry trying to survive in a harsh capitalistic world? Or perhaps to turn out my pockets and cough up my last Slovakian *krona* as a ransom before reclaiming my sorry little dinghy? Or perhaps this ugly crew were in need of a cabin-boy after the last one had expired under the duties expected of him, and I would fit the bill nicely all the way to Odessa?

Well, no, not exactly. I was sat down at a table along with ten other men, all of them dark-browed, swarthy, and smoking what smelt like tarmac, and was poured a large tumbler of schnapps. A bowl of hot soup appeared, and a platter of bread; the soup was a sort of broth full of root vegetables, white fish, black scaly fish skin, paprika and black pepper, and was ambrosial to my dazed senses. Then there followed another schnapps, burning like fire in my throat. A sizzling plate of fat rissoles, chopped tomato and salad appeared through the haze of blue smoke in front of me, and I fell on it with tears of joy and exhaustion. All this while, some of the crew were getting up from their dinners and moving outside to fix something. When I followed, I saw that they were rigging up a portable pump to sit in *Jack*'s waterlogged bottom to rid her of all the water that had washed aboard. Another man was handing out my sodden rucksack, my sleeping bag and my mattress in their sacks, and a third was inspecting some minor damage to the prow where the perspex bow-plate fitted by Peter in Coblenz had splintered into two. I moved to help but was ushered back down into the galley and poured a third schnapps by a man who, I suddenly realised, was speaking a thick guttural French, and was plying me with questions.

The next few hours passed in a tarry, schnapps-bright haze, and it was some twenty miles down the river again that they gently helped me into my dinghy, untied me from the stern and cast me adrift to make my own way again. The day had cleared, the river had narrowed down to a manageable size once more, and *Jack* and I were left alone to continue on our journey together. After a sheepish silence, *Jack* apologised to me for the truancy that had come so near to disaster that afternoon. I in turn did the right thing and said how sorry *I* was for abandoning her in Vienna and going off to art galleries and coffee shops without her and, with a little shake of her sails, she made it quite clear that all was now well between us. To change the topic, I pointed out how well we had done that day, breaking all previous personal records. We had come just over one hundred kilometres in a single day. And so it was with a surge of mutual pride, the best of friends again, we sailed at dusk that evening out of Slovakia and into the land of Hungary.

"Season of mists and mellow fruitfulness..."

Having got the whole of *The Eve of St. Agnes* under my belt, I had turned back to some of Keats' shorter works to memorise and, as before, I found that day by day the words took shape around me in the landscape I was passing through. The land about me was flat but mellow with old golds and purple copses, and a haze of wood smoke hung in the bright air from morning to dusk. Two more days of steady rowing brought me to the town of Esztergom, the ancient spiritual heart of Hungary. In my ignorance, I had never heard of it, but the very name conjured up something Byzantine and mosaic. You never see it written in any way other than like this:

ESZ✝ERG⊕M

...and this gave me an inexplicable thrill about the place. High over the town looms a rounded hill, and this is capped by the green-domed Dom. I wandered up through the massive fortifications of the Burg one morning; a wet night had left the ground soggy with large, sad leaves which lay like soiled paper bags all over the unkempt grass and slippery paths. The place felt very Eastern Bloc, with cracked concrete and damp stone, and the Dom was cavernous and cold. I paid a small sum to climb up to the top of the dome and from there could see the whole length of the river, the Duna as we must call it now, sweeping backwards to the brown haze of Slovakia and onwards to the Great Bend a few miles ahead. Here the river, after so many hundreds of miles forging eastwards, turns sharply south to Budapest and beyond. Where it does so, gentle hills on either side are clothed with fruit trees and orchards, vineyards and little homesteads; here is a place where Keats could well have written his *Ode to Autumn*, especially as here still, as in the poet's day, cider-presses ooze the slow hours and reaping-hooks still spare the last twinéd wreath of flowers. But not here in Esztergom. Here the distant yapping of dogs in back lanes, the faint pervading smell of open drains and the soggy trees argued a poverty very different from the well-brushed landscapes of Austria.

Wandering back down through the ramparts and the four hundred steps to the river, I was suddenly baled up by five dogs. Three were snarling about my ankles and another two were on a parapet above me, engaged in a frenzy of barking and teeth-baring at the level of my head. I scrabbled in panic at the handle of an old wooden door set into a corner tower and, to my surprise, the door swung open and I fell through into the darkness beyond. When I had recovered and stood up and brushed myself down, I was startled all over again by realising that an ancient crone was sitting less than two feet away from me, hidden in the shadows of the small dimly lit chamber I had stumbled into. After gazing at me intently from hooded eyes, she made a sweeping gesture with her arm towards a hanging curtain, like some gypsy fortune teller at a fair, and cackled something like "Enter, stranger, and gaze upon your doom," though I may have imagined this bit. Pushing aside the curtain, I found myself in a large circular room which had been converted into a temporary photographic art gallery, of all things. My mind full of *Macbeth*, I had been expecting a torture chamber at the very least. I am neither very knowledgeable nor interested in photography, but these were extraordinary because not one of the exhibits had been produced on ordinary commercial film. The artists had instead somehow projected their image onto a bizarre variety of materials – hessian, corrugated iron, bleached wooden slats, muslin – instead of onto the usual glossy paper. The images were grainy or patchy, coarse, splashy, brush-stroked or mottled, and had the power of all things primitive. To see a landscape of winter trees and frozen puddles projected onto a sheet of rusting tin, or to see the figure of a Bosnian refugee mother and child caught in the fibres of a piece of dusty weave of sacking like some latter day Turin Shroud, was a strangely moving experience. I thought of Herr Wulf and his pinhole camera-shots and how much he would have enjoyed experimenting in the same way.

By the time I left, the dogs had moved on to terrify some other poor traveller, and I was free to go. Despite the dogs, despite the decay, I found myself suddenly liking Esztergom and its people. I have in my diary a fatuous note that they seemed brave and cheerful and smiled a lot, though now I cannot remember meeting any but the witch in the tower. Perhaps it was just the way the name was written after all.

Now that I have left western lands behind, the river is rather wild in its appearance. Towns and villages are far and few between, and there are long stretches of the Duna that make me think of "*Huckleberry Finn.*" There are watery forest groves, lonely islands in midstream, swampy backwaters and the odd ramshackle hut swathed in fishing nets on poles. Strange splashes and gurgles from the banks cause me to wonder, not entirely flippantly, about the possibility of 'gators. I write letters as I drift along, too lazy to row. I catnap, I read, I doze off again... and so come slowly down the great river to Budapest.

If you took Christopher Wren, injected just a little Turkish blood into him, gave him some warm siennas and umbers to work with rather than the slate-greys and sooty hues of the Thames, and then let him get on with it, he would have come up with something like Budapest instead of London. From the river, the similarity is striking. It is like a condensed version of London with all the best bits left in, St. Paul's, the Houses of Parliament, Big Ben, the Tower and so on, but all the long grimy concrete-and-glass stretches left out. On the morning that I left it, four days after I arrived, this is what I was thinking, along with how much I suddenly admired the place. As for the four days of actually being there, well, that is another story.

Firstly, it rained torrentially for the entire four days. The weather sent me scuttling to a Youth Hostel where the first night was spent fighting for possession of the bunk that I had paid for with a drunk Irishman who was so blotto on vodka that he kept forgetting that he had checked out the night before and was meant to be on a train to Warsaw by now. The next few nights I managed to get a single room, but was alarmed to find myself woken three or four times a night by a mysterious flash seeming to come from somewhere in the room itself. It was as though there was a sudden spontaneous crackle of lightning filling the room with a brief but highly charged flash. It was of the same sort of intensity that you see on the overhead lines as a tram passes, but it had nothing to do with the light-switch or the bulb as far as I could make out. It didn't do any harm, nor make more than the tiniest of fizzling pops, but it left the whole room feeling charged and potent each time, and me wide awake and staring. I never did find out what it was. Static? St. Elmo's fire? Whatever it was, it was better than the Irishman.

Secondly, I found myself all at sea with the language. Now I've always prided myself on being able to make some good guesses at foreign words; a smattering of Latin from those choral masses we used to sing in choir, a basic understanding of Grimm's Sound Laws which lets one treat *p*'s as *f*'s and *t*'s as *d*'s and so on, and allows *Pisces* to transmute into *fish* at the drop of a syllable, and one can waltz through Europe from Wales to Greece without accidentally ordering anything too startling on the menu. But not when it comes to Hungarian, oh no. It belongs to a class of languages entirely unconnected with anything Indo-European, and the only people likely to make a stab at understanding the Hungarians are the Finns. Was it purely coincidental then, that when I went to a bar and tried striking up a conversation with the lively group on the next table, they all turned out to be a party from Finland? Having not the faintest idea about the language gave me a small insight into what it must be like to be illiterate. How do I find a book shop? Look in all the windows as I pass. How do I order food in a restaurant? Point to an item and pray that it's not pig's liver. What's the sign for *Metro Station* in the city underground system? Not a clue, so just follow the people.

This brings me to my third reason for getting fed up with Budapest. On the way back from a bar one night, the one with the Finns, I found myself on a tube-train that at every stop, filled up with more and more football fans on their way back from somewhere. Their behaviour was increasingly loutish as their numbers swelled, and at each station they would swirl off and on the train in gleeful high spirits, chanting and pushing and shoving and generally being obnoxious. Finally at one Underground station below Deak Square, the central plaza of the city, the commotion reached riot proportions, and amongst the milling fans I could suddenly see the green uniforms of the police. There was an almighty bang, and the fans who had swirled off the train suddenly turned and attempted to scramble back on again, jamming the doors and preventing the train from pulling out. There was at once a cloud of gas, and the cabin filled with choking, acrid fumes, as though someone had splashed a vat of ammonia or bleach down the stairwell: tear gas, no less, released by the police. My eyes started watering, and every gasp I took seared my nostrils and throat, and for a moment I could not think of anything but getting out of there. To step out onto the platform was impossible – the hooligans were still scrabbling in the doorways and, besides, I didn't fancy running through the incomprehensibly signposted tunnels of the Metro like an illiterate rabbit in a gassed warren. Another bang exploded and I saw through the crowd someone collapse on the platform. The report did the trick, however, of clearing the doors, and the fume-filled carriage was able to pull away from the platform. When the gas had cleared a little, I turned to the animated group of fellow travellers next to me, and asked in croaky pidgin-English what had happened. To my surprise, they ignored me, but continued to chatter in fume-strangled voices amongst themselves. Again I asked, and a second time I was ignored, even though they had lapsed into silence by this time. Perhaps they were more bloody Finns. A third time I spoke, loudly and directly to the nearest chap, and then saw where the hitch was. They were a small party of deaf mutes, and hadn't heard a word I'd been saying. Once they realised, they signed and mimed their apologies and what I assume was their shared wonder and bewilderment at the little adventure we had just been through. To be honest, I didn't get all the meaning, but one gesture was universal enough for anyone to understand. The leader of the group raised a fist, pointed his forefinger at me, cocked it and pulled an imaginary trigger. It was as I had suspected. The bang I had heard had been that of one of the rioters being shot dead before my eyes. After that, I didn't need to know the Hungarian word for *Metro*. I rather preferred to walk.

The rest of my stay in Hungary is quickly told. I drifted on down the Duna for two more days, between banks that were a solid screen of silvery osiers and willows. There was nothing to report, nothing to do, nothing to distract me from the task of reciting the complete works of bloody Keats to the empty sky in sheer desperate boredom. At one point a kind fisherman pulls alongside and wants to share a couple of beers with me. When I thank him and clink my bottle on his as a salute before swigging I am stopped in mid-swig by the expression on his face. He has gone quite pale, and looks as though I have just accused his deceased mother of a predilection for stable-animals for her marital needs. After a visible effort to control himself, my host explains. "In Hungary, we never do that, the clinking of the drinks. It is a grave insult. In the Austro-Hungarian rebellion in the 1800s, each time that the Austrians..." - here he spat fulsomely into the river - "hanged a Hungarian rebel, they would do that... that clinking thing... with their schnapps. Please, you were not to know, but never again, Kapitan, never again..."

He also talked about more recent history. I had not realised but it was Budapest that bore the brunt of the first Nazi pogroms, and such things have not been forgotten. German tourists still find a cold welcome there, almost as much as people who callously and wilfully clink their glasses before drinking.

Two last notes about Hungary. One is that every dish is cooked with copious amounts of paprika - steak and paprika, roast goose and paprika, cheese and paprika, popcorn and paprika. They even have little cruets of ground paprika on the tables where we have pepper. I am not averse to a little paprika as a rule, but by the time I left Hungary I was beginning to turn a distinct shade of orange. The second is that all the women are strikingly beautiful, but all have deep purple hair. I have no idea why. It was all just part of the incomprehensibility that dogged my stay in Hungary. Finns. Deaf mutes. Hungarian street signs. Sharing my room with ball-lightning. It was time to move on to somewhere that made more sense.

Proud Hearts and Empty Pockets

'Alas, poor country, -
Almost afraid to know itself! It cannot
Be called our mother, but our grave: where nothing,
But who knows nothing, is once seen to smile;
Where sighs and groans, and shrieks that rend the air,
Are made, not mark'd: where violent sorrow seems
A modern ecstasy...'

William Shakespeare - *Macbeth, Act IV, Sc.3*

My first stop in Yugoslavia was just at nightfall where I came to the border-control of Bedpans. I don't think it was actually called that but it may as well have been, as it was both clinical and foul at one and the same time. There in a dismal and monumental building I spent an hour doing the passport shuffle between ill lit offices where lounged dangerous criminals armed with rubber stamps. The cracked floors seeped with water, the light bulbs, where there were any, were a peculiar type of Yugoslavian five-watt kind, and in the main office the strip-light flickered on and off like an irregular strobe for the entire hour I was there until I felt my brain seeping out through my maniacally blinking eyes. I felt as though I was in an old black-and-white silent movie set in the Gulag. It was even worse than getting a busking license in Linz.

There was no pontoon to moor to, so I hitched up to a midstream buoy, and, too dispirited even to put up my awning, slept under the night sky. The stars were brilliant that night, the ice-cut constellation of Taurus with his ruby eye and the faint glitter of the Pleiades, silver fish caught in a heavenly net. But with the beauty came the cold, and I lay in an aching shiver of wakefulness, too cold to sleep, too cold to get up and do anything about it. When dawn came, and the sun poured warmth and life into my bloodless limbs, I felt as a dragonfly must, when, first emerging from the cocoon, he feels his wings shiver and spread as the life-fluid pumps through cell and fibre and gauze. I didn't even wait to perform my daily routine. I simply unhitched, and floated away from Bedpans on the current in my pyjamas and sleeping bag, feeling more like Huck Finn than ever.

By lunchtime I had reached Apatin, the first place where I could go through all the tedious but important process of changing money, using my Visa Card to replenish my scanty funds, and stock up on bread and tomatoes and salami and perhaps a nice bottle of some Yugoslavian plum wine. The only place to moor up along the steep rocky bank was right next to a huge glistening pile of cow's intestines, silver-black with buzzing flies. A professional soothsayer may have been able to read the augury; I did not wait to try. Besides I would know soon enough. A visit to a large gloomy bank elicited the following interesting facts:

1) The handful of Hungarian forints I had brought with me out of Hungary were not exchangeable for Yugoslavian dinar. Indeed the very thought caused a ripple of mirth around the otherwise joyless staff there. Forints?

Pah.

2) Yugoslavia was, it seemed, the one place in the known Galaxy that did not accept Visa, Mastercard, American Express, or indeed any credit card at all. This was despite the fact that the banks and shops all displayed large signs in several languages saying "VISA WELCOME HERE."

It took me a little while to establish with the lady behind the counter that these two facts were really, honestly, actually, truly the case. Having done so, I stepped out into the street again and gawped. I just stopped dead beneath the plane trees and my jaw sagged open as I contemplated with horror my present situation. I had no money except for about twelve dollars worth of useless Hungarian forint, my credit cards were invalid, and I had about three hundred miles of slow river travel across Yugoslavia to accomplish without starving to death. I was a bit stuck.

Actually, I say 'horror', but this realisation of having just made a disastrous move in the game of Life was accompanied, as is often the case, by a rising glee, a sort of irrepressible feeling that the next fortnight would hold adventure at least, if not meals and hot showers. I found myself singing Purcell's "Bell" anthem and the words from Philippians. It is not often that we are given the opportunity to live like the lilies of the field, but now that the time had come, and I could do nothing about it, there came a strange exhilaration as I walked back to the dinghy, half wondering if cow's intestines were in any way easily rendered edible.

On the way back, I passed a large and glossy building, the only sign of anything glossy besides the intestines that I had seen in the country so far. I thought at first that it might be a smart hotel, and I had an inkling that the very smartest of hotels might be able to do things with a Visa card that couldn't be done by common banks. I asked the clerk behind the counter if I could see the manager, and soon a smartly dressed businessman came and without any questions ushered me along a corridor and into a beautifully furnished office. It could have been in the heart of Paris or Frankfurt. He spoke excellent English and courteously asked how he could assist me. A little abashed by all this opulence, I stumbled out my story, explained about *Jack* and the trip from England and then asked whether his hotel could allow me to use Visa to withdraw some much needed cash for the weeks ahead. Without another word, he spoke briefly into an intercom and then beamed at me. "I am sorry to tell you, my friend, that this is not a hotel. In any case you would not find a hotel in all of Yugoslavia to help you, alas. Perhaps one in Belgrade, I don't know...You see, for the last few months, we have been under an embargo laid down by Nato and much of the Western World, to which, alas, it appears we no longer belong." He smiled sadly and shrugged his shoulders. "Your country and America feel it necessary to interfere with the way we are running our country, and have seen fit to punish our people for the follies of our President. We are all but cut off from the rest of Europe now, and I fear there are dark days ahead."

He was putting into words the facts that I had been only vaguely aware of on my media-free trip down the river. This was late September, 1998, and over the next few weeks, NATO were to begin their threats of air bombardment in response to the Kosovo situation, threats that came within twelve hours of being carried out in the days ahead. When, a year on, I saw the news coverage of shattered bridges and bombed towns along the Danube I recognised every one of them, and saw in my mind's eye the ghost of a little yellow dinghy threading between the twisted girders. I did not find it easy to join in the anti-Serbian chatter that milled about my colleagues and friends a year later. The reason why will become apparent, I hope, in the next few pages.

"But meanwhile," my host was continuing, "not all is bad. This is not a hotel, but it is something better! It is a brewery. And, my friend," he whispered, "it is the best brewery in Eastern Europe!" At that, in came a clerk with six bottles of Apatin beer. "I have a little job for you," said the manager, beaming. "I need an impartial taster to try out our latest brew," and with that bottles were opened, glasses produced, and the rich dark foaming beer was poured out. A good while later, after comparing and sipping and commenting on colour and taste and texture, it was time for me to go. But before I did, my host said, "You mentioned something about forint? It is true that one cannot exchange forint here for dinar, but I? I go across the border to Hungary three times a week. Let me exchange your money for you." And at that, he pulled out his wallet, counted out a wad of Yugoslavian dinar and took my useless forint in exchange. I now had at least twelve dollars worth of cash in hand, and need not scavenge those cow's intestines after all. What is more, just as I was leaving, he said, "But wait! I have not paid you for your tasting advice," and at that he put three large bottles of Apatin beer into my hand and led me to the foyer. "Good luck!" he called and waved, and I walked off down the dusty road light of heart and beginning to feel already arrayed like Solomon in all his glory. Perhaps it was the beer...

When I get back to the dinghy I encounter another side to Yugoslavia. There are a small crowd gathered around the boat and two policemen in generalissimo outfits of slate blue. Before I can stow my belongings, I am ushered into a battered police car and driven off to the police station. There a balding officer with hooded eyes like a vulture (he looks like Commandant Klink from *Hogan's Heroes*) questions me about my presence. I show him my visa duly stamped, and the papers that I had had signed in triplicate the night before in Bedpans, and he reluctantly accepts that I am legal. I should, however, have reported to him instantly on arrival. On the wall behind his desk is a large and detailed wall map showing the next forty miles of river. Being without any map at all, I try making out what lies ahead: towns, splits in the river, the Croatian border on the right-hand bank. He sees me looking at it and angrily tears it off the wall. "No! This is my map," he says, "not yours." I am turned out, and must walk the mile back to the river.

As I set off down the wide and sunlit river, I am unsure what lies ahead, but I am pretty sure it won't be boredom.

I felt that I had at last come to Wilderland, the upper reaches of mighty

Anduin beneath the eaves of Mirkwood. The river, now the Dunav, ran through seemingly endless forests on either side, and there in the fastness it was easy to imagine that Radagast the Brown dwelt, taming his birds, or that Beorn wielded his mighty axe amongst his monstrous bees, living on honey and cream. One night I pulled in under the overhanging boughs to a tiny fishermen's camp, a timber hut under the dank trees, and a small cluster of long wooden canoes tied to poles. They all seemed to have something resembling a seven-pronged Jewish candelabra in them. There some men were cooking fish in a rich and scaly stew in an ancient black cauldron over an outside fire of red-hot coals. An old man with a face like a long walnut, the keeper of the hut, lets me eat my supper of bread rolls and tomato at his rough wooden table by the light of a smoky kerosene lantern. As I eat, he keeps silently bringing tidbits from his own cupboard to supplement my meal: a boiled egg, some mustard, some smelly cheese, and then the inevitable schnapps. A large black Polish hound called Nox keeps begging for scraps. Around the walls are jar upon jar of pickling paprika, buckets and tubs and basins full of the stuff, glowing as scarlet in the lamplight as the embers outside. Afterwards, the three fishermen come inside smelling of woodsmoke and join in the schnapps and take out a much thumbed deck of cards. These are not the usual suits that we are used to, the simple diamonds, clubs, hearts and spades, but antique symbols: acorns, staffs, leaves and baubles, all in curly greens, scarlets and golds. They look to my unfamiliar eyes as ancient and enchanted as the first set of Tarot cards out of old Romany. The men keep filling up my glass with more schnapps, but otherwise ignore me, as though I am sort of daft old grandfather with whom they are completely familiar. That night, I fall asleep in a rough bunk under coarse grey blankets that the old man has set up for me. I explain as best as I can that I have no money, but he waves that aside with a grunt. The only toilet is a hole off in the woods with a single sign over it saying TELEFON. It is altogether wonderful.

As I row on the next day, a daring and ridiculous plan forms in my mind to acquire some funds. Soon I am to come to a point where the right-hand bank will be not Serbia but Croatia. It is just possible that:

a) Croatia will not be under the same embargo as Serbia
b) I might be able to withdraw some money from a bank there using my Visa card.
c) Question: Do I have a visa for Croatia?
d) No.
e) But I may not need one(?!)
f) I think you've entered the realms of fantasy, Corporal Jones…
g) Even if I am allowed into Croatia, my visa for Serbia is a single-entry one only, and it is unlikely that I would be allowed back in again once having set foot on foreign territory.
h) Assuming I am allowed into Croatia, I will have to withdraw deutschmarks, of course, or US dollars as the Croatian krona is even less likely to be accepted in Serbia than the much-sneered-upon forint.
i) If they let me back into Serbia, that is. (See Point g.)

j) Which I very much doubt.
k) This is assuming they let me into Croatia in the first place, of course
l) Which I very much doubt. Again. (See Points c. through to f.)

In short, I must somehow persuade someone official in the next town coming up on the Croatian side (a town called Vukovar) to let me enter Croatia illegally, not be stamped in, remove large slabs of German currency from a local bank, tiptoe out again, once more without being officially stamped out of the country to give the game away, and merrily go and spend it all in an enemy country. What is more, I have to explain all this using only the five words I know that might be understood by a Croatian (*pasaporte*, *visa*, *problema*, *banca* and *nema* meaning *not*) and possibly a good deal of vivid mime.

The whole plan was, of course, out of the question... so I decided to give it a go.

To the great credit of the Croatian police in Vukovar, who must play an awful lot of charades in their spare time, the white-haired Kapitan whose office I was marched off to as soon as I set foot on Croatian soil seemed to understand the whole thing perfectly. He didn't speak a word of English, but sat patiently while I conducted my carefully thought out little mime. I mimed a river running down the middle of his office with many a gurgle-gurgle noise. I mimed a little boat sailing down the middle of the carpet river, and leapt jauntily from the desk (Serbia) to the window (Croatia) and back again. I mimed being penniless with much rubbing of my stomach and turning out of pockets, and then did several masterful impersonations of strict, unsmiling Serbian immigration officers and their reaction on finding no second-entry visa in my passport. So carried away did I become at one point that I think I found myself miming being stood up against a wall and shot. Never has being a drama teacher, that most dilettante of all trades, become so useful in action. All this was of course accompanied by an improvised script of plenty of *problemas* and *nema visas* interspersed at crucial points: hardly Shakespeare, but the best I could manage. Finally, after a last little bow, I stood waiting for the verdict.

Which was for the Kapitan to call a guard, rap out some curt instructions, and five minutes later I was being driven around Vukovar in a decrepit police jeep looking for a bank to extract money from. We found one, but they could not help me. It seemed that a bank fifty miles inland might have been able to help me, but nowhere in Vukovar was able to process my card. Despite the anticlimax, I was thrilled by the kindness and understanding of the Croatian police, who as I had requested, omitted to sign me either in or out of the country so that the Serbs would have no reason to know that I had ever left Serbia.

Vukovar itself was a touching sight. Some years ago, it had been the centre of Serbian bombardment, and still many buildings were shell-shattered and blitzed. Children played noisy games in rubble-filled lots, and I saw one block of apartments where one half sported bright curtains flapping and washing hung out to dry from high windows, but in the other half, gaping holes and twisted iron reinforcement rods sticking from demolished walls showed where the war had scarred the town. The physical damage was still there, and I was to learn over the next few weeks that the hatred between these neighbouring countries is as intense and scalding as it has ever been. When the Serbs speak of the atrocities in the Second World War, they are referring not to the Nazis but to the barbarisms allegedly perpetrated by the Croatians. The Croatians of course do the same.

Just after sailing away from Vukovar with my illegal international money-laundering scheme failed, I found myself almost by accident floating down a little side channel on the Croatian bank. It was lovely to be out of the wide, sunny glare of the main river, and rowing between crowding banks where trees covered in vines shaded the water and gave to the river an almost Amazonian feel. After several hours, I passed an island where a single white shack stood, and there were some fishermen cooking something. Excitedly they hailed me and beckoned me over, and when I rowed over to moor up I recognised two of the men. One was the young guard who had driven me around looking for a bank, and the other had been witness to my vivid mime in the Kapitan's office. It was clear that they were now off duty and had come down to join their friends in an evening of schnapps and grilled fish. This I was invited to join, and spent the next hour sitting in the late afternoon sunshine enjoying their hospitality, while the two policemen reduced their friends to stitches of laughter. I could not of course understand the content, but I suspect I was the main topic of conversation.

The fish, I was told, was *babushka*, a prize delicacy of the river. It is served with a plate of raw onion just chopped in half and a bowl of rock salt. The onion is dipped into the salt, placed whole in the mouth, and the tender slivers of fish shovelled in after, skin and all. The schnapps helps considerably in this taste-assault course. It struck me that this was the second time I had been on Croatian soil, both times illegally... and both times with the connivance of the police. These are my sort of officials. I was not to meet many more like them as I sailed onwards down into the heart of the still-vex'd Balkans.

So precious are the memories of my time in Serbia and of the overwhelming kindness and simplicity of the Serbian people that I am tempted to relate in detail each new encounter, each new bend of the river, each new friend met on the way. I feel that if nothing else it would be a tribute to these people who have suffered much of late, not least being maligned by the World press. But as ever, the deeds of the few in power, the politicians and generals, are not representative of the common folk, and from purely personal experience, I found them to be the warmest and most spontaneously hospitable of people.

However, I shall limit myself to the briefest of sketches of that golden time. For golden it was. The sun shone warm and bright with September gold, flaming in the poplars and willows that lined the banks, and silvering the threads of gossamer that drifted in airy swathes across the river to festoon my rigging with fairy pennants. The low, level light made the river always a molten shimmer of silver haze, and at times it felt as though I was rowing into Paradise, or the album cover for a Handel Oratorio. Still the endless trees marched on either side, at times thick and tangled where I was delighted to see wild pigs rooting at the river's edge, unaware of my gliding presence yards away. A species of eagle with a distinct white tail could often be seen sailing across the river and emitting squeaky yelps more suited to a plastic baby's toy than a keen-eyed monarch of the skies. At times the air would turn even hazier and yellower than the autumn sun could account for, and stink of sulphur - a distant factory chimney above the trees would provide the unromantic explanation.

In one particularly lambent wood, I remember, there came a sweet chiming from somewhere high in the goldy-green treetops, a plangent jingling of bells as though elfin wind chimes were sounding. It was remote and musical and faint, unearthly above the clunk-splash of the mortal oars, and I wondered for a moment if I was dreaming. I have no idea what it was, so far from anywhere, and still wonder if perhaps in some odd geographical side-slip, I had passed by Lorien all unknowing.

Another night's stop was somewhat less poetic. South of Novi Sad, I had stopped in another fishermen's camp, but far busier than the previous one. Here I met three university students, Ivan, David and Sonja; they were keen to practise their already excellent English, and we talked for a long while about the present troubles in the country. Once, they said, just a few years ago, Yugoslavian students had had the run of Europe and Asia Minor for their holidays. In fact, so unrestricted were the Yugoslavians in where they could go in the world that a Yugoslavian passport had been the highest priced of all stolen passports on the Black Market. Now, they were restricted only to Hungary and Romania. The rest of the world was closed to them, and these young people were finding the cultural claustrophobia unbearable. They condemned their president's actions in Kosovo, but were angrier still at the stance of the United States and Britain. They were not children, they said.

Our talk was interrupted by a high, ear-splitting squeal from just behind me, and as I jumped in my seat I exclaimed the old cliché, "Goodness me, it sounds like a pig having its throat cut!" When I turned I saw that that was exactly what it was. Just yards away, a fisherman had a little pink pig propped between his booted knees and had just gashed a great steel knife across the poor creature's throat. As the blood gushed out in spurts my attention was transfixed by the expression on the poor creature's face; it was not so much agonised as faintly hurt and bewildered, a gently confused expression one would associate more with Pooh Bear wondering where his last pot of honey had got to than with an animal being slaughtered. "Why is the light dimming so fast, Mother?" it seemed to say, "and why am I feeling all so floppy and listless all of a sudden?" Poor piggy. Poor me. It was all rather too ethnic for us sensitive English-Drama teaching types.

The last day before I reached Belgrade, where I hope to replenish my vanishing money supplies, is a beauty. The forest has ended, and now sandy cliffs rear high on the southern bank, the home of thousands of sand martins and swifts. Near lunchtime I am hailed by two fishermen on the bank in a grassy meadow at the foot of the cliffs: Jan and Estovich. Jan is fifty-ish, Estovich is a hundred-and-two. They ply me with beer and peanuts, and though their English is as non-existent as my Yugoslavian, we seem to communicate with ease. Later they light a little fire and make a pot of coffee, the same river silt which I find hard to like, but drink gamely. Then when I show them a magic trick as a thanks, Jan is so overcome with excitement he does three somersaults in the long meadow grass like a child. I am tickled pink. When I finally indicate that I must sail on they solemnly present me with a large glass bottle of something that they call 'Paradijo.' It is most gorgeous, rich orange-red, opaque, and full of little golden-yellow seeds suspended in it, and I think it is made from tomatoes and paprika. Over the next four days, I treasure it, savouring each mouthful; the taste is a little like tomato juice, but there is a rich, burning afterglow that goes right to the belly. I could not work out whether it was alcoholic or not – I think on balance not – but it had the same warming effect, as did my memory of the middle-aged Jan tumbling for glee in the green grass whenever I swigged that precious stuff.

That night, I came to a tiny scattering of huts beneath a cliff, a squalid assortment of boat sheds and dank hovels, and sat on my dinghy preparing the last bit of bread and some salami that I had discovered in the bows. This was left over from Linz and still going strong... stronger by the day, in fact. I was just about to retire, when a huge man came out of one of the nearby huts and called me over. What I had thought was a private home was in fact a rough sort of taverna; a concrete floor, an open kitchen, but full of guests sitting at the cheap little tables with plastic red and white cloths and bowls of bread. Silently he pointed to a table in the corner, and his daughter brought a bowl of bread.

"Nema dinar..." I explained.

"Nema problema," he replied.

Before I had finished the bread, the girl had reappeared with a bowl of crumbed egg-plant.

"Um... thank you, but nema dinar..."

"Nema problema," she chirped, and tripped away.

These were people who did not know who I was or where I had come from. I had not yet had a chance to explain my story, nor do anything as impressive as the magic-hanky-into-toy-rabbit trick nor play a haunting air on my tin whistle. And yet throughout the rest of the night as they bustled around, serving their legitimate guests, each time they passed a new dish was set down before me – spiced meats, a dish of paprika in oil, grilled chops, a sweet thing made of poppyseeds, and three beers. It was all done so wordlessly that I couldn't help thinking that there must be a catch somewhere. My worst fears were confirmed when after the fifth apologetic rendition of "Look, I'm terribly sorry, there must be some mistake, I don't have any money and I appear to have eaten a four course dinner," my massive host put an arm around my shoulders and guided me into the kitchen area. There he showed me a framed photo of himself as a younger man dressed in a white kimono, grinning and holding up a trophy.

"Me, Europe karate champion ,1956. Chop, chop! Hyaaii!!"

Then he led me gently back to my seat. I translated that as meaning, "Mess with me, laddie, or try that old *not–got–any–cash–on–me* routine, and I'll kick your kidneys out your ears before you can say chop-suey, chum!"

But no, at the end of the evening, when the rest of the guests had departed, he came and sat at the table where I was rolling like a porpoise, poured the inevitable schnapps, and sat proudly telling me in incomprehensible Yugoslavian about karate, the 1956 Olympics, his beautiful daughter, and what a pleasure it was to have met me. It was all thoroughly puzzling. All I could do in payment was make a little painted origami book the next morning and leave it for them to find – just the sort of thing that is useful and valuable in a country plunged in economic and political disaster on the brink of bombardment, I always think...

I am going to race through Belgrade. It has a huge number of bookshops, but most of the books are on the occult. It has a marina called the Dorcol, meaning 'four corners' – it is where they used to quarter people using four horses all going in different directions. The marina is shabby but exceptionally friendly – I keep being given plum brandy by different people on old boats, poured out of coloured glass bottles shaped like St. Nicolai, the patron saint of sailors. The Hyatt Hotel, though hugely luxurious, will not give me cash but will allow me to use my Visa card for services. The clerks at reception are immune to both my logic and my charm. They are just charming back. I sit and have a hugely luxurious afternoon tea in a fit of pique and sit and write letters while Handel's Trio Sonata tinkles away in the background. I make long, expensive calls to England. I have a large, piggy dinner. I stop myself actually staying there that night, and sleep on the dinghy and regret it as a lashing thunderstorm soaks me through. I trudge around every bank in Belgrade, telling them to bloody well take down their Visa signs if they're not going to cough up. I climb the great park-like hill of Kalemegdan and watch the junction of the River Sava and the Dunav glow under a post-thunderstorm sky of orange and rose and purple, and all the trees and grass as unnaturally tinted as a Chesterton landscape. It is the Sava down which the beastly Croats sent the corpses of Serbs with nails knocked through their skulls, according to the Serbs I met later, and they fetched up here in Belgrade. The Serbs call it Beograd, which means "White City" though now it is sooty and grey, and sorry, but I hate it. While I am spending a penny behind a bush near the marina, a large brown snake glides away through my legs, and I am not in a position to do anything about it. The subsequent instinctive clenching does something to my bladder that makes it difficult to pee for several days afterwards. Now that we are back in a country where the language has some tenuous roots connected with Latin and Anglo-Saxon, the alphabet capriciously changes to the Cyrillic one, so I remain as baffled as I was in Hungary. For example, the perfectly guessable-at 'RESTORAN' for 'restaurant' transliterates as 'PEΣTOPAN' which sounds like something you boil jam in. I am thoroughly fed up, so let us leave Belgrade.

There, that was quick, wasn't it?

Over the next three days, things begin to get a little desperate. I have run out of food, and the supply of people on either hand to dole out provisions when needed is suddenly thin. So am I. The landscape slowly changes from pretty vineyards and orchards on gentle slopes (where I am sorely tempted to steal some grapes and apples) to a harsher, drier landscape as I near the Carpathian Mountains and the Iron Gates. This is where the Dunav carves its way through the last great obstacle before the final run to the sea. It does so in a great gorge, sheer sided and tortuous, the grim gateway into old Transylvania. But whether I will make it there before starving to death, I am not sure. Being hungry is not nearly as adventurous and romantic when you are actually in mid-fast.

The need to get to Bulgaria and to a bank presses me on, past the leaning fortress towers of Smederevo, past the fortress of Ram, through unfriendly Jugovo where in the dark streets men sit and play dominoes and chess with all the grunting and jeering and raucous noise more associated with wrestling matches; through a smart little riverside resort where a hugely fat man bathing with his family shouts out things in a purple rage at the sight of my two little Union Jacks. It still has not occurred to me that my little dinghy flying the British ensign could possibly enrage or offend the people whom Britain were on the point of bombarding. I suppose I might also have been seen as the very first flagboat of an invading British navy, sent out just to reccy round and report back. The point is driven home when I sleep aboard in the town of Veliko Gradiste and wake the next morning to find that someone in the night has slashed both my Union Jacks to shreds. I am furious, furious at the vandal that has done this. Then a sudden thought sobers me. Sleeping just three feet lower down, I am lucky not to have met a similar fate.

I am more fortunate. A doleful-looking Serb called Branko comes along, introduces himself and invites me back to his mother's house for lunch. His English is good... good enough to tactfully enquire whether I might like a hot bath first. The grubby ring around the bath when I have finished would grow root vegetables. Roast pork, potatoes, paprika (I really am a little tired of the paprika), vodka, damson-cake and wine and then a cycle ride out to a local beauty spot. On the way we run over two snakes, and see three more. I tell Branko of my snake experience in Belgrade, and he explains that yes, there appears to be a plague of them this summer. There are two possible explanations, he says. One is that it is a plot by the CIA, an experiment in biological warfare as an entrée before the main bombardment. The second and more likely one, he says with a perfectly straight face, is that God is punishing the Serbs for their wickedness. That opens the way for a long talk about Serbia and its problems, which are legion. Chief of these is corruption. Every town, every village has its local Mafia boss. Extortion on even the smallest, most local scale is rife. No one owns a business, not an apple cart, not a newspaper stand, without paying a large cut to the hired thugs of the resident Mr. Big. Those who resist meet with violence and terror tactics. Much of this stems from Milosevic and his ministers; the Kosovo problem is just one very visual symptom of the sickness in the land. The poverty I was seeing everywhere – and I was, often worse than I had seen elsewhere in Africa or Laos – was a recent phenomenon. Yugoslavia had been a rich and prosperous country until ten years ago, when the first blockades were imposed. Oh, it had never been as rich as Germany or Austria, for sure, but its farms had been productive, its orchards tended, its vines fruitful. Now everywhere there was filth and waste, and the people were confused and angry. That was the problem with the embargoes and blockades, Branko said. They drew the people's anger outwards to the States and Britain, muddying the issue. It was so easy for the politicians to blame all the country's woes on the evil superpowers, and deny responsibility for their own policies.

"Why do the people not rise up against Milosevic if it is clear that it is his actions bringing about the embargoes?" I asked.

"Because," he said with a sigh, "Serbs watch only Serbian television. You don't think Milosevic allows any truth to creep into the news coverage, do you? NATO is blockading us because they are jealous of us, or because they are afraid of us, or because they want to steal all our fruit. Not because of anything our glorious leader has done – dear me, never! Hence the CIA and the snakes," he added, looking more doleful than ever. "It is all very sad."

When I continued on my way that afternoon, I did so with a huge bag of apples, a clove of garlic and a great jar of home-made honey, a present from Branko's mother Dora. But I also took with me a new insight, a new thoughtfulness – I understood a little, just a little, about my slashed flags now.

That night, I met the local Mr. Big, I think. Just ten miles downstream I moored up in a tiny inlet overlooked by a large, isolated restaurant. This was spanking new, with the bulldozers still lurking in the shrubbery, freshly laid gravel and plastic white umbrellas at each beer garden table. The place seemed deserted, but when I sat and munched on my last bread roll at one of these tables, a man looking exactly like Danny de Vito came out, and after some sharp questioning in broken English, invited me into the front bar for a drink. There two young and sexy barmaids were sent off with a cheeky pat on the bottom each to fetch us food and more beers while the manager smirked at me, asking me what I thought of them, eh? Eh? Over the next hour, he too discussed politics. Kosovo? Too right there was a problem. The Muslims ought to be shot, every one of them, sneaking into Serbia with their dirty ways. The only problem was that Milosevic wasn't being allowed to get on with the job quicker. Sure, he was no saint, but to run this country you need to take a firm hand. Now look at me, people whinge and moan about the economy, but with a bit of initiative, a bit of push, you could make ends meet. More than, in fact. Two Mercs. A town house up in Belgrade.

The wife doesn't know about these little crackers, of course, (Sofi, another beer here, darling!) but what can a man do, eh? It'd only make her miserable.

Outside, the evening was turning colder and damper, the expanse of river lonely and wild... and infinitely preferable to the warm geniality and leering confidentiality of my host. *Come, friendly bombs*, I thought...

"And get that man with double chin
Who'll always cheat and always win,
Who washed his repulsive skin
In women's tears.

And smash his desk of polished oak
And smash his hands so used to stroke
And stop his boring dirty joke
And make him yell."

On an irrational impulse which I am still trying to analyse, I took out my last ten dinar that I had been saving, and insisted on paying for the drinks and the meal. It probably wasn't enough, and my host waved it aside with a laugh, but I left it on the bar before I departed. No painted book, but hard cash for the one Serb I had met so far who clearly had no need of it. I had not rowed very far that day, but felt the need for a bath all over again.

At last, the Carpathian Mountains come in sight. They lie across a great grey expanse of water where the Dunav spreads out into a lake. On the further shore are the high, bare hills of Romania, dusty grey and scored with ravines and gullies, a hostile and forbidding terrain. On the nearer shore, the right-hand or southern bank, the hills of Serbia seem greener and gentler. But today there is nothing gentle about the expanse of water that lies between the two. It has been whipped into a savage frenzy by a wind blowing straight out of the jaws of the Iron Gates Gorge, a mere notch in the hills seen dimly through veils of blowing spray and squalling rain five miles away across the lake. For hours I have been battling into this headwind, tacking to and fro all morning, and I am exhausted. The dinghy is three-quarters full of water, and seems to be taking on more than when she was out at sea. Is this something to do with the buoyancy of salt water? Or am I being fanciful? After two more hours, I realise that I am not going to make it to the Gorge, and so run in to shore where sits the little town of Golubac. There I change into dry clothes, retire to a surprisingly large hotel for such a small place, and, penniless though I am, beg for a corner in the reception area to sit and write. Three days later I am still there.

For three days the fierce north-easter blows straight out of the Gorge like the leaden breath from some frozen stone dragon. Three times I fool myself into thinking that the wind has eased off a little, and three times get a hundred yards out before having to turn back once more. Normally I would be no more than mildly frustrated by the enforced delay, but with no money, no food, and the nearest Visa outlet in Bulgaria beyond the mountains, I find the weather loaded with unnecessary spite.

Of course, I do not go hungry. The kindness of the people continues unabated. The hotel housekeeper, a motherly soul also called Dora who teaches very rudimentary English at the local primary school, takes me home to stay with her the first night. She lives with her elderly, gracious mother, and her two dark-eyed children, and we sit and drink linden tea made from the dried flowers of the lime tree. It is bright orange and very refreshing, scented like summer. We spend the evening looking at her old home Dubrovnik which, as it is part of Croatia now, she cannot return to. I am put up that night on a fold-out sofa bed which has clearly been designed by someone unfamiliar with the concept of sleeping: a whale-shark perhaps. It is like sleeping on a floppy mattress draped sideways over two gymnasium parallel bars and to be honest, it is the least comfortable night's sleep I have ever had. I do not tell Dora this, of course, and I don't think she notices that as I walk around the next morning my whole frame is bent into a Σ shape. Breakfast is a large bowl of honey eaten neat, straight off the spoon. At the other end of the sweet-bitter scale is the usual black coffee that tastes like asphalt, but has me wideawake and ready to face anything, even another bowl of honey.

Three miles along the lake road, right at the mouth of the Gorge, is the ruinous fortress of Stari Grad. Here seven rotting towers of grey stone loom over the lake, and I walk along and explore them the next afternoon. The weather is so foul that it is impossible to see the other side of the lake now, and it feels as if I am on the shores of a great sea. Grey waves crested with yellow foam pound the rocky shore, tossing the flotsam of plastic detergent bottles and polystyrene lumps to and fro onto the shingle. The marine effect is heightened by the sight of fishermen casting nets into the shallows. I have never seen this type of net before, but I watch fascinated. Each net is small and circular, no bigger than a little round tablecloth that you might spread for afternoon tea. The fisherman stands on the shore and with a pretty twirling twist, halfway between a bullfighter and a discus thrower, casts the net into the water. Barely has it settled than the fisherman pulls a drawstring, the net furls itself up like a shrinking jellyfish, and out the whole thing comes again. The astonishing thing is that each and every time the net was thrown in and pulled out, an operation that took about ten seconds, it would come up with fifteen fish at least. These were only small things, about the size of playing cards, but I was amazed that every six cubic feet of water seemed to yield so much life. It was as strange as if every random sweep of a butterfly net through the air should catch twelve butterflies.

It was not only fish they caught. One load brought up a huge and indignant frog in green and black, and for a brief moment of stupidity I thought, "Goodness, a new species! A salt water frog!" before remembering that the 'sea' was in reality just the old Danube in disguise.

I dared not go back to the hotel because I did not want Dora to think that I was angling for free Bed and Breakfast again, so I turned into a rough little taverna on the other side of the village. Here I walked in on a group of burly boar hunters who were so far gone on the schnapps that they seemed to think I was one of their party, and plied me with hunks of roasted boar and schnapps, all the while calling me Vlad. The taverna owner kept winking at me as if to say, "Just humour them, they're always like this, and besides they've got knives," so I did, and retired to my dinghy later that night yet again replete.

My third day in Golubac was spent listening to a breathless, fascinating and five hour long lecture on Serbian history by a young piano player called Alen who clearly had been waiting seventeen years to try out his English on someone. His English was flawless, his delivery engaging in its sheer enthusiasm, and the subject matter fascinating, though readers will forgive me if I do not now recall it all here and now. We started with the Turkish invasions in the 12th century and worked our way steadily up from there, omitting very little it seemed. The main gist of what Alen was saying was that of course the Balkans had always been troubled; they were at the crossroads of Europe and Asia, the main gateway into Europe for the Muslim hordes. It was not surprising therefore that the Serbs were an aggressive race; they had been keeping Europe Christian with their swords for a thousand years, the valiant gate-keepers of the West. He was not defending the actions in Kosovo – he was merely pointing out that it was just the latest in an endless history of defence.

The greatest tragedy in Serbian history occurred just before the Second World War, he explained. King Peter at the time had made one of the only sensible political decisions in the history of the Balkans. He had decided to divide up the country into small autonomous states, and had set a scheme in place to make sure that the boundaries were exactly where people wanted them, virtually getting his surveyors to walk along the proposed borders with a bit of chalk and having the local villagers on either side saying, "Left a bit, right a bit, that's it, straight on." This generous and far-sighted scheme was all set to go ahead when some fool in Dubrovnik shot the good king (what is it with these Serbs?) and the whole thing never happened. King Peter's heir was only a boy at the time, a regent had to be appointed, and by the time people had got back to their theodolites and chalk, World War II had broken out. It has all been a pig's dinner ever since.

Alen had come to Golubac to play the piano for his Serbian Folk Band that evening in the hotel, and he asked me along. Halfway through the feasting and the drinking, the jazz solos and the slow waltzes the band leader got up and announced the latest news: NATO were going to bombard the country in twenty-four hours unless Milosevic capitulated. The reaction of the assembled guests was odd; I do not know how they were all feeling amongst themselves, but the band to whom Alen had introduced me all gathered around me and expressed their concern... for me. Was I all right? Couldn't I perhaps leave the little boat here in Golubac and flee the country before the bombing started? The saxophonist had a van – he could have me to Bulgaria by the next morning if we left now. Surely I wanted to ring home at least...

I was astonished by these people. Their country in ruins, maligned by the World, under threat of immediate attack by Britain and the States, nevertheless they were busy worrying about the safety of a chance traveller from those very countries threatening them. I did not know of Walt Whitman's poem *"Song of the Open Road"* at the time, but when I came across it a few years later I felt how much I would love to have said to those people that night.

...All seems beautiful to me,
I can repeat over to men and women, You have done such good to me I would do the same to you,
I will recruit for myself and you as I go,
I will scatter myself among men and woman as I go,
I will toss a new gladness and roughness among them,
Whoever denies me it shall not trouble me,
Whoever accepts me, he or she shall be blessed and shall bless me...

You have done such good to me, you people of Yugoslavia, and I hope that one day I can say that I have done the same to you.

The next morning, the gale had blown itself out, the lake was a blue dream, and the Iron Gates stood to welcome me across the water.

High craggy precipices of white limestone rise straight out of water as deep green as bottle-glass. At times the sky is nothing but a thin blue ribbon far overhead against which occasionally an eagle can be seen soaring. Often I can see no more than a hundred yards ahead, the view blocked by yet another crumbling buttress of the gorge wall, or a free standing pinnacle of rock in midstream. One of these is the Babukai Rock, the Rock of the Sorry Wife. Legend has it that a man sick of his nagging wife took her and marooned her on the rock. Every day he would row out to her and call, "Are you sorry, wife?" and the answer would come back, fainter by the day, "No, husband, I am not! Are you?" until there came a day when there was no reply at all. Then perhaps the man was sorry. Perhaps not. Her ghost still sits on the barren pinnacle, waiting for a boat to pass by, hoping it will ferry her off. I hurry on past - it is easy to believe in such torments in such a place.

The current is not as fierce as I had been expecting. Had I been doing this trip fifty years earlier, I would have been swept down through the gorge on a turbulent mill race of white water, which would have been rather fun, if a little fatal. Now, however, a huge hydro-electric dam forty miles downstream has turned the torrent into one long and serpentine lake, allowing the safe passage of river boats in both directions. Even now, however, it is difficult to see how some of the great Danube barges could manoeuvre their mighty length around the tight kinks in the canyon.

At times the gorge would widen into pockets of almost Swiss-looking scenery – hayricks in shaven meadows backed by steep pine woods, and little red-roofed farmsteads, all held between the white knuckles of savage limestone rising to the sky. Then around another bend and the echoing stone would close in and the cold shadows lie across my shoulders once more.

But the wind was behind, and the going was good:

> "*Let us roll all our strength and all*
> *Our sweetness up into one ball,*
> *And tear our pleasures with rough strife*
> *Thorough the Iron Gates of Life...*"

I misquoted merrily to *Jack* as we bowled along, children in a giant's kingdom.

Towards dusk, after a long stretch through a broader section of woods and gentler slopes, we entered a further section of canyon. Again the walls closed in, and again I felt that I was entering some story of adventure. Just then, round a bend we came across a place where the river ran between two sheer cliffs of stone, and the current quickened. On the right-hand bank stood out a great column of stone, a natural tower some four storeys high, and this had been carved into a great brooding face, like the Mount Rushmore Presidents. This face, however, was no George Washington or Lincoln. It was a monstrous Apache face, hawk-nosed, heavy-browed, primitive and watchful. It reminded me suddenly of the Gates of the Kings on the River Anduin just above Rauros Falls, past which Aragorn guided the Fellowship in their elven boats.

Opposite this great guardian of stone was something smaller but more remarkable. Set into the cliff, just above the level of the river, was a plaque of white marble, beginning to gleam in the faint moonlight that was now suffusing the blue dusk. This was the Tabula Trajana, cut by the Emperor Trajan himself almost two thousand years ago, and set here to stamp the presence of Rome even in this, the wildest part of the wild east. Here it still stands; no road or path passes it by, no tourists crowd from their coaches to snap photographs. Even the great busy barges hurry by, I suspect, keeping to the safer northern bank, and never close enough to read it. I am quite sure I am wrong in this, but I liked to fancy to myself there in the moonlight, my torch picking out the carved letters in the dusk, that only dinghy sailors were privileged to read the antique Latin, and then only those who had come a long way to do so. It was for me a strangely special moment in the voyage, and I am still not sure why.

Guardian of the Iron Gates

Ever since my Union Jacks had been slashed in Veliko Gradiste I had flown as a flag my beloved red-and-white spotty handkerchief, a leaving present from Mair, the nursing sister back in Ellesmere. That night it saved my life; that and the fact that I still read my Swallows and Amazons regularly. Soon after sailing away from the Tabula Trajana, the breeze died to nothing as the last light faded, and I rowed on for another two hours in deepening darkness. The gorge widened out to a long valley and I remember that night as being utterly beautiful. The moonrise over the high cliffy hills, a single perfect puff of cloud sculptured in silver and blue shadow by the moon, and a solitary star, very bright and clear, that hung at the moon's breast. It was all so pure and still and perfect that I simply stopped rowing for half-an-hour just to drink it all in.

Finally, rowing on, I came in sight of the lights of Tekja, a small town on the right-hand side of the valley, and pulled hard for the distant twinkle that spoke of warmth and company and a place to tie up for the night. *Jack* and I both needed a rest. In fact, even as I pulled hard at the oars, one of them slipped from its rowlock, sending the rowlock tumbling into the darkened bottom of the dinghy amidst the debris of ropes and sponge and baler. I cursed, turned around and bent to grope for it. Now boating at night is a foolish thing to do – it is impossible to see what you are doing, impossible to judge distances, and you yourself are well-nigh invisible to others, unless you have the full set of proper navigation lights; red for port, green for starboard and a white light on the stern. I had none of these. It was with some alarm then that as I scrabbled around for the invisible rowlock, I realised that the lights twinkling across the black water ahead were not those of the pier or the town, but were those of a moving vessel... and one that was a good deal closer than I had realised. It was in fact one of those barges, an iron monster, churning silently through the darkness, only about thirty yards away, travelling fast and heading straight for me. The lights told me that last fact; I could see the two lights in a row – green and red from left to right – and even I, who am spatially dyslexic, could work out in three agonised seconds what that meant. Those three seconds had brought the Behemoth another ten yards nearer, and I realised that unable to row out of the way, and without showing a light, I had no chance at all. My torch was still handy and grabbing it and yelling into the darkness, I shone it straight at the wheelhouse of the barge.

But hang on! A boat showing only a single white light is a mystery to another vessel. If anything, it is the stern light of a retreating vessel, and therefore no cause for altering course. In actual fact I should be showing a red light, a port light to show that I was directly ahead but moving across their bows to their left, warning them to steer to starboard with all speed. I was, in fact, in precisely the same predicament in which the Swallows found themselves in "*We Didn't Mean to Go to Sea*" when they were adrift in a yacht on the North Sea and about to be run down by a liner. There the resourceful children had shone a torch straight through a red Woolworth's plate, and avoided disaster. I had no Woolworth's plate, nothing red except... the hanky. There it hung, limply drooping from the port stay. I lunged across the dinghy, jammed the torch into its folds and shone the now reddened light at the great hulk of the barge, now only yards away. Would they see it? Would they respond? Still the green-red pattern showed, doubly reflected in the curling black bow wave of the approaching monster. But then... ah, at last... the green winked out, and left only the red light dancing... The instinctive reaction of a skipper steering to starboard at the sight of a red light ahead had kicked in, and the great barge thundered by less than ten feet away. I was safe.

Even so, the passing wake knocked me off my feet and into the bottom of the dinghy. From the barge, a hastily activated searchlight swivelled and pin-pointed me like a moth on a board, floundering in the barge's wash. Someone on a megaphone shouted something incomprehensible out of the darkness, and I was for a moment glad that I did not speak Romanian or whatever it was. But I lay there sloshing in the bottom of the dinghy blessing Mair and her hanky and the Swallows over and over again before re-fixing my oar and rowing to the safety of the shore.

At the great dam wall of Derdap I had to wait for several hours the next morning before a passing barge came along and the first of two locks was operated. I whiled away the time by washing all my clothes in the river and spreading them to dry in the warm sunshine. A young security guard called Nenad came and chatted to me all the while; he spoke good English and was a thoroughly likeable fellow, and he told me some interesting facts. During Ceaucescu's dictatorship in Romania just across the river, many hundreds tried to flee the country, and the most obvious route was here across the Dunav to Yugoslavia where the river was narrow and isolated. In fact, Nenad himself had done some smuggling across the river-frontier himself, bringing exiles fleeing from the great cruelties of Ceaucescu's reign. But many Romanians had attempted to swim the gorge unaided, and had simply been shot by the border patrols from the cliff-tops as they floundered in the water. Their bodies had drifted down and fetched up here, right where I had been washing my socks. The Romanians disclaimed any knowledge of the pitiful corpses, and they had been buried in the little graveyard full of unmarked tombs just up the hill from where we sat. Ceaucescu had in his later days of power, Nenad told me, decreed an edict banning curtains in restaurants, so paranoid was he that people might be plotting against him in public places. I can't help thinking that if you need to make laws like that you know you're getting something wrong. It is also comforting to think that dictators themselves inevitably live in fear, caged in by paranoia and misery. Do they all, like Macbeth, come to the realisation that in their sere, their yellow-leaf,

"*That which should accompany old age,*
As honour, love, obedience, troops of friends,
I must not look to have; but, in their stead,
Curses not loud but deep, mouth-honour, breath,
Which the poor heart would fain deny, and dare not"?

One can only hope so.

I moored that evening at Kladovo below the dam, tying up to a girder thrust out over the water to make a rough pier. In the middle of the night, through my slumber I heard my name being called. "Sandy? Sandy? Are you there?" I was fairly sure I didn't have any relatives or ex-students in... where was I?... Kladovo?... but poking my head out, saw that it was Nenad, my friendly security guard, and his wife and his sister who had come along to invite me for a late night supper. We went off to a dim little bar in town, I in my pyjamas I'm afraid, and afterwards, rather touchingly, they told me that they wanted to show me their favourite view. We drove up a gentle hill in the darkness, and stopped at a lay-by near the top. The view was simply back over the town, a meagre cluster of streetlights below; neither very high, nor very steep, nor very expansive, nor winsomely tiny. It was just a town at night. But we all got out, breathed deeply and Nenad said, "Isn't it beautiful?" The two girls nodded their agreement.

I too agreed. There are different types of beauty, and one of them was here, standing on the dark hill with me, the unpretentious admiration and love of someone for home, and for ordinary existence. Later, when they are saying goodbye, Nenad's sister (an astrophysicist, by the way) produces a bag of goodies: some gateau, some grapes and pears and a wonderful-smelling cheese pie which I stow away for the morrow.

"Funny things, accidents," says Eeyore. "They never happen till you're having them." Later that night, half-asleep in the darkness, it seemed to me that *Jack* was heeling over slightly. I dismissed the fancy and rolled over. A while later, the illusion that *Jack* was tipping seemed even stronger, so I redistributed my weight, shifted my rucksack from one side to the other and went back to sleep. I woke an hour later with water lapping nearly over the gunwale at my ear, and the very clear realisation that we were somehow listing almost forty-five degrees over, and about to tip completely. The reason was soon plain enough; the water level had sunk by two or three feet in the night - so near the dam, I should have thought of this - and *Jack*'s mooring lines were stretched as tight as violin strings, holding her starboard side out of the water and allowing the port side to drop away at a dangerous angle. If the water dropped any further, she would be dangling from the girder high and dry.

I tried loosening off the mooring lines, but where they were attached to the boat they had pulled into stiff knots, iron-hard with the strain of *Jack*'s weight. They would have to be released from the top. But it was here that I discovered the real quandary. With the sinking water level, the pier top was now some seven or eight feet above me, and what had been an awkward scramble before was now impossible. I simply couldn't reach the girder, let alone climb onto it.

Eventually, out of sheer desperation, I just jumped. I stood precariously on *Jack*'s raised gunwale, bent my legs and sprung vertically into the air, knowing that if I missed my target, I would drop into the black river, possibly concussing myself on the way back down. As it happened, by some miracle I did what I had never been able to do in gym class in Grade Five and gripped the edge of the girder above me with my fingernails. I then somehow managed to do a sort of chin-up... followed by a chest-up, and a final scrabble, rust-stained and sweating onto the top of the iron beam. It was then an easy matter to ease off the mooring lines and allow *Jack* to settle once more onto the dark water's breast. The whole silly incident left me shaking and sleepless at how close I had come to disaster, but rather impressed at how fit I must have gradually become over the last year to perform the gymnastics required. Jolly fit, in fact. My self-congratulations were cut short by my discovery that somewhere in the gymnastics I had trodden heavily on the cheese pie.

The last run of a hundred or so miles to the border is uneventful, and takes three more days. The chief feature of these days is the hunger. I spend the last two dining on nothing but honey from the large jar given to me by Branko's mother, and the small clove of garlic. This I peel carefully, piece by piece, and munch raw. With the honey it is not too bad. This is, after all, Transylvania, though vampires seem thin on the ground. The landscape has flattened out, and on the northern bank the Romanian pastures are wide and empty, though with the occasional glimpse of gypsy camps and horses. Many of the scenes are like some Children's Illustrated Bible – shepherd boys tending flocks, wandering, wicked-eyed goats, dry sandy cliffs where the sand martins breed, the occasional tall moustachioed patriarch with a black crook. In the final two days the weather comes in, a thick chilling murk and a blustering easterly, so that I can barely see the passing landscape. Hatless and freezing, I take my red-and-white spotty handkerchief and tie it tightly over my head as a scarf, in the manner of Headmaster's wife standing on the touchline of the House Rugby Tournament. In the moment of deepest misery I remember the little clinking package given to me in Vienna. It is somewhere tucked away in the forelocker. When I unwrap it with numb fingers I discover that it is five little bottles of something called Barenliquor, or Bear's Mead. It is wonderfully warming and reviving, burning into my veins and fingertips and restoring my feeble spirits as though it were made by Beorn himself.

My last night in old Yugoslavia is at Prahavo, a dismal dead end of almost disused railway sidings, a container port, some big factories and a solitary grimy bar. There I go, starving and wet and cold, and for the first time actually bring myself to beg for a little bread. Even here at the most miserable spot in the country, two factory workers pool their funds and buy me a bowl of paprika soup. I squirrel some of the bread away for later. I sleep that night in a deserted waiting room in the railway station just by the river – it is too cold and wet for sleeping aboard – and keep stirring uneasily in my sleep at strange, furtive rustlings and whisperings. They seem to be emanating impossibly from beneath my very head, propped on my little knapsack as a pillow, and I put them down as delusions caused by fatigue and an overdose of paprika. It is only the following day when I go to fetch out the bread rolls I have stored there that I discover there is nothing left but a few gnawed crumbs... and a large rat-nibbled hole right through the bottom of the knapsack. Rats! And, judging by the size of the hole, the size of dachshunds hereabouts. I was very glad that I had not woken fully in the night. In fact, my diary records that it was there that I had the sweetest

of dreams, all about a white horse and the holy island of Iona, so sweet, so piercing,
I wrote, that like Caliban, "I cried to dream again."

And so at last a final day of headwind slogging, revived faintly by the last of
the Barenliquor and the honey, and over the border into Bulgaria. I am stopped
at the actual border by a grey patrol boat that shoots out from behind the river
bank bushes and accosts me in midstream. I am not worried. The Australian
Consulate in Vienna had assured me that I did not need a visa for Bulgaria. The
border guards think differently. I cannot enter.

"I cannot go back," I point out, too exhausted and wet to be diplomatic.

"You have no visa."

"No."

"Where have you come from?" they ask, guns cocked.

"England."

"No, no, where have you come from in this boat?"

"England," I repeat, and show them my map.

There is some discussion.

"You may continue to Vidin, twenty miles down the river. There you must
report immediately to the police. Do you understand? Immediately."

"Yes."

And they put their guns away and roar off.

Welcome to Bulgaria.

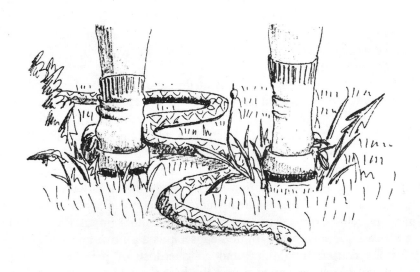

Bad Times in Bulgaria

'When I sally forth to seek my prey,
I help myself in a royal way:
I sink a few more ships, it's true,
Than a well-bred monarch ought to do…
For I am a Pirate King!
Hurrah! Hurrah! For our Pirate king!
And it is, it is a glorious thing
To be a Pirate King!'

W.S. Gilbert - *The Pirates of Penzance*

There was no way I was going to report immediately to the police. I arrived in Vidin after dark, cold, damp, starving and exhausted. The last thing I was going to do was sit in a draughty police station for a couple of hours, only to be told at the end of it that I must leave immediately. I needed a hot shower, a square meal and a good night's rest, preferably without rats banqueting in my pillow as I slept. And for all this I needed money.

The cash machine was next door to the police station.

Right.

Right. I put on my large shapeless cagoule without putting my arms in the sleeves, pulled out my red-and-white spotty handkerchief, tied it in a headscarf over my head, persuaded myself that I looked just like your average Bulgarian peasant woman out doing some late night shopping, and marched up to the machine under the eye of an idle policeman and extracted a great wad of glorious money. Then I marched into the nicest hotel I could find and proceeded to spend it all. (I turned back into a man first.)

The following morning, I mailed letters, phoned England, phoned Australia, did a ton of laundry, went back to bed until midday, and did all those things that are not possible to do while being deported for not having a bloody visa. Having got all that out of the way, I marched off to see the police, a smile hitched high on my lips and my face full of the winning charm that never fails to build insurmountable brick walls when it comes to border officials. Four hours later I was being granted a visa. It was simple after all; they just needed a lot of money for the paperwork. And it needed to be in US dollars. Unmarked. In a brown paper bag.

Back I went to the bank and discovered the first of many extraordinary things about Bulgaria that are designed to baffle or repel visitors. The fact is that in Bulgaria alone of all the nations of the Earth a nod of the head means "no" and a shake of the head means "yes," an oddity of communication that very nearly brought the bank-teller and me to blows. Over the next week or so I found this unique trait of the Bulgarian people incredibly frustrating. Even knowing the truth, the visual signal of a nod or shake is so much stronger than the verbal one that I was often left baffled by the simplest exchanges.

"Can I buy some bread?" I'd enquire, and at the shopkeeper's shake of the head I'd be out of the shop and down the road sadly looking for another place before I remembered that I'd just been told 'yes.' What the poor shopkeepers must have thought, I can't imagine. That there was a mad Englishman just going around checking on the availability of everything but never stopping to buy anything? And he looked so hungry, poor man...

In the midst of all these challenges, I was lucky to have a contact in Sofia, the country's capital, two hundred miles from the river. The father of one of my Ellesmere students worked as head of the Raffeisen Bank in Sofia and had invited me to look him up as I was passing, so I left *Jack* tucked up in the grimy river port of Orjahovo and headed off on the early morning bus to Sofia. I was instantly plunged from the primitive world of river travel to the giddy life of high finance for a bizarre but comfortable few days: a businessmen's lunch with the new British Ambassador; a newspaper interview for the Sofia papers in the upholstered luxury of the Sheraton Hotel; a gypsy and his dancing bear with tiny sad eyes and blistered snout who revolved drearily for pennies in the Square; hot baths and washing machines in David's comfortable flat, and a chance to explore the city. The greatest luxury was reading English books. I had fairly exhausted the potential of Keats and *The Tempest*.

But still the feeling that this was a sad country persisted. I learnt that of all the Eastern Bloc countries, Bulgaria had been the most fervent disciple of Communism and the most reluctant to let the regime go.

Then suddenly things improved. As I neared the eastern end of Bulgaria, my spirits revived, the people and the weather became sunnier, and I was attacked by pirates. What more could one ask?

I had spent a longish but lazy couple of days rowing and sailing down the broad stretches of river under wide sunny skies, stopping in villages that were less marred by the heavy Soviet style than upstream. Ruse, for example, several days' sailing downstream, was unexpectedly pleasant, almost Parisian in its wide boulevards, its plane trees, its pavement cafés, its classical statuary rather than the chunky Soviet kind. Ruse is only important to this chapter because I sat in a sunny square and wrote a postcard to a friend in Holland, and this is what I wrote:

Voyage nearly over now. Another week or so will see me to the Black Sea, I guess. All jolly good, I suppose, but rather dull, looking back on it. I would have liked just a few more adventures; discovering the princess of a lost island-kingdom, perhaps, or being captured by pirates. Still, mustn't complain, I suppose...Speak to you soon.

Love Sandy.

They say that the gods destroy us by granting our prayers. The following day, I was indeed captured by pirates, and cursing the whim that led me to voice such an ill-made wish.

Romania lies along the northern bank, Bulgaria along the south. The river here is very wide and empty and scattered along either shore are countless islands, tangles of dense reeds and willows and osiers. All morning the breeze has been blowing gently from the west, a perfect following wind, so I have been able to set the sails, put the tiller on autopilot (a carefully propped shoe) and lie back in the dinghy propped up on cushions and read. I have done my daily memory exercises, this time saying the whole of *The Eve of St. Agnes* in different accents for each part; Irene Handl for the nurse, Llangollen Welsh for Porphyro, and just for the fun of it, fair Madeline in gruff Yorkshire. I am happy but – as is probably clear - very, very bored.

The gossamer, I muse, has become a bloody nuisance. It's all very well seeing it at first as a magical hint of autumn, airy silver strands of finest silk festooning the rigging with fairy pennants. It's all very well musing that in the brilliant October sunshine *Jack* is now an enchanted barge out of Elf-Land,

> "*...a ship of leaves and gossamer*
> *With blossom for her canopy,*"

...sailing along, trailing clouds of glory, straight out of an Arthur Rackham illustration into the world of Mortals.

The fact is that all these things are fine in moderation, but here, on the lower reaches of the Danube, the fairies don't know the meaning of the word. The great poets who have dealt with the theme of gossamer have failed to mention one or two salient points about the stuff, such as its stickiness, its tendency to drape over and around anything in its way, its habit of clogging and clotting together in one's ears and eyes and mouth, the way that every swipe of the arm to clear the blasted stuff from one's tickled nostrils simply brings more of the sticky fibres floating in to drape themselves in great swathes across the face and eyelids; and, perhaps most importantly of all, the fact that it comes out of spiders' bottoms and is therefore accompanied by tiny pinhead baby spiders in their thousands. These lose no time in crawling into every facial orifice, nesting in one's hair, eating their way no doubt deep into the middle ear there to rear their horrid brood and generally colonise the human cranium, until I and my boat, so lately poetic and enthusiastic about the fairy nature of gossamer, resemble Miss Havisham's wedding cake on a bad-hair-day.

Engaged in such thoughts, I ripple along in the sunshine, all unknowing of what lies ahead. At this point there are several long wooded islands in midstream, but the only channel where the wind is blowing steadily is along the left-hand stretch of water between the islands and the Romanian shore. I am halfway down this strait when from out of the reeds and willows appears a

Romanian fishing boat manned by two fishermen. They hail me, and beckon me over with a handwave. I really do not feel like stopping, so I give a cheery but hello-and-goodbye sort of wave, call out "Engleski", and turn my attention back to the sailing. I am startled a minute later by their sudden appearance alongside my boat – they clearly want to chat for a bit.

Ah well, so be it.

On closer inspection, I found that I was playing an extra in an episode of *"Last of the Summer Wine."* One of the fishermen was exactly like Compo - short, grizzled, a smiley clownish face and a filthy beanie jammed down over his head. The other, manning the little outboard in the stern, was surprisingly like the quiet character of the same series played by Bill Sallis – a broad face, a gentle rueful smile and crinkled eyes. They were jabbering away in Romanian, and before I knew it had grabbed my bow-painter and lashed me alongside their boat. Smiles. Laughter. Handshakes all round. The offer of some lethal dark purple murky-looking liquor out of a lemonade bottle (declined)... and before I realised it, we were heading for the Romanian bank.

Puzzled I tried to indicate that I didn't want to go there... indeed, was not allowed to go there (*Ne visa Romania, es problema!... Bulgaria, es okay, ne problema... but Romania, ne! Ne! Ne visa!*) but Mr. Sallis at the helm stolidly ignored my pleas and we chugged on to the Romanian shore.

Very soon, they have me jammed up against the Romanian bank, the hoisted sail tangling dangerously in the overhead branches, and I am getting cross. They indicate with gestures and another burst of Romanian that I should take down the sail. I pretend not to understand. Again they jabber and point, and though their meaning is very obvious, I still play the uncomprehending idiot. It seems to me that the hoisted sail is in their eyes the one obstacle preventing them taking me where they like; perhaps they feel that to tow me along with it up is dangerous or perhaps conspicuous. Please understand that at this stage all is still in a state of genuine confusion. They are still smiling away, offering me the purple murk between long, loud swigs, and for all I know are just waiting to take me off to a surprise party they have prepared in the woods. But after almost half-an-hour of stalling, they begin to lose patience. I have asked them over and over again to let me go on my way; they keep mentioning Giurgu, a Romanian town some twenty miles back upstream. I am damned if I am going to let them take me all the way up there. The sail stays up. Finally Compo picks up a large brown catfish from where it is lying in the bottom of the boat and draws out a large, purposeful knife from his belt. Carefully, deliberately, he slits it from chin to tail, reaches in and pulls out a handful of dark red guts and hurls them straight at my head. I duck, and they splat into my sail. Then he holds up the knife, points to me, and draws a finger across his throat.

"Oh, the *sail*? Take it *down*? You should have said..."

...and a minute later, I have bundled the now stinking sail, boom and gaff together and hauled them out of the way up the mast. Sallis starts the decrepit little motor, and off we head up the river.

Even now, I am more puzzled and cross than frightened. But as we chug up the channel several things begin to alarm me. When I go to loosen off the rope that is lashing us together, Compo raises a stout black paddle above his head threateningly and I quickly desist. When I decide that if he is going to have a knife, I might as well have mine handy, and reach down to unpack it from its tupperware box, he again barks a threat and I turn the action into a little harmless tidying up of twigs and debris fallen into the boat. But between whiles, all is so friendly, so matey - smiles and laughs and drinks all round. To try and lighten the mood, I play my tin whistle, a Mozart medley, which they love. I even let them have a go on it. I offer them half a chocolate bar each. They grin and accept... but any move to liberate myself and Compo raises the paddle once more.

After a while, we chug out from behind the long island and into the main shipping channel, and there, oh joy! oh salvation! is a huge Danube barge half a mile away across the water. Surely if now I stand up and shout for help, the two fishermen will be unable to prevent me. But too late. They too have spotted the barge, and quick as a flash have wheeled around and we are racing back behind the sheltering screen of the island. My fears are confirmed. Whatever it is they are up to, they do not wish the World to see.

For the next hour we chugged along side by side back down the channel I had originally been on, hugging the Romanian shore, out of sight of any traffic on the main river. I spend the hour considering my options, every one of which now seems impossibly melodramatic. One such scheme is to pick up my oar, push Compo overboard with it, smack the outboard as hard as I could in an attempt to disable it, and get Sallis on the back-swing. Another scheme involves something I read years ago in *The Day of the Triffids* where the hero disables an engine by pouring a jar of honey into the petrol tank. I still have half a jar of Dora's honey, but cannot think of a plausible way of getting it into the outboard. Or could I suddenly drop the hoisted boom on Compo's head and...? No, no, I have it! The motor is started, I have noticed, by a detachable ripcord. If I can do some of my magic rope tricks, ask to borrow that ripcord once they are mesmerised by the magic, and then fling it overboard so that... that what? Another great idea bites the dust.

And the truth is that I cannot bring myself to do any of these things. There is a strong and unshakeable conviction in most people, I think, that as long as one can keep things on a civil level, a friendly, reasonable level, nothing dramatic can go wrong. This, more than their stupidity, is what prevents me ultimately from carrying out of any one of the plans so far, which would involve *me* getting far nastier and more dramatic than my captors had so far been: oars through skulls and so on. This is probably true of most crimes that end in tragedy for the victim; the perpetrator never makes it clear that this is going to go all the way to the end. He doesn't hand out business cards saying 'Murderer.' He operates step by step, each step a perfectly reasonable request. *Got a light, mister? What's your name then? Just step behind this bus shelter for a minute, would you? Just let's look at your wallet, eh? Where's the harm in looking, eh?* At each step the victim is presented, not with a life-and-death choice, but an ever-so-reasonable request. The only choice is whether to comply with it or kick up a dreadful, hysterical fuss in a fit of unreasonableness to the embarrassment of all concerned. And so the respectable lamb is led on until the throat is cut. *Just turn around a minute, would you? No harm in that, is there?*

Such thoughts were tangling in my mind as the two boats zoomed on through the water. But they were clarified a little when Compo leant over and rubbed his fingers together in an international signal. "Dollars? Deutschmarks? Leva? Krona?" He pointed at me, and at himself again.

"No, I'm afraid I don't have any money," I said in a voice a little too loud. Then it was my turn to receive the *Mr-Wiggins-lets-us* look from both Compo and Sallis, the amused certainty that I was trying it on. (So familiar was this look, it struck me for a wild moment that these two were perhaps Housemasters too, in some St. Fagin's Academy for Gypsy Thieves, Boarding and Day, Scholarships available. Then the smell of Compo reached me all over again and my head cleared.) But at least now they had shown their colours. They were pirates of a sort. Not, I admit, the sort I'd been hoping for, with a parrot, a peg-leg and a penchant for lace at cuff and knee. These two were hardly likely to break into a G&S chorus of "*Pour, Oh Pour the Pirate Sherry*" and let me off for being an orphan. In fact I am quite sure that they were usually fishermen. But today, I think they had decided to indulge in a little quiet piracy, and where it would end, I did not want to think.

I had just decided on a much easier plan than all that mucking about with honey and dropping booms. I could push both men overboard with a swift one-two of the oar, leap into their boat and take off with all speed until I was thirty miles downstream, only then stopping to cut myself free and carry on my way. Yes. That was it. That is what I would do.

Only of course I couldn't.

To this day I do not know whether I would ever have plucked up the sheer primitive indecency to do this, but suddenly the decision was taken out of my hands. The two men had for some while been searching the near bank for something (an inlet? a comrade?) and now at a shrill whistle from the shore, it seemed that they had found something they recognised. A horseman had emerged from the thick woods and was hailing them across the water. Any action I might have taken was now impossible – the man had a Sten gun held at the ready.

(Oh all right, I have no idea what sort of gun it was. What is a Sten gun anyway? But this one had enough handgrips and shoulder-guards and magazines draped about it to make it quite clearly not a rook rifle, or the sort of gun you have to reload with a ramrod each time while the Zulus get closer and closer. It was a gun that meant business.)

Within minutes we were ashore. The horseman was quite young looking, but was otherwise the coldest looking man I had ever seen. He also looked like the King of the Gypsies, and my two captors bowed and scraped before him, clearly in fear of him. He was clad in tatty khaki, but about his head he wore a bandanna of dirty crimson. His horse too had a red gypsy-knot tied in its bridle and a hundred jingling brass charms winking on its harness. A long argy-bargy followed, the rider smiling lazily all the while, and eyeing me up and down in cold amusement. If it were not so ridiculous to think so after the event, I would say that he was mentally undressing me, and I began to feel very uneasy indeed. Questions and answers were flung to and fro in curt Romanian, and at one point my bag was grabbed from the dinghy by one of the fishermen and handed to the horseman. He looked through it lazily: Keats poetry book, passport, tin whistle, wallet - all were examined with the same smiling scrutiny. Then a decision was made. This cock-a-hoop fellow gave an order and the men towed my dinghy round into a nearby creek, screened from the main river by willows and a half fallen poplar. There it was tied, and the fishermen pirates were dismissed. There was some grumbling about this at first, but the horseman stared coldly into the mid-distance and the whining petered out to silence. Finally Sallis said something curt to Compo, and they climbed in their filthy little boat and motored away out of sight downstream. Perhaps they would get their share of the booty later, back in the gypsy encampment.

Once they had vanished, the horseman, - gypsy-king, robber-chief, mercenary thug, whoever he was - motioned that I should walk into the forest ahead of him. I then did the only brave thing that day, and ignoring his obvious signals not to, walked down to *Jack* to tie her up properly – the fools had simply looped a line over a log, and already she was drifting loose. Then straightening up, on an impulse I took out of the boat a single oar and walked back up to where the man and horse were waiting. I received a faint sneering smile from the man – the horse didn't comment – and we commenced our walk into the heart of the forest.

Fear is a most peculiar thing. Once when I was walking up the aisle to read a lesson at an important service in the Cheltenham College chapel, I was suddenly overcome by an irrational and extraordinary fit of nerves. It was irrational because I have never had any fear of reading in public, and it was extraordinary because it split me like a knife into two... or even three... quite separate people. One was the physical body. I was acutely aware of the fact that my palms were sweating, my hands were trembling and I had even got one of those embarrassing quivers of the left leg which you only normally get when pulling yourself over the last ice-ledge of the Cuillin Ridge a thousand feet above a precipice and nearly not making it. The second Me, quite, quite separate from this pitiful jelly, was simply getting on with reading the lesson, slowly, sonorously, pausing at the right time, modulating the voice, and attempting to inject some degree of interest into what was otherwise one of the duller lists from Deuteronomy. I was doing quite well actually. But the third Me, and this felt like the real Me at the time, was watching the other two Me's with a heightened awareness and a sense of curious wonder. This new Me watched the furiously shaking leg, and the little boy in the front pew who stared fascinated at it throughout. This new Me carried on an amazed conversation with itself about the state of my sweaty palms. It critically evaluated the reading, the lilies in the side-nave, the azure lozenge of light cast on the far wall. It even looked with utter astonishment on its own existence, the like of which it had never even suspected before. It had super powers, was light and bright and alert, and a complete stranger to me.

There in the woods of Romania, he came back, along with all his friends. The body that scuffed its way through the yellow leaves clutching its ridiculous oar was sweating and nauseous and shaking like a jelly. But this didn't matter a bit, because that wasn't the real Me at all. The real Me was, I am almost ashamed to say, enjoying itself enormously. I was fizzing with daring ideas, all to do with my trusty oars and horses' legs, none of which my incompetent body would have been capable of putting into action. That didn't matter though. The leaves are so yellow here, and smelling deliciously of plum cake, rich and earthy. The horse is a noble beast. How could people ever eat them? I was alert and vibrant, almost gleeful… and intensely, excitedly curious.

This will sound both melodramatic and morbid, but I was excited because I thought I would soon know the outcome of death. I was sorry of course – sorry for my parents who would be really very upset. Sorry too for whoever found my corpse, if anyone. I hoped it would not be in too ghastly a state, and I worried, for some reason, that it would be a little girl playing dollies in the forest.

After several miles of walking through the forest – leggy nettles, swampy willows, dead brittle grey branches – we came to an impasse. Across the rutted muddy path, a side-arm of the hidden creek lay. My captor who had been riding along behind me, gun at the ready, reined up beside me and urged that I should wade across. But when he rode through, the murky water came up to the horse's thigh, and would have come up to my neck. This was as far as the road went for me. Ridiculous though it seems, I really didn't want to get all wet and muddy, even if it meant that the time had come for me to turn around and face a tree. This, I was sure, was it.

There is a part in one of the Narnia books where the children are about to go into great danger, from which it is likely that none of them will come out alive. "Let us go now," says one of the characters, "and take what adventure Aslan sends us." I have always loved that bit. An adventure! To see Aslan, or God, as the sender of good adventures, even the adventure of Death, seems an admirable and comforting way of viewing things. That was what it was like then: accepting an adventure whose outcome I had no idea of, beyond an odd certainty that the Sender of Adventures was all-loving, all-good.

And now having built all that up, though as honestly as I could, let me now confess right away that this is where the anti-climax starts. I for one am quite glad that things took an anti-climactical turn. I trust my readers will not be too disappointed with the outcome. For on my refusal to cross the ford, my sneering horseman suddenly looked a little at a loss. After some cogitation, he held up three fingers, said something that might possibly have been 'kilometros,' another thing that might have been "Kapitan," and indicated that I should wait there. Then he turned back across the ford, spurred his horse and trotted off up the rise into the trees.

I too was suddenly at a loss. My theory that he was the King of the Gypsies or intending to rob or kill me suddenly seemed a little shaky. True, he had my bag and all my valuables, but his deference to this 'Kapitan' was puzzling. As was his cavalier abandonment in the forest with the expectation that I would calmly await his return. If he thought that, he was sorely mistaken!

Or was he?

I thought again. If I bolted back to *Jack* now and took off down the river, I would do so without passport, wallet or money. Compo and Sallis might be waiting, guarding the boat. Never mind them – I would, after the recent feelings of fear and desperation during my walk in the forest, have absolutely no qualms whatsoever about using my oar on those two if they stood in my way. I was not going to let the adrenaline subside to civil, reasonable levels again. As for the money and passport, the bloody gypsies were welcome to them...

But what if I had been mistaken in all this? I still thought that the horseman was a cold-eyed killer, but what if this Kapitan was a more genial man, a sort of Robin Hood of Romania who would be so impressed by my feats of derring-do on the high seas that, after a firelit meal of venison pasties and a bed for the night under the greenwood tree, he would return all my possessions with a mocking bow – minus a small donation for the widows' and orphans' fund perhaps – and send me on my way again to tell the World of the magnanimous Gypsy-King? Or something along those lines?

And I'm afraid to confess that even my highly coloured imagination did entertain the uneasy feeling that all this was just another brush with immigration and a mix-up with border regulations.

I finally decided that my best course was to climb a tree. There was a very good one just by the ford, easy to climb to a fair height but well screened from the path's approach by broad leaves. There I would hide, wait until I had assessed the situation further when the horseman returned, and either reveal myself or continue hiding as I thought best. Yes. That is what I would do. So up that tree I climbed, still clutching my oar, and sat down to wait in my leafy bower.

Half-an-hour later, I was so intent on peering through my screen of leaves at the ford in front of me, that I was oblivious to all else. Then there came a polite cough from behind and below me. There stood a small party of men who had approached from the opposite direction to the ford – they were within ten yards of my tree, and I was in full view of them. One was in the smart green uniform of a police officer while the others were in various items of khaki, and looking up at me with the sort of gazes you too would use if you found a man up a tree with an oar. "Humour him," the looks said. "He is possibly confused."

I turned in alarm, nearly fell from my perch, caught myself just in time, and clambered hastily down out of the tree, brushing twigs and leaves from out of my hair and attempting to rub moss-stains out of my trousers. At a word from the officer, one of his men stepped forward warily and took my oar from me. Another helped me down the last five feet. The game was up.

Man Up Tree With Oar

To my relief, the officer looked not only competent but kind. He was a man of about my own age with a tanned face, fairish brown hair and clear grey eyes. The neat uniform suited his grave and courteous air – this was no tin-pot generalissimo running a racket. In fact, he had a look about him of a Roman officer: conscientious, a good leader, a Marcus Aurelius serving duty on the eastern frontier. And to my even greater relief, after one or two false starts, we made the mutual discovery that we both spoke French.

The rest of the story is swiftly told. I was taken a little way through the forest to a bend of the creek where was moored a speedboat, surprisingly new. This took us up the log-jammed creek at a terrifying speed to where it petered out on the further side of the forest. Here a lonely police outpost stood, surrounded by pigsties, and an office was quickly cleared of its chess-playing recruits. Strong black coffee was ordered, my horseman was sent for to join us, and the interview began.

The police chief – his name is Florian – is as good as he seems. Very slowly, very clearly, he questions me about that afternoon's movements. Very slowly, very clearly, I tell my tale. When I have finished, he tells me that there are one or two discrepancies he would like to clear up. The two fishermen, he says, claim that they found me on Romanian soil. Is this true?

No, I explain calmly but very clearly. I was certainly in the channel between the island and the shore – this is not a problem, the river is free to everyone, he reassures me - but I was certainly nowhere near the bank and had no intention of landing.

Ah. He smiles. They, the rascals, have told the horseman, (who is, by the way, a border patrol policeman, and not, despite his dress, a gypsy-king) that they had found me on Romanian soil and feared I was a spy. For the love of their country and as good, honest citizens, they had taken the first opportunity to seek out the police and hand their spy over to the proper authorities. There would, perhaps, be a small reward?

No, adds Florian to his narrative, but there might now be a small fine. The two opportunists would be found and punished. Bit by bit we piece together the events. We come to the conclusion that probably the two fishermen had hoped to take me somewhere quiet and rob me – hopefully nothing worse – but that their plan had been foiled at the appearance of the patrol-rider who had come along and seen them towing me and the distinctive *Jack* along. Knowing that if there were now any trouble, they would be the first to be questioned, they had quickly changed their plan. They knew that I had no visa and that I spoke no Romanian. Thus they quickly concocted their story about their captured 'spy' and spun it to the rider, hoping for a reward. (We must remember that at this time of trouble over the border in Yugoslavia the notion of spies – and the potential of them to do real work – was not as fanciful as it seems.) The rider accordingly had taken charge from that point on, perhaps over-zealously, and decided to bring me at gunpoint to the Kapitan. It was ironic that I had in fact been perfectly safe from the moment the horseman had arrived on the scene – the appearance had been quite the opposite.

But now the ordeal was over. We had another coffee - as gritty and black as ever, but oh! how I enjoyed it – and Florian handed me back my belongings and accompanied me back to the speedboat. Then there was another nightmare speed-race through the floating logs and low boughs of the secret creek until *Jack*'s bright buttercup hull and furled red sails came in sight, tethered to where I had secured her several lifetimes ago. Then they kindly towed me out into the main river, now a burnished gold in the late westering sun, and cast me off. The nearest town was Tutrakan on the Bulgarian side, some twelve miles down the river, they explained, before zooming off into the golden glare. The adventure was over.

Those last twelve miles were spent driving my boat along across a molten river under a molten sky with strokes still fuelled with adrenaline. As the miles passed, the sky deepened to apricot, then carmine, and then dying-ember crimson until starry darkness covered the heavens from west to east. Slowly my pace slackened, steadied, and I fell to singing every deep, glad, solemn hymn I know to keep time to the strokes. The lights of Tutrakan crept nearer and nearer, and I passed the last two miles improvising an anthem-like tune, Byrd or Palestrina in style perhaps – it was hard to tell. But the words were those of my favourite prayer, that which we said at evensong and Friday night choir practices with old

Mr. Finlay when I was a boy.

Lighten our darkness, we beseech thee, O Lord;
And by thy great mercy
Defend us from all perils and dangers of this night;
For the love of thy only Son,
Our Saviour, Jesus Christ,
Amen.

Amen, and again I say Amen!

The tale has one brief sequel. The following day was a particularly gossamer-clogged one, and otherwise utterly windless and still. I had nothing more than a fifty-mile slog of steady rowing down to the last town before the Romanian border, the town of Silistra. Much of this day was spent thinking about the events of yesterday, and as my fear subsided, so my dissatisfaction with the whole adventure grew. It had not after all been a terribly dramatic adventure when one came to look at it - a couple of cheeky opportunists, a mistake on my part as to the nature and motives of the horseman. I had not even had a chance to try out any of the really clever plans such as the one with the honey or the magic ripcord. Even the term 'pirates' seemed a little excessive now, here on this wide and tranquil stretch of the river. It was when I was only about three miles up from the town at the end of the day when it happened. A familiar looking boat shot out from the reeds and willows on the Romanian bank, and headed steadily straight for me. This in itself was not a worry. There were plenty of these little black skiffs on the river, and besides we were now some sixty-two miles downstream from the events of yesterday. I was quite safe. It couldn't possibly be them...

To be sure, it did look a little like them. The short one with the beanie in the bows, the darker one at the back... but no. Yesterday's fisherman had a flag, I seemed to remember, a grubby rectangle of green, red and white, whereas this boat...

... had one too. There it was suddenly rippling out in the breeze of their speeding progress. My pace quickened. I glanced over my shoulder to see how far the first buildings of Silistra were. Another two and a half miles of empty river bank and nowhere to hide. Still I told myself not to be silly. Here were two fishermen out on the river plying their trade. Of course they'd have a flag. Of course they'd travel in pairs. Of course the skipper's mate would wear a filthy beanie. Standard gypsy fisherman's uniform really. My friends from yesterday were a day's journey away, even now being fined by the police and locked up for a couple of nights. This pair had nothing to do with me.

At that point there came an unholy yell of glee across the water. Compo was standing in the bows of the speeding boat, pointing straight at me and yodelling a war chant across the glassy two hundred yards of river between us. It *was* the *bastards*, and they had been so upset by the outcome of yesterday, they had motored sixty miles down the river just to finish things to their satisfaction.

I turned to my oars and rowed. In a sudden returning rush of rage and fear and adrenaline, I pulled *Jack* through the water in great weltering surges, almost lifting her bodily out of the water with each frantic stroke. It must have looked like those Asterix comics where Obelix makes the rowing boat skip across the water in a series of leaps and bounds, the oars a blurry windmill of pen-strokes. Nearer and nearer the Bulgarian shore drew, but a disturbingly isolated and empty stretch. Nearer and nearer drew the pursuing boat, its crew still yelling out their menacing war-cry across the water. It was going to be a close thing. Sweat poured into my eyes, my arms were trembling with pain, and my lips were moving in sudden agitated prayer, "Oh please God, not again, not again."

Suddenly I knew I really wasn't going to make it. The pirates had changed course slightly to steer around behind me and get between me and the Bulgarian bank, and had already cut me off. The town was still a mile away and the river was deserted. I was at their mercy. Quickly I glanced around and grabbed any loose lines and stowed them out of reach in the bottom of the dinghy. I made sure my Leatherman knife was handy, and I took one of the oars out of its rowlock. This time, any knuckles attempting to grab onto my gunwale would be smashed to a pulp. I was frightened – no mystical calmness this time – but I was also shaking with rage. Come and try it!!

And suddenly it was over. As they swerved close to my stern I saw that the beanie'd chap wasn't my Compo of yesterday after all, and nor was the steersman Sallis. Still they were hooting and jeering and looked as menacing as one could wish for, but it was not for my benefit, and they gave me barely a glance as they skimmed by, heading back to the opposite bank.

It took another two hours for me to stop shaking, and that night I lay uneasily awake with my knife under my pillow. But the lesson had been learnt. Do not ask for real adventures unless you are ready to deal with them. You are no hero, but a dreamer. Be content with those that your dreaming mind and the loving World have given you.

I have lived and I have loved.
I have waked and I have slept.
I have sung and I have danced
I have laughed and I have wept.
I have won and wasted treasure,
I have had my fill of pleasure.
And some of it were weariness
And most of it were dreariness.
And all these things but two things
Were emptiness and pain.
And love it was the best of them
And sleep worth all the rest of them.

And sleep worth all the rest of them. And now, dreamer, sleep.

The Wings of the Morning

'This is the way the world ends,
Not with a bang but a whimper.'

T.S.Eliot – *The Hollow Men*

And so the long journey draws near to its end. I calculate that there are 376 kilometres to go, or half that distance depending on which route I take. About forty kilometres down the river, a canal cuts away to the right, heading straight for the Black Sea and emerging at Constanza on the coast. The longer route takes me further north before swinging eastward into the Danube Delta where the river spreads out into a maze of little channels, any of which will take me down to the Black Sea. Crazy though it seems now, I was in serious doubt as to which of the two routes I would take. The spirit of adventure which should have cried out for the mazy wilderness of the Delta, one of the world's greatest wetlands, was now nearly extinguished. I was tired and grubby, on the verge of madness from the sheer boredom of my own company, and I think the events of the past few days had shaken me more than I cared to admit. The straight canal to Constanza would have me finishing within three days, and I could be back in England by the weekend, sitting down in clean clothes amongst good company and never have to recite *The Eve of St. Agnes* again. I decided to take the shorter route.

Signing out of Bulgaria with the Silistra Police Chief that first morning was a surreal experience. Yes, the visa was in order, yes, I would have no trouble entering Romania, but the problem was with the boat. Where were her Ship's Papers?

Her what?

"Her Ship's Papers, Kapitan. Every vessel has Ship's Papers and without seeing them, I cannot let you continue."

"Look, she's only a dinghy," I explained, and led him out of his harbour side office to peer over the jetty at the little tub floating below. "There isn't even a motor."

He was not moved. "As I say, every vessel has a set of Ship's Papers, and I must see them. Otherwise," he added with a challenging stare, "how do I know that you have not stolen this boat?!"

What, and rowed it three thousand miles just to escape? I muttered under my breath. *There are easier ways to acquire a boat.* But I didn't voice my thoughts out loud. The police chief was a fat, smug man who looked quite content to sit there chewing toothpicks for the next few decades if needs be, waiting for the Ship's Papers so that he could stamp them for his records.

After another half-hour of this sort of impasse, I had an idea. I dug out my pencil case and a clean sheet of paper from my sketchbook. I sat down on the sunny steps at his door and drew a rather nice heraldic crow entwined with an anchor at the top as a letterhead. Then I wrote neatly in black ink:

Name of Vessel:	*Jack de Crow*
Class:	*Mirror Dinghy*
Reg. No.	*...er...180463 (my birthday, by coincidence)*
Ship's Owner:	*Alexander James Mackinnon*
Insurance:	*Oh, surely...*
Cargo:	*Tin whistles, watercolour paintboxes, parrot-embroidered cushions, honey-pots, magictricks, silken handkerchiefs, gossamer, Autumn leaves.*

I did all this while the Police Chief watched me through narrowed eyes, even getting up out of his chair to suggest a couple of curly mermaids at the top to flank the nautical crow. When I had finished, I said, "Oh, Ship's Papers? You mean *these* Ship's Papers. Yes, here they are, sorry, wasn't with you for a moment there."

He said "Yes, Ship's Papers. I told you they'd be somewhere." Then he stamped them, copied the details from them, signed the copies three times, stamped my passport and bid me farewell. "I'm a busy man," he said, and went back to his toothpick jar and his desk. I returned to *Jack*, showed her the proof of her new official status, and we sailed off down the river into Romania. Let's get this whole thing over with.

"Two roads diverged in a wood, and I,
I took the one less travelled by,
And that has made all the difference."

Well, in my case those roads were actually watery streams, and they ran down either side of a little island in midstream, clustered with thick yellowing trees. I took the left-hand channel on a whim – a white egret had flapped slowly off down that side – and discovered twenty minutes later that what I thought was an island had in fact been a peninsula, splitting the Danube into two. The branch I was on was the lesser of the two streams in width, but was in fact the Borcea River, and it ran another sixty miles in a meandering course before it re-joined the main Danube… thirty miles beyond the Constanza Canal turn off. It looked as though I was going to the Delta after all.

I am not actually too unhappy about this. The lesser Borcea is a prettier route as it winds between sandbanks and green pastures where herds of fine-looking horses graze. Tall clumps of poplars raise their golden towers like steeples over the landscape, and it reminds me vividly of my first few days on the little Vyrnwy in the pleasant pastures of North Shropshire. Every now and then I see the rising smoke of some settlement off in the trees, or closer to the bank large round conical huts made of larch poles all leaning together to an apex, the gaps stopped with moss and grass. They look a little like the charcoal burners' tepees that Ransome describes in the Lake District of his childhood, and a little like Mongolian yurts. Everywhere is a great and spreading silence. Along the banks are fading sedges, bone-white and buff-coloured, and the only sound is the thin hiss and rattle of the breeze sifting through their stiff stems. Far, far overhead I see three huge black and white birds, legs and necks outstretched in three great crosses. They are storks, I think, sailing eastwards to the Delta. It does not seem far now.

I moor one night on the outskirts of a dark and almost lightless town next to a rusting barge. The owners, Niko and Georgi, invite me to bunk down in a cosy cabin on board. We set off after dark into the town to find something to eat, and Niko and Georgi each take a stout club. I wonder why, but soon find out as we reach the outskirts. Two snarling dogs launch themselves out of the darkness in attack, but are sent yelping into the darkness by savage blows of the clubs. It is all quite unnerving. Even more so is passing by an open concrete drain, one of those huge cylinders of concrete that you see forming culverts under roads. From inside there is a light flickering, and as I stoop to glance in, I see that there is a whole family living there: a mother wrapped in rags, two thin children and a baby, huddled against the curving concrete walls to avoid the slimy trickle of dampness that runs down the middle of this, their home. In the darkened town, nothing is open, so we return to the barge and I am plied with brandy.

Communication is limited, but surprisingly, Romanian is easier to guess at than any other language so far between France and here. I learn later that the Romanians proudly claim their descent straight from Rome, the purest line there is, and their language reflects this. Here at the utter end of Europe, we are back to Latin roots and a recognisable alphabet. By some accident of geography and history, they have become islanded in a sea of Slavs, with whom they do not deign to mingle. They are a good-looking race, tanned and straight-nosed and clear-eyed with brown curling hair and frank grins – what can be discerned under the grinding lines of poverty, that is. For there is no doubt about it, Romania is crippled by poverty to an extent I had not guessed at. It was hard to believe that they shared the same continent with glittering Vienna or prosperous Frankfurt.

Over the next few days, nothing of any interest happens, except that as the towns are few and far between, I use my food sparingly. I spend one night sleeping on *Jack* under a rookery full of incontinent rooks, another in an almost identical cosy barge cabin on the invitation of another Georgi – I think for a minute that I have gone in a large circle – and then a day of racing winds and bright skies has me hurtling down the river through two large and surprisingly modern towns with gleaming white apartment blocks. Then I come at last to the very apex of the Delta. Tomorrow I will be in its wild heart, and the next day it will all be over. Let me spin this out a little, *Jack* and I, for the sake of fond memories and the end of things.

We stopped at dusk in the middle of a wild part of the forest. Here a gnarled willow tree thrust out old roots into the river to form a natural mooring spot, a promontory of earth and grass and fallen trunks behind which *Jack* could nestle. That night I gathered together great chunks of rotten wood and kindling, built a fireplace of stones and lit a fire. Soon I had a great blaze going, red against the blackness of the forest beyond, and over it I toast some bread and cheese on pointy sticks. It is not terribly successful – the chunks keep dropping off or charring – but I also open the bottle of wine that I have been saving since Vienna. Alfons and Uli gave it to me, and I think of their exquisite and spotless flat as yet another cheesy lump dribbles down my shirt-front. They would be very polite, I think, if they were here, and offer me a linen napkin. Vienna seems a long way away.

The wine is excellent, and soon I am finished with supper and sitting enjoying the fall of glowing coals, the sudden crackle of the tinder-dry wood and the sparks rushing up into the night sky. A little night breeze has sprung up and breathes cold on my back, but my front, my face, my outstretched palms are warm and glowing. I wonder that this is the first time I have made an effort to do this on the whole trip, now that it is so close to finishing. It is perfect. I picture myself on a map of Europe, sitting alone in the forest on the very eastern edge, and marvel at the fact that I am here. It seems such a bizarre place to be.

As I gaze into the embers, I am reminded of the tale one of my ex-students told of his grandmother who was a Welsh witch. She used to do a spell for him when he was a little boy, when they were sitting before a coal fire in her parlour on the west coast of Wales. She would say the magic words of the spell, and there in the coals, Gwilym would suddenly see tiny figures, tiny pictures, scenes from an ancient story that the grandmother would begin to tell each time. He remembers these as vividly real, not just the creations of an imaginative mind, and the story was always the same: a cave of rubies, a red dragon curled at the back, a young warrior with a white horse and a gleaming sword, and a harp of red gold that played by itself for the young man's death, the bronze and copper strings snapping and writhing to nothing as the spell ended.

I did not know the spell, but in the falling caves and glowing grottoes of ash and ember, I saw the pictures of that day: the women I had seen that morning in

Galati in the church of St. Nikolai, for example. An Orthodox priest with a long grizzled beard and looking like St. Peter was standing reading out aloud from a great book, and the headscarfed women, shawled and beaded, knelt in a cluster at his feet, touching his robes, reaching to touch the Bible's binding and kissing the priest's stole. The coals shifted and I saw another scene: a young man poling a reed-boat across the river, bare chested even in the blue wind, leading a herd of swimming horses across the deep, broad river. Their rolling eyes and snuffling nostrils were close enough to be seen, an inch out of the water like a line of water-kelpies led by a naked brown Pan. A log falls and ashes fly up. I see in them a great swirling dark cloud against a red sunset which as I draw nearer resolves into a myriad of winged specks: a swarm of rooks flocking homewards to roost in a clamorous rookery, a thousand strong.

The bottle is half gone now and the fire is dying. It is getting cold. I place another log on the fire and stoke it up, but then go and climb into my little boat. The mattress is laid out on its decking, the awning is up, but its open triangle is facing towards the fire. As I fall asleep, I can gaze out into the night and see my toes in the sleeping bag silhouetted against the rosy glow of the heaped fire. I wiggle them to get them warm, and listen to the gurgle and chuckle of the water around the willow roots. I am as happy as a King. No, I am as happy as Ratty and Tom Sawyer and Doctor Dolittle all rolled into one, and that is something better.

I awake the next morning to a thick grey ghostly mist over the river. It is as thick and blinding as wet wool, and it strikes me that in a year's travelling this seems to be the one classical story-book hazard I have not yet encountered. It has been saving itself for the one part of the trip where I am not following a single river course but must find my way through a network of channels in the Delta's maze.

I set off rowing, hugging the southern bank so as not to miss the channel to Sulina, the small port at my journey's end. If I end up traversing the northern part of the Delta, I will pass into the Ukraine, and I have had enough of illegal frontier crossings. Phantom ships loom up out of the fog, gaunt, rag-rigged things crewed by scrawny skeletal pirates jeering raucously as they approach… and then turn into drifting felled trees, their dead branches smothered in cormorants. My determination to stick to the southern bank soon leads me down a side-arm, a very graveyard of ships and barges all rusting, derelict, broken-windowed, caved in, half-sunk under the overhanging boughs of the crowding forest… but not abandoned entirely. A chained dog, a draped line hung with grubby dishcloths, a flicker of an oil lantern from behind yellowed glass shows that some at least of these hulks are inhabited. It is an eerie place, a Sheol of ships and their ghost masters, gibbering and squeaking in the mist.

Soon the graveyard arm re-joins the main river, and the mist begins to lift, burning off the water in spectacular wisps and curlicues of steam. When we finally manage to round the gravel-spit into the main channel to Sulina, we are very nearly both killed instantly. Around the bend at the speed of a jet-boat comes a hydrofoil, huge and grey and metallic, perched up on its front skis like something out of *Thunderbirds*. I have no time to lurch out of the way. Three seconds of high-pitched roaring is all the warning I get, and then the hydrofoil is upon me. Luckily, *Jack* and I are over to one side of the canal at the time. Had we been in mid-channel, we would now both be stork-fodder.

The channel to Sulina runs through the very heart of the Delta, but I must confess to being a little disappointed. I had expected something like the Okavango Swamp, reedy channels where the wildfowl nested in their thousands, clapping up like thunder at my passing. I expected geese and ducks, storks, ibis, egrets, and the croak of a million bullfrogs. I expected houses, if there were any, to be perched on long poles above the marsh and have nets drying on frames and wickerwork ladders down to the little punts of the fisherfolk dwelling there. I was fully prepared to put up with the constant swarm of midges and mosquitoes, gnats and flies, and horseflies that could sting through leather. I was half hoping to contract malaria.

As it was, the whole place was like one of the drearier corners of Essex. There was the odd farmhouse, neither decrepit enough to be quaintly ethnic nor luxurious enough to be the ex-king of Romania's shooting-lodge. There were a few villages, more ordinarily middle class than anywhere else I had seen in Romania, and the most rustic thing I saw was an ox cart being driven along the top of the dyke, but it was loaded with used tyres. There was not even a chance for a last campfire vigil that night, communing with the darkness. I arrived at a village called Maluc at dusk and could go no further that night. At Maluc there was a disproportionately large hotel right by the river bank, and everything conspired to tempt me to try its hospitality that evening. It had begun to drizzle, I was damp and suddenly desperate for a warm bed and a hot shower, and I was also very hungry. My last supplies had been the toasted bread and cheese the night before. Ignoring *Jack*'s reproachful look, I booked myself in for the night with the manager who spoke French.

Once I have handed over huge amounts of grubby Romanian notes, I retire to my room to find that there is no hot water. When I come down to see about that, I find that they are not serving any food either. You see, m'sieur, the hotel is actually closed for the Winter. Hm, not too closed to relieve me of a small fortune, I see. At this point I become rather schoolmasterly. I briskly march him off to find the water-heating system and together we work out how to light it. Then I spot Mme. Hotelier wandering through the foyer with a plate of fried eggs, and rather spoil the briskly efficient effect by making the same sort of mistake I had made all those months ago with Alain and Benedicte just outside Calais.

"I shall have un plat des oeils, s'il-vous plait," I order firmly.

My use of the word 'oeil' causes the Manager some consternation.

"Les… oeils? Pour manger?" he asks tentatively.

"Yes, yes," I snap back in a voice threadbare with impatience. "Les oeils frites… votre femme a les oeils, n'est-ce-pas?"

"Erm, les oeils de ma femme?… frites?"

The poor man is beginning to sweat and turn a little green at the thought of his wife's eyeballs frying in butter and being served up nice and runny on toast. At last I twig that I have got the damn word wrong again.

Oeufs. Oeufs. Oeufs. What is it with that word? I change my order to something less grisly, and the poor man hurries off relieved, and really happy now to provide anything, anything at all for the gentleman if he will just assure them that they will still be alive in the morning.

When I wake the next morning I am excited and apprehensive... nervous even. I know that today I will reach the Black Sea. I put on a suit of clean clothes and shave properly with soap and water, as though I am due to meet with royalty: the Dark Queen, the Mare Neagra herself.

The morning is grey and still, even with the odd drizzle, very light and fine. The banks continue flat and dull, but as the day progresses give way to reed beds where the sedges grow almost mast-high. They rattle like sabres on either side. The famed wildfowl continues to be conspicuous by its absence; the only birds are an ugly species of hooded crow and the odd heron. As I row along, I ponder again a long-considered question – namely, what will I do about *Jack de Crow* when I get to the end. Reluctant though I am to admit it, this will certainly be the end of our long acquaintance. I cannot possibly arrange to take her back with me. Various plans have come and gone in my mind over the last year. The wildest and loveliest of these is to give her a Viking send-off. I have visions of standing on the edge of the Black Sea and loading her with cedarwood and sandalwood, and dousing her with scented oils. Then, gently, I would set her sails and push her from the shore, letting the west wind take her out to sea. At the last minute, just before she gathered speed I would fling a burning brand into her from the shore, and she would sail into the east all afire, blazing like a comet until she dwindled from sight.

This vision had always in my dreams been swiftly followed by a vivid picture, however, of the burning *Jack* bumping straight into a Russian oil tanker bound for Odessa, igniting it in one titanic explosion and precipitating World War Three. Perhaps then I could do the whole thing but without the fire, simply setting her off on a captainless last voyage to sail to the land of the Golden Fleece, the far Caucasus. I really wasn't sure about the whole thing. Another idea had been, and I am not joking, not to stop at all, but to keep sailing down the coast, round to Istanbul, across the Aegean, on and on and on, a restless Odysseus sailing on until the boat fell to pieces under him. Sometimes I still dream of that, and someday I may do it. But to be honest, *Jack* had already reached the falling-to-pieces stage. Her decks were flaky with old varnish, her gaff was splitting and she was no longer as dry and watertight as she had been. There was hardly a fitting on her that was not working loose; they had all been screwed on and re-tightened so many times that the wood was rotting away around them. She had done extraordinarily well, covering 4900 kilometres, traversing 282 locks, and visiting twelve different countries, but I had been no careful, loving master, and she had suffered breakages and bumps, rough handling and bodily dragging, frayings and chafings and scrapes. It was time to retire.

The last six miles before Sulina saw a new idea creep into my mind. The sight of two small boys on the bank, their faces alight at the sight of me and *Jack*, made me wonder whether I could not hand *Jack* over to the local school. There must be one in Sulina, surely, and stuck between the river-marsh and the sea, I was sure that the inhabitants must lead a fairly maritime existence. Was it possible that *Jack* could end up as she had started, being used to teach youngsters to sail? The more I pondered the idea, the more I liked it. Even if *Jack* was used for nothing more exciting than allowing the local school teacher to get to outlying regions of the Delta where untaught children lived, she would serve the purpose. It was a splendid idea, and when I told it to *Jack*, she heartily agreed. She hadn't wanted to hurt my feelings before, but she now confessed that she had never really been too happy about the Viking funeral-pyre send-off after all.

In the mid-afternoon of that gentle grey day, the 26th of October, 1998, we sailed into the little town of Sulina on the Black Sea. It was a pleasant little place – there were few of the new Soviet-style buildings around and many of the older ones had remained intact, classical edifices with pillars and curly architraves, including a beautiful domed church built by none other than our old friend King Ludwig, who, I suspect, for all his sanity, rather thought that he owned the entire Danube. He certainly took a proprietorial and paternal interest in the whole river from its source in the Alps to here in the Delta.

I stopped at the river wharf in the centre of town a mile before the actual marine harbour and found the Harbour Master, ready to see what he thought of my scheme to donate *Jack* to the local school. I had reckoned without the cold hand of bureaucracy, deadening and blighting all under its grip, not only here but stretching over all Europe and Britain and the civilised world. The Harbour Master was a fatherly man, and nice enough, but his first response was with much rueful headshaking.

"No. This is not possible. What about Import Tax?"

I stared at him. "Import Tax? On the boat? What Import Tax?"

"You bring a boat here, you say you want to leave it here? Then you have imported it. On this, there is a tax. It is simple," he said.

I gaped.

"And," he went on, warming to his theme, "what about insurance?"

"Insurance?!"

"Yes, my friend, insurance. Who will pay that?"

I didn't know.

"This is the law in our country, my friend. All boats must be insured. I am sorry."

"I really think that…"

"And another thing. You say you leave your boat here as a gift. Perhaps you change your mind, eh? You come back. In six months time, you come back and you say, 'Where is my boat, you thieves?' What then?"

"Look, I can assure you that I won't be coming back, either in six months time or ever. I…"

"Ah, my friend, my friend. You say you are a school teacher. Hah! I believe you. You are clearly not a businessman!"

At this point I was exasperated and nettled by all this needless obstructionism. "Look, I'm sorry," I said, "but tomorrow I am walking out of here and not taking my twelve foot dinghy in my rucksack with me. For me, a very simple solution to *my* problem is to get up early tomorrow morning, cut her adrift and simply walk away. But that, I think, is where *your* problem will start: a vessel adrift in your main channel, a hazard to shipping and God knows what else besides. I won't be here to fix it. *You* will be. Can't we be sensible about this?"

The Harbour Master sat back in his chair and looked at me for a long, long time. Then he came to some sort of decision. "You are right. These laws are stupid, but I see a way around them. As Harbour Master, I have certain ... immunities ... to these laws. If I say I need a dinghy for my job, then I need a dinghy. No import tax, and the insurance is covered by the Harbour authorities. Even if I then decide in my wisdom to lend it to the local school, you understand? Which," he added, looking at me sternly, "I am not saying I will do. Maybe, maybe not. That is the best we can do, I think. Yes?"

It seemed to be the only solution. I was in no position to argue, especially when you understand that this whole exchange did not take place exactly as I have set it down, but in a much longer and more tedious batting to and fro of French, Pidgin English and Romanian sign-language.

So a piece of paper was brought out, typed up to his dictation but translated into French for me, and then duly signed by me. It read something like this:

I, Alexander James Mackinnon, owner and master of the sailing vessel Jack de Crow, *do hereby give her unreservedly as a gift to the Harbour Master of Port Sulina for his use in carrying out his duties, as of this day, 26ᵗʰ October, 1998, and henceforth have no further claim on her or any part of her, nor expect any payment in hiring fees or purchase price from the aforementioned Harbour Master.*
Signed this day, 26ᵗʰ October, 1998, Sulina, Romania.

(I have no idea, by the way, whether the Harbour Master later followed up his hints that the dinghy would get to the school after all, no questions asked. A sceptical side of me makes me fully aware that I had just signed away my boat to an opportunist who had done rather well out of the deal - but then again, I had just spent an entire year proving the extraordinary generosity and goodwill of ordinary people from Shropshire to the Black Sea. He seemed a kindly man after all. It seemed not only grudging of spirit to take this cynical view, but contrary to all experience to think thus. I saw no reason why the unlikely goodness of people should suddenly stop here at the furthest edge of Europe. I am content to think therefore that *Jack* is being of some use to the children of Sulina, and I never need to know one way or the other.)

Back in the Harbour Master's office, I signed the contract ...and then broke it immediately. I asked the Harbour Master if I could borrow her for the next few hours. There was still something to be done and *Jack* and I had to do it together. We had not, after all, yet reached the Black Sea.

Beyond the town, the land peters out into marshland and reed beds. The main river-channel, widened and deepened for shipping runs through this in a gently curving mile between built up dykes of rock and earth, the left-hand one of which continues right out into the Black Sea itself as a long, sturdy breakwater. However, long before I had rowed to this point, I noticed a little break in this dyke, just where the ruins of a stumpy little lighthouse stood overlooking a stunted willow. Beneath the very trailing fronds of this tree, the waters poured away in a smooth funnel, and on an instinct I quickly allowed *Jack* and myself to go with them. There was a rush and a gurgle, a brushing of willow-wands on cheek and sail, and we found ourselves in a secret little world of reeds and pools and channels behind the dyke wall. It was as though we had slipped out of the scullery door of some grand house rather than out of the main front doors, and instead of finding ourselves on the broad bland gravel of the coach-drive, had found ourselves in the cabbage-and-nasturtium cosiness of the kitchen garden, smelling of dew and turned earth.

Here at last was what I had expected the Delta to be like. Tall reeds hemmed us in either side, rustling with little birds that chirped and darted in their dry denseness. The channel we were on was barely ten yards wide and split into two just ahead. Which way to take? Try the right-hand one. Ah, no, this was curving back towards the sea wall so... but wait, here was another branch, and another. This one looked promising... but no, a few wiggling bends later and it stopped in a wall of sedges. The next half-hour was a blissfully happy hunt through the maze of reed beds for the channel that would take me out to open water. Soon even the sea wall and the top of the lighthouse were lost behind the screening reeds and I was alone in a secret world under the mild grey sky. And then an opening showed ahead in the wriggling channel, a glimpse of clear horizon and open water, and a minute later *Jack de Crow* and I rowed out onto the calm waters of the Black Sea. The reed-marsh was behind us, and clearly visible a mile away was the dyke and the stump of the derelict lighthouse, but before us, the sea stretched to the horizon.

It did not look like a sea, actually. It was so flat, so grey-silver, so calm that it looked more like a vast freshwater lake under the steely sky. I dipped a finger in the water to taste it. It *was* fresh. A good steady breeze was blowing from the north-east, so *Jack* and I decided to spend our last few hours together sailing out to find where the real salt sea began.

Back Door to the Black Sea

Well, we never found it. I learnt later that such is the volume of water coming down the Danube that the Black Sea remains completely fresh for almost seven miles out from Sulina, but those last couple of hours were some of the happiest I have ever spent. We skimmed to and fro over the burnished water, this way and that, now skimming close to a reed bed to investigate a likely coot's nest, now sailing out again to clear waters. It suddenly struck me that for the first time in a year, I was actually sailing purely for pleasure. I had no course that I had to follow, no distant mark that I was trying to bring closer inch by inch, no hemming land to shift the wind at every turn. I could tack up into the wind purely for the pleasure of turning around and sailing downwind again. I could zigzag here and there at a whim. For the first time in a very long time, I could sail on a reach – that is, across the wind rather than into or down it – and rediscover that this is the pleasantest sailing of all. The boat is lightly balanced, the sails trimly set, and the tiller resting with a comfortable pressure in the fingertips.

And here at last were the birds. Battalions of geese gathered on the glass-grey waters and paddled gabbling away as I approached. A fleet of white swans dipped and glided amongst the fringes of the reed beds and then took flight, oaring overhead with silver necks outstretched, wings whistling and creaking into the east. Smaller birds, sandpipers and dunlins, turnstones and knots, pattered and whirred on the mud-flats in the distance and a marsh harrier hawked over the reeds. And everywhere, commoner than all the others, were the homely ducks, bobbing like toy boats amongst the rushes.

After an hour or two, the skies to the north and east had darkened to charcoal, but the west was watery yellow with the setting sun. At one point a faint rainbow glimmered out in a far-off shower against the leaden sky: a brief thing, but as unearthly as they come. It was time to head back to Sulina.

One last little adventure remained to us. Finding my way back to the 'back-door' by the lighthouse was easy enough, rowing through the winding channels between the tall reeds, but when it came to passing through that doorway back onto the main river, the difficulties began. The current pouring down either side of the willow tree on its tiny island was far too strong to row against. Time and time again I would aim *Jack*'s prow for one or other of the gaps, row like smoke, and at the last minute be deflected sideways by the onrush of the stream. Back I would go, spinning down the channel like a leaf on the flood. The dusk was deepening and rain was threatening, and unless I could get beyond this miniature Charybdis, I would be spending the night out here on the marshes, with the Harbour Master convinced I had absconded with what was now technically his boat. Finally, with a change of tactics, I managed to drive *Jack* up into the tiny triangle of quiet water in the lee of the willow'd islet, between the two torrents racing down either side. Then there was nothing for it. We were back to the Morda Brook all over again, here at the very end of our journey. I took down the rigging, lowered the mast, emptied her of all my luggage, removed the oars and bodily dragged poor *Jack* up onto the knobbly roots of the tiny eyot. Then, clumsily and painfully, I hauled her over the twenty feet or so, dragging her under and through the low, grabbing branches of her old enemy, the willow. Twigs and leaves rained down into her, branches clawed at her, roots rose up to batter her keel, but scratched and leaf-spattered we made it eventually to the upper side of the island. Our last problem was how to launch off into the main river again without instantly being swept either side back down through the doorway.

There was a good evening breeze blowing in from the sea and up the river. With oars and sail together, we might just make it clear of this trap. The problem was that even here the willow tree spread its branches out over the water, so that it was impossible to raise the mast and sail while still on shore. I would have to row clear of the island; only then would come the task of somehow getting the mast up and the sail unfurled before the current could sweep us back down past the willow-isle and into the marshes again.

Very carefully, I set everything in place. The mast-foot was ready to slot into its step on the foredeck, and I blessed the day I had bothered to put my pulley-system on the forestay. The mainsail was ready to haul aloft at a second's notice, and the oars were in their rowlocks ready to do their job. I patted *Jack* on the gunwale, whispered 'good luck!' and tugged her down into the water. Then with an almighty push, I sent her flying from the bank, floundered aboard, and started rowing as hard as I could out. We had to get away from that island and its encircling twin currents. I heaved and hauled at the oars, but they were not enough. I was fifteen yards from the island but already beginning to slip backwards, sideways, spun by the current. I abandoned the oars, threw myself at the forestay pulley and hauled, slotting the mast-foot into place with the other hand. Teeth and hand, teeth and hand, I pulled away and the mast rose upright and stood firm. Ten yards to the gap. Seven yards. Like lightning I cleated the pulley rope and flung myself at the halyard. Five yards. Four yards. The halyard came in hand over hand and the gaff rose up the mast taking the scarlet sail with it. Never had she risen more smoothly or wonderfully to the task. The wind filled the sail, the boom swung wide, and, with just five yards before we vanished down the sluice again, *Jack* stopped her backward drift and began to inch forward once more. We had done it. Setting to the oars again, and now aided by the good sea breeze, we made our way slowly back up the river to the lights of Sulina shining in the distance.

Earlier that afternoon I had had a vision. It was no mystic wonder, just another fanciful flight of the imagination such as the thousand others recorded here. It had been on the last stretch of river before reaching Sulina, perhaps five miles upstream from where I was now. As I had been rowing along, facing back up the river as usual, I had been struck by the powerful notion that there before me lay the whole vastness of Europe; it unrolled in my mind's eye like a map. Over there to my left somewhere, the rocky-white promontories of Greece, deckle-edged and with the map-maker's Mediterranean blue coloured in up to each tiny crinkle. Over to my right, the plains and forests of Russia stretching away, a blank paper wilderness, and straight ahead the little ridge of the Carpathian Mountains cut by the notch of the Iron Gates gorge, inked in tiny detail. Beyond that the great Magyar plain of Hungary and Yugoslavia, smudged and torn here and there by a careless hand, but dotted with the colours of plum and apple ripening on the tree. Then the Alps, tiny and perfect and sharp, like things seen in a globe of glass; the solemn temples, the gorgeous palaces, the cloud-capped towers of Austria and Bavaria. And so to the wavy line of the Rhine and the lesser line of the Moselle, wiggling up the map on a golden-green background, the colour of new vines - and so to France, scattered with woods and fields and the bright sprinkle of poppies. But the map does not end there. A narrow bar of painted sea and there is England as John of Gaunt saw it, a precious stone set in a silver sea. The White Cliffs are there, and London, and Oxford, every detail on the Magdalen Tower to be seen under the cartographer's glass. And there on the very furthest edge, where the paper is curling off the table, the green meadows and blue hills of Wales.

And through all this runs a single thread. At times it is the brandy-brown of country brooks; elsewhere it is salt-green flecked with white. Sometimes it is a thread of softest wool, dyed blue-grey. Elsewhere it is stretched steel wire, scratched and harsh. In places it is a ribbon of midnight-blue, spangled with the sequins of stars; or a thread of pure gold that catches the light and runs it up and down its length like liquid in a glass. It is threaded with beads and trinkets along its length: the carved stones of cathedrals, or white quartz beads as cold as marble. There are rich gems strung on the stone: garnets red as fire-coals, sapphires flashing like kingfishers, topazes set in gold. But in all its length, it is unbroken, a single thread of water-green laid from one end of the map to the other.

As I sail the last mile back up to Sulina in the gathering dusk, I recall the vision of that afternoon briefly, and then it fades again. There are things to do. As I sail along in the dusk, willow twigs are thrown overboard, leaf-mulch and breadcrumbs and all the debris of the riverbanks that collects so easily in the boat's bilges. I straighten her lines, coil her painters and halyards, and sponge the worst of the mud off her decks and bottom-boards. She's not a bad little boat really. By the time we have arrived at the town pier, it is completely dark, but the job is done. *Jack de Crow* is ready for her new life, and I for mine.

Photograph by
Frank Clarke

Full name: Alexander James Mackinnon
Nationality: Australian
Date of Birth: 18th April 1963
Profession: Teacher of English and Drama
Current Job: Geelong Grammar School, Victoria

Sandy Mackinnon was born in Australia in 1963. He spent his childhood between England and Australia, travelling as a small boy with his family on the last P&O liners to sail between the two countries, a factor to which he attributes his life-long love of maritime travel.

He finished his education at the University of Adelaide, completing a Diploma in Education and a Bachelor of Arts in English Literature, Linguistics and Anglo-Saxon. His teaching career started at Westminster school, Adelaide, where he taught English and Drama for four years. After this time he travelled overland to England by yacht, hitch-hiking, river-canoe and even horseback - spending a brief time in a Chinese prison after accidentally swimming into China, and being attacked by Komodo Dragons, amongst other experiences.

England provided a somewhat tamer existence as he taught at the prestigious schools of Sherborne and Cheltenham, before becoming Head of Drama at Ellesmere College, Shropshire, for six years where he also taught English at all levels.

In September 1997, ready for more adventure, he set off in a twelve-foot open sailing dinghy from the school gates at Ellesmere, and nine months later had managed to row and sail all the way to Romania and the Black Sea - a journey of some four thousand miles, passing through twelve different countries and involving shipwreck, arrest, capture by pirates and becoming lost in the English Channel.

His interests include painting, philosophy, writing, conjuring and home-made fireworks, and he has written and directed a number of plays and musicals.

He is currently enjoying his English and Drama teaching at Geelong Grammar School, Australia, where he continues to coach sailing to staff and students.